ALTERNATIVE CHRISTS

Few, if any, individuals have had such a profound influence on Western culture as Jesus, even though not a single detail of his life or teaching can be confirmed with certainty. This lack of reliable biographical data has left his life open to broad interpretation. Jesus, gnostic and apocryphal sources insist, never truly died on the cross since he was a divine being, whose human frame was an illusion. Muslim sources affirm that Jesus was a prophet of God and will return at the end of time. Jörg Lanz von Liebenfels formulated racial theories in which Jesus was a redeemer for Aryans only, while the Renaissance polymath Guillaume Postel was convinced that Christ had returned as a Venetian woman.

This book explores these and other views without taking sides in any theological arguments and presents research on a variety of alternative Christologies.

OLAV HAMMER is Professor, History of Religions at the University of Southern Denmark. He is co-editor with James R. Lewis of *The Invention of Sacred Tradition* (2007).

ALTERNATIVE CHRISTS

EDITED BY

OLAV HAMMER

CAMBRIDGE
UNIVERSITY PRESS

CAMBRIDGE UNIVERSITY PRESS
Cambridge, New York, Melbourne, Madrid, Cape Town, Singapore, São Paulo, Delhi

Cambridge University Press
The Edinburgh Building, Cambridge CB2 8RU, UK

Published in the United States of America by Cambridge University Press, New York

www.cambridge.org
Information on this title: www.cambridge.org/9780521889025

© Cambridge University Press 2009

First published 2009

Printed in the United Kingdom at the University Press, Cambridge

A catalogue record for this publication is available from the British Library

Library of Congress Cataloguing in Publication data
Alternative Christs / edited by Olav Hammer.
p.   cm.
Includes bibliographical references and index.
ISBN 978-0-521-88902-5 (hardback)
1. Jesus Christ.   I. Hammer, Olav.   II. Title.
BT304.9.A44   2009
232.9 – dc22   2009014241

ISBN 978-0-521-88902-5 hardback

Contents

Figures

Notes on contributors

JASON BEDUHN is Associate Professor of Religious Studies at Northern Arizona University, Flagstaff, USA. He specializes in Ancient and Asian Christianities, with particular focus on the Manichaean religion. In addition to his many articles on these subjects, he is the author of *The Manichaean Body: In Discipline and Ritual* (2000) and *Augustine's Manichaean Odyssey: Conversion and Apostasy in the Late Fourth Century* (2009), and co-editor of *Emerging from Darkness: Studies in the Recovery of Manichaean Sources* (1997), *The Light and the Darkness: Studies in Manichaeism and its World* (2001), and *Frontiers of Faith: The Christian Encounter with Manichaeism in the Acts of Archelaus* (2007).

JEAN-PIERRE BRACH is Professor of Religious Studies at the École Pratique des Hautes Études, Paris. His research concerns esoteric currents of the early modern period. His publications include *La symbolique des nombres* (1994) and *Des admirables secrets des nombres platoniciens*, an annotated edition of a text by Guillaume Postel (2001).

ROELOF VAN DEN BROEK is Emeritus Professor of History of Christianity at the University of Utrecht, the Netherlands, a member of the Royal Dutch Academy of Arts and Sciences and honorary doctor of the École Pratique des Hautes Études (Sorbonne, Paris). He is the author of *The Myth of the Phoenix According to Classical and Early Christian Traditions* (1972), *Studies in Gnosticism and Alexandrian Christianity* (1996), Dutch translations of gnostic and hermetic texts (1986, 1990, and 2006), and numerous articles in academic journals and collective volumes. He is one of the co-editors of the *Dictionary of Gnosis and Western Esotericism* (2005), to which he also contributed a considerable number of articles on ancient gnosticism and hermetism.

DOUGLAS DAVIES is professor at the Department of Theology and Religion, Durham University. His research interests include funerary rites,

Mormonism and Anglicanism. His research in the area of Mormonism has resulted in *An Introduction to Mormonism* (Cambridge University Press 2003) and *The Mormon Culture of Salvation* (2000) along with other books, chapters and encyclopedia entries.

NICHOLAS GOODRICK-CLARKE is Chair of Western Esotericism at Exeter University and Director of the Centre for the Study of Esotericism (EXE-SESO) in the School of Humanities and Social Sciences. His numerous publications include studies of Ramon Llull, Paracelsus, John Dee, Cornelius Agrippa, Emanuel Swedenborg, and Helena Blavatsky, as well as a trilogy of monographs on the millenarian-esoteric connection, *The Occult Roots of Nazism*, *Hitler's Priestess*, and *Black Sun*. He is General Editor of the "Western Esoteric Masters" Series published by North Atlantic Books, Berkeley. His most recent book is *The Western Esoteric Traditions* (2008).

OLAV HAMMER is Professor of History of Religions at the University of Southern Denmark. He has published extensively on various aspects of religious innovation in the modern West, in Swedish as well as in English. His most recent publications include *Polemical Encounters* (edited with Kocku von Stuckrad, 2007) and *The Invention of Sacred Tradition* (edited with James R. Lewis, Cambridge University Press 2007).

WOUTER J. HANEGRAAFF is Full Professor of History of Hermetic Philosophy and related currents at the University of Amsterdam, the Netherlands. He is the author of *New Age Religion and Western Culture: Esotericism in the Mirror of Secular Thought* (1996/1998), *Lodovico Lazzarelli (1447–1500): The Hermetic Writings and Related Documents* (2005; with Ruud M. Bouthoorn), *Swedenborg, Oetinger, Kant: Three Perspectives on the Secrets of Heaven* (2007), and numerous articles in academic journals and collective volumes.

JAN HJÄRPE is Emeritus Professor of Islamology at the Department of History and Anthropology of Religions, University of Lund, Sweden, PhD in History and Psychology of Religion. He has published extensively on Islam, mainly in Swedish; his recent books include *Tusen och en natt och den elfte september: Tankar om islam* (2003), *Shari'a, gudomlig lag i en värld i förändring* (2005), and *Profetens mantel: den muslimska världen 2001–2006* (2007).

JAMES R. LEWIS has taught Religious Studies and Philosophy at the University of Wisconsin since 1999. He is the author of *Cults: A Reference*

Volume, Legitimating New Religions, and *The Encyclopaedia of Cults, Sects and New Religions.* He is the editor of *The Oxford Handbook of New Religious Movements* and the forthcoming *Scientology.* He is also the co-editor, with Olav Hammer, of *The Invention of Sacred Tradition* and, with Sarah Lewis, of the forthcoming *Sacred Schisms.*

BRADLEY MALKOVSKY is Associate Professor of Comparative Theology at the University of Notre Dame, USA and is the editor of the *Journal of Hindu-Christian Studies.* His scholarly expertise is in the Hindu-Christian doctrinal and spiritual encounter, with a specialization in Advaita Vedanta. He is the editor of *New Perspectives on Advaita Vedanta: Commemoration Volume for Richard De Smet, S.J.* (2000) and the author of *The Role of Divine Grace in the Soteriology of Samkara* (2001).

MIKAEL ROTHSTEIN is associate professor at the Department of Cross-Cultural and Regional Studies, University of Copenhagen, Denmark. He specializes in the study of new and emerging religions, not least so-called UFO religions, and has published extensively on the subject. His other field of research is the religions of indigenous peoples.

JAMES A. SANTUCCI is Chair and Professor of Comparative Religion at California State University, Fullerton. He has a PhD degree from the Australian National University (Canberra), is the author of *An Outline of Vedic Literature* and *La società teosofica,* and is editor of *Theosophical History* and *Theosophical History Occasional Papers.* Dr. Santucci is also a contributor to the *Intercontinental Dictionary Series,* now housed at the Max Planck Institute.

URSZULA SZULAKOWSKA is an art historian at the University of Leeds whose specialism is the history of alchemical illustration in the Renaissance. She has published extensively in this field, most recently *The Sacrificial Body and the Day of Doom: Alchemy and Apocalyptic Discourse in the Protestant Reformation* (2006). She has written numerous critical and scholarly papers on contemporary art. She is currently preparing a monograph on the appropriation of alchemy and magic by contemporary artists.

EINAR THOMASSEN is Professor of Religion at the University of Bergen, Norway. His most important publications are *Le traité tripartite* (with Louis Painchaud, 1989) and *The Spiritual Seed: The Church of the 'Valentinians'* (2006). In addition he has published textbooks and numerous articles on Gnosticism, ancient religions in general, and Islam.

CHAPTER I

Alternative Christs: an introduction

Olav Hammer

Few if any individuals have had such a profound influence on Western culture as Jesus. Or rather, few if any cultural icons have had a comparable importance. For those who are intent on determining who Jesus really was, the status of the sources poses apparently insurmountable problems. Books on his life are plentiful, and range from the ultra-skeptical extreme of denying that Jesus even existed, to the literalist one of accepting the Gospel stories (in suitably harmonized form) as a historically accurate record. Even a cursory acquaintance with this literature shows that there is no consensus regarding even one single detail of his life or teachings.

Mainstream churches, from Late Antiquity to the present day, have traditionally relied on the works included in the New Testament canon to provide them with a picture of the life of Jesus. These works, however, are documents of faith rather than of history. They were composed several decades after the death of their main protagonist, display numerous internal inconsistencies, are spotty in their coverage, and promote ideological agendas. The extracanonical sources are plentiful, but are for the most part composed at even later dates, and are at least as ideologically biased. In short, even the earliest accounts of the life of Jesus interlace whatever historical kernel they may contain with abundant legendary material.

Jesus legends form part of the core mythology of various religious groups. The human being Jesus is also, among other things, the mythologized bearer of a religious message and the flesh-and-blood manifestation of a transcendent being: Christ. The scriptures of early Christianity are not formulated as systematic theological tracts, and the precise relationship of Jesus the human being, Jesus the purveyor of a divine message, and Jesus as Christ is never spelled out in precise detail. A number of religious currents nevertheless agree on the basic proposition that Jesus was all of these, and elaborate the details in widely divergent ways. It thus makes only limited sense to separate legends of Jesus from myths of Christ – they form part and parcel of the same religious discourses.

What from one perspective could be seen as historically problematic sources and vague doctrines can also be construed as opportunities for religious innovation. The numerous gaps in the earliest texts on the life of Jesus were soon filled in with further details; the tantalizing clues to what it meant for Jesus to be Christ soon led to a dazzling variety of Christologies.

Already in the New Testament texts of the late first century, there are clues to the effect that the first followers of Christ understood him in different ways. The First Epistle of John polemically distinguishes "correct" opinions from "false" ones:

> Hereby know ye the Spirit of God: Every spirit that confesseth that Jesus Christ is come in the flesh is of God. And every spirit that confesseth not that Jesus Christ is come in the flesh is not of God: and this is that spirit of antichrist, whereof ye have heard that it should come; and even now already is it in the world (1 John 4.2–3, KJV).

More abundant sources from the second and third centuries CE show that by that time, theological divergence was rampant. These early sources document a variety of opinions that in time received their own appellations, of which a few can be mentioned here.[1] *Adoptionism* is the name given to the view that Jesus was in essence a human being and became the Son of God through God's adoption of him, for instance at his baptism. *Separationists* similarly understood Jesus as a human, who had become savior by receiving an influx of divinity, the Christ, into his person. *Patripassianist* or *modalist* writers suggested that Jesus was identical to God the Father, and that it was the latter who had descended to earth in human form, had suffered, died and had risen again. *Docetism* was the opinion that Christ as a divine being did not have an ordinary human body during his incarnation, but only appeared to do so; in particular, he did not really suffer and die on the cross. *Arianism*, which arose a few generations later, that is in the fourth century, affirmed that Jesus was a perfect or even transcendent being, but that he was nevertheless different from and less divine than God the Father.

Each of these terms in turn covers a gamut of opinions. This can, for instance, be seen from various gnostic Christologies, myths which can generally be placed in the separationist and docetic camps, but nevertheless display many differences of detail. Recently, the appropriateness of affixing a shared label to such a diverse set of religious traditions has been

---

[1] The following thumbnail sketches of early Christologies is dependent on J. N. D. Kelly, *Early Christian Doctrines* (5th edn., London: A. & C. Black, 1977), Bart Ehrman, *The Orthodox Corruption of Scripture: The Effect of Early Christological Controversies on the Text of the New Testament* (New York and Oxford: Oxford University Press, 1993) and Charles Kannengiesser, S. J., "Arianism," in Mircea Eliade (ed.), *Encyclopedia of Religion* (New York: Macmillan 1986), vol. I, 405–406.

questioned.[2] The main argument against the term is that it masks a plurality of currents united by little more than an unreflective adoption of orthodox Christian heresy charges. However, it is clear from the sources that there were Christians who considered gnosis, a particular religious insight, necessary for salvation. The term can be used as shorthand for the various divergent opinions that emerge from a careful reading of those sources. In his chapter, Roelof van den Broek discusses a variety of views which are documented in gnostic texts, or can be tentatively reconstructed from the arguments of their opponents. Christ plays a variety of different roles in the cosmic emanation mythologies that portray the emergence from the highest divine principle of a number of *aeons* or divine qualities. Gnostic writers were confronted with the question of how this spiritual figure could possibly be related to the historical person of Jesus. Some adopted the view that Christ had never been incarnated at all, and that his human body was only illusory. Such a non-corporeal being could of course not have resurrected in the flesh. Others, however, understood the divine and human natures to have been united in Jesus, with little attempt to solve the difficulties inherent in this position.

This early period also saw the development of biographical Jesus legends that came to be excluded from the emerging canon. Various extracanonical sources, examined in the chapter by Einar Thomassen, present an array of Jesus legends. Readers of these apocrypha will find details of Jesus' physical appearance, and stories that affirm that Jesus had the miraculous ability to shift shape at will. There are details regarding the birth of Jesus and his childhood that fill in missing details in the Gospel traditions. Other extracanonical sources portray Jesus as a teacher of secret wisdom, and provide tantalizing clues as to the relationship between Jesus and Mary Magdalene. Christological themes are presented in ways that complement or contradict canonical passages: various texts deny that Jesus suffered on the cross, follow him as he descends into Hell, and extend the stories of Jesus' appearances after his resurrection in new directions.

Together, these two contributions document the plurality of religious options in Late Antiquity. It took political processes culminating in the fourth and fifth centuries CE to produce a certain degree of uniformity in the emerging church; the acceptance of "mainstream" views was, however, never absolute. The processes that led to this partial streamlining have

---

[2] For attempts to deconstruct the "Gnosticism" label, see Michael Allen Williams, *Rethinking "Gnosticism": An Argument for Dismantling a Dubious Category* (Princeton: Princeton University Press, 1996) and Karen King, *What is Gnosticism?* (Cambridge, Mass.: Belknap Press of Harvard University Press, 2003).

been described in a vast literature, and need only be recapitulated in their barest essentials, as a background to subsequent developments. Conflicts between rival groups, especially between those who claimed that Christ and God the Father were of the same substance, and those who espoused the view that Christ was not essentially divine, but had been created by God, led to a protracted series of conflicts. The council of Nicaea (325) led to a tentative formulation of orthodoxy, a view of Christ as fully divine and fully human that was enforced as binding at the council of Constantinople (381). Emperor Theodosius attempted to outlaw the opposing Arian point of view in the 380s, without succeeding in eradicating it entirely. If these councils managed to create consensus about the relationship between Christ and the Father, the precise nature of the connection between human and divine in Christ was still a matter of heated discussion among the religious elites. The council of Chalcedon (451) attempted to formulate a definitive answer, but did so by excluding other alternatives. By the mid-fifth century, leading spokespersons for Western Christianity had arrived at the formulation of an orthodox position, according to which Christ is one with and of the same substance as the Father, a single person with fully human and fully divine natures.

Despite the attempts at these church councils to formulate and enforce a binding doctrine regarding the nature of Christ, emerging orthodoxy never succeeded in suppressing alternative understandings. Two of these non-orthodox fifth-century Christologies were particularly influential. *Nestorians* regarded Jesus Christ as containing two distinct natures: divine and human; *Monophysites* held that the two natures had fused into one single unitary being. These perhaps arcane distinctions became identity markers for various regional churches. Nestorian churches were established in – among other places – Syriac-speaking parts of the Middle East, the Coptic Church opted for the Monophysite creed, while Arianism for another century or two remained the preferred option among various Germanic peoples, such as the Goths. The Western church continued to combat residual "heresies" in its territories; even within the confines of the orthodox formulation, however, enough leeway was left for religious creativity to blossom – views of Jesus that will be pursued no further here, but which are amply documented in the existing literature.[3]

The differences between adherents of emerging orthodoxy, of Arianism, Nestorianism, and Monophysitism may strike a modern reader as matters

---

[3] See, e.g., Jaroslav Pelikan, *Jesus through the Centuries: His Place in the History of Culture* (New Haven and London: Yale University Press, 1985 and many reprints).

of detail, truly "alternative" only for those involved in the power struggles and schisms of the fourth and fifth centuries. However, a number of much more divergent "non-orthodox" views survived and flourished by becoming important elements of organizationally distinct religions.

Jason BeDuhn discusses the Jesus legends of the Manichaeans, and documents a number of Christological developments that gave the version of the Christian tradition constructed by Mani (216–ca. 277 CE) and his followers a quite distinct character. The double mythological role, found also in mainstream Western Christianities, of Jesus as crucified savior, forms the basis of various aspects of Manichaean Christology. In his role as one saved, Jesus shares a common nature with all living things. There is no essential difference between the divine and the soul entrapped in matter and in need of salvation – indeed, the extensive use of crucifixion metaphors includes the idea that the soul is everywhere crucified in the material world. As savior, Jesus delivers the directives of Christ that guide each person's life, and by his example he offers a paradigm for the Manichaean believer, who is encouraged to live his life in imitation of Christ. His role as savior is also manifest in his role as inspiration to all prophets throughout history, his task as psychopomp (helping the soul on its journey into the afterlife), and in his function as judge at the end of time.

In the seventh century CE, Jesus appears in the text of the Qur'an, and becomes the basis of a series of Islamic reflections on Jesus as prophet. Jan Hjärpe's chapter surveys the ways in which the figure of Jesus (known as 'Isa in the Islamic tradition) is presented in the Qur'an, enters the hadith literature (the traditions regarding the sayings and actions of the prophet Muhammad and his followers), passes on to the traditions created in Sufi milieus and in popular piety, and finally appears in new guises in contemporary literature, literary fiction and in ethical debates. The emphasis placed in Islam on the oneness of God rules out any implication that Jesus is in any way consubstantial with the godhead. Rather, Jesus is considered a prophet, one among many who have received a revelation from God. Nevertheless, Islamic sources share numerous other motifs with various Christian concepts: Jesus as miracle worker, as eschatological figure, and as ethical role model.

The process of incorporating Jesus into distinct religious traditions has continued up to our own time. Although Christians have been present in southern India since at least the third century CE, the incorporation of Christ in Hindu traditions is a much more recent phenomenon, in particular emerging in the nineteenth century. Hindu Christologies of the colonial period have been discussed in a number of previous studies. Bradley

Malkovsky, in his chapter "Christ in Hinduism," breaks new ground by moving beyond these classical Hindu assessments of Christ and bringing us up to date with more recent developments, not only in regard to the formulation of Hindu Christologies, but also and especially in reference to the method used by contemporary Hindus as they question both standard Christian and standard Hindu understandings of Christ.

With the remaining contributions in this book, we return to the Christian and post-Christian West. As we will see, Christ has over the centuries been understood, among other things, as a purveyor of secret knowledge for the initiated few, as an equivalent of the philosophers' stone, as a feminine redeemer, and in many other roles. This plurality is all the more remarkable, given that Christology has been a topic so central to the dominant religious ideologies of the West that the borders of the acceptable were for many centuries policed with extraordinary zeal.

Some alternative Christologies managed to survive, albeit temporarily, by being part of what could anachronistically be called subcultures, networks of people whose distinct interests allowed for the circulation of rather unorthodox opinions. Urszula Szulakowska's chapter "Christ and the alchemical mass" discusses the ways in which writers on alchemy forged novel views of Christ. During the sixteenth century, the image of Jesus Christ was used to symbolize the philosopher's stone, while his passion and crucifixion became an allegory of the laboratory process. The philosopher's stone was understood to be a substance both material and spiritual, immanent and transcendent like Christ himself. The stone's alternative designation was "quintessence," an aetherial matter, spiritual in nature but with a physical body. The alchemical stone was believed to be the Christ-savior of the mineral kingdom, turning base matter into gold. It became mystically identified with the glorified body of the resurrected Christ. In fact, the stone's transformative effect on the metals was mirrored by its redemption of the body and soul of the alchemist himself.

Other "alternative" Christologies were formulated or defended by individuals who managed with varying degrees of success to navigate difficult political waters. The two following chapters deal with Christologies that emerged from the religious creativity of such people. In Jean-Pierre Brach's chapter we are introduced to the Renaissance polymath Guillaume Postel (1510–1581), who created one of the most extraordinary Christologies of the early modern age. The medieval mystic Bernard de Clairvaux had in the twelfth century proclaimed the appearance of Christ in three distinct phases: once on earth as Jesus, once in the final apocalypse, and between these two in a third, invisible state in the Eucharist. Early in his career, in 1547, Postel elaborated on this Bernardian theme by adding a fourth coming of Christ. Postel had met the Messiah come again – this time in the person of a poor Venetian woman. This led to new and often remarkably heterodox theological statements on Postel's part regarding salvation, the doctrine of the Eucharist, and the nature of Christ's celestial body. His writings proved so unpalatable to church authorities that Postel was summoned to appear before an inquisitorial court, barely escaping with his life by being declared insane.

Emanuel Swedenborg (1688–1772) was a visionary whose religious doctrines are deeply indebted both to traditional Christian theology and to a radical type of Enlightenment rationality. Wouter Hanegraaff's chapter shows how Swedenborg combined these two seemingly incompatible approaches. His Christology rejected orthodox trinitarianism in favor of an appeal to God's unity, claiming that it was God Jehovah himself who was incarnated in the person known as Christ. Swedenborg's innovative understanding of Christ was based upon his peculiar combination of strict biblicism, a relentless pursuit of logic and consistency, and a personal conviction of being the chosen instrument of divine revelation.

Yet other "alternative" views of Christ materialized as new church organizations began to emerge. Douglas Davies' chapter "Christ in Mormonism" identifies a series of images of Christ that exist within the Church of Jesus Christ of Latter-day Saints, that is the Mormon Church. Various images have dominated at different periods of the Church's history: Christ in the Plan of Salvation, in visionary appearance, as Jehovah, and as Elder Brother; the pro-active Christ of Gethsemane and the passive Christ of the cross; Jesus as the Christ in resurrection appearances in the Holy Land, in America and to the Lost Tribes of Israel; Jesus in his Second Coming as King of the world.

Swedenborg and the Mormon prophet Joseph Smith were innovative religious figures in a repressive age. Because of restrictions on the freedom of the press in Sweden, Swedenborg published all of his religious works outside of his native country, primarily in Holland and England. Neither this fact nor the fact that he did not try to organize a church enabled him to escape controversy with the church in Sweden. Toward the end of his life two men who had accepted his teachings became embroiled in a heresy trial as a result of propagating the new ideas. Similarly, Joseph Smith and the church that he founded were from the very inception enmeshed in conflicts with surrounding society, and were repeatedly persecuted and driven out of their settlements. By the late nineteenth century, such repressive measures against religious dissidents were no longer the norm. The decreasing ability of the theological mainstream to enforce discipline through legal means has allowed new narratives to spread with little opposition, and the rate of innovation has accelerated in the last century and a half. Cheaper means of mass distribution have made it possible for a much broader range of people to contribute with their own voices to the discussion of "who Christ really was." In the last few years, anybody with a computer with Internet access and the modest technical know-how necessary in order to set up a website has been able to disseminate their own Jesus narratives. The last five chapters of this book illustrate a number of very diverse understandings of Jesus Christ that have emerged from the 1870s to today.

As shown in James Santucci's contribution to this book, the conception of the Christ in the theosophical tradition reflects attitudes and teachings more allegorical than historical. The teachings of the various theosophical authors are not homogeneous, but there are two observations that are for the most part accepted: the fundamental distinction between Jesus and the Christ and the subordinate role of Jesus to the Christ. As one "overshadowed" by the Christ, Jesus assumes importance as a teacher sent by a brotherhood or spiritual hierarchy to guide human evolution. The teachings of the atonement, crucifixion, resurrection, ascension, and the second coming all take on a meaning summarized by theosophist Annie Besant (1847–1933) as enabling "every man . . . to become a Christ."

Ariosophy, described in the chapter by Nicholas Goodrick-Clarke, is a Christian variant of the *völkisch* (nationalist-racialist) ideology widespread among the intellectual precursors of the Third Reich in the period 1900 to 1935. Conceived by the former Cistercian monk, Jörg Lanz von Liebenfels (1874–1954), Ariosophy expounded a form of Christianity based on the idea that the Aryan race was divine. Lanz's racial theology described a clash between these god-like Aryans and various demonic dark races, a scenario he supported by referring to a decidedly idiosyncratic biblical exegesis. Lanz also assimilated aspects of the natural sciences, and in particular understood electricity as a form of divine revelation and inspiration. In his book *Theozoologie* (1905), he suggested that the divine ancestors of the Aryan race had possessed extraordinary electrical powers such as telepathy and omniscience. Lanz identified Christ as just such an "electrical" being, who came to redeem a fallen humankind from bestial miscegenation through a revival of the racial gnosis.

Metaphysical Christianity is a term which includes a variety of currents, ranging from New Thought denominations to churches oriented more toward theosophy and spiritualism. These movements reject traditional theological views regarding, among other things, sin and hell, and embrace a view of the human being as basically good. We are all part of God, and we will all eventually be "saved." In most systems of metaphysical Christianity, Christ becomes a divine principle and Jesus becomes a human being who is honored as the person who best exemplified the Christ principle in his life. Jesus thus does not save us by "atoning" for our sins. Instead, he serves as a model for human striving by demonstrating perfect "at-one-ment" with God. James R. Lewis' chapter concentrates on the Christology of one such metaphysical Christian group, the Church of the Movement of Spiritual Inner Awareness (MSIA).

The Aetherius Society, the subject of a chapter by Mikael Rothstein, is one of the largest and certainly oldest UFO religions. It was founded by the late George King in London in 1954 when he, according to the movement's founding myth, was approached by extraterrestrials and told to serve as their prophet or "Terrestrial Channel." One of these benevolent space creatures is, according to The Aetherius Society, the same entity as the Jesus of the New Testament. Hence, George King had on several occasions been in direct contact with Jesus, either when he visited Earth or during trips in Commander Jesus' space ship Mars Sector 6. Rothstein's chapter attempts to explore the mythological reformulation of Jesus in various aspects of the religious life of the Aetherius movement: texts, rituals, hagiography, iconography, and so forth. He argues that the Jesus of The Aetherius Society is different from, yet in some ways very similar to, the Jesus of "traditional" Christian mythology, a fact that suggests that religious symbols can be quite stable over time, yet allow for very variable interpretations.

The final chapter surveys a number of contemporary Jesus legends, but does so principally in order to discuss and illustrate some theoretical points: how do such narratives relate to more general processes of religious innovation? Although the title of this book stresses the "alternative" nature of these and other understandings of Jesus Christ, the scare quotes alert us to a potential pitfall with the term. Vestiges of earlier heresiological thinking still influence prevalent theorizing on the development of "alternative" understandings of Jesus Christ. Major sociological theories, such as Colin Campbell's concept of the cultic milieu, presuppose that there is a dominant, nearly monolithic culture, in opposition to an underground of divergent and rather marginalized innovations.[4] Other theories, developed by cultural anthropologists over the last several decades, afford opportunities to understand religious innovation differently.

The concept of "culture" in early anthropological writings tended to be described as a fixed set of ideas, behaviors, artifacts, values, and so forth:

---

[4] Colin Campbell, "The Cult, the Cultic Milieu and Secularization," *A Sociological Yearbook of Religion in Britain* 5 (1972), 119–136.

each ethnic group, in this view, had a distinct culture shared by its members. Alfred Kroeber and Clyde Kluckhohn in a seminal text defined culture in such terms: "Culture consists of patterns, explicit and implicit, of and for behavior acquired and transmitted by symbols, constituting the distinctive achievement of human groups."[5] The idea of a fairly monolithic religious landscape in the West, with the markedly distinct products of heterodox individual agency relegated to a separate countercultural cultic milieu, closely fits this view of culture.

Since at least the late 1970s, however, the representation of cultures as stable systems regulating individual behavior has been the subject of considerable critique. The assumption that a particular group shares a culture has been seen as masking the hegemony of the dominant strata of that group, and being blind to variability and diversity. Anthropologists such as Roy Wagner,[6] George Marcus, James Clifford,[7] Tim Ingold,[8] and many others have from a variety of perspectives suggested that "culture" is a problematic term, an abstraction created by the anthropologist in order to describe the manifold things that people do, rather than a monolithic model of and for behavior that people collectively inherit and embody.[9]

A number of different metaphors could be useful to conceptualize this more recent approach to culture and cultural variability. The one employed here is that of culture as a profuse repertoire of discourses and practices, that is, what other authors have labeled a "tool kit,"[10] or a "surfeit of cultural material."[11] The repertoire metaphor is helpful both in describing synchronic variation and change over time. Synchronic variation, as Fredrik Barth argues, is part of any complex society that encompasses people with different levels of expertise, different received traditions, local variations, various social strata and various pragmatic interests.[12] In the specific domain of religion, agents with different competences and interests can pick and choose different elements from the repertoire.

[5] Alfred Kroeber and Clyde Kluckhohn, *Culture: A Critical Review of Concepts and Definitions* (Cambridge, Mass.: The Museum, 1952), 357.

[6] Roy Wagner, *The Invention of Culture* (2nd edn., Chicago: University of Chicago Press, 1981).

[7] George Marcus and James Clifford, *Writing Culture: The Poetics and Politics of Ethnography* (Chicago: University of Chicago Press, 1986).

[8] Tim Ingold, "Introduction to Culture," in Tim Ingold (ed.), *Companion Encyclopedia of Anthropology: Humanity, Culture and Social Life* (London: Routledge, 1994), 329–349.

[9] The genealogy of the term "culture" is far more complex than can possibly be sketched here. For a background to the classic statement by Kroeber and Kluckhohn and to the debate of the 1980s and 1990s, see Adam Kuper, *Culture: the Anthropologists' Account* (Cambridge, Mass.: Harvard University Press, 1999).

[10] Ann Swidler, "Culture in Action: Symbols and Strategies," *American Sociological Review* 51 (1986), 277.

[11] Fredrik Barth, *Balinese Worlds* (Chicago: University of Chicago Press, 1993), 4.

[12] Barth, *Balinese Worlds*, 4–5.

Diachronic change arises because religions, like "cultures" more broadly, have no essential components that are inherently stable over time: old doctrines are replaced by new ones, existing rituals die out in favor of ritual innovations, and organizational structures are transformed. Innovations arise when the selection of religious elements from the repertoire changes, when existing elements are discarded or new elements are introduced. In various branches of the Christian tradition, the tension between conservatism and innovation is seen in the ways in which various issues subsist over time, become contested or are rejected: Is Scripture inerrant? Is Hell a physical location? Do demons truly exist? Are there witches? Are rituals of exorcism a core element of Christianity? Should heretics be compelled by force to convert? Must good Christians reject Darwin's theory of natural selection? Should only men be accepted as members of the clergy? Is homosexuality an abomination in the eyes of God? In the past (sometimes the not-too-distant past), these questions would be answered in the affirmative by most people who identified themselves as Christians. Today, the responses to such questions become identity markers that distinguish different denominations, for example "conservative" from "liberal."

The metaphor of religions as vast repertoires from which a limited selection is made suggests a number of constraints on variability and change, including the composition of the repertoire, the social and historical context that makes a particular selection from this repertoire relevant, the individual creativity of particular agents, and the ability of dominant players in the religious ecology to enforce their own selection on others.[13] The final chapter by Olav Hammer surveys aspects of these four basic issues of religious innovation, as they are relevant to innovative opinions on Jesus Christ in the modern age. They are, nevertheless, valid for earlier historical periods as well.

The total religious repertoire is truly immense. Classical theological approaches to Christianity tend to highlight a particular transmission of discourses and practices, and to see this as constituting the Christian tradition. Christian writers of any age have, however, at their disposal a much broader set of religious elements: the entire fund of previous narratives and practices with which they happen to be familiar, from the earliest canonical and extracanonical texts to voices of their own time. Indeed, even the resulting vast corpus of accumulated "tradition" is by no means coterminous with the entire repertoire. Religions have no impermeable,

---

[13] There are other constraints, e.g. of a cognitive nature, but these would require a separate, extensive treatment.

fixed and stable borders vis-à-vis others.[14] Discourses and practices are regularly transported across the putative boundaries of the various religions and of various social domains. Innovations in Christian doctrine can be constructed by selecting and combining themes from biblical passages, eschatological currents, philosophical concepts drawn, for example, from Platonism, Stoicism, and Aristotelianism, the natural sciences, texts known from Judaism, Hinduism, Buddhism, and other religious traditions, and so on.

Many innovations strike the observer as adaptations to prevalent social and historical forces. The philosopher Alasdair MacIntyre once remarked that "Christians behave like everyone else but use a different vocabulary in characterizing their behaviour, and so conceal their lack of distinctiveness."[15] Many of the shifts in what constitutes "Christianity" can be seen as ways to reduce distinctiveness vis-à-vis the wider socio-historical context. Has the inerrancy of the holy texts come under attack? The "essence" of liberal Christianity no longer needs to include this tenet. Have social attitudes regarding gender equality and tolerance toward others changed? Christianity can be reconstructed as a religion that accepts pluralism and embraces equal opportunities for all.

Other shifts appear less motivated by such external pressures, and are presumably irreducible ethnographic data that can best be attributed to the ideas of individual religious spokespersons. Jean-Pierre Brach's chapter on Guillaume Postel documents how Postel depended on previous and contemporary opinions, but also how truly original, not to say eccentric, the resulting idea of a feminine Messiah was. Nicholas Goodrick-Clarke's contribution similarly demonstrates the thorough assimilation of contemporary natural science, archaeology, anthropology, and biblical exegesis in the construction of a racial gnosis, but also how dependent this Ariosophical gnosis was on the unremitting efforts of its originator Jörg Lanz von Liebenfels.

Despite all efforts at adapting inherited Christ myths to changing circumstances, and despite the vast amounts of individual creativity deployed, various restrictions put a break on forces that would otherwise fragment "tradition" completely. Innovations and loans are rarely wholesale rejections of existing structures and adoptions of radically novel ones: religions do display a measure of conservatism. Conservatism can be the net effect

---

[14] This understanding of the porous religious and social boundaries owes much to the German discussion of a specific field of European history of religions; see, e.g., Burkhard Gladigow, "Europäische Religionsgeschichte," in Hans G. Kippenberg and Birgitte Luchesi (eds.), *Lokale Religionsgeschichte* (Marburg: Diagonal Verlag, 1995), 21–42.

[15] Alasdair MacIntyre, *Against the Self-Images of the Age* (London: Duckworth, 1971), 24.

of religious spokespersons insisting on the vital importance of safeguarding the particular selection of elements that they have been socialized into and which they prefer. Cognitive constraints (not all innovations are plausible or memorable enough to be transmitted), market mechanisms (not all innovations are equally welcomed by a readership), and not least disciplining forces (resistance from established churches, critique by skeptical writers) are further mechanisms that keep the creative imagination in relative check. Like all other religious discourses, Jesus narratives are subject to these forces. Although, as we have noted, even the earliest Jesus narratives are thoroughly imbued with legendary material, a lingering feeling remains with many writers that they are in some sense not only historically prior, but also more genuine accounts.

Academic writing surveying non-orthodox Jesus legends and Christ myths is not immune from this tendency. Many published studies enter the fray of textual polemics: not only are they historical chronicles of alternative beliefs, they are often composed with the explicit purpose of debunking such stories. An early classic of the genre, Edgar Goodspeed's *Strange New Gospels* (1931), presents this aim in the preface: to point out "their failure to meet the simple and familiar tests of antiquity and genuineness." Later examples of this literature pursue the same goal of refuting the claims contained in modern Jesus narratives, and occasionally do so in a decidedly hostile language.[16] All of these works are highly informative, but most have a theological goal that the present volume does not share. A critical analysis of such texts as Notovitch's *The Unknown Life of Jesus Christ*, which purports to tell of Jesus' travels to India, will readily reveal clues that the document cannot be a historically accurate record of the life of Jesus. Books such as Levi Dowling's *The Aquarian Gospel of Jesus the Christ* do not even purport to be ancient documents, but function as revelatory narratives.[17] As such, they are hardly very different from the canonical texts relating to

---

[16] The accounts span a broad spectrum. There are numerous decidedly theological refutations such as Douglas Groothuis, *Jesus in an Age of Controversy* (Eugene, Oreg.: Wipf & Stock Publishers, 2002) and Ron Rhodes, *The Counterfeit Christ of the New Age Movement* (Grand Rapids, Mich.: Baker Publishing Group, 1990). Other works are combinations, in varying proportions, of descriptive and critical-normative approaches; see, e.g., Per Beskow, *Strange Tales about Jesus: A Survey of Unfamiliar Gospels* (Philadelphia: Fortress Press, 1983; translated from the Swedish original *Fynd och fusk i Bibelns värld* [Stockholm: Proprius, 1979]), Günter Grönbold, *Jesus in Indien: Das Ende einer Legende* (Munich: Kösel, 1985), Arild Romarheim, *Kristus i vannmannens tegn: Nyreligiøse oppfatninger av Jesus Kristus* (Oslo: Credo, 1992) and others. Yet others are scholarly surveys with a touch of disapproval, e.g. John Saliba, *Christian Responses to the New Age Movement* (London: Geoffrey Chapman, 1999), 198–201. Among the few entirely non-polemical accounts, see the brief overview in Wouter J. Hanegraaff, *New Age Religion and Western Culture: Esotericism in the Mirror of Secular Thought* (Leiden: Brill, 1996), 314–318.

[17] Both of these books are discussed at greater length in the final chapter of the present volume, "Modern Jesus legends."

the life of Jesus. The books in the scriptural canon also present historical inaccuracies and internal contradictions. They too are considered by many insiders to the Christian tradition to be divinely inspired, that is, revelatory texts. In short, all Jesus narratives, whether ancient or modern, are the products of the religious imagination, and can be analyzed as such.

This book takes for granted what the critical literature sets out to prove, namely that Jesus narratives are legends and not historically accurate chronicles; that Christologies are theological constructs, the truth claims of which we can surely bracket. The stories of Jesus and conceptions of Christ documented here have been chosen because they are "alternative" in a social and historical sense, not because of any theological divergences from a putatively more "authentic" understanding. The mythologies of the scriptures and the elaborations of the various Christian churches, the conceptions of Jesus Christ from the Gnostics to the age of UFOs are the manifold results of the indomitable religious creativity of our species.

BIBLIOGRAPHY

Barth, Fredrik, *Balinese Worlds* (Chicago: University of Chicago Press, 1993).

Beskow, Per, *Strange Tales about Jesus: A Survey of Unfamiliar Gospels* (Philadelphia: Fortress Press, 1983; translated from the Swedish original *Fynd och fusk i Bibelns värld* [Stockholm: Proprius, 1979]).

Campbell, Colin, "The Cult, the Cultic Milieu and Secularization," *A Sociological Yearbook of Religion in Britain* 5 (1972), 119–136.

Ehrman, Bart, *The Orthodox Corruption of Scripture: The Effect of Early Christological Controversies on the Text of the New Testament* (New York and Oxford: Oxford University Press, 1993).

Gladigow, Burkhard, "Europäische Religionsgeschichte," in Hans G. Kippenberg and Birgitte Luchesi (eds.), *Lokale Religionsgeschichte* (Marburg: Diagonal Verlag, 1995), 21–42.

Grönbold, Günter, *Jesus in Indien: Das Ende einer Legende* (Munich: Kösel, 1985).

Groothuis, Douglas, *Jesus in an Age of Controversy* (Eugene, Oreg.: Wipf & Stock Publishers, 2002).

Hanegraaff, Wouter J., *New Age Religion and Western Culture: Esotericism in the Mirror of Secular Thought* (Leiden: Brill, 1996).

Ingold, Tim, "Introduction to Culture," in Tim Ingold (ed.), *Companion Encyclopedia of Anthropology: Humanity, Culture and Social Life* (London: Routledge, 1994), 329–349.

Kannengieser, Charles, S. J., "Arianism," in Mircea Eliade (ed.), *Encyclopedia of Religion* (New York: Macmillan 1986), vol. I, 405–406.

Kelly, J. N. D., *Early Christian Doctrines* (5th edn., London: A. & C. Black, 1977).

King, Karen, *What is Gnosticism?* (Cambridge, Mass.: Belknap Press of Harvard University Press, 2003).

Kroeber, Alfred and Clyde Kluckhohn, *Culture: A Critical Review of Concepts and Definitions* (Cambridge Mass.: The Museum, 1952).

Kuper, Adam, *Culture: The Anthropologists' Account* (Cambridge, Mass.: Harvard University Press, 1999).

MacIntyre, Alasdair, *Against the Self-Images of the Age* (London: Duckworth, 1971).

Marcus, George and James Clifford, *Writing Culture: The Poetics and Politics of Ethnography* (Chicago: University of Chicago Press, 1986).

Pelikan, Jaroslav, *Jesus through the Centuries: His Place in the History of Culture* (New Haven and London: Yale University Press, 1985 and many reprints).

Rhodes, Ron, *The Counterfeit Christ of the New Age Movement* (Grand Rapids, Mich.: Baker Publishing Group, 1990).

Romarheim, Arild, *Kristus i vannmannens tegn: Nyreligiøse oppfatninger av Jesus Kristus* (Oslo: Credo 1992).

Saliba, John, *Christian Responses to the New Age Movement* (London: Geoffrey Chapman, 1999).

Swidler, Ann, "Culture in Action: Symbols and Strategies," *American Sociological Review* 51 (1986), 273–286.

Wagner, Roy, *The Invention of Culture* (2nd edn., Chicago: University of Chicago Press, 1981).

Williams, Michael Allen, *Rethinking "Gnosticism": An Argument for Dismantling a Dubious Category* (Princeton: Princeton University Press, 1996).

CHAPTER 2

The gnostic Christ

Roelof van den Broek

INTRODUCTION

In almost all esoteric movements in which Christ plays a role of any
importance, he is primarily a teacher of hidden wisdom – a wisdom that
implies salvation for those who accept it. This also holds for the gnostic
type of Christianity that was current in the first three centuries of our
era. That there were Christians who considered the possession of spiritual
insight (Greek: *gnōsis*, "knowledge") an indispensable means of salvation is
abundantly testified to by original gnostic documents, the Nag Hammadi
Codices (NHC) in particular, and the vehement polemics by anti-gnostic
Christian writers, such as Irenaeus of Lyon (ca. 180) and Hippolytus of
Rome (ca. 220).[1] Already the Pseudo-Pauline *First Letter to Timothy* (ca.
100 CE) warned against "the contradictions of what is falsely called 'Knowledge'" (6.20), although the exact nature of this knowledge is left in the dark.
In recent research, historians of the early church tend to describe the gnostic
movement as an original Christian heresy. But that view of Gnosticism is
too limited, since it accounts neither for closely related phenomena outside
the Christian world, such as Mandaeism, nor for those ancient gnostic texts
which do not show any (or only some superficial) Christian influence, nor
for the spontaneous emergence of gnostic ideas through the ages, without
any connection with those of the early Christian gnostics. However, the

---

[1] See the editions mentioned in the bibliography. For an overview and succinct discussion of the
primary sources for the study of Gnosticism, see Roelof van den Broek, "Gnosticism II: Gnostic
Literature," in Wouter J. Hanegraaff *et al.* (eds.), *Dictionary of Gnosis and Western Esotericism* (2
vols., Leiden: Brill, 2005 and, in 1 vol., 2006), 417–432. In the following, the Nag Hammadi
Codices are mostly quoted (with sometimes slight alterations) after the translations in Marvin Meyer
(ed.), *The Nag Hammadi Scriptures: The International Edition* (New York: Harper, 2007). Some
recent introductions to Gnosticism are: Karen L. King, *What is Gnosticism?* (Cambridge, Mass. and
London: Harvard University Press, 2003); Christoph Markschies, *Gnosis: An Introduction* (London:
T&T Clark, 2003); Roelof van den Broek, "Gnosticism I: Gnostic Religion," in Hanegraaff *et al.*
(eds.), *Dictionary of Gnosis*, 403–416; Birger A. Pearson, *Ancient Gnosticism: Traditions and Literature*
(Minneapolis: Fortress Press, 2007).

ideas and traditions that are usually held to be gnostic show such a great diversity that the question has been raised whether we should not stop using the term "Gnosticism" altogether, since it (and the term "gnostic" as well) has lost any specific meaning.[2] There are, however, no serious objections against maintaining the (modern) term Gnosticism in a neutral, non-pejorative sense, as long as it is not taken as referring to a monolithic religious system or as the heretical counterpart of ecclesiastical orthodoxy. It can be used as an umbrella term for the many, variegated, and often conflicting views that emphasized the salvific role of secret spiritual knowledge, which in particular found expression in the great gnostic systems of the second and third centuries. In my view, it should better be avoided with respect to the gnostic and esoteric ideas and currents that arose in the West after Late Antiquity, to which, however, the terms "gnosis" and "gnostic" are perfectly applicable.

That the gnostic movement was not merely a Christian heresy is clearly demonstrated by the fact that there are gnostic systems in which the revealer of the saving knowledge is not Christ, but quite another heavenly figure. A well-known example is Derdekeas, who in the *Paraphrasis of Shem* (NHC VII, 1) plays the role of revealer and savior. Other gnostic writings are only superficially Christianized, for instance the *Holy Book of the Great Invisible Spirit* (NHC III, and IV, 2), in which Seth manifests himself as the savior who appeared at various occasions in the course of history and finally in the person of Jesus. But there are also many gnostic texts which present Christ as the revealer and savior *par excellence*. Some important ideas contained in these texts will be the subject of the following discussion.[3]

THE HEAVENLY CHRIST

The gnostic views on Christ have to be discussed and can only be rightly understood within the context of the early Christian debate on

---

[2] Michael A. Williams, *Rethinking "Gnosticism": An Argument for Dismantling a Dubious Category* (Princeton: Princeton University Press, 1996). A discussion of the problem of definition (and a rejection of Williams' proposal) in van den Broek, "Gnosticism I," 403–405, and Pearson, *Ancient Gnosticism*, 8–12; according to King, *What is Gnosticism*, 213–216, Williams did not go far enough.

[3] On Gnostic Christology and soteriology in general: Kurt Rudolph, *Gnosis: The Nature and History of Gnosticism* (San Francisco: Harper, 1987), 148–171; Giovanni Filoramo, *A History of Gnosticism* (Oxford and Cambridge, Mass.: Blackwell, 1990; many reprints), 101–127; Majella Franzmann, *Jesus in the Nag Hammadi Writings* (Edinburgh: T&T Clark, 1996); on the Valentinian views in particular: Einar Thomassen, *The Spiritual Seed: The Church of the Valentinians* (Nag Hammadi and Manichaean Studies, 60; Leiden: Brill, 2006). A thorough discussion of the relevant texts on the Passion of Christ can be found in Dietrich Voorgang, *Die Passion Jesu und Christi in der Gnosis* (Europäische Hochschulschriften, Reihe 23: Theologie, 432; Frankfurt am Main: Peter Lang, 1991).

the relationship between God and Christ, and that between Christ and the historical Jesus. In the second and third centuries, almost all Christians shared the belief in the divine origin of Christ, his appearance on earth in the person of Jesus, and his return to the divine realm, but the interpretation of these beliefs was a matter of fierce dispute. The only dissenting opinion was that of the great majority of the Jewish Christians of Palestine and Syria, who refused to assign a divine status to Christ. They preferred to see him as a special prophet of God who had brought God's final revelation, after having received the Holy Spirit at his baptism in the river Jordan.[4]

In the course of the second century, the relationship between God and Christ's divine nature became a burning question. The simplest and most widely accepted answer was to make no distinction at all, which in any case saved the monotheistic concept of God. In Antiquity, opponents called this view "monarchianism"; modern scholars mostly speak of "modalism," because in its mature form Father, Son, and Spirit were considered three modes in which the one God manifested himself. It was "a simple way of expressing the essential beliefs that God is one and Christ is God."[5] In fact, it was an early form of the later doctrine of the two natures of Christ: the historical Jesus was thought to have been real God and real man in one person, who had really suffered. Ignatius of Antioch (before 117 or ca. 170) did not hesitate to speak of "the suffering of my God" or "the blood of God."[6] And Zepherinus, the bishop of Rome (198–217), stated: "I know only one God, Jesus Christ, and except him no one else who was born and suffered."[7] Although our information is scarce, there also seem to have been gnostics who adhered to a modalistic concept of the Godhead. If Irenaeus is to be trusted, there were Simonian gnostics in Rome who said that Simon Magus, whom they glorified as the supreme God, had taught

---

[4] On the Jewish Christians, see now Oskar Skarsaune and Reidar Hvalik (eds.), *Jewish Believers in Jesus: The Early Centuries* (Peabody, Mass.: Hendrickson Publishers 2007).

[5] Geoffrey W. H. Lampe, "Christian Theology in the Patristic Period," in Hubert Cunliffe-Jones (ed.), *A History of Christian Doctrine* (Edinburgh: T&T Clark, 1978), 53. On monarchianism as the most common form of Christian belief in the second century, see the important studies by Reinhard M. Hübner, *Der Paradox Eine: Antignostischer Monarchianismus im zweiten Jahrhundert* (Supplements to Vigiliae Christianae, 50; Leiden: Brill, 1999).

[6] Ignatius of Antioch, *Epistle to the Romans* 6.3 and *Epistle to the Ephesians* 1.1 (cf. *ibid.* 18.2: "our God Jesus Christ was conceived by Mary from the seed of David on the one hand and the Spirit of God on the other"). On the authority of Eusebius, *Ecclesiastical History* 3.36, Ignatius is usually dated to the reign of the emperor Trajan (96–117), but Hübner, *Der Paradox Eine*, 132–206 ("Die Ignatianen und Noet von Smyrna"), has made a strong case for a much later date, between 165 and 175.

[7] Hippolytus, *Refutatio omnium haeresium* 9.11.3.

that he had appeared as Son among the Jews, had descended as Father in Samaria, and had come as Holy Spirit among the other nations.[8]

More intellectual Christians, however, gnostics and non-gnostics alike, rejected the monarchian position as too naïve. On the non-gnostic side, the so-called Apologists, of whom Justin Martyr (d. 165) was the most influential, distinguished between God the Father and his Son, the pre-existent Christ, whom they identified with the Logos of Greek philosophy (Stoa, Platonism) and Alexandrian Jewish religious speculations (Philo of Alexandria, and already in John 1.1–4, 14). In second-century theological speculations, the Holy Spirit played only a minor role. It was primarily seen and experienced as the spirit of God or Christ that manifested itself in the individual or communal life of the Christians. The divine Logos was God's manifestation in creation and revelation, who for the sake of salvation had become man in Jesus Christ.

The gnostic Christians also distinguished several hypostases within the one Godhead but they usually distinguished more aspects of the divine than the three "Persons" that became customary in non-gnostic, ecclesiastical theology. The great gnostic myths of the second century describe the development of the divine world out of the highest divine principle into a great number of divine qualities, called aeons, which together form the Fullness (*pleroma*) of God. The *Apocryphon of John*, the basic document of what is often called Sethian Gnosticism,[9] puts the Son Christ in the third position after the Unknown Father and his First Thought, the Mother Barbelo. But there is a fair possibility that originally the tradition only spoke about the Son as the Light that was anointed with the Father's goodness (*chrēstotēs*), which may have led to its identification with Christ.[10] In any case, the Sethian description of the Pleroma does not give an indication that Christ is to play a role of any importance in the process of salvation. As

---

[8] Irenaeus, *Adversus haereses* 1.23.1. These Simonian speculations have nothing to do with Simon's original teaching: they betray a distinct influence of late second-century Christian monarchianism, although the Simonians denied that Christ had a real, material body. On Simon Magus and Simonian Gnosticism, see my article "Simon Magus" in Hanegraaff *et al.* (eds.), *Dictionary of Gnosis*, 1069–1073 (with references to relevant literature).

[9] Standard edition of the *Apocryphon* by Michael Waldstein and Frederik Wisse (eds.), *The Apocryphon of John: Synopsis of Nag Hammadi Codices II, 1; III, 1; and IV, 1 with BG 8502, 2* (Nag Hammadi and Manichaean Studies, 32; Leiden: Brill, 1995). On Sethianism, see Michael A. Williams, "Sethianism," in Antti Marjanen and Petri Luomanen (eds.), *A Companion to Second-Century "Heretics"* (Supplements to Vigiliae Christianae, 76; Leiden, Brill, 2005), 32–63, and Winrich A. Löhr, "Sethians," in Hanegraaff *et al.* (eds.), *Dictionary of Gnosis*, 1063–1069.

[10] On the very complicated tradition of the "Sethian" Pleroma, see my study "Autogenes and Adamas. The Mythological Structure of the Apocryphon of John," in Roelof van den Broek, *Studies in Gnosticism and Alexandrian Christianity* (Nag Hammadi and Manichaean Studies, 39; Leiden: Brill, 1996), 56–66.

a matter of fact, there was no need of a savior in the original perfect Pleroma of God. According to the *Apocryphon*, it was only after the attempt by the lowest aeon Sophia to imitate the creative activity of the Unknown Father, which entailed the creation of the world and humankind, that Barbelo sent a female savior and revealer, the luminous Epinoia (not Christ), to control and finally repair the damage.[11]

The situation is more complicated in the second great gnostic myth, that of the Valentinians. The teaching of Valentinus himself (ca. 140 CE) cannot be reconstructed to an acceptable degree of certainty anymore, but we have much information about the ideas of his pupils, both through original Valentinian texts and more or less reliable reports by opponents.[12] Both kinds of sources agree with respect to the structure of the Valentinian Pleroma: from the Unknown Forefather, called "Depth," and his Thought, also called "Silence" (or more monadic: from the Forefather who rests in Silence) derive thirty aeons, who are arranged in three groups of respectively four, five and six pairs. Theletos ("Will") and Sophia ("Wisdom") form the last pair that appeared.[13] In this aeonic system, too, there is no organic place for Christ or any other saving figure, because it is perfect in itself. In this connection, a detailed discussion of the various Valentinian views on the "fall" of Sophia and the measures taken to correct it would carry us too far. Suffice it to say that Sophia sought to understand the Father but that her intention and passion became a miscarriage, which was put outside the Pleroma and there formed the lower Sophia. Thereupon Christ and the Holy Spirit came into being, either within the Pleroma or outside it; in the last case as an emanation from the lower Sophia, from whom Christ loosens himself and returns to the Pleroma. In both cases Christ restores the equilibrium of the Pleroma by teaching the knowledge of the Father to all the aeons.

---

[11] *Apocryphon of John*, Synopsis 53, 19–54, 18 (ed. Waldstein & Wisse, 116–119). The revealing activity of Christ is only mentioned in the introductory and concluding framework and in a series of seven questions by John and answers by Jesus, which point to a Christianization of originally non-Christian material.

[12] For a full discussion of all Valentinian traditions and their sources, see Thomassen, *Spiritual Seed*; recent overviews by Jens Holzhausen, "Valentinus and Valentinians," in Hanegraaff *et al.* (eds.), *Dictionary of Gnosis*, 1144–1157, and Immo Dunderberg, "The School of Valentinus," in Marjanen and Luomanen (eds.), *Companion*, 64–99.

[13] Irenaeus, *Adv. Haer.* 1.1–2 (Valentinians in general), 1.11.1 (Valentinus). The more monadic view of the source of being, with other differences, in Hippolytus, *Refutatio* 6.29–30, and, among others, the *Valentinian Exposition*, NHC XI, 23.19–21: "This, then, [is the] root [of] the All, the Monad before whom there is none. He is also the Dyad, dwelling in Silence and speaking only with himself." For a penetrating study of Valentinian "protology," see Thomassen, *Spiritual Seed*, 193–326.

It is a characteristic feature of Valentinian Gnosticism that Christ acts already as a savior in the pneumatic realm of the Pleroma. The next step is made by the production of "the common fruit of the Pleroma" or the savior Jesus, a second Christ, who descends to the lower Sophia and brings her knowledge and delivers her from her emotions, which results in the psychic form of being and in matter. Moreover, she gives birth to pneumatic seeds that are sowed in a certain number of (but not all) human beings. These seeds are in a state of ignorance and must be saved, that is, brought to knowledge, too. This is done by the earthly Christ, in whom the savior Jesus takes a human form, albeit not a fleshly body. Thus, the Valentinians acknowledged three Christs who acted within the three realms they distinguished: the pneumatic Christ restored the Pleroma, the savior Jesus saved the lower Sophia in the psychic realm and Jesus Christ brought saving knowledge to the spiritual seeds in the world of matter.

The discovery of a number of authentic Valentinian documents has shown that Valentinian Gnosticism was much more variegated than the reports of the anti-gnostic writers suggested. In this context, only the *Tractatus Tripartitus* (NHC I, 5) may be mentioned, a distinctly Valentinian systematic treatise.[14] Its unknown author, who probably wrote in the first half of the third century, must have been an original theologian and a powerful thinker. He has some distinctive features in common with the Valentinian theologians Theodotus and Heracleon (both second half of the second century CE) and with the non-gnostic theologian Origen (185–254). The work can be seen as an attempt to approach the non-gnostic theological positions as closely as possible without giving up the essential Valentinian views on the Godhead and the salvation of man. Among its most characteristic features are the trinity of Father, Son, and Church and the absence of Sophia as initiatrix of the developments within and outside the divine Pleroma. The Father is unknowable, the Son is his self-reflective Thought and the Church is the congregation of the aeons, conceived as the divine qualities of the Father as expressed in the thinking of the Son. The disturbance of the Pleroma is not caused by Sophia but by the Logos, who was the youngest aeon (NHC I, 75.17–77.11). It was with good intentions that this Logos "rushed forward to give glory to the Father, even though he undertook a task beyond his power." It is even said that this impulsive act and its consequences did not happen without the will of the Father, "rather the Father had brought him forth for the things that he knew must take place." Nevertheless, the Logos reached too high and, just

---

[14] See Thomassen, *Spiritual Seed*, 46–61, 166–187.

as in the case of Sophia, his presumptuous thought triggered a course of events that led to the genesis of a psychic and a material world. The savior is the product of the Pleroma, he enlightened the fallen Logos, who in his turn gave birth to the spiritual seeds (the spiritual church above), and breathed a particle of this seed, the "breath of life," into the first human being, who was made out of material and psychic elements (104.18–106.25). In accordance with the pneumatic, psychic, and the material levels of being there are three kinds of human beings: pneumatics, psychics, and hylics (118.14–119.27).

THE BODY OF JESUS AND THE PASSION

In the second and third centuries, Christian thinkers began to realize that the relationship between the divine and the human in the historical Jesus Christ posed a serious problem. We have to keep in mind, however, that the great majority of Christians were not intellectuals who wanted to understand and to know, but simple believers who experienced their salvation through participation in the mysteries of the church: the baptismal rite and the Eucharist. Christianity was primarily a mystery religion that promised its adherents remission of sins and eternal life after death. It taught that this had been realized by the appearance of God himself in Jesus Christ, who had suffered on the cross and had risen from death. Most Christians seem to have simply maintained the unity of Jesus of Nazareth and the divine Christ, without reflecting about how this unity had to be understood. But for Greek intellectuals this assumption became increasingly problematic because of the philosophical premise that the divine world of being and the material world of becoming were strictly separated and could not unite, which made the unity of God and man in Jesus Christ inconceivable. This problem became still more complicated by the common Christian view that the Son of God had appeared in the material world without being contaminated by it. This led to different ideas on the nature of Jesus' body.

One of the first attempts to solve this problem was to deny the reality of Christ's incarnation. As testified by the epistles ascribed to John, this view was already well known about 100 CE. The author writes: "Every spirit which acknowledges that Jesus Christ has come in the flesh is from God, and every spirit which does not thus acknowledge Jesus is not from God. This is what is meant by 'Antichrist'" (1 John 4.2–3). The same is expressed in 2 John 7, which speaks of "many deceivers" who have gone out to teach this doctrine. These people apparently propagated what is customarily called a "docetic Christology" (from Greek *dokeō*, "to seem," *dokēsis*, "appearance"), which means that Christ had only seemingly possessed a human body. This idea was not gnostic in itself, for it was primarily inspired by the Greek view of the unbridgeable gulf between unalterable being and ever-changing matter. But the idea of a "docetic Christ" fits very well in with the gnostic view on the nature of the created world. According to the great gnostic myths, the material world, the human body included, was an imperfect imitation of the divine world and its inhabitants. It had not been created by the highest God, but by a lower, imperfect or even bad demiurge, in order to incarcerate the divine spark that by a tragic accident had become the inner self of man.[15] It is this divine element that is the object of salvation; the material body, no more than a prison designed to confine it, is destined to perdition. There are several gnostic texts that expound the docetic view that Christ had only seemingly possessed a material, mortal body, and, as a corollary, had not really suffered at the crucifixion. To mention only one clear example, the *Second Treatise of the Great Seth* has the savior speak about his seeming passion: "I did not give in to them as they had planned. And I was not hurt at all. Though they punished me, I did not die in actuality but only in appearance." The crucifixion is not denied, but Christ explains that in reality it was Simon of Cyrene (cf., e.g., Mark 15.21 and parallels in other Gospels) who suffered, whereas Christ was rejoicing in the height and laughing at the ignorance of the evil powers (NHC VII, 55.14–56.19). Irenaeus of Lyons ascribes a very similar description of the passion to the Alexandrian teacher Basilides (first half of the second century): Christ was sent to the world in a human shape (*in forma hominis*), he performed miracles, but he did not suffer. Simon of Cyrene was transformed by him so that he was thought to be Jesus himself, whereas Jesus took the form of Simon and laughed at those who thought they crucified him.[16]

However, as said above, most Christians adhered to a rather unreflected form of Christology, which held that God and man had formed a union in the historical person of Jesus Christ. He had been really God and really man at the same time, who had suffered and died. This inevitably led to such antithetic, almost liturgical expressions as found in Ignatius of

---

[15] The classic form of this gnostic creation myth is found in the *Apocryphon of John*; it is extensively discussed by Alastair H. B. Logan, *Gnostic Truth and Christian Heresy: A Study in the History of Gnosticism* (Edinburgh: T&T Clark, 1996), and Karen L. King, *The Secret Revelation of John* (Cambridge, Mass. and London: Harvard University Press, 2006).

[16] Irenaeus, *Adversus haereses* 1.24.4. Whether Basilides was a gnostic (as Irenaeus describes him) or not is a matter of dispute; for recent overviews with earlier literature, see Winrich A. Löhr, "Basilides," in Hanegraaff *et al.* (eds.), *Dictionary of Gnosis*, 164–168 (not gnostic), and Birger A. Pearson, "Basilides the Gnostic," in Marjanen and Luomanen, *Companion*, 1–31 (gnostic).

Antioch, *Letter to the Ephesians* 7.1: "There is one physician, composed of flesh and of spirit, generate and ingenerate, God in man, authentic life in death, from Mary and from God, first passible and then impassible, Jesus Christ our Lord." In the same letter (20.2) Ignatius speaks of "Jesus Christ who is from the race of David according to the flesh, the Son of Man and the Son of God." Contrary to its original meaning, the Greek Christians of the second century took the biblical and Jewish term "Son of Man" as an indication of Christ's human nature.[17] The same interpretation is found among the gnostics, who, however, sometimes applied the term to the heavenly Christ too.[18] According to Clement of Alexandria (ca. 200), the Valentinians concluded from Jesus' testimony that the Son of Man "had to be rejected, outraged and crucified" (cf. Mark 8.31 and parallels in other Gospels), that he apparently spoke about the Son of Man "as about another, apparently the one who was subject to passion."[19] And in the Valentinian treatise *On the Resurrection*, NHC I, 44.21–33, the unknown author says that Jesus Christ was Son of God and Son of Man: "Rheginus, the Son of God was a Son of Man. He embraced both aspects, humanity and divinity, so that by being a Son of God he might conquer death, and by being a Son of Man the Pleroma might be restored."[20]

The gnostic Christians usually shared the generally Christian view that Jesus had been a man of normal human flesh and blood, who had really suffered on the cross. But there were some very influential dissidents who taught that Jesus had possessed a heavenly body. Marcion (ca. 140), who in many respects was not a gnostic, but just as the gnostics radically separated the God and Father of Jesus Christ from the Jewish Creator God, ascribed a heavenly, angelic body to Jesus: he was not born from a woman but came down from the heaven of the good God in the fifteenth year of the emperor Tiberius (29 CE; cf. Luke 3.1).[21] The Valentinians also taught that Jesus had a heavenly body, though they held different views on this point. According to Hippolytus, the Western, Italic, school of Valentinianism (Ptolemaeus, Heracleon, and others) taught that Jesus had possessed a psychic body

---

[17] See, for instance, also Irenaeus, *Adversus haereses* 3.20.2: the Logos dwelled in man "and became a Son of Man," i.e. a human being.

[18] Franzmann, *Jesus in the Nag Hammadi Writings*, 97–98.

[19] Clement of Alexandria, *Excerpta ex Theodoto* 61.4.

[20] See on this passage and on the Christology of *On the Resurrection* in general, the notes by M. L. Peel, in Harold W. Attridge (ed.), *Nag Hammadi Codex I (The Jung Codex): Notes* (Nag Hammadi Studies, 23; Leiden: Brill, 1985), 146–156.

[21] Testimonies in Adolf von Harnack, *Marcion: Das Evangelium vom fremden Gott* (2nd edn., Leipzig: J. C. Hinrichs Verlag, 1922; reprinted, together with Harnack's *Neue Studien zu Marcion*, Darmstadt: Wissenschaftliche Buchgesellschaft, 1960, 1996), 184. On Marcion, see Gerhard May, "Marcion," in Hanegraaff *et al.* (eds.), *Dictionary of Gnosis*, 765–768, and Heikki Räisänen, "Marcion," in Marjanen and Luomanen (eds.), *Companion*, 100–124.

to which the Spirit had descended at the baptism in the river Jordan. At the cross, the Spirit had left Jesus' psychic body, which thereupon had died and had been raised from the dead, as an indication that the psychic Christians could be saved. The Oriental Valentinian school (Theodotus and others), however, taught that Jesus had possessed a pneumatic body from the beginning, to which the demiurge had somehow given a psychic form.[22] In his report on the Valentinians, Irenaeus says that there were "many" of them who taught that Jesus' body was composed of three elements: a pneumatic element from the lower Sophia, a psychic element from the demiurge, and another psychic component, which made his body visible and passible.[23] In a similar context, Irenaeus says that, according to the Valentinians, Christ went through the Virgin Mary "as water through a pipe" (*kathaper hydōr dia sōlēnos*).[24] Many other writers used this simile too, to indicate that Christ's heavenly body was by no means contaminated by its birth from the Virgin Mary.[25] In the *Gospel of Truth*, which may be a work of Valentinus himself, it is only said that Christ "came in the likeness of flesh, and nothing blocked his way, for incorruptibility cannot be grasped" (NHC I, 31.4–9). As we will see, however, this does not mean that Christ's body did not really suffer. Valentinus' own ideas about the body of Christ are no longer known: Irenaeus ascribes to him at least three different views.[26] But Clement of Alexandria has preserved a fragment of a *Letter to Agathopus* by Valentinus himself that at least shows that Christ did not have a common human body: "Jesus practiced his divinity, he ate and drank in a special way, without excreting his viands. His capacity for continence was so great that the nourishment in him was not corrupted, for he knew no corruption."[27] Valentinus did not deny that Christ ate and drank, which was generally held to be an indication of his real humanity,

---

[22] Hippolytus *Refutatio* 6.35.5–7. For a discussion of the problems raised by this report, see Jean-Daniel Kaestli, "Valentinisme italien et valentinisme oriental: leur divergences à propos de la nature du corps de Jésus," in Bentley Layton (ed.), *The Rediscovery of Gnosticism*, vol. I: *The School of Valentinus* (Studies in the History of Religions, 41; Leiden: Brill, 1980), 391–403. See also Thomassen, *Spiritual Seed*, 30–31, 39–45. The sources surrounding the two branches of Valentinianism have been scrutinized by Joel Kalvesmaki, "Italian versus Eastern Valentinianism?," *Vigiliae Christianae* 62 (2008), 79–89.

[23] Irenaeus, *Adversus haereses* 1.6.1.   [24] Irenaeus, *Adversus haereses* 1.7.2.

[25] All testimonies and a study of the background of this expression are in Michel Tardieu, "'Comme à travers un tuyau.' Quelques remarques sur le mythe valentinien de la chair céleste du Christ," in Bernard Barc (ed.), *Colloque international sur les textes de Nag Hammadi (Québec, 22–25 août 1978)* (Quebec/Louvain: Les presses de l'Université Laval/Editions Peeters, 1981), 151–177.

[26] Irenaeus, *Adversus haereses* 1.11.1. See on this report, Thomassen, *Spiritual Seed*, 23–28, and on Valentinus and the Valentinians, *ibid.*, 417–508.

[27] Clement of Alexandria, *Stromateis* 3.59.3. See Christoph Markschies, *Valentinus Gnosticus? Untersuchungen zur valentinianischen Gnosis mit einem Kommentar zu den Fragmenten Valentins* (Wissenschaftliche Untersuchungen zum NT, 65; Tübingen: J. C. B. Mohr /Paul Siebeck, 1992), 83–117; Thomassen, *Spiritual Seed*, 457ff.

but at the same time he maintained that Christ's body was not affected by any kind of corruption. Clement quotes this letter with approval, and elsewhere he shows that his views on this point were even more radical than those of Valentinus: it would be ludicrous, he says, to contend that Christ ate to sustain his body, for his body was sustained by a holy Power. He simply ate to prevent the idea of a docetic Christology![28] This shows that around the year 200 the ideas about the nature of Christ's body were still very divergent, at least in Alexandria. Ecclesiastical orthodoxy was still in the making. Origen, the greatest (anti-gnostic) Alexandrian theologian (185–254), thought it inconceivable that divinity and humanity could be united in Christ without an intermediate element that was not affected by sin. Just as the gnostics, he taught a pre-cosmic spiritual world, in which the souls had fallen away from God the Logos by a decision of their own free will. Only one soul kept itself pure and remained wholly attached to the Logos, and it was in perfect union with this pure soul that God the Son was born from the Virgin: "Without a mediator, the union of the nature of God and a material body was impossible."[29]

The non-gnostics liked to emphasize more strongly the unity of God and man in the historical Jesus Christ, even though this caused insurmountable logical problems. Anticipating the Christological decisions of the fifth century, Tertullian of Carthago (ca. 200) was the first to find a formula which consciously integrated the internal contradictions of traditional Christology. In his view, the two "substances" formed a union in Jesus Christ but preserved their own qualities and activities, which led to his famous definition: "We observe a twofold condition, not confused but conjoined (*non confusum sed coniunctum*), Jesus, in one person (*in una persona*) at once God and man."[30] Except for the strict docetists, all Christians, gnostics and non-gnostics alike, believed that at the passion Jesus' body had really suffered but that his divine element had remained unimpaired, for the divine is unchangeable and cannot suffer and die. According to the non-gnostic Christians, the divine element remained with Christ's body in its suffering and death and was responsible for its resurrection. Irenaeus, the staunch opponent of the gnostics, wrote:

Just as he was man in order to be tempted, so he also was the Logos that he might be glorified. The Logos was at rest during the Lord's temptation, dishonoring, crucifixion and death, but he was closely connected with the man (or: the man was swallowed up by the Logos) in his victory, his merciful perseverance, his resurrection and his assumption into heaven.[31]

---

[28] Clement of Alexandria, *Stromateis* 6.71.2.   [29] Origen, *De principiis* 2.6.3.
[30] Tertullian, *Adversus Praxean* 27.   [31] Irenaeus, *Adversus haereses* 3.19.3.

THE RESURRECTION OF CHRIST

Whereas the non-gnostic Christians attached great importance to the bodily resurrection of Christ, as the precondition, model, and guarantee of the resurrection of the dead, their gnostic co-religionists did not believe in the resurrection of the carnal body of Jesus, just as they rejected the resurrection of the flesh in general. For that reason they mostly assumed that the divine component of Christ had left him before he died at the cross. This gnostic interpretation of the passion is one of the main topics in the *Apocalypse of Peter*. In a vision Peter sees Jesus being nailed to the cross and at the same time he sees another Christ who is laughing above or near the cross. Christ explains:

The one you see smiling and laughing above the cross is the living Jesus. The one into whose hands and feet they are driving nails is his fleshly part, the substitute for him. They are putting to shame the one who came into being in the likeness of the living Jesus. Look at him and look at me (NHC VII, 81.14–24).

The one who was crucified is the creation of the demiurge,

the firstborn, the abode of demons, the stone vessel in which they live, the man of Elohim, the man of the cross, who is under the law. But the one who is standing near him is the living Savior, *who was in him at first and was arrested but was set free . . .* The one capable of suffering must remain, since the body is the substitute, but *what was set free was my incorporeal body* (NHC VII, 82.21–83.8).

The incorporeal body is the heavenly Christ, the divine element in Jesus, which has to be set free before he dies. The same idea is expressed in other gnostic texts, for instance in the *Gospel of Judas* 55.19–21, where Jesus says to Judas: "You will sacrifice the man who bears me," which means: by making my crucifixion possible you will be instrumental in liberating the divine element within me. And in the *First Apocalypse of James*, the risen savior says: "I am the one who was *within me*. Never did I suffer at all, and I was not distressed. These people did not harm me. Rather all this was inflicted upon a figure of the rulers and it was fitting that this figure should be destroyed by them" (NHC V, 31.17–26). The "rulers" are the archons, the evil powers of the demiurge, who tried to kill Christ at his crucifixion but only killed their own creature, the man of flesh of blood, who was the earthly envelope of the heavenly Christ. From this perspective, the crucifixion and the death of Jesus were the decisive defeat of the powers of evil. Their failure to destroy Christ revealed the fundamental weakness of their nature. In this sense, the gnostic Christians could attribute a redemptive meaning to the death of Jesus too, as is clearly testified by the

Gospel of Truth. In this Valentinian writing the author says that Christ enlightened those who were in the darkness of forgetfulness:

For this reason Error was angry with him and persecuted him, but she was restrained by him and made powerless. He was nailed to a tree, and he became fruit of the knowledge of the Father. This fruit of the tree, however, did not bring destruction when it was eaten, but rather it caused those who ate of it to come into being (NHC I, 18.21–29).

And elsewhere he says:

For this reason the merciful, faithful Jesus was patient and accepted his suffer-ing . . . since he knew that his death would be life for many . . . Oh what a great teaching! He humbled himself even unto death, though clothed in eternal life. He stripped off the perishable rags and clothed himself in incorruptibility, which no one can take from him (NHC I, 20.10–34).

At first sight, this view on the death of Jesus would hardly seem offensive to non-gnostic Christians, but on closer inspection a clear reference to the resurrection of Jesus' body is conspicuously absent. The author's ideas about the resurrection did probably not differ much from those of the Valentinian *Treatise on Resurrection*, which says:

The Savior swallowed death. You must know this. When he laid aside the per-ishable world, he exchanged it for an incorruptible, eternal realm. He arose and swallowed the visible through the invisible, and thus he granted us the way to our immortality.

And in the same context the author says of the human Christ, the Son of Man: "We believe that he arose from the dead. We say of him: 'He became death's destroyer'" (NHC I, 45.14–46.19). Just as Paul in 1 Cor. 15, the author closely connects the resurrection of Christ and that of the Christian believer and states that in both cases it is not a carnal but a pneumatic body that arises.

The gnostic sources evince on the one hand that there were gnostics who flatly denied any kind of resurrection of Christ or the Christian believer. If they anyhow mentioned the resurrection, they meant the liberation of the divine Christ before the death of Jesus or that of the divine spark in man from the bonds of matter and ignorance. But, on the other hand, there were also gnostics who professed the resurrection of Jesus and the Christian, albeit not in a fleshly but a spiritual, pneumatic body. In the second century, there was a heated debate about the reality of the resurrection, which finally resulted in the confession of the Old Roman Creed (about 200 CE):

"I believe in the resurrection of the flesh." In the second century this question was still undecided. The gnostic views are part of the inner Christian discussion on the meaning of the resurrection, both of Christ and the Christians.

As a whole, the gnostic Christians tended to downplay the importance of the passion and resurrection of Christ.[32] They saw Christ primarily as the teacher of saving knowledge, for in their view the human condition was not characterized by sin but by ignorance. Humanity has fallen into a state of forgetfulness: it knows neither its origin in the divine realm, nor the cause of its miserable present situation. The savior, Christ, has come down into this material world of ignorance to enlighten those who are open to it and are worthy of it, as it is said in the *Gospel of Truth*, NHC I, 18.16–21: "Jesus Christ enlightened those who were in darkness because of forgetfulness. He enlightened them and showed the way, and that way is the truth he taught them." This is the core and kernel of the gnostic understanding of Christ. In contrast to the non-gnostic Christians, the gnostics saw him almost exclusively as the revealer who lifted the veil of ignorance. That became one of the main reasons for the split between incipient orthodoxy and the gnostics. For them, salvation consisted in the saving knowledge revealed by Christ, the spiritual understanding of our divine origin and the world we live in. It is knowledge of God and knowledge of oneself in one saving act, or, as it is put in the *Testimony of Truth*, NHC IX, 44.30–45.6: "When man comes to know himself and God, who is over the truth, he will be saved and crowned with the unfading crown."

BIBLIOGRAPHY

SOURCES

Bibliothèque Copte de Nag Hammadi (Quebec: Les Presses de l'Université de Laval, 1977–). Edition of the Nag Hammadi Library and the Berlin Gnostic Codex, with French translations and extensive commentaries; still in progress, about 40 texts published.

The Coptic Gnostic Library (Leiden: Brill, 1975–1996; paperback edn. 2000). Complete edition of the Nag Hammadi Library and the Berlin Gnostic Codex, with English translations.

Foerster, Werner, *Gnosis: A Selection of Gnostic Texts*, vol. I: *Patristic Evidence* (Oxford: Clarendon Press, 1972).

Holl, Karl (ed.), *Epiphanius, Panarion haer.*, 3 vols. (Leipzig: Hinrichs, 1915–1923; rev. edn. of vols. II and III by Jürgen Dummer, Berlin: Akademie Verlag, 1980).

---

[32] See also Voorgang, *Die Passion Jesu*, 241–246.

Kasser, Rodolphe *et al.* (eds.), *The Gospel of Judas, Together with the Letter of Peter to Philip, the Book of James, and an Unknown Book of Allogenes, from Codex Tchacos. Critical Edition* (Washington, D.C.: National Geographic Society, 2007).

Marcovich, Miroslav (ed.), *Hippolytus: Refutatio omnium haeresium* (Berlin and New York: De Gruyter, 1986).

Meyer, Marvin (ed.), *The Nag Hammadi Scriptures: The International Edition* (New York: Harper, 2007). Complete English translation of the Nag Hammadi Library.

Rousseau, Adelin and Louis Doutreleau (eds.), *Irénée de Lyon: Contre les Hérésies*, 10 vols. (Paris: Éditions du Cerf, 1952–1982).

Sagnard, François (ed.), *Clément d'Alexandrie: Extraits de Théodote* (Sources Chrétiennes, 23; Paris: Éditions du Cerf, 1970).

Waldstein, Michael and Frederik Wisse (eds.), *The Apocryphon of John: Synopsis of Nag Hammadi Codices II, 1; III, 1; and IV, 1 with BG 8502, 2* (Nag Hammadi and Manichaean Studies, 32; Leiden: Brill, 1995).

LITERATURE

Attridge, Harold W. (ed.), *Nag Hammadi Codex I (The Jung Codex): Notes* (Nag Hammadi Studies, 23; Leiden: Brill, 1985).

Broek, Roelof van den, *Studies in Gnosticism and Alexandrian Christianity* (Nag Hammadi and Manichaean Studies, 39; Leiden: Brill, 1996).

"Gnosticism I: Gnostic Religion," in Hanegraaff *et al.* (eds.), *Dictionary of Gnosis*, 403–416.

"Gnosticism II: Gnostic Literature," in Hanegraaff *et al.* (eds.), *Dictionary of Gnosis*, 417–432.

"Simon Magus," in Hanegraaff *et al.* (eds.), *Dictionary of Gnosis*, 1069–1073.

Dunderberg, Immo, "The School of Valentinus," in Marjanen and Luomanen, *Companion*, 64–99.

Filoramo, Giovanni, *A History of Gnosticism* (Oxford and Cambridge, Mass.: Blackwell, 1990; many reprints).

Franzmann, Majella, *Jesus in the Nag Hammadi Writings* (Edinburgh: T&T Clark, 1996).

Hanegraaff, Wouter J. *et al.* (eds.), *Dictionary of Gnosis and Western Esotericism* (Leiden: Brill, 2005 [two volumes] and 2006 [one volume, same pagination]).

Harnack, Adolf von, *Marcion: Das Evangelium vom fremden Gott* (2nd edn., Leipzig: J. C. Hinrichs Verlag, 1922; reprinted, together with Harnack's *Neue Studien zu Marcion*, Darmstadt: Wissenschaftliche Buchgesellschaft, 1960, 1996).

Holzhausen, Jens, "Valentinus and Valentinians," in Hanegraaff *et al.* (eds.), *Dictionary of Gnosis*, 1144–1157.

Hübner, Reinhard M., *Der Paradox Eine: Antignostischer Monarchianismus im zweiten Jahrhundert* (Supplements to Vigiliae Christianae, 50; Leiden: Brill, 1999).

Kaestli, Jean-Daniel, "Valentinisme italien et valentinisme oriental: leur divergences à propos de la nature du corps de Jésus," in Layton (ed.), *The Rediscovery of Gnosticism*, vol. I, 41, 391–403.

Kalvesmaki, Joel, "Italian versus Eastern Valentinianism?," *Vigiliae Christianae* 62 (2008), 79–89.

King, Karen L., *What is Gnosticism?* (Cambridge, Mass. and London: Harvard University Press, 2003).

    The Secret Revelation of John (Cambridge, Mass. and London: Harvard University Press, 2006).

Lampe, Geoffrey W. H., "Christian Theology in the Patristic Period," in Hubert Cunliffe-Jones (ed.), *A History of Christian Doctrine* (Edinburgh: T&T Clark, 1978), 21–179.

Layton, Bentley (ed.), *The Rediscovery of Gnosticism*, vol. I: *The School of Valentinus* (Studies in the History of Religions, 41; Leiden: Brill, 1980).

Löhr, Winrich A., "Basilides," in Hanegraaff *et al.* (eds.), *Dictionary of Gnosis*, 164–168.

    "Sethians," in Hanegraaff *et al.* (eds.), *Dictionary of Gnosis*, 1063–1069.

Logan, Alastair H. B., *Gnostic Truth and Christian Heresy: A Study in the History of Gnosticism* (Edinburgh: T&T Clark, 1996).

Marjanen, Antti and Petri Luomanen (eds.), *A Companion to Second-Century "Heretics"* (Supplements to Vigiliae Christianae, 76; Leiden: Brill, 2005).

Markschies, Christoph, *Gnosis: An Introduction* (London: T&T Clark, 2003).

    Valentinus Gnosticus? Untersuchungen zur valentinianischen Gnosis mit einem Kommentar zu den Fragmenten Valentins (Wissenschaftliche Untersuchungen zum NT, 65; Tübingen J. C. B. Mohr/Paul Siebeck, 1992).

May, Gerhard, "Marcion," in Hanegraff *et al.* (eds.), *Dictionary of Gnosis*, 765–768.

Pearson, Birger A., *Ancient Gnosticism: Traditions and Literature* (Minneapolis: Fortress Press, 2007).

    "Basilides the Gnostic," in Marjanen and Luomanen (eds.), *Companion*, 1–31.

Räisänen, Heikki, "Marcion," in Marjanen and Luomanen (eds.), *Companion*, 100–124.

Rudolph, Kurt, *Gnosis: The Nature and History of Gnosticism* (San Francisco: Harper, 1987).

Skarsaune, Oskar and Reidar Hvalik (eds.), *Jewish Believers in Jesus: The Early Centuries* (Peabody, Mass.: Hendrickson Publishers 2007).

Tardieu, Michel, "'Comme à travers un tuyau.' Quelques remarques sur le mythe valentinien de la chair céleste du Christ," in Bernard Barc (ed.), *Colloque international sur les textes de Nag Hammadi (Québec, 22–25 août 1978)* (Quebec/Louvain: Les presses de l'Université Laval/Editions Peeters, 1981), 151–177.

Thomassen, Einar, *The Spiritual Seed: The Church of the Valentinians* (Nag Hammadi and Manichaean Studies, 60; Leiden: Brill, 2006).

Voorgang, Dietrich, *Die Passion Jesu und Christi in der Gnosis* (Europäische Hochschulschriften, Reihe 23: Theologie, 432; Frankfurt am Main: Peter Lang, 1991).

Williams, Michael A., *Rethinking "Gnosticism": An Argument for Dismantling a Dubious Category* (Princeton: Princeton University Press, 1996).

"Sethianism," in Marjanen and Luomanen (eds.), *Companion*, 32–63.

CHAPTER 3

Jesus in the New Testament apocrypha

Einar Thomassen

INTRODUCTION

Unlike "the Apocrypha of the Old Testament," which refers to a fixed number of writings (texts included in the Septuagint but not found in the Hebrew Bible), and which are valued by the Christian churches even if not considered (fully) canonical, the so-called "Apocrypha of the New Testament" are a vaguely defined mass of documents, of which only a few have attained some degree of ecclesiastical approval. Modern collections of New Testament apocrypha offer a bewildering variety of texts, and exactly which texts are included differs significantly from one collection to the other.[1] What the texts all have in common, however, is that they profess to give information about Jesus and/or the apostles, without having been found worthy of inclusion in the New Testament canon. As a rule, moreover, the genres of these texts – actual or self-proclaimed – correspond to those occurring in the New Testament: they are "Gospels," acts of apostles, epistles, and apocalypses.

Doctrinally, the New Testament apocrypha display great diversity. They represent many different kinds of Christianity, from gnostic or otherwise "heretical" documents, which for that reason were excluded from the corpus of canonical texts, to texts that were acceptably "orthodox" in content but not considered sufficiently authentic as far as apostolic authorship was concerned to merit inclusion. Consequently, the images of Jesus found in this heterogeneous mass of texts vary widely as well. It would scarcely be

---

[1] The most authoritative and recent collections are: Wilhelm Schneemelcher (ed.), *Neutestamentliche Apokryphen*, 2 vols. (6th edn., Tübingen: Mohr-Siebeck, 1990, 1997), of which there is an English translation of the 5th German edition edited by R. McL. Wilson, *New Testament Apocrypha*, 2 vols. (London: James Clarke; Louisville: Westminster John Knox, 1991, 1992); *Écrits apocryphes chrétiens*, vol. I, edited by Francis Bovon and Pierre Geoltrain, vol. II edited by Pierre Geoltrain and Jean-Daniel Kaestli (Paris: Gallimard [Bibliothèque de la Pléiade], 1997, 2005); J. K. Elliott, *The Apocryphal New Testament* (Oxford: Clarendon Press, 1993). For the theme of this article, the collection of texts in J. K. Elliott, *The Apocryphal Jesus: Legends of the Early Church* (Oxford: Oxford University Press, 1996) is particularly helpful.

meaningful to present them all under a single heading simply as "apoc-ryphal." In this chapter I shall largely disregard the set of texts generally called "gnostic," which have their own characteristic Christological notions, and which, moreover, are discussed in a separate contribution to this vol-ume, and concentrate instead on the more "orthodox" apocrypha. On the other hand it must be acknowledged that the boundaries between "gnos-tic" and "non-gnostic," and even more so those between "orthodox" and "heterodox," are far from clear-cut, and cannot therefore be rigorously observed in the following discussion.

Apocryphal writings not infrequently say things about Jesus that we are not told about in the canonical Gospels. What they say in this regard, however, is not always to be understood as alternative images of Christ. Often they are better described as supplementary to the canonical presen-tations of Jesus. There are, after all, notable lacunae in the biographies of the Christ offered by the canonical Gospels: his childhood, for instance, or his relations with his own family. Some texts just intend to fill in some of the gaps left in the canonical narratives. At other times motives of a more seriously theological nature underlie the attempt to supplement or even revise the canonical accounts. What is the case in each instance, however, is not always obvious, since the texts are open to varying interpretations and even in Antiquity were used to support different theological positions. The reception of these documents is in this sense as important as their original authorial intentions. This question will be dealt with in each case in the following.

THE POLYMORPHOUS CHRIST

It is somewhat surprising that no ancient source provides a description of Jesus' physical appearance.[2] Several texts, on the other hand, elaborate one peculiar aspect of Jesus' presence in the world: his ability to appear in diverse forms.[3] Perhaps the best-known example is found in a section of the *Acts of John*. There, a certain Drusiana, who had been locked up in a tomb

---

[2] For the rather vague references to Jesus' outward appearance in ancient literature, see the remarks by Walter Bauer, *Das Leben Jesu im Zeitalter der neutestamentlichen Apokryphen* (Tübingen: Mohr [Siebeck] 1909), 311–314, and in E. Hennecke, *New Testament Apocrypha*, English translation ed. R. McL. Wilson, vol. 1 (SCM Press, 1963), 434. In a Christian context, only the late medieval *Letter of Lentulus* undertakes to describe the actual physiognomy of Jesus in detail. For this apocryphal letter, purportedly written by a Roman official under Tiberius, see Elliott, *Apocryphal New Testament*, 542–543.

[3] See in particular Gedialahu G. Stroumsa, "Polymorphie divine et transformations d'un mythologème: L'Apocryphon de Jean' et ses sources," *Vigiliae Christianae* 35 (1981), 412–434; Eric Junod and Jean-Daniel Kaestli, *Acta Iohannis* (Corpus Christianorum: Series Apocryphorum, 1–2; Turnhout:

by her husband because he disapproved of her conversion to Christianity, reports that the savior had shown himself to her both in the form of John and of a youth. This is nothing unusual, John replies,

For when he had chosen Peter and Andrew, who were brothers, he came to me and to my brother James, saying, "I have need of you, come unto me." And my brother said, "John, this child on the shore who called to us, what does he want?" And I said, "What child?" He replied, "The one who is beckoning to us." And I answered, "Because of your long watch that we kept at sea you are not seeing straight, brother James: but do you not see the man who stands there, fair and comely and of a cheerful countenance?" But he said to me, "Him I do not see, brother; but let us go and we shall see what it means." . . .

And when we left the place, wishing to follow him again, he again appeared to me, bald-headed but with a thick and flowing beard; but to James he appeared as a youth whose beard was just starting. We were perplexed, both of us, as to the meaning of what we had seen . . . And sometimes he appeared to me as a small man and unattractive, and then again as one reaching to heaven . . . (chs. 88–89; trans. J. K. Elliott)

In this text, Jesus is able to appear as a child, a young man, a mature man or an old man, ugly or handsome, a short man or an immensely tall one. Moreover, not only is he able to appear in different forms on different occasions, but he can also show himself in multiple shapes simultaneously to different people.

As was already noted, several early Christian texts present similar ideas. These ideas cannot be reduced to a single motif; rather, they constitute a cluster of individually distinguishable motifs that produce various combinations in the texts. Thus, the revelation of Jesus as a child (outside the nativity and infancy narratives) exists as a motif in its own right.[4] It is to be distinguished from, even if it sometimes tends to be conflated with,[5]

Brepols, 1983), vol. II, 466–493 (with a good bibliography at 470, note 1); more recently Peter J. Lalleman, "Polymorphy of Christ," in Jan N. Bremmer (ed.), *The Apocryphal Acts of John* (Studies in the Apocryphal Acts of the Apostles, 1; Kampen: KokPharos, 1995), 97–118; *The Acts of John: A Two-Stage Initiation into Johannine Gnosticism* (Studies in the Apocryphal Acts of the Apostles, 4; Leuven: Peeters, 1998), esp. 165–167, 170–172; Paul Foster, "Polymorphic Christology: Its Origins and Development in Early Christianity," *Journal of Theological Studies* 58 (2007), 66–99.

[4] *Acts of Andrew and Matthias* 18, 33; *Apocalypse of Paul* (Nag Hammadi Codex V), p. 18; perhaps Valentinus in Hippolytus, *Ref.* 6.42.2. The *Gospel of Judas* 33.21 perhaps says that Jesus sometimes appeared to his disciples as a child, but the reading is uncertain. Jesus certainly manifests himself as a child, however, in the newly discovered so-called *Gospel of the Saviour* (Charles W. Hedrick and Paul A. Mirecki, *Gospel of the Saviour: A New Ancient Gospel* [Santa Rosa, Cal.: Polebridge, 1999], 41 lines 58–60; Stephen Emmel, "Preliminary Reedition and Translation of the *Gospel of the Saviour*," *Apocrypha* 14 [2003] 9–53 at 41, no. 73; cf. Stephen Emmel, "Ein altes Evangelium der Apostel taucht in Fragmenten aus Ägypten und Nubien auf," *Zeitschrift für antikes Christentum* 9 [2005], 86–99 at 91).

[5] E.g., the *puerulus speciosus* in Euodius, *De fide contra Manichaeos* 38.

Jesus' appearance as a (handsome, often radiant) young man.[6] In the latter instance, the epiphany recalls that of an angel,[7] and Christ seems in this context especially to perform the role of a guardian or a helper in distress. Jesus' appearance as a child on the other hand seems not to have such connotations. The motive behind the child epiphany is not certain, but it may perhaps be interpreted as an abbreviated variant of still another motif, namely that of the multiple appearance of Christ as a child, a young man and an old man. One example of this was already seen in the passage from the *Acts of John* quoted above. Another example is found in the *Acts of Peter* (21), where Christ simultaneously and variously appears as a boy, a young man, and an old man to individual women among a group of blind widows. In the gnostic *Apocryphon of John* Jesus similarly appears to John successively as a child, an old person, and a "servant."[8]

Variables other than age are also found. Thus, Christ may appear as a figure of gigantic size,[9] or as ugly as well as handsome.[10] Further variations on Christ's appearance which may be cognitively imaginable seem not to be attested.[11] On the other hand the phenomenon of Christ's polymorphism is sometimes commented upon as such. In the *Acts of Thomas* Christ is actually called *polymorphos*.[12] Christ's polymorphism may also signify that Christ adapted his appearance to the various categories of beings who were to "receive" him. Thus, the *Gospel of Philip* states that Jesus assumed all shapes, appearing to the small as small, to the great as great, to angels as an angel, and to humans as a human being.[13] This idea is also familiar to Origen.[14] Another variant is the idea that, by

---

[6] In the *Acts of Peter* 5 Christ appears to Peter at sea as a radiant young man; the *Acts of Paul* 9.19 (Ephesus episode; Elliott, *Apocryphal New Testament*, 378–379) lets a handsome *pais* appear to Paul in prison; also *Acts of Thomas* 27, 154, 155; further, Erik Peterson, *Frühkirche, Judentum und Gnosis* (Rome: Herder, 1959), 191–193.

[7] Foster, "Polymorphic Christology," 91.

[8] Nag Hammadi Codex II, p. 2. The "servant" appears only in the long version of *Apocalypse of John*, and only in one of the three manuscripts (the other two have lacunae at this point); the short version of the Berlin Codex has only the child and the old man. For a discussion of the Coptic word used, see Stroumsa, "Polymorphie divine," 419, who thinks, moreover, that the "servant" alludes to Phil. 2.7 (425–427).

[9] *Acts of John* 89, quoted above; *Gospel of Peter* 39 (cf. Foster, "Polymorphic Christology," 79–80); the so-called *Gospel of the Saviour* also contains a vision of Christ as a gigantic figure whose head reaches into heaven (Emmel, "Preliminary Reedition," 39, no. 33; cf. *ibid.*, 34, note 80).

[10] The only example of an ugly Christ that I know of is in the text from *Acts of John* 89, quoted above.

[11] Christ was said to have appeared as a woman to a Montanist prophetess, according to Epiphanius, *Panarion* 49.1.3. Variations of skin color etc. do not appear, as far as I know.

[12] Ch. 48 (Greek version), 153.   [13] *Gos. Philip* 26 (Nag Hammadi Codex II, 57–58).

[14] "[H]is appearance was not just the same to those who saw him, but varied according to their individual capacity" (*Contra Celsum* 2.64; trans. Chadwick; further references to the theme in Origen by Bauer are in Hennecke, *New Testament Apocrypha*, 434). As an example, Origen

adapting his appearance to the ones who saw him, Christ concealed his true nature.[15]

This "shape-shifting" Jesus is not an idea found in the New Testament. However, certain passages in the canonical writings probably served as an inspiration and a justification for its development in the apocryphal texts. In particular, the transfiguration scene of the synoptic Gospels (Matt. 17.1–8; Mark 9.2–9; Luke 9.28–36) was probably a point of reference. Here, Jesus took some of his disciples to a high mountain, where "he was transfigured before them, and his face shone like the sun, and his garments became white as light" (Matt. 17.2).[16] Moreover, the phrase "he appeared in another form" in the longer ending of Mark (16.12) also points in the direction of polymorphism. However, it is clear that the apocryphal texts that elaborate on Christ's ability to appear in multiple forms introduce a new accent in Christology. If Christ is depicted as a being that can take on different bodily shapes at will, and even several bodies at the same time, it is evident that Jesus as a human and historical person has been replaced by an eternal being who is essentially other than the forms in which he empirically manifests himself. Christ's ability to appear in various human forms is an expression of his transcendently eternal nature: he can take on various shapes at will precisely because as an eternal being he is not bound to any of these temporal human forms.[17] Theologically, this Christology is liable to the suspicion of "Docetism," the heresy of not regarding the humanity of Christ as "real" (more on this below). On the other hand, Christian theology has always had to balance the notion of Christ's "full" humanity with that of his "full" divinity – two propositions that to a non-theological mind seem difficult to reconcile and which often give rise to ambiguities. Thus, it may be argued that, instead of detracting from the importance of Christ's human incarnation, the idea that he appeared in many different human forms actually enhances it: by these multiple appearances Christ embraced humanity in all its diverse forms. On the other hand it must be repeated that Christ's polymorphic epiphanies cannot be reduced to

---

refers to the transfiguration on the mountain. Lalleman ("Polymorphy," 102, with note 23) thinks Origen took the idea from Philo, who states that God reveals himself in different ways to different people.

[15] This theme is found in the *Ascension of Isaiah* 10 and the *Physiologus* 1, and is applied to Simon Magus in Irenaeus, *Adv. Haer.* 1.23.3 (Jean Daniélou, *The Theology of Jewish Christianity* [The Development of Christian Dogma before the Council of Nicaea, 1; London: Darton, Longman & Dodd, 1964], 206–214; Lalleman, "Polymorphy," 103). In *Gos. Philip* 26 the two themes exist side by side.

[16] The influence of the transfiguration story on the accounts of Christ's polymorphism is stressed by Foster, "Polymorphic Christology."

[17] Thus Peterson, *Frühkirche, Judentum und Gnosis*, 183–208.

a single motif. If he manifests himself in multiple forms, it is sometimes to make himself more easily accessible, at other times to conceal his true nature, while at other times again the purpose of the text may just be to create a sense of the miraculous and wonderful. Sometimes Christ appears as a guardian angel in the shape of a handsome young man, at other times as a child or successively as a child, a young man, and an old man, expressing how he encompasses all ages. At any rate, the apocryphal texts in these cases explore dimensions of Christology that at best are only rudimentarily present in the canonical texts.

THE BIRTH OF JESUS

The Gospels of Matthew and Luke each tell the story of Jesus' birth. Though their versions differ considerably, they have been fused in tradition and popular imagination into a more or less coherent narrative. Alternative, or supplementary versions of the nativity story existed, however, already in antiquity, and they also contributed to this narrative fusion.[18] Most important of these alternative accounts is the so-called *Protevangelium of James*, composed in Greek probably in the late second century.[19] Its main focus is on the birth and early life of Jesus' mother Mary, but it also contains an account of the birth of Jesus that varies in some respects from those given in Matthew and Luke. Thus, the *Protevangelium* specifies that Mary gave birth to Jesus in a cave on the road to Bethlehem (17.10ff.) and not in the familiar stable in Bethlehem itself. Leaving Mary in the cave, Joseph goes looking for a midwife (18.2ff.). While walking, Joseph has a vision of time suddenly standing still: clouds and birds stop in midair, people's movements are momentarily frozen. This impressive scene signals the birth of Jesus, a cosmic event whereby eternity breaks into temporal human history.[20] Joseph then goes on to find a midwife, but when they together arrive at the cave, which is now filled with a bright light, Mary has already given birth (19) – the human assistance of a midwife was clearly not needed at this miraculous and painless birth. The midwife performs a

---

[18] A helpful collection of texts is J. K. Elliott, *A Synopsis of the Apocryphal Nativity and Infancy Narratives* (New Testament Tools and Studies, 34; Leiden: Brill, 2006).

[19] A convenient edition is found in Ronald F. Hock, *The Infancy Gospels of James and Thomas* (The Scholars Bible, 2; Santa Rosa, Cal.: Polebridge, 1995). For a commentary, see H. R. Smid, *Protevangelium Jacobi: A Commentary* (Apocryphi Novi Testamenti, 1; Assen: Van Gorcum, 1965). For the dating, see Hock, *Infancy Gospels*, 11–12.

[20] On this episode, see François Bovon, "The Suspension of Time in Chapter 18 of *Protevangelium Jacobi*," in Birger A. Pearson (ed.), *The Future of Early Christianity: Essays in Honor of Helmut Koester* (Minneapolis, Minn.: Fortress, 1991), 393–405.

different, important function, however, since she can attest that a miracle has happened: the mother is still a virgin. This point is elaborated in a following episode which involves still another character, Salome,[21] who refuses to believe what the midwife tells her. Salome is told to see for herself by putting a finger into Mary. As she does so, however, her hand begins to burn. She desperately cries for mercy, and an angel appears and tells her to pick up the child. By touching Jesus, Salome is healed and converted, and she proclaims that she will henceforth worship him as the new king of Israel (20).

The *Protevangelium* is clearly familiar with the nativity stories of Matthew and Luke,[22] but the freedom with which they are treated shows that the canonical writings are not assumed by the author of the writing to give the definitive account of the birth of Jesus. As a matter of fact, the canonical quality of the nativity stories has never been a matter of textual exactness; rather, the story functions more like a myth that lives through the popular imagination, being constantly reproduced and subject to variation through oral transmission, visual representation and ritual enactment. The account in the *Protevangelium* is effectively part of the canon in this sense.[23] Thus, depictions of the nativity set in a cave are frequently found in church art, especially in eastern churches.[24] The midwife and Salome may appear in such representations as well, sometimes displaying "the miracle of the withered hand," though the two characters are as a rule conflated.[25] That Jesus was born in a cave is, it may be added, a very old tradition, attested to as early as Justin Martyr in the middle of the second century.[26]

The popularity of the *Protevangelium* did not, however, save it from being formally rejected in the Western church, most significantly in the *Decretum Gelasianum* in the sixth century.[27] In the East, the writing,

---

[21] Two Salomes are known from other early Christian sources: it is the name both of a disciple of Jesus (Mark 15.40; 16.1) and of a daughter of Joseph from his first marriage (Epiphanius, *Panarion* 78.8.1; 78.9.6; *Ancoratus* 60.1). See Richard Bauckham, "Salome the Sister of Jesus, Salome the Disciple of Jesus, and the Secret Gospel of Mark," *Novum Testamentum* 33 (1991), 245–275, who argues that the Salome of the *Protevangelium* is Joseph's daughter.

[22] See, e.g., Hock, *Infancy Gospels*, 22–25.

[23] This is also, and even more so, true with regard to the *Protevangelium*'s account of the birth and early life of Mary, which had an enormous influence on later Mariology and church art.

[24] See Gertrud Schiller, *Ikonographie der christlichen Kunst* (Gütersloh: Gütersloher Verlagshaus Gerd Mohn, 1966–1991), vol. I, 72–75. See also Ernst Benz, "Die heilige Höhle in der alten Christenheit und in der östlich-orthodoxen Kirche," *Eranos Jahrbuch* 22 (1953), 365–432.

[25] Schiller, *Ikonographie*, vol. I, 74–75.

[26] *Dialogue with Trypho* 78. Further, Origen, *C. Celsum* 1.51, and other authors; see Bauer, *Das Leben Jesu*, 61–67; Schmid, *Protevangelium Jacobi*, 125–127. As Schmid points out, the suggestion that this account was inspired by the myth of the birth of Mithras is not very likely.

[27] For the *Decretum Gelasianum*, which contains a list of all canonical and non-canonical books, see Schneemelcher and Wilson, *New Testament Apocrypha*, vol. I, 38–40.

though never canonical in the technical sense, continued to be esteemed. Through indirect channels, however, the *Protevangelium*'s version of the nativity story nevertheless came to have a profound influence even in the West. A Latin writing, the so-called *Gospel of Pseudo-Matthew* (originally composed perhaps ca. 600, but later expanded several times), incorporated the account of the *Protevangelium* so as to produce a harmony of that text with Matthew and Luke.[28] Thus, for example, *Pseudo-Matthew* lets Mary leave the cave after two days and relocate to a stable; there she places the child in a manger, and an ox and an ass come to adore Jesus (ch. 14). This account has, of course, been enormously influential, being reproduced in art and Christmas plays, to such an extent that many people are now surprised to learn that the canonical narratives do not, strictly speaking, mention a stable at all, nor the adoring animals at the manger.[29]

In this case, the apocryphal stories about Jesus are not really "alternatives" to the canonical ones, but rather supplements to them or have even in some respects themselves come to provide the authorized version of the sacred narrative.

JESUS AS A CHILD

The canonical Gospels tell us nothing about the early life of Jesus, save for the story about the visit of the twelve-year-old boy to the temple, where he amazed the teachers with his knowledge and wisdom (Luke 2.41–52). The *Infancy Gospel of Thomas*, however, knows more about Jesus the child.[30] It is a collection of anecdotes about the divine wonder boy. One group of stories describes Jesus as a precocious schoolboy, who knows much more than his teacher and puts him to shame with his questions. Other stories tell about various miracles performed by the child, some of them quite shocking to a modern mind: when little Jesus became angry with the other children, he put curses on them so they died. His despairing parents did not know what to do with this difficult child. Later, however, Jesus explains

---

[28] Relevant extracts are translated in Elliott, *Apocryphal New Testament*, 84–99; Elliott, *The Apocryphal Jesus*, 23–28.

[29] The notion of the stable is an extrapolation from the statement in Luke 2.7, that Mary laid the child in a manger because there was no room in the inn. (Matthew knows nothing about a stable either, but lets the *magoi* visit the child in "the house" [2.11].) The presence of the ox and the ass is justified by *Pseudo-Matthew* by quoting Isa. 1.3 and Hab. 3.2 (LXX, Vulg.) as prophecies of the nativity. The motif is current in Christian art already from the fourth century (Schiller, *Ikonographie*, vol. I, 70, 71–72).

[30] Greek text and English translation in Hock, *Infancy Gospels*. See also Stephen Gero, "The Infancy Gospel of Thomas: A Study of the Textual and Literary Problems," *Novum Testamentum* 13 (1971), 46–80.

that he did these things in order to make people understand who he really is, and he then brings the dead children back to life. From then on he uses his divine powers for the good of his neighbors, healing and reviving people in critical situations, and performing little everyday miracles such as stretching a beam to make it fit the size of the bed his carpenter father has been commissioned to make.

The motif of the divine, miracle-working and often unruly child is spread across many cultures – recall, for instance, the Homeric Hymn to Hermes, or Krishna of the *Puranas.* That of the precocious child is even more widespread.[31] Direct channels of cross-cultural influence do not have to be postulated in order to recognize the common human interest lying behind this motif. The *Infancy Gospel* wants to emphasize the extraordinary and superhuman nature of Jesus, but also, no doubt, to entertain and amuse.

The text must have existed in some form or another already in the second century, since one of its stories is mentioned by Irenaeus (*Adversus Haereses* 1.20.1). Its later dissemination was considerable: it was translated from its original Greek into many languages both in the East and in the West and was reused in other writings.[32] Unlike the *Protevangelium of James*, the *Infancy Gospel of Thomas* never seems to have acquired any kind of ecclesiastical recognition and did not inspire Christian art.[33] The stories it told must nevertheless have enjoyed wide popularity. In one of them, for instance, the five year old Jesus plays at a stream and molds birds from clay; he then bids the birds to come alive and they fly away. This story is attested in such diverse contexts as the Qur'an[34] and Norwegian folklore.[35] Though frowned upon by the religious authorities,[36] the miracles of Superboy Jesus lived on for many centuries in popular imagination and storytelling.

---

[31] See, e.g., Bauer, *Das Leben Jesu*, 95–97; Gero, "Infancy Gospel," 47, note 1; Hock, *Infancy Gospels*, 98–99.

[32] Translations into Latin, Syriac, Ethiopic, Georgian and Slavonic; used as a source by an Arabic *Infancy Gospel,* certain recensions of *Pseudo-Matthew* and an Irish verse narrative: see Elliott, *Synopsis*, 132–170.

[33] An exception of sorts to the latter are the cartoon-like "Tring tiles" (fourteenth century, England), on which see Mary F. Casey, "The Fourteenth-Century *Tring Tiles*: A Fresh Look at their Origin and the Hebraic Aspects of the Child Jesus' Actions," *Peregrinations* 2(2), http://peregrinations.kenyon.edu/vol2–1.pdf.

[34] Sura 3.49. See Neal Robinson, "Creating Birds from Clay: A Miracle in the Qur'an and in Classical Muslim Exegesis," *Muslim World* 79 (1989), 1–13.

[35] See Brita Pollan, *Jesusbarnet og andre hellige barn* (Oslo: Emilia forlag, 2002), 38, 40–41. The full cross-cultural spread of these stories in oral and written tradition has not, to my knowledge, been charted.

[36] E.g., Irenaeus, *Adv. Haer.* 1.20.1, and John Chrysostom, *Homilies in John* 17.3, who denounce these stories as fables and inventions.

JESUS AS A TEACHER OF SECRET WISDOM

Writings that portray Jesus as a revealer or teacher of wisdom are abundant in early Christianity. Many of these writings belong to the genre of "revelation dialogues," where Jesus appears in conversation with the disciples, or with one disciple in particular, but a text such as the *Gospel of Thomas*, which largely consists of sayings of Jesus without a context, also conveys an image of Jesus as primarily a revealer of hidden knowledge. This scenario is especially common in so-called "gnostic" literature,[37] but it can also be found in more "orthodox" apocryphal works such as the *Questions* (or *Gospel*) *of Bartholomew* and the *Epistle of the Apostles*.

Of course, the canonical Gospels portray Jesus as a teacher as well, and contain many dialogues between Jesus and his disciples. The apocryphal works in question can therefore be regarded as simply continuing to use a literary form for which the authoritative texts serve as a model. To a large extent the difference between the canonical and the apocryphal texts lies more in the specific doctrines the apocrypha let Jesus teach than in his role as a teacher as such. It may also be said, however, that the canonical Gospels evince a certain ambiguity in their presentation of Jesus, who is on the one hand portrayed as a teacher and on the other as a divine savior. With Jesus the teacher the focus lies on understanding the meaning of his spoken words and parables; with Jesus the savior his incarnation, atoning death and resurrection are essential, his saving "work" which may be appropriated by the believer through personal devotion to Jesus. Though theologians have always wished to minimize this ambiguity by insisting that Jesus is himself the essential message of his own teaching, it is nevertheless the case that the early traditions about Jesus give room for two in principle distinct interpretations of his character.[38]

For Jesus' role as a teacher a trajectory may be traced that starts from the earliest traditions about Jesus as the author of "sayings" and leads to the instruction and revelations made in the apocryphal revelation dialogues of later centuries. Primitive sayings materials were incorporated into the narratives of the canonical Gospels – especially the famous hypothetical *Quelle* (Q) of Matthew and Luke – but a number of further sayings attributed

---

[37] A number of the Nag Hammadi tractates belong to the genre of the revelation dialogue. See in particular Pheme Perkins, *The Gnostic Dialogue: The Early Church and the Crisis of Gnosticism* (New York: Paulist Press, 1980).

[38] For the portrayal of Jesus as a teacher, see Bauer, *Das Leben Jesu*, 368–377; Friedrich Normann, *Christos Didaskalos: Die Vorstellung von Christus als Lehrer in der christlichen Literatur des ersten und zweiten Jahrhunderts* (Münsterische Beiträge zur Theologie, 32; Münster: Aschendorff, 1967).

to Jesus can be found scattered elsewhere in ancient Christian literature as well.[39] The various revelation dialogues in turn put sayings of Jesus into a question-and-answer framework, sometimes reusing older sayings, more frequently inventing new ones. Notwithstanding the differences of style and content, a continuity in the image of Jesus as a teacher is evident from the earliest sayings traditions, where he appears as a teacher of wisdom, a prophet, or a speaker of oracles,[40] to the later texts, which portray him as a revealer of cosmic secrets or saving *gnosis*. In this literary tradition, the accent lies on the saving capacity of the doctrines taught by Jesus at least as much as on the message of his saving passion and resurrection. An illustration of this understanding of Jesus is given by the *Gospel of Thomas*, which opens thus: "These are the hidden sayings that the living Jesus spoke and Judas Thomas the Twin recorded. And he said, 'Whoever discovers the interpretation of these sayings will not taste death.'"

Evidently, the figure of Jesus as a teacher was a highly useful vehicle for the propagation of doctrines that were thought to be insufficiently treated in the canonical reports about Jesus. This explains the popularity of this motif in apocryphal works that argue for special interpretations of the Christian message. Such works put these special interpretations into the mouth of Jesus, as instructions given by the Lord to his disciples – often divulged to them in secret, which explained why these doctrines were not generally known. As already mentioned, the so-called "gnostics" made extensive use of this device, but a more "orthodox" text such as the *Questions* (or *Gospel*) *of Bartholomew* also employs it, in order to supply additional information about various points of doctrine: Jesus' descent to Hades during the crucifixion, the description of Paradise, how the earthly woman Mary could give birth to a divine being, the fall of Satan, the nature and number of the angels, and miscellaneous questions concerning cosmology and salvation.

The literary fiction of the secret gospel, in which Jesus teaches otherwise unknown doctrines, continued to be attractive in later periods, being used in several "neo-apocryphal" compositions from the Muslim *Gospel of*

---

[39] Collections of such sayings are William D. Stroker, *Extracanonical Sayings of Jesus* (Resources for Biblical Study, 18; Atlanta, Ga.: Scholars Press, 1989), and Mauro Pesce, *Le parole dimenticate di Gesù* (Rome: Fondazione Lorenzo Valla/Mondadori, 2004).

[40] Some controversy exists as to whether the early sayings of Jesus should be understood as wisdom sayings or as prophetic or some other form of oracular utterances, see Migaku Sato, *Q und Prophetie: Studien zur Gattungs- und Traditionsgeschichte der Quelle Q* (Wissenschaftliche Untersuchungen zum NT, 2/29; Tübingen: Mohr Siebeck, 1988), and the discussion between James M. Robinson, "Die Logienquelle: Weisheit oder Prophetie," *Evangelische Theologie* 53 (1993), 367–389, and Migaku Sato, "Q: Prophetie oder Weisheit?," *ibid.*, 389–404.

Barnabas in the sixteenth century to Edmond B. Szekely's *Essene Gospel of Peace* in the twentieth century.[41]

HERETICAL CHRISTOLOGIES IN THE APOCRYPHA

The orthodox dogmas about Christ, as laid down in the councils of Nicaea (325), Constantinople (381), and Chalcedon (451), are that he is one with and of the same substance as the Father, not subordinate to him, and that he is fully human and fully divine, a single person possessing two inseparable natures. Numerous views about Christ that diverged from these later dogmas were proposed, however, during the early centuries CE.[42] Of these "heretical" Christologies, two in particular are relevant for the purposes of this chapter: *adoptionism*, the view that Christ was born as a human being and became the Son of God through adoption, either at his baptism or on some other occasion, and *Docetism*, the opinion that Christ as a divine being did not have an ordinary human body during his incarnation, but only appeared to do so – in particular, that he did not really suffer and die on the Cross.

Traces of such views about Christ can sometimes be found in the New Testament apocrypha. Thus, the adoptionist interpretation of Jesus' divine sonship seems to have been propounded in the Jewish-Christian *Gospel of the Ebionites*, a writing which today is known only from a few quotations in Epiphanius.[43] According to one of the texts quoted, the Holy Spirit descended on Jesus at his baptism, and a voice was heard crying out, "This day I have generated you."[44] Further details about how Jesus was seen in this Gospel are not provided by the extant fragments, but according to Epiphanius, "these people" say that Jesus was born from Joseph and Mary, and "they insist that Jesus was really a man . . . and that Christ came

---

[41] See Per Beskow, *Strange Tales about Jesus: A Survey of Unfamiliar Gospels* (Philadelphia: Fortress Press, 1983). There is a new Swedish edition of this book: *Fynd och fusk: Falsarier och mystifikationer omkring Jesus* (Örebro: Libris, 2005).

[42] For an introduction to these alternative forms of Christianity, see Bart Ehrman, *Lost Christianities: The Battles for Scripture and the Faiths we Never Knew* (Oxford: Oxford University Press, 2003). A clear survey of heterodox Christologies is also found in his *The Orthodox Corruption of Scripture: The Effect of Early Christological Controversies on the Text of the New Testament* (New York and Oxford: Oxford University Press, 1993).

[43] The extant fragments of the Jewish-Christian Gospels (*Gospel of the Nazoreans, Gospel of the Hebrews, Gospel of the Ebionites*) are collected in A. F. J. Klijn, *Jewish-Christian Gospel Tradition* (Supplements to Vigiliae Christianae, 17; Leiden: Brill, 1992). On the Ebionites see, most recently, Sakari Häkkinen, "Ebionites," in Antti Marjanen and Petri Luomanen, *A Companion to Second-Century Christian "Heretics"* (Supplements to Vigiliae Christianae, 76; Leiden: Brill, 2005), 247–278 (on their Christology, 266–270).

[44] Epiphanius, *Panarion* 30.13.7; Klijn, *Jewish-Christian Gospel Tradition*, no. IX, 70.

into being in him because he descended in the form of a dove."[45] Epiphanius here attributes to the Ebionites a "separatist" version of adoptionism, according to which the divine Christ is a figure distinct from the human Jesus, with whom he united at baptism. This kind of theory is found among some gnostic groups, and may be inaccurately attributed to the Ebionites by Epiphanius, who is notoriously unreliable, but whatever the details, it is likely that the *Gospel of the Ebionites* propounded a Christology where Jesus was born as an ordinary human being and was elevated to or transformed into the Messiah, Son of God only at his baptism.

It may be added that adoptionist Christologies of various kinds were not uncommon in the early phase of Christianity.[46] Such ideas can in fact be found in the canonical Gospels themselves.[47]

"Docetist" Christologies are characteristically found in Marcion and certain "gnostic" varieties of early Christianity.[48] In other apocryphal literature, one striking example is provided by the *Acts of John*, whose polymorphic Christology has already been commented on above.[49] To the author of this text, Christ himself is clearly always another person than what he appears to be. This also applies to his suffering:

Therefore I have suffered none of the things which they will say of me . . . For what you are, you see that I showed you; but what I am, that I alone know, and no one else . . . You hear that I suffered, yet I suffered not; that I suffered not, yet I did suffer, that I was pierced, yet was I not wounded; hanged, and I was not hanged; that blood flowed from me, yet it did not flow; and, in a word, those things that they say of me I did not endure, and the things they do not say those I suffered (*Acts of John* 101; trans. Elliott).

Christ is a divine being who has manifested himself on earth in a human shape, but he did not possess a body that was subject to pain and suffering.[50]

---

[45] Epiphanius, *Panarion* 30.13.7; cf. Klijn, *Jewish-Christian Gospel Tradition*, 72.

[46] Cerinthus, in Irenaeus, *Adv. Haer.* 1.26.1; Hippolytus, *Ref.* 7.33.1–2, 10.21.2–3; cf. Roelof van den Broek, "Cerinthus," in Wouter J. Hanegraaff *et al.* (eds.), *Dictionary of Gnosis and Western Esotericism* (Leiden: Brill, 2006), 252–254. Further, Theodotus of Byzantium, in Hippolytus, *Ref.* 7.35.1–2, 10.23.1–2; Eusebius, *Church History* 5.28.6; Epiphanius, *Pan.* 54.

[47] E.g. Luke 3.22, where most of the oldest and best textual witnesses just like the *Gospel of the Ebionites* read "this day I have generated you" in connection with the baptism of Jesus (actually a quotation from Psalm 2.7). Anti-adoptionist concerns apparently motivated ancient copyists to change the text to "with you I am well pleased." For the whole issue, see Ehrman, *Orthodox Corruption*, 47–118.

[48] For surveys of early instances of Docetism, see, e.g., Ehrman, *Orthodox Corruption*, 181–187; Gedialahu G. Stroumsa, "Christ's Laughter: Docetic Origins Reconsidered," *Journal of Early Christian Studies* 12 (2004), 267–288 (esp. 267–275); both provide additional bibliography.

[49] A discussion of whether the Christology of the *Acts of John* should be called Docetist is given by Lalleman, *The Acts of John*, esp. 208–212, who concludes affirmatively.

[50] Cf. Lalleman, *The Acts of John*, 209: "The AJ in its final form suggests that the God Christ appears from heaven from time to time without really living an earthly life and of course without ever

Another, much discussed case of possible Docetism in the apocrypha is that of the *Gospel of Peter*. This apocryphal Gospel is mentioned in a letter by Serapion, bishop of Antioch c. 190, who warns against using it on the grounds that it is heretical and a forgery.[51] He explicitly says that the heresy is Docetism. A manuscript of this Gospel was discovered in 1887.[52] That manuscript does not, however, provide unequivocal evidence of Docetism. At most, the description of Jesus on the cross, "he held his peace as if he felt no pain" (4.10), may be construed in that way, but it does not have to.[53] It may simply refer to Jesus' noble endurance of his passion.

JESUS DESCENDS TO HELL

The passion narrative told by the *Gospel of Peter* varies in some respects from those of the canonical Gospels, but the differences are minor. Other apocryphal texts elaborate much more extensively on certain elements of the narrative. For instance, a considerable literature sprang up about Pilate, who is variously portrayed as a villain or as a witness to Jesus' innocence, and stories are told about such minor figures as Joseph of Arimathaea and Saint Veronica.[54] In particular, however, the idea became popular that in the interval between his death on the cross and his resurrection Christ went down to the Underworld and there redeemed the souls of righteous people who had lived before his own appearance on earth. It is uncertain whether the idea is present in the New Testament,[55] but the *Gospel of Peter* mentions it briefly (10.42–43), and theologians attest to it from the second century onwards.[56] Of course, the phrase *descendit ad inferna* became a part of the Apostles' Creed.

Extensive accounts of Christ's descent to Hades are given in the *Questions of Bartholomew* and the *Gospel of Nicodemus*, both composed in late antiquity or the early Middle Ages but containing earlier materials. Most

---

incarnating in a human body . . . The AJ completely denies the humanity of Jesus as depicted in the canonical Gospels and only gives an account of a divine Saviour."

[51] An extract of the letter is preserved by Eusebius, *Church History* 6.12.

[52] Some papyrus fragments discovered later have also been attributed to this Gospel. Doubts about the identification have been raised recently by Paul Foster, "Are there any Early Fragments of the So-Called *Gospel of Peter*?," *New Testament Studies* 52 (2006), 1–28.

[53] See Jerry W. McCant, "The Gospel of Peter: Doceticism Reconsidered," *New Testament Studies* 30 (1984), 258–273; P. M. Head, "On the Christology of the Gospel of Peter," *Vigiliae Christianae* 46 (1992), 209–224.

[54] See, e.g., Elliott, *The Apocryphal New Testament*, 164–225.

[55] Traditionally, 1 Peter 3.19 has been thought to refer to the idea, but this is now doubted; see Richard Bauckham, "Descent to the Underworld," *The Anchor Bible Dictionary*, vol. II, 145–159, at 156.

[56] Ignatius, *Magn.* 9.2; *Odes Sol.* 42.11ff.; Melito, *Pascha* 102; Irenaeus *Adv. Haer.* 4.27.1–2; etc.; see Bauckham, "Descent," 156–157.

influential by far was the *Gospel of Nicodemus.* This is a Latin writing that in its transmitted state consists of two independent parts: the first belongs to the tradition of the *Acts of Pilate* and tells about Pilate's interrogation of Jesus, whereas the second consists of the *descensus ad infernos* account (chs. 17–27). The description is highly dramatic. Jesus appears with a tremendous light before the gates of the Underworld, demanding to be let in. The ruler of that realm, the personified Hades himself, is terrified and deliberates with his associate Lord Satan what to do. Satan says that Jesus is a mere human and poses no threat. But, forcing open the mighty gates, Jesus nevertheless enters easily. Hades then realizes he is facing the King of Glory, submits to him and bitterly rebukes Satan. Jesus catches Satan and hands him over to Hades, eternally to be in his power, and then leaves, taking all the saints with him to Paradise.

The story of Christ's "harrowing of hell" was immensely popular in the Middle Ages. The *Gospel of Nicodemus* was translated into practically all the European vernacular languages and was well known in the East as well. More than 500 manuscripts of various versions of the text are known. It also inspired a large amount of church art.[57] Like the *Protevangelium of James*, the *Gospel of Nicodemus* acquired, in practice, a quasi-canonical status.[58] Theologically, the descent motif gave a solution to the problem regarding the salvation of the righteous who had lived in the age before the coming of Christ. Popular imagination was attracted to the image of Christ conquering Satan and Death, in an age when Christ was seen above all as the triumphant king ruling the world.

BIBLIOGRAPHY

SOURCES

Bovon, François and Pierre Geoltrain (eds.), *Écrits apocryphes chrétiens*, vol. I (Paris: Gallimard [Bibliothèque de la Pléiade], 1997).

Elliott, J. K., *The Apocryphal New Testament* (Oxford: Clarendon Press, 1993).
  The Apocryphal Jesus: Legends of the Early Church (Oxford: Oxford University Press, 1996).
  A Synopsis of the Apocryphal Nativity and Infancy Narratives (New Testament Tools and Studies, 34; Leiden: Brill, 2006).

Geoltrain, Pierre and Jean-Daniel Kaestli, *Écrits apocryphes chrétiens*, vol. II (Paris: Gallimard [Bibliothèque de la Pléiade], 2005).

---

[57] See Schiller, *Ikonographie*, vol. III, 41–66.

[58] Cf. Rémi Gounelle and Zbigniew Izydorczyk, *L'Évangile de Nicodème* (Apocryphes, 9; Turnhout: Brepols, 1997), 28–29.

Hennecke, E., *New Testament Apocrypha*, ed. W. Schneemelcher, English translation ed. R. McL. Wilson, 2 vols. (London: SCM Press, 1963–1965).

Schneemelcher, Wilhelm (ed.), *Neutestamentliche Apokryphen*, 2 vols. (6th edn., Tübingen: Mohr-Siebeck, 1990, 1997).

Schneemelcher, Wilhelm and R. McL. Wilson (eds.), *New Testament Apocrypha*, 2 vols. (London: James Clarke; Louisville: Westminster John Knox, 1991, 1992).

LITERATURE

Bauckham, Richard, "Descent to the Underworld," *The Anchor Bible Dictionary*, vol. II, 145–159.

"Salome the Sister of Jesus, Salome the Disciple of Jesus, and the Secret Gospel of Mark,"*Novum Testamentum* 33 (1991), 245–275.

Bauer, Walter, *Das Leben Jesu im Zeitalter der neutestamentlichen Apokryphen* (Tübingen: Mohr [Siebeck], 1909).

Benz, Ernst, "Die heilige Höhle in der alten Christenheit und in der östlich-orthodoxen Kirche," *Eranos Jahrbuch* 22 (1953), 365–432.

Beskow, Per, *Strange Tales about Jesus: A Survey of Unfamiliar Gospels* (Philadelphia: Fortress Press, 1983).

Fynd och fusk: Falsarier och mystifikationer omkring Jesus (Örebro: Libris, 2005).

Bovon, François, "The Suspension of Time in Chapter 18 of *Protevangelium Jacobi*," in Birger A. Pearson (ed.), *The Future of Early Christianity: Essays in Honor of Helmut Koester* (Minneapolis, Minn.; Fortress Press, 1991), 393–405.

Broek, Roelof van den, "Cerinthus," in Wouter J. Hanegraaff *et al.* (eds.), *Dictionary of Gnosis and Western Esotericism* (Leiden: Brill, 2006), 252–254.

Casey, Mary F., "The Fourteenth-Century *Tring Tiles*: A Fresh Look at their Origin and the Hebraic Aspects of the Child Jesus' Actions," *Peregrinations* 2(2), http://peregrinations.kenyon.edu/vol2-1.pdf.

Daniélou, Jean, *The Theology of Jewish Christianity*, trans. John A. Baker (The Development of Christian Dogma before the Council of Nicaea, 1; London: Darton, Longman & Dodd, 1964).

Ehrman, Bart, *The Orthodox Corruption of Scripture: The Effect of Early Christological Controversies on the Text of the New Testament* (New York and Oxford: Oxford University Press, 1993).

Lost Christianities: The Battles for Scripture and the Faiths we Never Knew (Oxford: Oxford University Press, 2003).

Emmel, Stephen, "Preliminary Reedition and Translation of the *Gospel of the Saviour*," *Apocrypha* 14 (2003), 9–53.

"Ein altes Evangelium der Apostel taucht in Fragmenten aus Ägypten und Nubien auf," *Zeitschrift für antikes Christentum* 9 (2005), 86–99.

Foster, Paul, "Polymorphic Christology: Its Origins and Development in Early Christianity," *Journal of Theological Studies* 58 (2007), 66–99.

"Are there any Early Fragments of the So-Called *Gospel of Peter*?," *New Testament Studies* 52 (2006), 1–28.

Gero, Stephen, "The Infancy Gospel of Thomas: A Study of the Textual and Literary Problems," *Novum Testamentum* 13 (1971), 46–80.

Gounelle, Rémi and Zbigniew Izydorczyk, *L'Évangile de Nicodème* (Apocryphes, 9; Turnhout: Brepols, 1997).

Häkkinen, Sakari, "Ebionites," in Antti Marjanen and Petri Luomanen, *A Companion to Second-Century Christian "Heretics"* (Supplements to Vigiliae Christianae, 76; Leiden: Brill, 2005), 247–278.

Head, P. M., "On the Christology of the Gospel of Peter," *Vigiliae Christianae* 46 (1992), 209–224.

Hedrick, Charles W. and Paul A. Mirecki, *Gospel of the Saviour: A New Ancient Gospel* (Santa Rosa, Cal.: Polebridge, 1999).

Hock, Ronald F., *The Infancy Gospels of James and Thomas* (The Scholars Bible, 2; Santa Rosa, Cal.: Polebridge, 1995).

Junod, Eric and Jean-Daniel Kaestli, *Acta Iohannis*, 2 vols. (Corpus Christianorum: Series Apocryphorum, 1–2; Turnhout: Brepols, 1983).

Klijn, A. F. J., *Jewish-Christian Gospel Tradition* (Supplements to Vigiliae Christianae, 17; Leiden: Brill, 1992).

Lalleman, Peter J., "Polymorphy of Christ," in Jan N. Bremmer (ed.), *The Apocryphal Acts of John* (Studies in the Apocryphal Acts of the Apostles, 1; Kampen: KokPharos, 1995), 97–118.

   The Acts of John: A Two-Stage Initiation into Johannine Gnosticism (Studies in the Apocryphal Acts of the Apostles, 4; Leuven: Peeters, 1998).

McCant, Jerry W., "The Gospel of Peter: Doceticism Reconsidered," *New Testament Studies* 30 (1984), 258–273.

Normann, Friedrich, *Christos Didaskalos: Die Vorstellung von Christus als Lehrer in der christlichen Literatur des ersten und zweiten Jahrhunderts* (Münsterische Beiträge zur Theologie, 32; Münster: Aschendorff, 1967)

Perkins, Pheme, *The Gnostic Dialogue: The Early Church and the Crisis of Gnosticism* (New York: Paulist Press, 1980).

Pesce, Mauro, *Le parole dimenticate di Gesù* (Rome: Fondazione Lorenzo Valla/Mondadori, 2004).

Peterson, Erik, *Frühkirche, Judentum und Gnosis* (Rome : Herder, 1959).

Pollan, Brita, *Jesusbarnet og andre hellige barn* (Oslo: Emilia forlag, 2002).

Robinson, Neal, "Creating Birds from Clay: A Miracle in the Qur'an and in Classical Muslim Exegesis," *Muslim World* 79 (1989), 1–13.

Sato, Migaku, *Q und Prophetie: Studien zur Gattungs- und Traditionsgeschichte der Quelle Q* (Wissenschaftliche Untersuchungen zum NT, 2/29; Tübingen: Mohr Siebeck, 1988).

Schiller, Gertrud, *Ikonographie der christlichen Kunst*, 5 vols. (Gütersloh: Gütersloher Verlagshaus Gerd Mohn, 1966–1991).

Smid, H. R., *Protevangelium Jacobi: A Commentary* (Apocryphi Novi Testamenti, 1; Assen: Van Gorcum, 1965).

Stroker, William D., *Extracanonical Sayings of Jesus* (Resources for Biblical Study, 18; Atlanta, Ga.: Scholars Press, 1989).

Stroumsa, Gedialahu G., "Polymorphie divine et transformations d'un mythologème: L''Apocryphon de Jean' et ses sources," *Vigiliae Christianae* 35 (1981), 412–434.

"Christ's Laughter: Docetic Origins Reconsidered," *Journal of Early Christian Studies* 12 (2004), 267–288.

CHAPTER 4

The Manichaean Jesus

Jason BeDuhn

INTRODUCTION

Although in many respects Manichaeism can and should be considered a distinct world religion, it belongs to the larger Christian tradition, broadly construed, through the special place it accords Jesus Christ in its ideology and devotional practices. Arising from the confluence of the early Christian mission with indigenous religious elements of third century CE Mesopotamia, the Manichaean religion can be understood as a distinctively "oriental" or "Asiatic" expression of the Christian tradition, and therefore as an alternative form of the faith in comparison with the Western, Hellenized version which has been historically regarded as the Christian mainstream. The religion's founder, Mani (216–ca. 277 CE), and those around him in the Iranian world were engaged in consolidating a construal of Jesus' message that put it in conversation with Zoroastrian and Buddhist thought at the same time that their contemporaries in the Roman world were undertaking a similar formalization in dialogue with Hellenic religious and philosophical antecedents. From these parallel processes emerged a battle over the legacy of Jesus as both of these Christianities sent missions into the territory of the other, each claiming to be the true disciples of Jesus.

Where should we turn for the Manichaean view of Jesus? If we mean the official dogma promoted by Manichaean authorities, then we might best turn to prose statements within canonical or other sanctioned texts. If we mean the place of Jesus in the religious life of the ordinary believer, then we might look to personal letters or onomastic records. Somewhere in between fall hymns and other devotional literature which, although often composed and collected with official *imprimatur*, can reflect accommodation to popular attitudes. We have sources of all these kinds to work with (as well as polemical reports of all kinds) by which to reconstruct the Manichaean Jesus, and consequently find some variety in how he is conceived.[1] Whether ultimately we will find a "logical" coherence, not just a "practical" one, among these various representations,[2] must for now remain an open question, particularly when we are dealing with over a millennium of historical development and a geographical spread from the Atlantic to the Pacific oceans.

Because the Hellenized Christianity of the Catholic-Orthodox tradition won the competition for historical dominance, and the Asiatic Christianity of the Manichaean tradition lost, the modern understanding of Manichaean Christology has been clouded by the dominant voice of the anti-Manichaean heritage of the Western intellectual tradition. Augustine of Hippo's polemical ridicule of the multivalence of the Manichaean Jesus (*Faust.* 20.11) has imposed an artificial division of the Manichaean Jesus figure in much of the discussion of this subject in modern publications. Only in the last thirty years have previous isolated voices[3] grown into a chorus in Manichaean studies challenging Augustine's construct and arguing for an essential unity in the religion's conception of Jesus,[4] even as they have continued to use Augustine's divisions to sort out different aspects of this complex and pervasive figure. The overall unity of the various elements of the figure of Jesus in Manichaeism, as Iain Gardner observes, is their common derivation from the Jesus narrative known to mainstream Christians and Manichaeans alike, combining both suffering and exaltation, victimization and triumph.[5] The division of the Manichaean Jesus into discrete figures, therefore, may be no more legitimate than carving up

---

[1] Abbreviations of primary texts used in this chapter as follows: *Alex. Lyc.* = P. W. van der Horst and J. Mansfeld, *An Alexandrian Platonist against Dualism: Alexander of Lycopolis' Treatise 'Critique of the Doctrines of Manichaeus'* (Leiden: Brill 1974); *Faust.* = Roland Teske, *Answer to Faustus a Manichean* (Hyde Park: New City, 2007); *Fort.* = Roland Teske, *The Manichean Debate* (Hyde Park: New City, 2006); *Hom.* = Nils-Arne Pedersen, *Manichaean Homilies* (Turnhout: Brepols, 2006); *Hymnscroll* = Tsui Chi, "Mo Ni Chiao Hsia Pu Tsan, The Lower (Second?) Section of the Manichaean Hymns," *Bulletin of the School of Oriental and African Studies* 11 (1943–46), 174–219; *Keph.* = Iain Gardner, *The Kephalaia of the Teacher* (Leiden: Brill, 1995); *Psalm-Book* = C. R. C. Allberry, *A Manichaean Psalm-Book, Part II* (Stuttgart: Kohlhammer, 1938).

[2] Nils-Arne Pedersen, "Early Manichaean Christology, Primarily in Western Sources," in Peter Bryder (ed.), *Manichaean Studies. Proceedings of the First International Conference on Manichaeism* (Lund: Plus Ultra, 1988), 157.

[3] E.g., Henri-Charles Puech, "The Concept of Redemption in Manichaeism," in Joseph Campbell (ed.), *The Mystic Vision* (Princeton: Princeton University Press, 1968), 280–281.

[4] E.g., Eugen Rose, *Die Manichäische Christologie* (Wiesbaden: Harrassowitz, 1979), 67–69; Iain Gardner, "The Docetic Jesus," in Iain Gardner (ed.), *Coptic Theological Papyri II* (Vienna: Hollinek, 1988), 67; Majella Franzmann, *Jesus in the Manichaean Writings* (London: T&T Clark, 2003), 133ff.

[5] Iain Gardner, "The Manichaean Account of Jesus and the Passion of the Living Soul," in Alois van Tongerloo and Søren Giversen (eds.), *Manichaica Selecta: Studies Presented to Professor Julien Ries* (Louvain/Lund: IAMS/CHR/BCMC, 1991), 85.

the mainstream Jesus according to his various epithets and roles in the life of the orthodox believer.

As we trace the historical development of Manichaeism and its regional variation, however, we do see the figure of Jesus expanding and contracting in its roles, depending on the setting and the manner of synthesis with local religious traditions. In the increasingly Christianized West, the Manichaean Jesus absorbed attributes and functions that in other regions were parceled out among a dozen or so divine figures. As observed by Werner Sundermann, most attributes ascribed to Jesus can be found ascribed to some other more circumscribed mythological figure of the Manichaean pantheon as well.[6] This fluidity has led some to question just how essential or central Jesus is to the Manichaean religion.

We are not yet in a position to draw many conclusions about the Manichaean religion in its distinct local forms. But we can say that devotion to Jesus in one form or another is a constant. The individual roles highlighted in the following discussion find wide attestation, and do not seem to be confined to only certain regions. At the practical level of devotion, Manichaeans consistently prayed to Jesus as an active savior, and so came to associate him with the sun and moon towards which they faced in their daily prayers.[7] Evidence for reverential devotion to Jesus on the part of the Manichaean faithful comes not only from hymns and the adopted religious names of adherents, but also from newly identified Manichaean devotional paintings of Jesus from Central Asia and from China, the latter showing his continued prominent place in the latest, most far-flung Manichaean community a millennium after the religion's foundation.[8]

In the Aramaic-speaking Mesopotamian environment in which Manichaeism originated, "Yeshu Meshiah" already figured as the ultimate authority behind a variety of Christianities. Mani had learned of the teachings of Jesus, and of his dramatic ordeal, and drew connections from both to his visionary experiences about the predicament of all living things. He saw the figure and story of Jesus reflected at every stage of salvation history.

---

[6] Werner Sundermann, "Christ in Manicheism," *Encyclopedia Iranica*, vol. V (London: Routledge & Kegan Paul, 1992), 536.

[7] From the Latin West, Faustus in *Faust*. 20.2; from Iranian Manichaeism, in the account of Mani's disciple Gabriab standing before the rising Jesus – i.e., the moon – in the evening to pray in TM 389a.R.23ff. (Werner Sundermann, *Mitteliranische manichäische Texte kirchengeschichtlichen Inhalts* [Berlin: Akademie Verlag, 1981], 47); in Turkic Central Asia, his identification as Kun Ai Tengri, the god of sun and moon.

[8] Zsuzsanna Gulacsi, "A Manichaean 'Portrait of the Buddha Jesus' (Yishu Fo Zheng): Identifying a 13th-century Chinese Painting from the Collection of the Seiun-ji Zen Temple, near Kofu, Japan," *Artibus Asiae* 69/1 (forthcoming).

Jesus' suffering and crucifixion – a narrative well known and often repeated in Manichaean texts[9] – provided the imagery for a mythological drama of cosmic proportions, even as his instructions offered the formula by which Manichaeans believed world suffering could be resolved. In the words of Iain Gardner, in Manichaeism "historical features of Christ have become universalized out of specific time and space, and made applicable to the totality of the divinity, whether needing to be redeemed or redeeming."[10]

This dual attention to Jesus as both paradigmatic victim and foremost liberator provides the foundation of a Manichaean Christology that finds its elaboration in the idea of Jesus as *salvator salvandus*, the savior who is himself saved.[11] As *salvandus*, the saved, Jesus shares a common nature with all living things, the essence of life. As *salvator*, the savior, Jesus is the ultimate revealer, the inspirer of all the prophets. In his own historic mission as one of those prophets, he delivers the *mandatum Christi*, the mandate of Christ that guides the believer's life; and by his example he offers the model of perfected (or better, restored) humanity, emulated by the believer in an *imitatio Christi*. His role as *salvator* finds further expression in his function as *psychopomp*, meeting the soul as it departs the body for the afterlife, as well as in his place as eschatological judge. At several points, these conceptions of Jesus as both savior and saved make contact with beliefs about him found in mainstream Christianity at either the official or popular level. Yet collectively they form a unique and strikingly alternative understanding of the nature and purpose of Jesus in the universe and in the life of the individual Manichaean believer.

JESUS *SALVANDUS*

Manichaeism shares with mainstream Christianity an interest in Jesus' intimate identification with those who need to be saved, "not unable to sympathize with our weakness, but tested in every way like us, apart from sin" (Heb. 4.15). But from that common concern arise two radically different

---

[9] See Enrico Morano, "My Kingdom is not of this World: Revisiting the Great Parthian Crucifixion Hymn," in Nicholas Sims-Williams (ed.), *Proceedings of the Third European Conference of Iranian Studies, Part 1: Old and Middle Iranian Studies* (Wiesbaden: Reichert, 1998), 131–145.

[10] Iain Gardner, "Manichaean Christology. The Historical Jesus and the Suffering Jesus with Particular Reference to Western Texts (i.e., Texts from a Christian Environment), and Illustrated by Comparison with Marcionism and Other Related Movements" (PhD Thesis, Manchester University, 1983), 32–33. This derivation of the Manichaean myth from the passion of Jesus was stressed simultaneously by Alexander Böhlig, "The New Testament and the Concept of the Manichaean Myth," in A. H. B. Logan and A. J. M. Wedderburn (eds.), *The New Testament and Gnosis: Essays in Honour of Robert McL. Wilson* (Edinburgh: T&T Clark, 1983), 90–104.

[11] Franzmann, *Jesus in the Manichaean Writings*, 48.

Christologies: on the one hand the orthodox "Two-Nature" Christology by which the transcendent Son of God "assumes" the human Jesus, on the other the Manichaean belief that no difference in kind exists between the divine nature and the soul in need of salvation. The latter, resident in all living things, belongs in its essence to the heavenly realm and shares a common nature with the forces sent from heaven to rescue it. Manichaeism in this way erases the gulf separating God and creatures, savior and saved, insisted upon by mainstream Christian dogma. In his one single nature, Jesus both encapsulates the plight of the imprisoned soul in this world and represents the totality of divine power active in redeeming it.

According to Manichaean belief, all living beings share in a common "light soul" or "living soul" that emanates from God. This divine life-force has entered into a condition of mixture with contrary negative forces. The mixture of these two antithetical properties yields the material world as we experience it, in which we suffer in our true divine identities as we are afflicted by contact with and dominance by evil. Manichaeans at times characterize this state as one of "crucifixion," and refer to the soul entrapped everywhere on earth as the "light cross."[12] "The cross of light that gives life to the universe, I have known it and believed in it; for it is my dear soul, which nourishes every man, at which the blind are offended because they know it not" (*Psalm-Book* 86.27–29). The African Manichaean Faustus refers to Christ's "mystic nailing to the cross, emblematic of the wounds of our soul in its passion" (*Faust.* 32.7). In the Coptic Manichaean *Psalm-Book*, the three days between Christ's death and resurrection are said to symbolize the three stages of ascent taken by the liberated "cross of light" (*Psalm-Book* 160.14–19), while Gregor Wurst has reported the same idea in still unpublished *Sunday Psalms* from the same codex ("He was suspended on the cross in the likeness of the soul that is in the universe," *Psalm* 123; "When Christ rose from the dead, he revealed the type of the soul that is in the whole world," *Psalm* 126).[13] The Iranian Manichaean "Hymns to the Living Soul," recently edited by Desmond Durkin-Meistererernst, similarly identify the trapped divine light soul with Jesus.[14] From the widespread use of crucifixion imagery in the religion's ideology, Enrico Morano has

---

[12] See Hans-Joachim Klimkeit, "Das Kreuzessymbol in der zentralasiatischen Religionsbegegnung," *Zeitschrift für Religions- und Geistesgeschichte* 31 (1979), 99–115; Alexander Böhlig, "Zur Vorstellung vom Lichtkreuz in Gnostizismus und Manichäismus," in B. Aland (ed.), *Gnosis: Festschrift für Hans Jonas* (Göttingen: Vandenhoeck & Ruprecht, 1978), 473–491; Gardner, "The Manichaean Account of Jesus," 80–82.

[13] Gregor Wurst, "A Dialogue between the Saviour and the Soul," *Bulletin de la Société d'archéologie copte* 35 (1996), 149–160.

[14] Desmond Durkin-Meistererernst, *The Hymns to the Living Soul* (Turnhout: Brepols, 2006), 61.

concluded that, "It is evident that the suffering and death of Jesus were to the Manichaeans important images of the suffering of the Living Soul bound to the *hyle*, and his resurrection refers to the liberation of the soul and its return to the Realm of Light."[15]

Manichaeans regard the suffering and death of Jesus, therefore, as proto-typical of the suffering of all living beings. What happened to the historical Jesus symbolizes and conveys a truth about the universe and about our-selves. It both portrays events that, at the beginning of time, caused the world to come into being, and reflects back to us our own present con-dition of captivity and suffering – a condition shared with sparks of the divine scattered throughout the natural world. The Catholic writer Evodius reports in the early fifth century that, according to the Manichaeans, Jesus is born, suffers, and dies in plants daily (*De fide* 34). Indeed, in the fourth-century Coptic Manichaean *Homilies*, Jesus' silence before Pilate is said to be illustrative of the silence of plants as they are harvested, despite their suffering (*Hom.* 91.28–32). "You are the life of the plants, the might of the mountains, the wealth of the seas; you are the primeval sacrifice," declares the Iranian "Hymns to the Living Soul."[16] Speaking for itself in the Coptic *Psalm-Book*, this Jesus-identified world soul says, "I am in everything . . . I am the life of the world. I am the milk that is in all trees. I am the sweet water that is beneath the sons of matter" (*Psalm-Book* 54.25–30). In the Greek *Cologne Mani Codex* (*CMC*), an eighth- or ninth-century manuscript that nonetheless preserves early traditions, the prophet figure Elchasai, "having taken soil from that earth which spoke to him, wept; he kissed (it) and placed (it) upon his breast and began to say: 'This is the flesh and blood of my lord.'" (*CMC* 97.3–10). Of the same period is the Chinese Manichaean *Hymnscroll*, far removed from an environment with a significant Christian cultural presence, which nonetheless says that the living elements constituting the divine soul trapped in the world are "the flesh and blood of Yishu" (*Hymnscroll* 252–254).

This pervasive imagery allows the Manichaean Faustus to inform his Catholic opponents that they "attach the same sacredness to the bread and wine that we do to everything" (*Faust.* 20.2), and to describe Christ as "suspended from every tree," echoing the rhetoric of the slightly older Coptic Manichaean *Psalm-Book*, which speaks of "Jesus who hangs on the tree" (*Psalm-Book* 155.24), and states that, "the trees and the fruits, in them

---

[15] Enrico Morano, "A Survey of the Extant Parthian Crucifixion Hymns," in R. E. Emmerick, W. Sun-dermann, and P. Zieme (eds.), *Studia Manichaica*, vol. IV: *Internationaler Kongreß zum Manichäismus* (Berlin: Akademie Verlag, 2000), 398.

[16] Durkin-Meisterernst, *The Hymns to the Living Soul*, 59.

is thy holy body, my lord Jesus" (*Psalm-Book* 121.32–33). Faustus famously coined the expression *Iesus patibilis*, "the vulnerable Jesus,"[17] to capture this aspect of Christ's identity. Even though the phrase is unique to Faustus, the underlying concept finds clear expression throughout the Manichaean world and in all strata of the tradition.[18] On the basis of this evidence, Iain Gardner has maintained that the identification of Jesus and the imprisoned living soul cannot be regarded as "a later accretion nor a regional variant."[19]

Indeed, Mani himself suggests such an identification in his use and elaboration of the last judgment scene of Matt. 25 in his *Shabuhragan*, a catechism prepared for an Iranian Zoroastrian audience. Closely following the original Gospel text, Mani depicts Jesus (here called "God of the Wisdom Realm") telling those who are saved,

I was hungry and thirsty, and you gave me food; I was naked and you clothed me; I was ill and you cured me. I was bound and you loosed me. I was a captive and you set me free; I was an exile and a wanderer, and you gathered me to your houses.[20]

As in Matthew, the saved humbly suggest that they could not have done such a thing: "Lord, thou art god and immortal, and greed and desire do not overcome thee, and thou dost not hunger or thirst, and pain and disease do not afflict thee."[21] But, Jesus corrects them, explaining his immanence in the community of believers. Admittedly, the *Shabuhragan* passage misses an opportunity for Jesus to express a broader identification with the entire imprisoned light soul, rather than with just "the religious" of the Manichaean community; but precisely such a broader identification found in many other Manichaean texts seems to build on the idea of reciprocity highlighted in Jesus' words here. Text after text identifies the fragments of soul liberated by human religious action with the agency that

---

[17] Gregor Wurst, "Bemerkungen zum Glaubensbekenntnis des Faustus von Mileve (Augustinus, *Contra Faustum* 20,2)," in R. E. Emmerick, W. Sundermann, and P. Zieme (eds.), *Studia Manichaica*, vol. IV: *Internationaler Kongreß zum Manichäismus* (Berlin: Akademie Verlag, 2000), 649, draws attention to this correct rendering of the Latin *patibilis* as "vulnerable" ("leidensfähiger"), not "suffering" ("leidender"), as it is often given in secondary literature.

[18] Wurst goes too far in emphasizing Faustus' coinage as "eine *ad hoc*-Bildung" that can "schwerlich als integraler Bestandteil manichäischer Christologie gewertet werden" (Wurst, "Bemerkungen," 653). Faustus simply applied a new term to an essential part of the Manichaean conception of Christ.

[19] Gardner, "The Manichaean Account of Jesus," 77; *pace* Franzmann, *Jesus in the Manichaean Writings*, 142.

[20] D. N. MacKenzie, "Mani's Šābuhragān," *Bulletin of the School of Oriental and African Studies* 42 (1979), 507.

[21] *Ibid.* Pedersen, "Early Manichaean Christology," 173, wrongly takes this rhetorical objection as the point of the *Shabuhragan* passage, missing Jesus' rejoinder here, as in Matt. 25, that good done to others is done to him.

in turn liberates those humans. Manichaeans are encouraged to "purify the light soul so that it may save you."[22] The trapped light soul, addressed as "lord Jesus," is told, "With happiness are you saved, soul; raise us, too, to paradise."[23] Jesus is "new redeemer and new redeemed one" (M28). In a single hymn he can be addressed as messiah and judge, while also being the "saved creator," the "saved light soul," and in that respect both "first and last."[24]

Manichaeism, therefore, seems to retain the image of Christ as paradigm of all believers that mainstream Christianity has always struggled to maintain against the gulf it posits between the divine and human. The orthodox Christ is always in danger of becoming a *tertium quid*, a third thing different from both the purely divine and the purely human, whose experiences and abilities stand so apart from the human plane that they offer no model of our reality and hope. Drawing on the same early Christian sources, the Manichaeans gave a new understanding to human experience by assuming its close correlation to Christ's. The African Manichaean Fortunatus pointed out to his Catholic opponent Augustine of Hippo the instruction given by Paul in Phil. 2.5: "Think with respect to yourselves that which also (you think) with respect to Christ Jesus."[25] Paul follows this instruction with an outline of Christ's descent into human form, his suffering and death, and his resurrection and ascent to glory. How else could Paul mean his instruction other than that Christ's story somehow is Everyman's story? Fortunatus draws the inevitable conclusion:

We have this same thought about ourselves, then, as about Christ who, though he was established in the form of God, became subject even to death in order to show his likeness to our souls. And just as he showed the likeness of death in himself and that, having been raised up from among them, he is in the Father and the Father is in him, so we think it will also be the same way with our souls. For we shall be able to be set free from this death through him (*Fort.* 7).

It followed for the Manichaeans that Jesus revealed an essential identification between the divine and the human when he, the son of God, repeatedly referred to those he was calling as, likewise, sons and daughters of God. Only by recognizing that Jesus is as much *salvandus* as *salvator* and that we are dealing with the same Jesus in both capacities, can we account

---

[22] Durkin-Meistererernst, *The Hymns to the Living Soul*, 23.
[23] Durkin-Meistererernst, *The Hymns to the Living Soul*, 105.
[24] Durkin-Meistererernst, *The Hymns to the Living Soul*, 63–65.
[25] It is clear that this is the meaning Fortunatus takes from the Latin *hoc sentite in vobis, quod et in Christo Iesu*.

for such devotional rhetoric as that found in the Coptic Manichaean *Psalm-Book*:

Cornerstone unchanging, unaltering, foundation unshakeable; sheep bound to the tree, treasure hidden in the field; Jesus that hangs to the tree; Youth, son of the dew, milk of all trees, sweetness of the fruits; eye of the skies, guard of all treasures . . . that bears the universe; joy of all created things, rest of the worlds: thou art a marvel to tell. Thou art within, thou art without; thou art above, thou art below; that art near and far; that art hidden and revealed; that art silent and speakest, too. Thine is all the glory. (*Psalm-Book* 155.20–39)

Here the juxtaposition of *salvator* and *salvandus* finds unmistakable expression, even as the paradoxical character of the idea is acknowledged. The paradox here is not that of some *tertium quid*, but one intended to shine a light into a mystery of all living things.

JESUS *SALVATOR*

Jesus is more than a reflection of the mortal condition; he also represents its solution. The Manichaeans held that the entrapped light soul is consubstantial (*homoousios*) with the divine forces of the Realm of Light from which the soul descended. Individuated souls on earth possess heavenly "twins" with which they can be reconnected. The exact quantity of soul sent out by God was providentially determined to allow it to be absorbed into mixture with evil. It works from within the mixture to weaken evil and render it powerless. The descended soul is awakened and empowered by an infusion of additional soul from the Realm of Light. This infusion of soul-power is personified as Christ (*Alex. Lyc.* 4; *Faust.* 20.2), whom we might characterize as the "over-twin" of the entire descended mass of the light soul. In a variety of ways, Jesus provides the necessary aid and supplement to the soul's own divine nature that allows for its ultimate liberation.

In the cosmic scheme of things, Manichaeans postulated a series of emanations from God, each charged with a particular phase of resolving the dualistic conflict of the universe. Previous emanations from God repelled the assault of the minions of darkness on the Realm of Light and put this world of mixed light and darkness into an order designed to gradually separate the two antithetical forces. All of nature functions as a great purification machine. But salvation also requires the gathering of fragmented light souls into conscious beings guided to the path back to the Realm of Light. Jesus is emanated to direct this final stage of liberation. He is "the releaser and redeemer [of] all souls" (*Keph.* 29, 82.20–21), through providing the sort of conscious awakening that empowers souls to "collect" and "form" themselves into agents of their own liberation.

In one of many heuristic schemes of describing Jesus' pervasive role in salvation, he is the "third father" who generates (or "summons") three distinct agencies (or "evocations") that carry out the various tasks involved in bringing imprisoned souls to awareness (*Keph.* 7, 35.18–34). First is the Light Mind, the actual infusion of conscious empowerment that allows human beings to shake free from enslavement to evil inclinations, that gathers them into religious communities, and that inspires them to work towards the salvation of themselves and all other living beings.[26] Second is the Great Judge, the agent of discriminating judgment that separates light from darkness, souls ready for liberation from those that need more development before they can rise up from the mixed world. Third is the Youth or Child (Coptic *p.lilou*), representing the initial inclination towards liberation sowed by Jesus among the fragments of the living soul, by which the individual soul responds to the summons of the light world.[27] While these agencies of salvation can at times be described as children of Jesus, or be fitted into various mythological schemes in relation to Jesus, at other times their functions are attributed directly to Jesus himself. Such fluidity of mythological personification is characteristic of Manichaean teachings.

Jesus' work began as soon as the world was formed and its natural processes set in motion. Entering into the celestial spheres from the realm of light, he assessed the condition of the light souls being released by the rotational movements of these spheres, and determined which were sufficiently pure to ascend, and which needed to be returned to the world for further purification (*Keph.* 19, 61.17–21; cf. 28, 80.18–25). He undertook the same work at each level as he descended through the layers of the sky, changing his form to conform to each kind of being, finally taking the "form of flesh" on the earth (*Keph.* 19, 61.21–25). There he sowed the seeds of liberation in the form of "Jesus the Youth," that is, the arising of awareness through the coming together of the divine summons with

---

[26] Cf. *Psalm-Book* 166.35.

[27] Cf. *Keph.* 38, 92.7–8. "So the Youth is an expression of a conscious will for salvation" (Pedersen, "Early Manichaean Christology," 177). Franzmann, *Jesus in the Manichaean Writings*, 123–124, expresses doubt that the "Youth" figure of Iranian Manichaean sources – e.g., M42 – is the same figure as Jesus the Youth in Coptic sources, and notes approvingly Siegfried Richter's proposition that in Coptic sources Jesus has been laid over an earlier generic figure embodying the trapped light (Siegfried Richter, *Die Aufstiegspsalmen des Herakleides: Untersuchungen zum Seelenaufstieg und zur Seelenmesse bei den Manichäern* [Wiesbaden: Reichert, 1997], 171–173).

the soul's response to it (*Keph.* 19, 61.25–28). On the human plane, Jesus served as the primordial revealer to the first human couple, Adam and Eve. Numerous versions of his appearance to them survive. In some of them, Jesus warns Adam away from Eve, since sexuality will perpetuate the imprisonment of light through reproduction of "mixed" human beings. In others, he apparently works through Eve to enlighten Adam (*Keph.* 16, 54.2–9; 38, 94.3–4).

Jesus continues to serve as the inspiring force behind all subsequent prophets and apostles who have brought truth into the world throughout time.[28] As "the introducer and guide and reliance, the original form and appearance of all the Buddhas, the king in the mind of all the wise, the real and true comprehension of all precious and solemn ones" (*Hymnscroll* 16–19), as "the father of all the apostles" (*Keph.* 28, 80.18–19; 73, 179.10–11), Jesus plays an active role throughout salvation history. Beside figures such as Zoroaster, the Buddha, and Mani, Manichaeans recognized that in each new land to which they came there were holy teachers of the past who represented further valid prophetic activity, however distorted in its subsequent transmission. In the Roman world, Hermes Trismegistus, Pythagoras, and Plato received such recognition, and in China, Lao-tzu. But Jesus stands apart from all such human teachers in Manichaean belief, even while serving himself as the historical prophet of "the West" in the first century CE.

Returning in his own person as the historical Jesus, he has the unique distinction of coming as an entirely spiritual being, without the typical human body made up of a mixture of good and evil. This gave extra authority to his teachings. The *mandatum Christi*, mandate of Christ, provided the formula for living a holy life guided by love, compassion, and service that remains always valid, even if the community he founded strays from them (*Faust.* 32.7).[29] The African Manichaean leader Faustus staked his claim to be, as a Manichaean, an upholder of "true Christianity" on his literal adherence to the values of the Sermon on the Mount (*Faust.* 5.1–3). In doing so, he was issuing a challenge to others who laid claim to being the "church" of Christ. According to Manichaean teaching, that separate church had already run its course by the time Mani received his calling as Jesus' successor in 240 CE. Now the new "church" of Mani would "complete the work," drawing to it the heritage of all former prophets. Mani was the "great interpreter" who gave definitive understanding to the

---

[28] See Franzmann, *Jesus in the Manichaean Writings*, 40ff.
[29] Franzmann, *Jesus in the Manichaean Writings*, 61–62.

teachings of Jesus. Even his death on the cross, far from being an atoning sacrifice for human sin, was interpreted by Mani as simply another act of instruction, revealing the "crucifixion" of all living soul throughout the material world. Henceforth Christ's revealing activity would operate through the Manichaean community, until the world's end.

Mani saw himself as "the apostle of Jesus Christ," and conducted himself accordingly; in the words of an important hagiography of Mani, the *Cologne Mani Codex*, he walked in the world "according to the image of our lord Jesus" (*CMC* 107.12–14). Through Mani and the missionary organization he created, it was believed that Jesus continued to enlighten and empower souls through the agency of the Light Mind. Jesus not only brings an awakening knowledge and recognition of the soul's true identity, as in Gnosticism, but also renovates the person – body and soul – into an agent in the struggle between good and evil. Souls that had evolved sufficiently in their previous lives to be called to Manichaeism received a direct infusion of consciousness and virtue that utterly transformed their being. The domination of evil over their lives was broken and replaced with a regime of ordered goodness, only occasionally interrupted by outbreaks of the remaining evil residue within the embodied mixture. The identification of Jesus with the five intellectual gifts that awaken and enlighten the believer (i.e., mind, thought, insight, intellect, and reasoning; *Psalm-Book* 166.38–167.2), as well as the five virtuous gifts that enable moral conduct (i.e., love, trust, contentment, patience, and wisdom; *Psalm-Book* 167.4– 9), provided the basis for an *imitatio Christi* – a modeling of one's life on Christ's example – by which Manichaeans sought to perfect themselves. Because of the divine nature they share with him, people can aspire to imitate Jesus in all respects, most especially in the patient endurance of their suffering as they serve in God's cause. The Manichaean emphasis on receiving virtuous qualities and the capacity for good action sets them apart from purely "gnostic" forms of Christianity. The gnostic emphasis on self-liberation is replaced in Manichaeism by a calling to serve for the liberation of all life from the grip of death.

Jesus completes his task of liberation in his supervision of the soul's departure from this life and ascent to heaven. Next to praise of him as a revealer, Manichaean devotional literature focuses most on Jesus' role as the psychopomp of the souls of the dead, coming to meet the departing soul, protect it from recapture by evil, and conduct it to its liberation. Funeral hymns preserved in both Coptic and Iranian invoke Jesus and express the belief that he will conduct the soul out of bondage and into paradise.

Hail, righteous judge, son of Christ that seest [the] universe. [As I come] now unto thee in the trust of my deeds, let thy power and thy authority arise and come unto me quickly, that I may be able to stand in thy presence, [loving] thee with all my heart. (*Psalm-Book* 83.2–7)

Parthian Manichaeans developed an elaborate funerary liturgy involving extensive performance of hymn-cycles that contrasted life in this world to the joys of paradise, and described in vivid detail the experience of the departed soul as it was threatened by evil and rescued by Jesus. With words of encouragement as well as active protection, Jesus is portrayed guiding the soul out of its post-mortem anxiety and towards the light.[30]

Mani taught that this process of liberation would reach its culmination with a final eschatological judgment of those souls that remain trapped in the world. As we have seen, Mani drew on the last judgment scene from Matt. 25 in imagining this end of world history in his *Shabuhragan*. Because he deliberately avoided overtly naming Jesus in a book written for a Zoroastrian audience, Mani referred to the eschatological judge as "God of the Realm of Wisdom" – a title transparent to the place of Jesus in the Manichaean pantheon. In the Sermon on the Great War written by one of his disciples, and preserved for us in the Coptic Manichaean *Homilies*, the same figure appears as the "Great Shining One," as well as the "Glorious One," and "Judge of Truth" (*Hom.* 35.12ff.). "He will descend and set up his *bema* [judgment seat] in the midst of the great inhabited world" (*Hom.* 36.30–31); from there he proceeds to judge the "sheep" and "goats" according to their deeds. "For I was [h]ungry and thirsty, [. . . and] not one o[f you he]lped [me]" (*Hom.* 38.22–23). The judgment seat was a central symbol of the Manichaean community, with its eye always upon the eschaton. At its annual Bema ceremony, while looking back to Mani's death and imagining him to momentarily occupy the judgment seat in order to receive the confession and repentance of the community of believers, that same community looked forward to the return of Jesus: "Thou art glorious, blessed Bema, that shall reign unto the end of the world, until Jesus shall come and sit upon it and judge all races" (*Psalm-Book* 25.24–26).

MANICHAEAN ENGAGEMENT WITH MAINSTREAM CHRISTOLOGY

Manichaeans leveled a withering criticism at mainstream Christian views of Jesus. They ridiculed the Christian emphasis on Jesus' miraculous birth as woefully misdirected, as if to believe that Jesus being born of a virgin

---

[30] See Mary Boyce, *The Manichaean Hymn Cycles in Parthian* (London: Oxford University Press, 1954).

was more important than heeding his teachings about how to live a holy life (*Faust.* 2.1, 5.2–3).[31] They subjected the Gospels to a critical analysis that in several respects foreshadows modern biblical criticism, denying that they had been written by Jesus' disciples, but instead "much later, by some unknown men who . . . gave their books the names of the apostles" and had added all sorts of unhistorical details that distorted Jesus' message (*Faust.* 32.2; cf. 17.1). For the Manichaeans, however, such critical analysis of pre-Manichaean sources on Jesus ultimately relied on comparison to the direct revelations vouchsafed to Mani, which provided the controlling terms within which Jesus was to be understood.

We cannot expect Manichaean Christianity to engage with "orthodox" Christology in the latter's terms or priorities. Attempts to derive a Manichaean position on familiar mainstream Christological questions are bound to encounter frustrating ambiguities in Manichaean sources. The Manichaeans did maintain that Jesus was a divine being, and on that basis made a failed bid for official tolerance by the Roman state as sufficiently "orthodox" to not fall under the ban of various "Arian" Christologies that treated Jesus as a created being. When it came to questions of Jesus' incarnation, physicality, and duality of nature, however, the Manichaeans found mainstream Christians and themselves engaged in fundamentally alien discourses. In mainstream Christianity, Jesus' possession of a human physical existence served a vital function in the redemptive purpose of his atoning death, even if this redemptive suffering was limited to his human nature, while his divine nature remained immune. Manichaeans, however, rejected the atonement theory of Jesus' death as deeply offensive to God's goodness. Human souls are not bought and paid for in some sort of bizarre judicial or business transaction, but are liberated by recognizing the essential identity of Jesus with themselves and acting accordingly, with divine aid that is simply a reinforcement of their inherent goodness. That very identity of nature between the human soul and Jesus made the entire orthodox concern with a divine *and* human nature in Jesus incoherent for Manichaeans. Since the human and divine natures are one and the same, any talk of "two natures" suggested to a Manichaean ear the opposing good and evil natures at war in all existence. For that reason, Manichaean sources scoff at talk of "two natures" in Jesus.[32] Because Jesus represents a fresh infusion of divine

---

[31] See *Psalm-Book* 120–121 for an anti-orthodox, oppositional outline of Christ's career.

[32] The most direct rejection of "two-nature" language is found in isolated passages quoted from supposed letters of Mani, long thought to be later Christian polemical forgeries; but close examination of their ideas and expression gives reason to regard them as genuinely Manichaean, even if not genuinely from the pen of Mani. See Iain Gardner and Samuel N. C. Lieu, *Manichaean Texts from the Roman Empire* (Cambridge: Cambridge University Press, 2004), 174–175.

nature into the world in order to give trapped souls the boost they need to achieve liberation, by definition he is a single pure nature, unsullied by prior or present mixture with evil. Because the human body takes its form and character from its mixed origin, however, Jesus took on the appearance (*schēma*) of just such a mixed body in order to interact with human beings and effectively communicate his message and example to them.

Researchers in the field of Manichaean studies have not been able to come to a consensus on the question of whether "Docetism" is a useful term by which to understand Manichaean Christology. In other words, is it useful to categorize the Manichaean view of Jesus as one where he *appears* to be, but is not really, human and subject to all the vulnerabilities of humanity, but in reality transcends them? The chief Catholic critic of the religion, Augustine of Hippo, repeatedly attacks it for adhering to an unreal Jesus, a phantom that could not connect to our humanity. The assumption that he knew what he was talking about has generally held sway. Primary Manichaean sources, however, are ambiguous on this subject – at times emphasizing the transcendence of the historical Jesus, at other times dwelling on his suffering, in much the same way that the larger figure of Jesus can be both savior and saved in this tradition. We have to take seriously the possibility, raised particularly by Iain Gardner, that the diverse elements that formed the background of Manichaeism have left a set of tensions and even logical incompatibilities in the religion's handling of the physicality and vulnerability of the historical Jesus. Mainstream Christianity similarly has had to negotiate a variety of preexisting concepts in speaking of Christ as God – by definition immortal and immune to suffering – while emphasizing the reality of his suffering and death.

Imagery of Jesus' suffering pervades Manichaean discourse; yet several Manichaean sources apparently deny that Jesus could be in any way harmed. Some texts speak as if Jesus did not possess the sort of body that could be grasped or injured, so no actual crucifixion took place. Other sources allude to the substitution of another on the cross, the worldly Messiah Jesus son of Mary or even Satan himself.[33] Gardner has shown the complex pedigree of such alternative ideas of what really happened at the

---

[33] According to the African Catholic bishop Evodius, *De fide* 964.7–10, Mani wrote in his *Fundamental Epistle* that, "The enemy, indeed, who hoped to have crucified even this savior, the father of righteousness, was himself crucified, since at that time one thing was done and another was exhibited." The Coptic Manichaean *Psalm-Book* 123.5 similarly mentions "thy cross, the enemy being nailed to it." The idea that there were two Jesuses, the true one descended from heaven and the false one born to Mary who dies on the cross, appears in such Manichaean sources as M28, in the rather neutral report of the Islamic scholar an-Nadim, according to whom Mani wrote about "the son of the widow, who according to Mani was the crucified messiah whom the Jews crucified" (Bayard Dodge (ed.), *The Fihrist of al-Nadim: A Tenth-Century Survey of Muslim Culture* [Records of Civilisation: Sources and Studies, 83; New York and London: Columbia University Press, 1970],

crucifixion in the diverse range of Christianities predating Manichaeism.[34] But does this mean that Manichaeism had no coherent answer to whether Jesus actually suffered on the cross or not? If we find it so difficult to pin down our sources on this seemingly simple either/or question, it may be that we are asking the wrong question. Keeping in mind that coherence can only be addressed within the premises of a religion, we might better frame the question as: what was it about the role and function of Jesus in Manichaeism that allowed the either/or of physicality or Docetism not to arise among the religion's adherents?

The typical notion of Docetism relies on a matter–spirit duality characteristic of Western forms of Christianity under Platonic influence, which assumes that to truly suffer, Jesus must have had a body. If he did not have a body, if he only appeared to (i.e., had only a "Docetic" or apparent body), then he could not have suffered. This is a crucial issue in the mainstream Christian tradition, because Jesus must really suffer and die in order to serve as an atoning sacrifice for human sin. Moreover, a Docetic Jesus threatens to have no connection to human beings, since he would be entirely divine and not in any way creature.

But Manichaeism shared none of these premises. It neither accepted atonement as the purpose of Jesus' mission, nor worked with a matter–spirit duality that confines suffering to the body. Because Jesus' mission is not redemptive in Manichaeism, it does not require a physical embodiment capable of an atoning sacrificial death. For Manichaeans, Jesus' life on earth communicates the real suffering of all human and non-human souls.[35] To communicate this reality, it is irrelevant whether the historical Jesus suffers in his own person, or merely conveys the suffering of the entire living soul that he represents. The true suffering of the "son of God" is the universal suffering of all souls, revealed to the world through "the mystic nailing to the cross, emblematic of the wounds of the soul in its passion" (*Faust.* 32.7). Furthermore, because for Manichaeans what is essentially human is entirely divine, a "Docetic" Jesus is under no threat of losing his connection to humanity, but rather manifests the true nature of humanity precisely to the degree that he is free of the limits of material physicality.

Jesus' identification as *salvandus* with the light soul trapped in mixture with evil means that, in some sense, he has entered into the vulnerabilities

798), and in the orthodox Christian Long Formula of Abjuration against Manichaeism, which talks of two Jesuses, one born of Mary from the evil principle, and another from the good, "Jesus the unbegotten and the luminous who appeared in the likeness [*schēma*] of man" and anathematizes Manichaeans for saying "that our lord Jesus Christ suffered only in appearance and that there was one who was on the cross and another who stood at a distance from it and laughed because some other person was suffering in his place."

[34] Gardner, "The Docetic Jesus."   [35] Franzmann, *Jesus in the Manichaean Writings*, 71ff.

of human existence – that he is the "vulnerable Jesus" – from the beginning, long before his historical manifestation. Yet at the same time the transcendence he retains in his capacity as *salvator* makes possible his injection of knowledge and power into the trapped soul that allows the latter to overcome its enslavement to evil and sin. It is imperative to this saving function that Jesus arrives in the world undiluted with evil. Orthodox Christian polemicists directly state that Manichaeans denied the birth of Jesus; and that observation appears confirmed by Manichaean sources. Such a birth would make him a mixed being like the rest of us, and as such trapped and incapable of liberation through his own power. These same polemicists go on to argue, on the basis of their own metaphysical premises, that if Jesus was not born, he could not suffer and die. But there is no evidence that Manichaeans accepted this conclusion, or the premises on which it was based. Quite the contrary, the Manichaean Faustus objects, "Why could he not be both unborn and die?" (*Faust.* 28.1).[36] By insisting that Jesus did not have a body born of the mixture of good and evil as everything else does, the Manichaeans apparently did not mean to deny that Jesus could suffer. Mani's account of Jesus in *Kephalaion 1* both states plainly that, "he came without a body," and proceeds to describe his seizure and crucifixion without the slightest hint that it was anything but real. In the words of Majella Franzmann, "Otherness, in relation to ordinary humanity, is not a means by which Jesus avoids suffering."[37]

In fact, the only "otherness" Manichaeans posited for Jesus entailed a concentration of divine substance unparalleled in the fragmented portions of divine substance that constitute embodied souls in this world. In analyzing the two aspects of Jesus as saved and as savior in Manichaeism, we must be careful not to lapse into a mainstream "two-nature" Christology, which depends for its logic on a differentiation between deity and human soul whose denial stands at the heart of the Manichaean religion; nor should we impose on Manichaeans ideas that rely on distinctions between spiritual and material dimensions that they did not make.[38] Just as Jesus possesses both a vulnerable immanent aspect and an invulnerable

---

[36] *Quare non et non nasci potuerit et mori?* Both English translations of the *Contra Faustum*, Richard Stothert's of 1887 reproduced in the NPNF series and Roland Teske's of 2007 in the WSA series, follow a clearly defective reading of this clause which omits the second *non* and makes Faustus' remark nonsensical.

[37] Franzmann, *Jesus in the Manichaean Writings*, 75.

[38] Franzmann, *Jesus in the Manichaean Writings*, has difficulty avoiding both such lapses into mainstream models, e.g., 73: "Surely the comfort of the paradigm . . . for those who suffer physically is that Jesus the Apostle himself suffered physically, but his heavenly nature was not affected. Therefore, he could move beyond death just as the Manichaean soul could also triumph over death"; similarly, 86: "Because he combines in himself both a divine and human nature, he suffers and at the same time does not suffer."

transcendent aspect, so all suffering souls possess a transcendent "twin" with which they ultimately join in salvation. The suffering of the soul in this world results from a diminution and fragmentation of the substance that makes it vulnerable to the impingement of evil. God, for example, remains utterly immune to evil, not because he is different in kind from the vulnerable soul, but different in mass. Jesus does not have to assume some other nature than his original divine one in order to be connected to humanity; but he does need to retain his transcendence from "mixture" in order to have full liberty to aid humanity. That is the cusp on which Manichaean Christology balances, and it is a very different one than the one that concerns mainstream Christology. For Manichaeans, it is we mortals who have "two natures" – good and evil mixed together – the solution to which is to become as single natured as Jesus was and is.

Death sought in him, it found nothing belonging to it. It found not flesh and blood, the things of which it eats. It found not bone and sinew which it consumes daily. It found not its likeness in him – the fire, the lust. A vesture (*schēma*) is what it found, like a mask. It grieved, it wept, because of the deception that came to pass. He left them in their shame, he went up victorious (*Psalm-Book* 196.12–32).

In order for Jesus to really infuse souls with the power and awareness they need to be liberated, he must adopt a state that really enters into the world and makes a difference; he must by diminishing and emptying himself become a *dynamis pathētikē*, a vulnerable power and not just a transcendent one (*Alex. Lyc.* 4.24). Both the historical Jesus in his visible career and the living Jesus of the Light Mind in individual believers, must invest itself in the suffering human condition in order to enable individual souls to coalesce, cohere, and take on the agency that leads to liberation, while remaining sufficiently pure and unsullied by any mixture with evil to provide a reliable source of inspiration and guidance. There is, therefore, a paradox in Jesus' story, that of a transcendent, divine being that somehow becomes vulnerable to evil while never surrendering his divine identity and transcendent destiny.

> Amen, I was seized; Amen again, I was not seized.
> Amen, I was judged; Amen again, I was not judged.
> Amen, I was crucified; Amen again, I was not crucified.
> Amen, I was pierced; Amen again, I was not pierced.
> Amen, I suffered; Amen again, I did not suffer.
> Amen, I am in my father; Amen again, my Father is in me.
> But thou desirest the fulfilment of Amen:
> I mocked the world, they could not mock me.
> (*Psalm-Book* 191.4–11)

That very paradox reflects the story of every soul, and in reflecting on it, the Manichaean believer expected to find insight into his or her own true self, and hope for ultimate salvation.

BIBLIOGRAPHY

SOURCES

Allberry, C. R. C., *A Manichaean Psalm-Book, Part II* (Stuttgart: Kohlhammer, 1938).

Boyce, Mary, *The Manichaean Hymn Cycles in Parthian* (London: Oxford University Press, 1954).

Dodge, Bayard (ed.), *The Fihrist of al-Nadim: A Tenth-Century Survey of Muslim Culture* (Records of Civilisation: Sources and Studies, 83; New York and London: Columbia University Press, 1970).

Durkin-Meisterernst, Desmond, *The Hymns to the Living Soul* (Turnhout: Brepols, 2006).

Gardner, Iain, *The Kephalaia of the Teacher* (Leiden: Brill, 1995).

Gardner, Iain and Samuel N. C. Lieu, *Manichaean Texts from the Roman Empire* (Cambridge: Cambridge University Press, 2004).

van der Horst, P. W. and J. Mansfeld, *An Alexandrian Platonist against Dualism: Alexander of Lycopolis' Treatise 'Critique of the Doctrines of Manichaeus'* (Leiden: Brill 1974).

Hutter, Manfred, *Manis kosmogonische Šābuhragān-Texte* (Wiesbaden: Harrassowitz, 1992).

MacKenzie, D. N., "Mani's Šābuhragān," *Bulletin of the School of Oriental and African Studies* 42 (1979), 500–534; 43 (1980), 288–310.

Pedersen, Nils-Arne, *Manichaean Homilies* (Turnhout: Brepols, 2006).

Sundermann, Werner, *Mitteliranische manichäische Texte kirchengeschichtlichen Inhalts* (Berlin: Akademie Verlag, 1981).

Teske, Roland, *The Manichean Debate* (Hyde Park: New City, 2006).

Answer to Faustus a Manichean (Hyde Park: New City, 2007).

Tsui Chi, "Mo Ni Chiao Hsia Pu Tsan, The Lower (Second?) Section of the Manichaean Hymns," *Bulletin of the School of Oriental and African Studies* 11 (1943–46), 174–219.

LITERATURE

Böhlig, Alexander, "Zur Vorstellung vom Lichtkreuz in Gnostizismus und Manichäismus," in B. Aland (ed.), *Gnosis: Festschrift für Hans Jonas* (Göttingen: Vandenhoeck & Ruprecht, 1978), 473–491.

"The New Testament and the Concept of the Manichaean Myth," in A. H. B. Logan and A. J. M. Wedderburn (eds.), *The New Testament and Gnosis: Essays in Honour of Robert McL. Wilson* (Edinburgh: T&T Clark, 1983), 90–104.

Franzmann, Majella, *Jesus in the Manichaean Writings* (London: T&T Clark, 2003).

Gardner, Iain, "Manichaean Christology. The Historical Jesus and the Suffering Jesus with Particular Reference to Western Texts (i.e., Texts from a Christian Environment), and Illustrated by Comparison with Marcionism and Other Related Movements" (PhD Thesis, Manchester University, 1983).

"The Docetic Jesus," in Iain Gardner (ed.), *Coptic Theological Papyri II* (Vienna: Hollinek, 1988), 57–85.

"The Manichaean Account of Jesus and the Passion of the Living Soul," in Alois van Tongerloo and Søren Giversen (eds.), *Manichaica Selecta: Studies Presented to Professor Julien Ries* (Louvain/Lund: IAMS/CHR/BCMC, 1991), 71–86.

Gulacsi, Zsuzsanna, "A Manichaean 'Portrait of the Buddha Jesus' (Yishu Fo Zheng): Identifying a 13th-century Chinese Painting from the Collection of the Seiun-ji Zen Temple, near Kofu, Japan," *Artibus Asiae* 69/1 (forthcoming).

Klimkeit, Hans-Joachim, "Das Kreuzessymbol in der zentralasiatischen Religions-begegnung," *Zeitschrift für Religions- und Geistesgeschichte* 31 (1979), 99–115.

Morano, Enrico, "My Kingdom is not of this World: Revisiting the Great Parthian Crucifixion Hymn," in Nicholas Sims-Williams (ed.), *Proceedings of the Third European Conference of Iranian Studies, Part 1: Old and Middle Iranian Studies* (Wiesbaden: Reichert, 1998), 131–145.

"A Survey of the Extant Parthian Crucifixion Hymns," in R. E. Emmerick, W. Sundermann, and P. Zieme (eds.), *Studia Manichaica*, vol. IV: *Internationaler Kongreß zum Manichäismus* (Berlin: Akademie Verlag, 2000), 398–429.

Pedersen, Nils-Arne, "Early Manichaean Christology, Primarily in Western Sources," in Peter Bryder (ed.), *Manichaean Studies: Proceedings of the First International Conference on Manichaeism* (Lund: Plus Ultra, 1988), 157–190.

Puech, Henri-Charles, "The Concept of Redemption in Manichaeism," in Joseph Campbell (ed.), *The Mystic Vision* (Princeton: Princeton University Press, 1968), 247–314.

Richter, Siegfried, "Christology in the Coptic Manichaean Sources," *Bulletin de la Société d'archéologie copte* 35 (1996), 117–128.

Die Aufstiegspsalmen des Herakleides: Untersuchungen zum Seelenaufstieg und zur Seelenmesse bei den Manichäern (Wiesbaden: Reichert, 1997).

Rose, Eugen, *Die Manichäische Christologie* (Wiesbaden: Harrassowitz, 1979).

Sundermann, Werner, "Christ in Manicheism," *Encyclopedia Iranica*, vol. V (London: Routledge & Kegan Paul, 1992), 535–539.

Wurst, Gregor, "A Dialogue between the Saviour and the Soul," *Bulletin de la Société d'archéologie copte* 35 (1996), 149–160.

"Bemerkungen zum Glaubensbekenntnis des Faustus von Mileve (Augustinus, Contra Faustum 20,2)," in R. E. Emmerick, W. Sundermann, and P. Zieme (eds.), *Studia Manichaica*, vol. IV: *Internationaler Kongreß zum Manichäismus* (Berlin: Akademie Verlag, 2000), 648–657.

CHAPTER 5

Jesus in Islam

Jan Hjärpe

INTRODUCTION

The role of Jesus in Islam has evoked much interest with regard to both religious polemics and religious dialogue. So the literature on this topic is immense and continues to grow.[1] A search on the Internet shows that this is very much an ongoing polemic with firmly entrenched ideas, but also part of a serious dialogue oriented towards a search for common beliefs, and, last but not least, an ongoing scholarly endeavor in search of a complicated history of ideas.

Jesus ('Īsā) is regarded as a prophet and a messenger in Islamic doctrine. There are, however, several different lines taken, or layers to consider, in the Islamic tradition as to the role of Jesus in doctrine and in religious practice. We can distinguish between the picture of Jesus in the Qur'an, Jesus in the *aḥādīth* (the tradition regarding the sayings and actions of the prophet Muhammad and his followers), the narratives about Jesus in the Sufi tradition and in popular piety, and the role of Jesus in contemporary literature, literary fiction, and ethical debate.

JESUS IN THE QUR'AN: THE PROBLEM OF THE TRADITION'S ORIGIN

There is a feature in the Qur'anic text which poses a problem of a special kind. There are so many allusions to stories and narratives about biblical personages in the Qur'an (Ādam/Adam, Ḥawwā/Eve, Qābīl/Cain and Hābīl/Abel, Shīth/Seth, Nūḥ/Noah, the Patriarchs – especially Ibrāhīm/Abraham – Mūsā/Moses, Hārūn/Aaron, Dāwūd/David,

---

[1] For a large number of annotated references to both Christian and Muslim works as well as scholarly contributions, see Oddbjørn Leirvik, *Images of Jesus Christ in Islam: Introduction, Survey of Research, Issues of Dialogue* (Uppsala: Swedish Institute of Missionary Research 1999), 13–21, and the bibliography on pp. 254–265.

Sulaymân/Solomon *et al.*), but it is simultaneously very clear that the biblical text is not the source of these narratives and allusions. But the similarity with the versions to be found in the Jewish Midrash is very clear, especially with the narratives in the midrash on Genesis (*Bereshith Rabba*). The connection between these fragments and allusions in the Qur'an with regard to these midrash narratives of the Old Testament personages is easy to demonstrate and has been well established by scholars.[2] Added to this comes the fact that the early practice of Islam included many elements close to the Jewish practice (halaka): the method of slaughter, the first *qibla* (direction in which one prayed, towards Jerusalem), the emphasis placed on ablutions and ritual purity (*tahāra*), (male) circumcision, and the rules for fasting during the first years of Muhammad's preaching. The connection between early Islam and the Jewish tradition is thus obvious. But, simultaneously, there is in the Qur'an a considerable role given to New Testament personages, Zakariyā/Zacharias, Yaḥyā/John the Baptist, Maryam/Mary the mother of Jesus, and of Jesus himself, described with special traits, not identical with those in the New Testament.

The strong element of Jewish midrash and halaka is thus combined with a form of belief in Jesus which makes it possible to assume that there might be a connection between the message and practice during the first years of Islam and some form or forms of Jewish Christianity ("Judaizers"), the groups of early Christians who regarded the Old Testament Levitical laws as still binding, and thus retained the halaka and probably the midrash tradition too. The existence of those Jewish-Christian movements is testified by the polemics against them by Paul (especially in the Epistle to the Galatians) and by the church fathers. One criterion was the importance given to circumcision. These groups regarded Jesus as the Messiah and of course saw themselves as his pupils and as followers of his teachings. The doctrines and cosmology of at least some of these "Judaizers" included some gnostic elements. Baptisms and ablutions seem to have played a considerable role among them. As for one of the sects, the Ebionites, it seems clear that they existed east of the Jordan for a considerable time, that they rejected the epistles of Paul, retained the Mosaic law, used only one Gospel (either some version of the Gospel according to Matthew or a separate "Gospel to the Hebrews"), and had an adoptionist Christology. A similar

---

[2] Classical works on this issue include Abraham Geiger, *Was hat Mohammed aus dem Judenthume aufgenommen?* (2nd edn., Leipzig: Kaufmann, 1969 [1902]) and Heinrich Speyer, *Die biblischen Erzählungen im Qoran* (Hildesheim: Olms, 1961). As for the Old Testament personages in the Qur'an and in Islamic tradition, see respective articles in the *Encyclopaedia of Islam* (new edn., Leiden: Brill).

sect, the Elkesaites, is known for having rejected Paul's epistles, having a docetic Christology and keeping the Mosaic Law, and for stressing the role of baptism. The "Nazarenes" in Syria during the first Christian centuries was obviously a group with similar characteristics (note that the term for "Christians" in the Qur'an is *naṣārā*, a word with the same root as the pejorative term *noserim* used for Christians in the Jewish tradition).[3]

The Jewish-Christian (and gnostic) groups fled eastwards in response to the Roman–Jewish war in the years 66–70 CE, and existed there for some centuries east of Jordan and near Damascus and eventually continued into the inhabited parts of the Arabian Peninsula. Perhaps there is a relation with those "monotheists" who in later Islamic tradition were called hanifs (*ḥunafā'*), a term used in the Qur'an for Ibrāhīm/Abraham, as a monotheist (but not as a Jew or Christian, as he lived before both Moses and Jesus).[4]

This peculiarity, the close relation between the Jewish tradition and early Islam and with the Jesus in the Qur'an without the Western Christian doctrines of incarnation, and with a "docetic" view regarding the crucifixion, makes it reasonable to see a connection between Jewish Christianity – which had moved eastwards and was regarded as Christian heresy – and early Islam. The lack of source material makes it difficult or impossible, however, to get a clearer picture of such a relation. We must take into account also the influence operating in the Arab environment emanating from Jewish tribes and clans and from contacts with Greek and Syrian eastern Christianity and the Christian Arab tribes and dynasties, and the role of the commercial contacts, the caravan transportations of goods to and from Syria-Palestine and Mesopotamia, and the contacts with Ethiopia and Egypt. So influences from Orthodox, Nestorian, Jacobite, Ethiopian, and Coptic Christianity can be taken for granted. This we can see, for instance, from the considerable number of loanwords from Aramaic and other "Christian" languages in the vocabulary of the Qur'an.[5] The stories and ideas from Christian, Jewish, gnostic, and other movements during the centuries before Muhammad were widely spread, and they must have been rather well known in the pre-Islamic Arab milieu as the allusions to them in the Qur'an obviously were understandable for those who first listened to the message of the Islamic Prophet. One can also point out that

---

[3] For the Judaeo-Christian sects, see Jean Daniélou, *Théologie du judéo-christianisme* (Paris: Desclée 1958), esp. 68 ff., and *Judéo-christianisme: Recherches historiques et théologiques offertes en homage au cardinal Jean Daniélou* (Paris: Recherches de science religieuse 60, 1972).

[4] The discussion on the interpretation of the role of Ibrahim in the Qur'an is summarized by Rudi Paret in the article "Ibrāhīm," in *Encyclopaedia of Islam*, vol. III (new edn., Leiden: Brill, 1971), 980–981.

[5] Cf. Arthur Jeffery, *The Foreign Vocabulary of the Qur'ān* (Baroda: Oriental Institute, 1938).

there are some similarities between early Islam and Manichaeism (especially as to practice), as there is some possible connection between Mani and the Elkesaites. The text of the Qur'an also reflects elements of the conflicts and polemics between Jews and Christians which thus must have been known in the milieu.

JESUS IN THE QUR'AN[6]

In the fifth Sura, from the late period in Medina, there are a couple of verses that can be said to summarize the "Christology" of the Qur'an:

When God said: "O 'Īsā ibn Maryam! Remember My grace on you and your mother; when I strengthened you with the holy Spirit, you spoke to the people in the cradle and as older, and when I taught you the Book and the wisdom and the *Tawrāt* and the *Injīl*; and when you created from clay like the shape of a bird by My permission, and breathed into it and it became a bird by My permission, and you healed those born blind and the leprous by My permission; and when you brought forth the dead by My permission: and when I withheld the children of Israel from you when you came to them with the evidences, and those who disbelieved among them said: 'This is nothing but clear sorcery'."

And when I revealed to the disciples: "Believe in Me and My Messenger," they said: "We believe. And witness that we are submissive (*muslimūn*)!" (5.110/109–111)

After this follows the story of how the disciples ask Jesus about a special sign: to pray to God to send down a table with food from Heaven, a prayer which God answers favorably. Then we find the following dialogue between God and Jesus:

And when God said: "O 'Īsā ibn Maryam! Did you say to people: 'Take me and my mother as two gods instead of God!'?" He said: "Glory to You! It is not for me to say what is not true. If I had said that, You would have known it. You know what is in my soul, but I do not know what is in Your soul. Behold You are the Knower of the concealed.

I did not say to them anything but that which you had ordered me: 'Serve God, my Lord and your Lord!' And I was a witness over them as long as I stayed by them, but when You took me in, You were the Watcher over them. You are the Witness to all things.

If You chastise them, then they are Your servants, and if You forgive them, then You are the Mighty, the Wise." (5.116–118)

---

[6] Cf. Heikki Räisänen, *Das koranische Jesusbild: Ein Beitrag zur Theologie des Korans* (Helsinki: Missiologian ja ekumeniikan seura R.Y, 1971), Leirvik, *Images*, 22–41, and George C. Anawati, "'Īsā," in *Encyclopaedia of Islam*, vol. IV (new edn., Leiden: Brill, 1973), 81–86. For literature on the different Qur'anic verses, see the references in each case in Rudi Paret, *Der Koran: Kommentar und Konkordanz* (Stuttgart: W. Kohlhammer, 1971).

In this text Jesus is described as a messenger who has received a revelation from God, obeys God, and by God's permission is able to perform miracles, from being able to speak already as a newborn child in the cradle and as a child make living birds from clay to, as an adult, healing the sick and resurrecting the dead. But he is acting as a servant to God, obeying his orders, and he is not a god himself, and does not know the hidden things that God knows, God's secrets. Neither has he claimed such powers for himself or his mother (i.e. Mary) that they should be considered gods. The names of the revealed books are mentioned (*at-Tawrāt* and *al-Injīl*).

We also see here his most common appellation in the Qur'an: *Ibn Maryam*, "Son of Mary." This name for Jesus is common in some of the (eastern) Christian apocryphal Gospel traditions, and the miracle with the clay bird given life is found in the so called *Childhood Gospel of Thomas,* probably from the second century CE (not to be confused with the Coptic *Gospel of Thomas*), which has been one of the sources for the *Arab Childhood Gospel* which likewise is older than the Qur'an.[7] So the stories must have been known to those who listened to the revelations of Muhammad. The special status of Jesus (given the Holy Spirit) and his miracles are mentioned in other verses in the Qur'an too (e.g. 2.87/81, 2.253/254, 43.63). But more extensive are the accounts in Sura 19 and Sura 3.

The narratives of Mary's Annunciation and the birth of Jesus are to be found in Sura 19, from the period in Mecca, and it follows there after the story of Zakariyā/Zacharias and Yaḥyā/John the Baptist:

And remember Maryam in the Book; when she drew aside from her family to an eastern place.

And she took a veil (or: screen) [to hide] from them. And We sent to her Our Spirit and he appeared to her as a well-made man.

She said: "Surely I seek refuge from you in the Merciful, if you are God-fearing."

He said: "See, I am your Lord's Messenger to give to you a pure boy."

She said: "That I should have a boy – and no human has touched me? And I am not unchaste."

He said: "Even so." Your Lord has said: "That is easy for Me, and that We shall make him as a sign to people and a mercy from Us. And it is a decreed matter."

And she became pregnant with him and withdrew with him to a remote place.

And the pains drove her to the trunk of the palm-tree. She said: "Oh, would that I had died before this and that I had been quite forgotten!"

And it cried to her from beneath her: "Do not grieve; surely your Lord has made a stream beneath you!"

---

[7] For the legends of the childhood of Jesus in the Christian tradition, see Jean Daniélou, *Les évangiles de l'enfance* (Paris: Desclée de Brouwer, 1967), and J. K. Elliott, *The Apocryphal Jesus: Legends of the Early Church* (Oxford: Oxford University Press, 1996).

And shake towards you the trunk of the palm-tree! It will let fall on you fresh ripe dates.

So eat and drink and refresh (the) eye! And if you see a human being so say: 'Surely I have vowed to the Merciful a fast so I shall not talk to anyone today.'"

And she came with him to her family carrying him. They said: "O Maryam, you have surely done an amazing thing!

Sister of Hārūn, your father was not a bad man, and your mother was not unchaste!"

And she pointed to him. They said: "How could we speak to one who is a child in the cradle?"

He [=the child] said: "Surely I am God's servant (*'abdullāh*). He has given me the Book and made me a prophet (*nabī*),

and He has made me blessed wherever I may be, and has prescribed for me the Prayer (*aṣ-ṣalāt*) and the Charity (*az-zakāt*) as long as I live,

and to be reverent to my mother, and He has not made me oppressive, wretched.

And peace on me on the day as was born, and on the day I die, and on the day I am raised to life!"

This is 'Īsā ibn Maryam, the word of truth, about which (or: whom) they dispute.

It is not for God that He should take a son, glory be to Him. When He decides something, He only says "Be!" to it and it is. (19.16–35/36)

In this text we find the belief in Jesus as having been born in a miraculous way, without any father, his mother being a virgin, and the miracle of the child talking in the cradle to the people, declaring himself a prophet, a servant of God, and connected with the revelation ("the Book") and the religious duties of prayer and charity. In the latter respect he offers a parallel to Muhammad.

In the third Sura (from Medina) the themes are in some way more elaborated. The angels salute Mary (verse 42/37) "God has chosen you and purified you and chosen you above all women in the world!" In the following (verse 45/40) the annunciation is formulated in this way:

When the angels said: "O Maryam, God announces to you a word (*kalima*) from Him; his name is the Messiah (*al-masīḥ*) 'Īsā ibn Maryam, distinguished in this world and the hereafter, and [one] of those brought near [to God]."

The following repeats what is said in Sura 19 about his miracles, but to it is added:

And He will teach him the Book and the wisdom and at-*Tawrāt* and al-*Injīl*.
    And [make him] a Messenger (*rasūl*) to the children of Israel - - -. [3.48f./43]

Jesus is called "the Messiah" and is a "Messenger" (*rasūl*) like Muhammad, and has received as a revelation "the Gospel" (*al-Injīl*), regarded as a confirmation of the revelation to Moses (*at-Tawrāt*) and in its turn confirmed by the revelation to Muhammad.[8] The narratives about the earlier prophets very often belong to the period when the Qur'anic texts reflect the disbelief and doubts shown by Muhammad's compatriots: Muhammad is here met with disbelief just as the previous messengers were. The function of the stories is to show the similarity between the ones sent by God, the point being that they were met with similar reactions from their audiences. Thus it is said in the following verses:

And when 'Īsā perceived the unbelief (*al-kufr*) from them, he said: "Who are my helpers (*ansār*) [in the way] to God?" The disciples said: "We are God's helpers. We believe in God, and bear witness that we are submissive (*muslimūn*)."

Our Lord, we believe in what You have sent down and we follow the Messenger, and write us down with those who bear witness!" [3.52/45–53/46]

The disciples of Jesus are here called *ansār*, "helpers," the same term that was the appellation designating the inhabitants of Medina who supported Muhammad in connection with his migration (*hijra*) from Mecca to Medina. The audience who did not believe the message of Jesus are "kafirs" just as those who doubted the message of Muhammad.

In the following passage there is a remark of some importance as it connects Jesus with the idea of the Last Judgment, the coming Judgment Day, which is a very common feature of Jesus' role in later tradition. The text begins in this way:

When God said: "O 'Īsā, I shall take you away [or: I shall let you die] (*innī mutawaffika*) and raise you to Me and purify you from those who disbelieve and make those who follow you above those who disbelieve until the day of resurrection (*yawm al-qiyāma*). Then to Me you return, and I will judge (*ahkumu*) between you as to what you disagreed upon." [3.55/48]

The question of Jesus' miraculous birth is commented in a verse later on, 3.59/52:

Surely the likeness of 'Īsā before God is [that of] Adam; He created him from dust, then He said to him: 'Be!' and he was.

As Adam was created without a father, Jesus was God's special creation, created in the womb of Mary without a father. He was born by a virgin, but created, not "the son of God." This is stressed too in a rather polemical text in Sura 9:

[8] For the concept of "the Gospel" in the Qur'an and in Islamic tradition, see Bernard Carra de Vaux and George C. Anawati, "Indjīl," in *Encyclopedia of Islam*, vol. III (new edn., Leiden: Brill, 1971), 1205–1208, and Leirvik, *Images*, 53–54.

And the Jews said: "Uzayr (Ezra) is the son of God." And the Nazarenes/Christians (*naṣārā*) said: "*al-Masīḥ* is the son of God." [In] this their saying in their mouths they imitate the saying of those who disbelieved before. May God fight them! How they are turned away!

They have taken their scribes and monks as lords instead of God – and *al-masīḥ* ibn Maryam – although they were enjoined to serve one God only. No god but He. His glory – from what they associate [to Him]! [9.30–31]

The doctrine of monotheism – against the idea of Christ as God – is stressed in Sura 5.17/19f. as well as in 5.116.

Of importance is also the statement that Jesus did not die on the cross. The context of this is a polemic against the Jews, in the fourth Sura. Among the accusations is the following:

And their saying: "Surely we killed the Messiah ʿĪsā ibn Maryam, God's Messenger." And they did not kill him, and they did not crucify him, but it appeared (*shubbiha*) to them so, and those who have different opinions about it are in doubt as to it, they have no knowledge about it, but only conjecture to follow. And they did not kill him for sure.

Nay! God raised him to Himself. And God is Mighty, Wise.

And there is not [any] of the People of the Book (*ahl al-kitāb*) who will not believe in him before his death, and on the day of resurrection he will be a witness against them. [4.157/156–159/157]

Thus, the ascension of Jesus is there in the Qur'an, but not his death on the cross. Still, it is said that his day of resurrection is blessed. The solution to this problem is found in the tradition: Jesus will come back before Judgment Day, die and be resurrected – like all human beings – on the day of resurrection. We can see too that the term *ahl al-kitāb* for Jews and Christians (and other believers of earlier prophets) appears in this verse of the Qur'an.

A special case is the view on the crucifixion held by the founder of the Ahmadiyya movement, Mirza Ghulam Ahmad (1835–1908). He maintained that Jesus was really crucified, but was taken from the cross alive and after recovering went to Kashmir to preach. There he died at the age of 120 and was buried in Mohalla Khaniyar in Srinagar.[9] The tomb which is shown there is called Yūs Āsaf (probably a misreading for Būd Āsaf = Boddhisattva).[10]

---

[9] The theme is elaborated in the book by the founder of the movement Mirza Ghulam Ahmad, *Masih Hindustan Mein* (1899, 1908); English translation: *Jesus in India: Jesus' Deliverance from the Cross and Journey to India* (Tilford: Islam International Publications, 2003), cf. Leirvik, *Images*, 125–127.

[10] See David Marshall Lang, "Bilawhar wa-Yudasaf," in *Encyclopedia of Islam*, vol. I (new edn., Leiden: Brill, 1960), 1215–1217, cf. Per Beskow, *Jesus i Kashmir* (Stockholm: Proprius Förlag, 1981), 23–31.

One more mention of Jesus in the Qur'an is of special importance. It has to do with the idea of a series of prophets, Jesus predicting the advent of Muhammad:

And when 'Īsā ibn Maryam said: "O children of Israel! Surely I am God's Messenger to you, verifying what is before me of *at-Tawrāt* and giving the good news of a Messenger coming after me whose name is Ahmad." But when he came to them with the clear evidences they said: "This is evident sorcery!" [61.6]

"Ahmad" is a variant form of the word and having the same meaning as "Muhammad," "the laudable one." In Islamic tradition and theology this verse is most commonly regarded as an allusion to the promise of Jesus about the coming Paraclete, "the Comforter," in the Gospel of John 14.16 (cf. 16.13).[11]

Eleven times in the Qur'an Jesus is called *al-masīḥ*, the Messiah, but evidently without the special connotations that the word has in Christian (and Jewish) tradition. The virginity of Maryam is stressed in the Qur'an, as in the eastern Christian tradition and likewise in the apocryphal childhood Gospels. In the Qur'an, this theme (her virginity and that God breathed His Spirit into her) is seen for instance in Sura 21.91 and 66.12.

A special problem is the form of the name 'Īsā. Several explanations have been proposed: one that it is an influence from early Jewish polemics against Christianity, comparing Jesus with Esau (*'ēsāw*), another that it is from the Aramaic *yēshū'*, or as a parallel to the form Mūsā for Moses.[12]

JESUS IN THE *AḤĀDĪTH* (SAYINGS OF MUHAMMAD)[13]

Some of the themes from the Qur'an are more accented in the tradition. So, for example, the special nature of Jesus and Mary in the *ḥadīth* (in Bukhari's *Ṣaḥīḥ et al.*) saying that "every son of Adam when newly born is touched by Satan, except for Ibn Maryam and his mother . . ." But in general, the main feature in the *aḥādīth* is the eschatological role of Jesus, his return and fight against *ad-Dajjāl* ("the Impostor," Antichrist). There are many variations on the eschatological themes, and slightly

---

[11] For a discussion on this interpretation, see Räisänen, *Das koranische Jesusbild*, 52–56, cf. Leirvik, *Images*, 56–57.

[12] Cf. Anawati, "'Īsā," 81.

[13] Cf. Leirvik, *Images*, 42–52. References to texts containing themes relating to Jesus are to be found in A. J. Wensinck, *A Handbook of Early Muhammadan Tradition* (Leiden: Brill, 1971), 112–113. See also Anawati, "'Īsā," 84–85.

different versions as to the details, but the main picture can be summarized thus:[14]

A great number of calamities and trials will occur before "the Hour," and disbelief will increase, wars and huge battles will be fought, and *ad-Dajjāl* will appear. Immorality will grow. Nature will be in disorder. All these future events are described extensively, with many details in different versions. And so comes the return of 'Īsā, Jesus, to counteract the false teachings of "the Impostor." Jesus will descend from heaven to "the white minaret to the east of Damascus."[15] The *Mahdī* has already come, and Jesus will pray behind him, destroy the pictures of the cross and kill all pigs, and prohibit all things which are against Islam. Jesus will then establish the kingdom of God on earth, with a very harmonious and peaceful order according to the Islamic Sharī'a. He will establish a kind of "welfare state." Almost all people will accept Islam. He will marry and have a family. He will kill *ad-Dajjāl*. The mighty peoples of *Ya'jūd* and *Ma'jūd* (Gog and Magog, cf. Sura 18.94/93 and 21.96) will come and will kill and plunder, but with the help of Jesus they will perish. The believers will then have a good death; the unbelievers will be left behind. Jesus will die too, and be buried beside Muhammad in Medina. Then the general resurrection will occur, including the resurrection of Jesus, and Doomsday will have arrived.

The hadith tradition, too, gives a description of Jesus, as a person squarely built, of reddish complexion, very beautiful, and with long flowing hair.

STORIES AND WORDS OF JESUS IN HISTORIOGRAPHY AND IN THE SUFI TRADITION

In the rapidly expanding Islamic empire during the first Muslim centuries many influences came from different directions. It was a milieu where apocryphal Gospel narratives were present, sayings from and stories about (Christian) hermits and desert saints were spread; gnostic movements had their refuge in the deserts of the Arabian Peninsula, and of course the well-established churches of Eastern Christianity continued their life under the Islamic Caliphate. There were thus various sources to draw from, including the canonical Christian Gospels, their echoes in oral traditions and sermons, together with material from other traditions. Converts from

---

[14] See, for instance, the collection of traditions on the eschatological time and its signs in Fazlul Karim, *Al-Hadis; Mishkat-ul-Masabih* [text, translation, and commentaries], Book IV (Lahore: The Book House, 1938), 1–153. For the descent of Jesus, *ibid.* 79–82, cf. Leirvik, *Images*, 45–48.

[15] Karim, *Al-Hadis*, 57–59.

Christian groups certainly played a role in supplying narratives about Jesus.

During this time the Islamic Law, the *Sharī'a* tradition and its jurisprudence developed, as a necessity for the administration of the empire, and the hadith collections served as sources to establish the normative *sunna* of the Prophet. So this legal and doctrinal process can be seen as the context for the above mentioned hadith tradition on Jesus. This, however, means that there was a considerable change in the function of Islam, from the preaching and practices in the time of the Prophet, to a religion giving legitimacy to an empire, its leadership and court life. Tension was almost inevitable. Another context arose for stories about Jesus and his words: the early form of Islamic mysticism, *taṣawwuf*, with its emphasis on *zuhd*, asceticism. In these pious circles, which were critical of the mundane life at the princely courts, critical of the mighty and their tools, the *fuqahā'*, the jurisprudents, the "Narratives on the Prophets" (*qiṣaṣ al-anbiyā'*) as a literary genre developed. These stories were of interest both for the authors of comprehensive "world histories" as aṭ-Ṭabarī and his many followers during the centuries, and for the more specific Sufi collectors and writers, such as Abū Nu'aym, al-Yafi'ī, al-Makkī, at-Tirmidhī, and last but not least the great al-Ghazālī, to mention the more important ones. In Sufi circles the critique of the jurisprudents, the *fuqahā'*, could be expressed by means of variant versions of the polemic of Jesus against the Pharisees.[16] The stories about and words by Jesus in their works have been systematically collected and profusely analyzed by scholars since the nineteenth century up to now.[17]

From where do these stories and words ascribed to Jesus come in this living and growing "Muslim Gospel tradition"? The number of Jesus stories and sayings in the Muslim tradition is considerable, more than three hundred. Sometimes we can see sentences which are obviously traveling traditions, coming from other directions and ascribed to other personages such as Hermes-Idrīs, the pre-Islamic Arab sage Luqmān, the Christian desert hermits; there are sayings whose parallels are to be found in the Jewish *Pirke Avot* (in the Mishna), or even otherwise connected with pre-Socratic Greek philosophers, or are ascribed to one or the other of the early

---

[16] For the social setting of the different lines of traditions on Jesus, cf. the introductory chapter in Tarif Khalidi, *The Muslim Jesus: Sayings and Stories in Islamic Literature* (Cambridge, Mass.: Harvard University Press, 2001).

[17] To mention a few: Miguel Asín Palacios, Michel Hayek, Tor Andrae, and recently Tarif Khalidi, whose extensive collection is very useful in giving commentaries and references to the sources and the literature in each case. Cf. also Leirvik, *Images*, 58–102.

Sufi sheikhs. We recognize maxims from the genre of wisdom literature in general. Other material seems to have a connection with other apocryphal Jesus traditions (agrapha). But most of them, without doubt the absolute majority, are variants of stories and sayings which we find in the Gospels of the New Testament too. Much of it is very close to what we find in the Sermon on the Mount in the Gospel according to Matthew (and its parallels in Luke). In general there is an affinity to the words of Jesus in Matthew and Luke. There are some examples of passages running parallel to the text of the Gospel of John, whereas parallels to Mark seem to be almost entirely lacking.[18] This is so because early Islam was more interested in the sayings and sentences of Jesus than in the events of his life. So the content of the Muslim tradition on Jesus bears resemblance to the hypothetical text "Q," that is, the presumed source of the passages, mostly sayings of Jesus, in the Gospels where Matthew and Luke show a similarity to each other but not to Mark.

What is also lacking in the Muslim tradition is of course Jesus as the cosmic-mythological Christ, the incarnated God, and the cosmic savior of the Christian doctrine. Rather, we find Jesus as a prophet and sage, the hermit-ascetic, the "poor" (*faqīr*), the vagrant preacher, wandering in the land of Syria (*ash-Sha'm*) together with his disciples. He is the kind and cheerful prophet (in contrast to his relative Yaḥyā, John the Baptist, who is a severe and grave prophet).

There are some very typical traits in this Muslim tradition. Jesus is the "Prophet of the heart," the vagrant preacher and humble ascetic. He is sometimes called "the Seal of the Saints" (*khātam al-awliyā'*), as a parallel to the characterization of Muhammad as "the Seal of the Prophets" (*khātam al-anbiyā'*).

There is rarely a literal conformity to the wording to be found in the New Testament Gospels, even if there is sometimes a rather close affinity. It is quite clear that the source is not the text of the Bible but that the material comes from oral tradition, the sayings of Jesus as part of the immense number of proverbs and words of wisdom prevailing in the Middle East. Among them is the advice to "lay up for yourselves treasures in heaven, for where your treasure is, there will your heart be also" (cf. Matt. 6.20f.),[19] and the exhortation not to "throw pearls before swine, because the swine can do nothing with them" (cf. Matt. 7.6).[20] The application of this sentence, however, in the Muslim tradition is that wisdom should not be given to

---

[18] Beside the collection of Tarif Khalidi, cf. Tor Andrae, *I myrtenträdgården: studier i sufisk mystik* (Stockholm: Bonniers, 1947), 28–50.

[19] Khalidi, *The Muslim Jesus*, saying number 33.   [20] *Ibid.*, number 64.

those who do not want it, and that wisdom is more valuable than pearls and the one who rejects wisdom is worse than swine.

The commandment to love God and one's neighbor (cf. Luke 10.27) is combined with the Golden Rule to do (or not to do) whatsoever you want to be done (or not done) to you (cf. Matt. 7.12).[21] Here the Muslim version is rather long, giving the two *logia* as answers by Jesus in a conversation on goodness. The context is very often provided by someone coming to Jesus to ask a question or get advice (cf. Matt. 6.25f.).[22] The stress here is on *zuhd*, asceticism, but allusions to miracles also occur, for example when Jesus says that he who has faith can walk on water (cf. Matt. 14.25ff.).[23] Jesus is an example of turning one's cheek to one's enemy (cf. Matt. 5.39), but here in a longer version than in the New Testament text. Here Jesus and one of his disciples have to go through the Afiq pass where a man was preventing them from doing so unless he is allowed to slap them on the cheek. When the disciple did not accept this condition, Jesus did in his place and thus got slapped twice. At the end of the story there is a hint that God is the rightful avenger.[24] He shows that one shall pray for those who treat one badly – the one who does pray accordingly defeats Satan;[25] and in general, the virtue of humility is stressed in different ways. So we can find in the Muslim tradition a version of the story from the Gospel of John, chapter 13, of Jesus washing his disciples' feet, with just that point: Jesus prepares food for the disciples and washes their hands and feet, he acts as a servant to them.[26]

A sentence ascribed to Jesus and very prevalent in Muslim literature, and not to be found in the New Testament is the following: "*al-Masīḥ* said: 'The world is a bridge. Walk across the bridge but do not build your dwellings on it!'"[27]

Several of the stories tell about Jesus resurrecting the dead. But the point is then that the deceased comes to life in order to answer a question or to pronounce a word of wisdom or to illustrate the vanity of this world, and then dies again. Thus also these narratives belong to the genre of wisdom literature.

IN CONTEMPORARY TIMES

From the eighteenth century onwards the influence of printed Bibles, in different translations, can be seen in literature and in (polemic)

---

[21] *Ibid.*, number 48.   [22] *Ibid.*, number 15.   [23] *Ibid.*, number 35.
[24] *Ibid.*, number 66.   [25] *Ibid.*, number 211.   [26] *Ibid.*, number 269.
[27] *Ibid.*, number 99. The saying is to be found in different versions. Cf. Leirvik, *Images*, 59.

theology. This means that to the Muslim Jesus tradition is added an element of more direct acquaintance with the narratives in the Christian
Bible. Some renowned Egyptian authors have used the personage of Jesus
in literary works discussing ethical and philosophical issues, which has pro-
voked interest among Christian scholars.[28] So ʿAbbās Maḥmūd al-ʿAqqād
in his *ʿAbqariyyat al-masīḥ*, "The spirit of the Messiah" (1952), underlines
the message of love and the spirituality in the Gospels, and stresses the role
of the human conscience (in contrast to legal casuistic rules). Another is
Kāmiʾl Ḥusayn, in his novel about the trial of Christ, *qarya ẓālima*, "The
Iniquitous City" (1954), a meditation on the trial and verdict against Jesus,
a trial which he sees as a huge crime as he leads the reader to regard it
from the point of view of the Jews, the Apostles, and the Romans. The
perspectives on the events provided by the author are both psychological and moral, highlighting the role of the conscience and the relation
between religion and state, and so on. These works have been analyzed
and are known especially for the authors' use of the personage of Jesus
to pose these problems emanating from moral dilemmas, and from the
role of the individual conscience in relation to society. In the same way
Khālid Muhammad Khālid's *Maʿan ʿalā aṭ-ṭarīq, Muḥammad wa-l-masīḥ*,
"Together on the road, Muhammad and Christ" (1958) has been analyzed
from the perspective of how the concept of conscience is related to the
messages of Muhammad and of Jesus.[29]

In contemporary Muslim polemic, theology and literature use has been
made of the so called Gospel of Barnabas, which contains a Christology
rather close (if not identical) to that of the Qurʾan. The first English
translation in 1907 was followed by a great number of translations into
languages of the Muslim world.[30] This booklet, however, existing in Italian
and partly in Spanish, is evidently a forgery dating not earlier than the
fifteenth century. Its name is taken from a "Gospel of Barnabas," which
has not been preserved, but is mentioned in the *Decretum Gelasianum*
(sixth century). This Italian Gospel of Barnabas, in translations, has been
rather widely spread in the Muslim world in the late twentieth century,
and has played a considerable role in religious polemics, because it is often
regarded as genuine by Muslims. To it is then applied a story of its discovery

---

[28] Cf. Anawati, "ʿĪsā," 85. These works have been thoroughly analyzed by Oddbjørn Leirvik in his
doctoral thesis, *Knowing by Oneself, Knowing with the Other: Al-ḍamīr, Human Conscience and
Christian-Muslim Relations* (Oslo: Det teologiske fakultet, University of Oslo, 2002), 193–341.

[29] Leirvik, *Knowing by Oneself*, 241–305.

[30] For a presentation of the book, its contents and its use in polemics, and the arguments for and
against its authenticity, see Leirvik, *Images*, 127–139.

in the library of Pope Sixtus V in the late sixteenth century – a variety of the common story of the secretly hidden and recovered book. One of its details is that Jesus was substituted on the cross by Judas, and that Jesus vehemently denies that he is the "Son of God." Circumcision is stressed as necessary, and so is the prohibition of pork.[31]

The role of Jesus in Islam opens up the question of whether Islam can be seen as a part of the Christian tradition. So in an appendix to his very influential *Lehrbuch der Dogmengeschichte* (from 1885 and through many editions), Adolf von Harnack (1851–1930) argued that Islam was more likely to be regarded as a Christian sect than was the case with Manichaeism. And the Swedish theologian and archbishop Nathan Söderblom (1866–1931) had the intention (which was not possible to fulfill, however) to invite the Shaykh al-Islām of Turkey or a representative from him to participate in the vast ecumenical meeting in Uppsala and Stockholm in 1925 as *hospes*, representing "the eastern schism." Söderblom wrote to his correspondent in Istanbul: "Without doubt it seems that Islam in Constantinople is administering the heritage of our Lord in a way as lively [as the Christians]."[32]

BIBLIOGRAPHY

Anawati, George C., "'Īsā," in *Encyclopaedia of Islam*, vol. IV (new edn., Leiden: Brill, 1973), 81–86.

Andrae, Tor, *I myrtenträdgården: studier i sufisk mystik* (Stockholm: Bonniers, 1947).

Bernabé Pons, Luis F., *El texto Morisco del Evangelio de San Bernabé* (Granada: Universidad de Granada e Instituto de Cultura Juan Gil-Albert, 1998).

Beskow, Per, *Jesus i Kashmir* (Stockholm: Proprius Förlag, 1981).

Carra de Vaux, Bernard and George C. Anawati, "Indjīl," in *Encyclopedia of Islam*, vol. III (new edn., Leiden: Brill, 1971), 1205–1208.

Daniélou, Jean, *Théologie du judéo-christianisme*, vol. I (Paris: Desclée, 1958).
  Les évangiles de l'enfance (Paris: Desclée de Brouwer, 1967).

Elliott, J. K., *The Apocryphal Jesus: Legends of the Early Church* (Oxford: Oxford University Press, 1996).

Geiger, Abraham, *Was hat Mohammed aus dem Judenthume aufgenommen?* (2nd edn., Leipzig: Kaufmann, 1969 [1902]).

---

[31] The edition of the Italian text is by Lonsdale and Laura Ragg, *The Gospel of Barnabas, Edited and Translated from the Italian MS. in the Imperial Library at Vienna* (Oxford: The Clarendon Press, 1907). The modern text edition of the Spanish text is Luis F. Bernabé Pons, *El texto Morisco del Evangelio de San Bernabé* (Granada: Universidad de Granada e Instituto de Cultura Juan Gil-Albert, 1998).

[32] Quoted in Bengt Sundkler, "Nathan Söderblom, Johannes Kolmodin och ortodoxa kyrkan," in *Religion och Bibel*, XXVI (1967), 73.

von Harnack, Adolf, *Lehrbuch der Dogmengeschichte* (Freiburg: Mohr, 1885 [with several reprints]).

Jeffery, Arthur, *The Foreign Vocabulary of the Qur'ān* (Baroda: Oriental Institute, 1938).

Judéo-christianisme: Recherches historiques et théologiques offertes en homage au cardinal Jean Daniélou, Recherches de science religieuse 60 (1972).

Karim, Fazlul, *Al-Hadis: Mishkat-ul-Masabih* [text, translation, and commentaries], Book IV (Lahore: The Book House, 1938).

Khalidi, Tarif, *The Muslim Jesus: Sayings and Stories in Islamic Literature* (Cambridge, Mass.: Harvard University Press, 2001).

Lang, David Marshall, "Bilawhar wa-Yudasaf," in *Encyclopedia of Islam*, vol. I (new edn., Leiden: Brill, 1960), 1215–1217.

Leirvik, Oddbjørn, *Images of Jesus Christ in Islam: Introduction, Survey of Research, Issues of Dialogue* (Uppsala: Swedish Institute of Missionary Research, 1999).

   Knowing by Oneself, Knowing with the Other: Al-damīr, Human Conscience and Christian–Muslim Relations (Oslo: Det teologiske fakultet, University of Oslo, 2002).

Mirza Ghulam Ahmad, *Jesus in India: Jesus' Deliverance from the Cross and Journey to India* (Tilford: Islam International Publications, 2003).

Paret, Rudi, *Der Koran: Kommentar und Konkordanz* (Stuttgart: W. Kohlhammer, 1971).

   "Ibrāhīm," in *Encyclopaedia of Islam*, vol. III (new edn., Leiden: Brill, 1971), 978–979.

Ragg, Lonsdale and Laura Ragg, *The Gospel of Barnabas, Edited and Translated from the Italian MS. in the Imperial Library at Vienna* (Oxford: The Clarendon Press, 1907).

Räisänen, Heikki, *Das koranische Jesusbild: Ein Beitrag zur Theologie des Korans* (Helsinki: Missiologian ja ekumeniikan seura R.Y., 1971).

Speyer, Heinrich, *Die biblischen Erzählungen im Qoran* (Hildesheim: Olms, 1961 [1931]).

Sundkler, Bengt, "Nathan Söderblom, Johannes Kolmodin och ortodoxa kyrkan," in *Religion och Bibel* 26 (1967), 64–77.

Wensinck, A. J., *A Handbook of Early Muhammadan Tradition* (Leiden: Brill, 1971 [1927]).

CHAPTER 6

Christ and the alchemical mass

Urszula Szulakowska

INTRODUCTION

During the sixteenth century, the image of Jesus Christ made a controversial appearance in the alchemical literature. The psychologist Carl Jung was the first to identify this phenomenon. He attributed it to the Renaissance concept of alchemy as being a religious rite whose miraculous results were expressly ordained by God. The image of Christ was used to symbolize the philosopher's stone, while his passion and crucifixion became an allegory of the laboratory process.[1]

More recent studies, such as those by Stanton J. Linden[2] and the present author,[3] have contextualized the alchemical Christ within the widespread expectations in Protestant Germany regarding the imminent Day of Judgment. Prophets and astrologers were foretelling the impending return of Christ around the year 1600. In the Gospels Christ had foretold that, prior to his reappearance, he would reveal great secrets. Since they were (apparently) living in the Last Times, many German alchemists believed that Christ must have finally produced the keys to unlocking their perplexing mysteries.[4] It seemed to be a productive (and profitable) time to publicize those obscure arts that were now supposedly illuminated by the Spirit of Christ. Accordingly, alchemists, astrologers, and kabbalistic magicians produced enormous quantities of publications, at first mainly in Germany, England, and Holland. These were often richly decorated with expensive engravings and woodcuts.

---

[1] C. G. Jung, *Psychology and Alchemy* (London: Routledge and Kegan Paul, 1993), 396–404.
[2] Stanton J. Linden, "Alchemy and Eschatology in Seventeenth-Century Poetry," *Ambix* 31 (1984), 102–124.
[3] Urszula Szulakowska, *The Sacrificial Body and the Day of Doom* (Leiden: Brill, 2000).
[4] Robin Bruce Barnes, *Prophecy and Gnosis* (Stanford: Stanford University Press, 1988), 24ff.

CHRIST AS ANTHROPOS, THE FIRST MAN

In the late sixteenth century the Christ was specifically identified with an ancient mythical being known as "Anthropos." This was a semi-divine person who was regarded in several ancient religions and in Jewish kabbalism as God's first-created progeny. He had been made before the entirely human Adam. The myth of Anthropos, Son of Man, had been one of the most evocative religious stories inherited from the Middle East, specifically from Iran. The Greek name "Anthropos" is an abbreviated translation of the older form, "First Man," "Primal Man," or "Great Man,"[5] originally a nameless being. This pagan Anthropos figure had been transferred to a Judaic context in the apocalyptic texts of Daniel, Ezekiel, and Enoch 2, where he was known as "Bar Nasha"/ "Anthropos"/ "Son of Man." In turn, these scriptures had provided the model for New Testament authors in their account of Jesus Christ, called "Son of Man," who would be the executioner of God's justice on Judgment Day: "Behold, I see the heavens opened, and the Son of Man standing on the right hand of God." (Acts 7.56)

In a number of religious traditions in the Near East and North Africa during the Hellenistic period, Anthropos was regarded as being the source of the physical universe. He was the Cosmic Soul, or "Pneuma," "Ratio," "Logos," "Inner Man," or "Son of Man." Anthropos was also later encountered in gnostic religions of the late Hellenistic period as a heroic cosmic figure who struggled against the primal forces of evil, suffered, and died. It was through the sacrifice of his own body that Anthropos had made the world, reusing his own substance as its material.

CHRIST-ANTHROPOS AS THE ALCHEMICAL
PHILOSOPHER'S STONE

The image of the primal Christ-Anthropos was equated by sixteenth-century alchemists with their own philosopher's stone, a substance material and spiritual, immanent and transcendent like Christ himself. The stone's alternative designation was "quintessence," the fifth essence described by Aristotle as an aetherial matter, spiritual in nature but with a physical body. The alchemical stone was believed to be the Christ-savior of the mineral kingdom, turning base matter into gold. It became mystically identified with the glorified body of the resurrected Christ. In fact, the

[5] Carl H. Kraeling, *Anthropos and Son of Man* (New York: Columbia University Press, 1927), 108–109.

stone's salutary effect on the metals was mirrored simultaneously by its redemption also of the body and soul of the alchemist himself. According to these heretical beliefs, the laboratory process eventually transmuted the alchemist's own sinful humanity into a Christ-like form.[6] The process was modeled on the ritual of communion in the Roman Catholic mass in which Christ's presence in the bread and wine entered the body and soul of the communicant.

THE DEVELOPMENT OF THE VISUAL IMAGERY OF THE ALCHEMICAL CHRIST

The visual iconography of the alchemical Christ, his crucifixion, and resurrection began to develop in late fourteenth-century manuscripts.[7] According to Barbara Obrist, illustrations of Christ as Mercurius-philosopher's stone were first seen in a manuscript written by Gratheus, *La sagesse de Salomon* and were soon followed by those of Constantinus in *Le livre des secrets de ma dame alchimie*.[8] Here he was identified specifically with the concept of "Mercurius," the prime matter of the laboratory process. (The exact nature of this "mercury" was supposed to be kept a secret). Mercurius retained in alchemy his original pagan meaning as the dual-natured messenger of the gods, that is, he was both male and female, belonging equally to heaven and the underworld. In his basest form, Mercurius was identified with the serpent, or dragon, as the dangerous, life-threatening menstrual blood. Through the action of a chemical cleansing, the "menstruum" could become the elixir of life, the quintessence in liquid form.[9] Many alchemists, such as Heinrich Khunrath and Robert Fludd, regarded the elixir as being the alchemical equivalent of the blood of Christ in the mass. The Greek alchemist Zosimos in the fifth century CE had used the language of torture and sacrifice to describe the laboratory purification of mercury, a bloody process but one that eventually culminated in its rebirth as a supernatural being. His alchemical allegory was popularized and identified with the passion of Christ.[10]

A notorious image of the resurrection of the Christ-stone appeared in *Das Buch der heiligen Dreifaltigkeit* ("The Book of the Holy Trinity"),

---

[6] Szulakowska, *The Sacrificial Body*.

[7] Barbara Obrist, *Les débuts de l'imagerie alchimique (XIVe–XVe siècles)* (Paris: Le Sycomore, 1982), 126ff.

[8] See Obrist, *Les débuts de l'imagerie alchimique*, 67ff.; figs. 1, 2, 3, 4, 5, 11.

[9] F. N. L. Poynter (ed.), *Chemistry in the Service of Medicine* (London: Pitman, 1963), 5–26.

[10] Michèle Mertens (ed.), *Zosime de Panapolis, "Mémoires authentiques,"* vol. IV: *Les alchimistes grecs* (Paris: Les Belles Lettres, 1995), 36–39.

which was composed by a German alchemist at the time of the Council of Constance in 1414–1418. It contains several scenes drawn from Roman Catholic iconography, such as the coronation of the Virgin Mary; this image is used, however, to allude to the alchemical process of sublimation. Among these pictures there is an image depicting Christ crucified on the emblem of a lily, while the Virgin Mary sits at his feet on the down-turned crescent moon in the midst of sun-rays. These celestial elements signify that she represents the apocalyptic Woman in the Revelation of St. John.[11] It is a well-documented fact that many contemporaries and later readers objected to the *Book of the Holy Trinity*, claiming that it was heretical because it incorporated Christian doctrine into a magical context. Obrist has argued, however, against this interpretation, reading the work as merely a political allegory.[12] Another controversial image was made later for the *Rosarium philosophorum*, the most popular alchemical work of the period. The picture illustrates Christ rising from his tomb with a cross in his hands (fig. 1).[13] The earliest manuscript of this treatise dates from the early fifteenth century, though it was not illustrated at that date. It first appeared in print at Lyons in 1504, then later in Frankfurt in 1550 in a collection of works, the *De alchimia opuscula*. At that stage, twenty woodcuts were added including the image of the risen Christ.[14]

In Obrist's argument, the alchemists' appropriation of Christian iconography had been a political strategy designed for use in their battle against university scholars who were teaching the physical theories of Aristotle. He had taught that each type of metal constituted a species and that species could not transmute into one another. This meant that lead could not turn into gold through the action of the philosopher's stone. In response, the alchemists "proved" the truth of their claims in their development of visual imagery which they used in order to persuade the viewer. They presented him with a "vision" (as it were) of alchemical transmutation in the hope of convincing him of its reality. By using Christian iconography, they gave their illustrations the appearance of the sacred scenes experienced by Christian saints. In this manner, the alchemists moved their theories from

[11] Illustrated in Gustav Friedrich Hartlaub, "Signa Hermetis," *Zeitschrift des deutschen Vereins für Kunstwissenschaft* 4 (1937), 110, fig. 8.
[12] Obrist, *Les débuts de l'imagerie alchimique*, 117ff. See also Hartlaub, "Signa Hermetis," 93–162.
[13] "Rosarium Philosophorum," in *De alchimia opuscula* (Frankfurt, 1550), reprinted in *Artis auriferae* (Basel, 1593). See also "Rosarium philosophorum," in Eberhard Zetzner (ed.), *Theatrum chemicum*, vol. V (Strassburg: Heredium Eberhard Zetzner, 1622), 191.
[14] Lutz Claren and Joachim Huber (eds.), *Rosarium philosophorum*, vol. II (Weinheim: VCH, 1992), 180–186.

the ground of scholarly debate to that of the unquestionable truths of the Christian faith.[15]

HEINRICH KHUNRATH AND THE DEVELOPMENT OF ALCHEMICAL ILLUSTRATION IN REFORMATION GERMANY

In the sixteenth and early seventeenth centuries, it was Lutheran alchemists who developed these ideas further, especially by providing visual imagery to accompany their texts. Among these, the work of Heinrich Khunrath was of supreme importance in influencing later generations of mystics and magicians. In his treatise, the *Amphiteatrum sapientiae aeternae* ("The Amphitheatre of Eternal Wisdom," Hamburg, 1595), Khunrath produced a detailed description of Christ as the philosopher's stone, using for the first time concepts drawn from Renaissance kabbalism. Following his example, from the early 1600s there appeared a wealth of illustrated alchemical books in German cities associated with the Protestant reforms, above all in Strassburg, Frankfurt, Oppenheim, Hanau, and Augsburg. These alchemical works were published by printers of a liberal Protestant persuasion, in particular Lucas Jennis in Oppenheim, the de Bry family in Frankfurt and Strassburg, and David Franke in Augsburg.

Khunrath (1560–1605) was born in Leipzig, studied medicine first in his birthplace and later in Basel. From 1591 he attended Count Rosemberk of Trebona as court physician. Rozemberk was a prominent European patron of the magical arts. Later Khunrath became the physician of the Emperor Rudolf II in Prague at whose court he would have met the foremost philosophers and alchemists of his time.[16] The most surprising aspect of Khunrath's career is the length of time involved in the publication of his writings, which were printed very late in his career: the first version of the *Amphiteatrum sapientiae aeternae* appeared in Hamburg in 1595. This was followed by a few more books published in Magdeburg in 1599. His further treatises were printed only after his death in 1605, eventually appearing in Hanover (1609), Strassburg (1608), and Magdeburg (1616). The apparent difficulties in getting his work into print indicate that he was facing opposition. From the internal evidence of the texts and pictures, as well as from other contemporary writers, it is possible to conclude that both the Lutheran and the Catholic religious authorities were antagonistic to Khunrath.

[15] Obrist, *Les débuts de l'imagerie alchimique*, 5–65 and 248–249.
[16] R. J. W. Evans, *Rudolf II and his World: A Study in Intellectual History* (Oxford: Oxford University Press, 1973), 212, 214.

In fact, the manner in which Khunrath integrated Christian doctrine with alchemical theory evolved into an independent type of religious piety, one that did not rely on the spiritual ministrations of any established state religion. Khunrath was born in Saxony, the heartland of Luther's Reformation, but his own religious beliefs were those of a second generation of Protestants who felt that Luther's original reformation needed to be revised substantially.[17] For Khunrath this would result in a Protestant faith that could be practiced in private, through a direct appeal to the Holy Spirit of Christ, bypassing the official structures of the Lutheran church, its clergy, religious rites, and doctrine. He wrote in his works that he was an "enthusiast," that is, one filled with the presence of the divine. He felt himself to be inspired, literally "breathed-in" by the Spirit, a force that he identified with the alchemical "pneuma," the soul of the universe pervading all things animate and inanimate.[18]

SIXTEENTH-CENTURY ALCHEMY AND THE CHRISTIAN KABBALAH

Particularly objectionable to Khunrath's enemies may have been his adoption of the Christian kabbalah created by Johannes Reuchlin. The latter had managed to avoid official censure due to his friendship with the liberal humanist Philip Melanchthon, Luther's closest collaborator. In contrast, Reuchlin's own intellectual mentor Pico della Mirandola, a Florentine humanist, had been forced by the papal authorities to retract his ideas in the 1480s. (Pico had ventured to introduce a rudimentary kabbalism into Christian doctrine.) By the 1580s there were many Lutherans who similarly regarded the use of kabbalism to support Christian theology as, at best, superfluous and, at the extreme, as downright heretical.

Reuchlin had created a radical new theology through his transformation of the Jewish kabbalistic system into a Christian one based on the concept of the Trinitarian Godhead. The Christian kabbalah became the indispensable foundation of all later learned magic up to and including the nineteenth century. The name "kabbalah" ("received tradition") had originated in the circles of Rabbi Isaac the Blind in thirteenth-century southern France, with more detailed systems being worked out slightly later in Spain by figures such as, most notably, Abraham Abulafia (b. 1240; d. after 1291). The kabbalistic texts were based on the early chapters of the

---

[17] Thomas Klein, *Der Kampf um die zweite Reformation in Kursachsen, 1586–91* (Cologne and Graz: Böhlau, 1962).

[18] Urszula Szulakowska, *The Alchemy of Light* (Leiden: Brill, 2000), 79–152.

biblical books of *Genesis* and *Ezekiel*, but in the course of the Middle Ages further ideas were adopted from Christian Neo-Platonism. The kabbalists believed that the fundamental principles of all things were numbers, letters, and sounds.[19] The Hebrew alphabet itself was sacred since it was composed out of the divine flame of God, and the secret name of God "YHVH" (the "Tetragrammaton") was the major source of power.

Reuchlin transformed the original Judaic Tetragrammaton into a Christian sign by placing the Hebrew letter "shin" at its center. Thereby he created the form "YHSVH" ("Jesue"), thus locating Christ at the heart of the kabbalistic system. Pico della Mirandola in his *Conclusiones* had initiated the identification of the kabbalistic Messiah with Christ. Developing this idea much further, Reuchlin gave Christ a kabbalistic name on the model of the Jewish Book of Beresith (Gen. 1.2). In *De verbo mirifico* (1494) and *De arte cabbalistica* (1517) Reuchlin referred to Christ, the Creator-God, as the "Ruach-Elohim," the Spirit of the Lord moving over the waters of chaos. Following his example, Khunrath applied the same designation to his alchemical Christ, whom he identified with the universal spirit, the quintessence or "azoth," which composed the stone of the philosophers. In his system he prioritized the idea of Christ as the soul of the cosmos over that of the historical Jesus, the redeemer of humankind.

PARACELSIAN ALCHEMY AND MEDICINE

The main influence on German alchemists and radical theologians of the late Renaissance was Theophrastus Paracelsus von Hohenheim (1493–1541), who was both a doctor using alchemical medicines, as well as a radical theologian, or theosophist. There were constant attacks on Paracelsian spirituality and medicine by both Protestant and Catholic theologians and natural philosophers, such as Thomas Erastus (1523–1583) and Marin Mersenne (1588–1648). They recognized the fact that Paracelsian alchemists were transmitting unorthodox views that had been developed outside the doctrinal confines of the church. The Paracelsians, nonetheless, considered themselves to be true disciples of Jesus Christ and wrote to this effect. Erastus, however, accused Paracelsus of pagan regression due to his use of astral demons in preparing his medicines.[20] Paracelsus had claimed that his remedies were pervaded by the Holy Spirit, acting by proxy through

---

[19] Gershom Scholem, *Major Trends in Jewish Mysticism* (New York: Schocken Books, 1973), passim.
[20] Allen G. Debus, *The Chemical Philosophy: Paracelsian Science and Medicine in the Sixteenth and Seventeenth Centuries*, vol. I (London: Heinemann, 1977), 129–134.

angels (or "daemons") residing in the stars and constellations. The stars imprinted their form on these astrological medicines.

An image of the alchemical Christ in a theosophical and kabbalistic context appears in Khunrath's *Amphiteatrum sapientiae aeternae* (1595). The engraving displays a naked, male figure standing in the midst of a fiery light, his arms outstretched as in traditional imagery of the crucifixion (fig. 2). Below him hovers the dove of the Holy Spirit, emitting tongues of flame. He represents the kabbalistic "Ruah-Elohim" (the Spirit of God). The Hebrew alphabet, believed to be the primal language of Adam, is inscribed around the man who can also be identified with "Anthropos," or Macrocosmic Man. This image was modeled on the Greek *Corpus Hermeticum* (second century CE), a collection of seventeen religious and magical texts. It recounts the myth of the demiurge Anthropos, son of "Nous" (Mind), who unites with "Phusis" (Nature) to create matter.[21] Khunrath names his figure the "Makrokozmou Filius" (the son of the Macrocosm) which is his term for "Anthropos."[22] Inscribed on the engraving there are other texts revealing him to be Jesus, the true Son of God ("Vere filius DEI erat IPSE") who is the sign of victory ("SIGNO VINCES IN HOC"). In 1608 the meaning of Khunrath's emblem was further explained by Johannes Arndt (1555–1621),[23] a respected Lutheran theologian who also admired Paracelsian theosophy, alchemy, and kabbalah.[24] He explained that the Hebrew names in Khunrath's engraving were those of the "angel" standing within the circle. This identification was drawn from Reuchlin's account in *De arte kabbalistica* (1517) of the angel Metatron, the prefiguration of the Messiah.[25] Hence, Khunrath's Macrocosmic Man is also Christ the Messiah.

THE ROSICRUCIAN MANIFESTOS

After 1615 many German alchemical texts proclaimed their admiration for the Rosicrucian Manifestos. These were two short tracts, the *Fama* (1614) and *Confessio* (1615), that were published anonymously in Kassel

---

[21] Brian P. Copenhaver, *Hermetica* (Cambridge: Cambridge University Press, 1992), 3–4.

[22] Heinrich Khunrath, *Amphiteatrum sapientiae aeternae* (Hanau, 1609), 198.

[23] Johannes Arndt, "Judicium über die vier Figuren des grossen Amphiteatrum Henrici Khunraths," in Heinrich Khunrath, *De igne magorum philosophorumque*... (Strassburg: Lazarus Zetzner, 1608), 107–123.

[24] Hermann Geyer, *Johann Arndts "Vier Bücher vom wahren Christentum"*... (Berlin: Walter de Gruyter, 2001).

[25] Johannes Reuchlin, *De arte kabbalistica (1517)* (Stuttgart: Friedrich Frommann Verlag, 1964, facs. of 1517 edn.), 33, 143.

where the ruler, Moritz of Hesse, encouraged alchemy and other eso-teric studies.[26] Recent research, such as that of Dickson and Tilton, has ascertained that the Manifestos had originated in the circles of Johann Valentin Andreae at the University of Tübingen in the 1590s.[27] The Man-ifestos announced the existence of a secret society created by the mythical philosopher Christian Rosencreutz. It was Protestant in religious sympa-thies, but also equally inspired by pagan Greek magic, kabbalism and the alchemical theory of Paracelsus.[28] It is unlikely that such a Rosi-crucian Society ever existed in reality, but its admirers nevertheless pro-duced a flood of publications in its name. These would-be fellow-travelers employed a common idiom, as Frances Yates has shown, that of Paracelsian alchemy.[29]

MICHAEL MAIER AND THE ALCHEMICAL MASS

The work of Michael Maier (1568–1622) was the next important contri-bution to the textual and visual discourse of the alchemical Christ. He belonged to the second generation of Paracelsian alchemists to display Khunrath's influence. Maier's most famous treatise was a collection of illustrated alchemical emblems known as *Atalanta Fugiens* (published in 1617–1618). He structured his alchemical theory in the form of allegorical stories, poems, music, and songs designed to entertain a courtly audience. Although Maier himself was a member of the central European aristocracy, he worked as a physician at the court of Rudolf II in Prague. He was among the first to publish a supportive commentary on the Rosicrucian Manifestos in his *Themis aurea* (1618).

In his biography of twelve European alchemists, the *Symbola aureae duodecim nationum* (1617), Maier included a paraphrase of an earlier treatise composed by Melchior Cibinensis, a Hungarian alchemist of the early sixteenth century. According to Jung, Cibinensis can be identified with Nicolaus Melchior Szebeni of Hermannstadt (formerly Sibiu, or Cibiu). Cibinensis had been chaplain and astrologer from 1490 to Louis II (1516–1526). After the defeat of Louis II by the Turks at the battle of Mohács

---

[26] Bruce T. Moran, *The Alchemical World of the German Court: Esoteric Philosophy and Chemical Medicine in the Circle of Moritz of Hesse* (Stuttgart: Franz Steiner Verlag, 1991).

[27] Donald R. Dickson, *The Tessera of Antilia* (Leiden: Brill, 1998), 32–36. See also Hereward Tilton, *The Quest for the Phoenix: Spiritual Alchemy and Rosicrucianism in the Work of Count Michael Maier (1569–1622)* (Berlin: Walter de Gruyter, 2003).

[28] Roland Edighoffer, "Rosicrucianism," in Wouter J. Hanegraaff *et al.* (eds.), *Dictionary of Gnosis and Western Esotericism*, vol. II (Leiden: Brill, 2005), 1009–1014.

[29] Frances A. Yates, *The Rosicrucian Enlightenment* (London: Routledge and Kegan Paul, 1972; repr. 1986), 92–102.

in 1526, Cibinensis fatefully joined the court of Emperor Ferdinand I in Vienna where he was executed for heresy in 1531. He wrote an unpublished treatise in which the rite of the communion mass, the Eucharist, was compared to alchemical transmutation.[30] He had dedicated this work to the Reformation of the church, although Jung has argued that it predates 1516, having been written before Luther's rebellion of 1517.[31]

Maier commissioned a set of engravings for the *Symbola aureae* from the artist Matthieu Merian. The engraving accompanying the biography of Cibinensis depicts a Roman Catholic mass and contains allusions to the Book of Revelation.[32] It consists of the image of a Roman Catholic priest dressed in liturgical garments (fig. 3). This is embroidered with an image of Christ hanging from the cross. The priest has turned his back to the congregation. To the left of the picture, hovering in the air, is a young women suckling an infant. Her bare head and loose blonde locks indicate that she is an unmarried virgin. The author of the Book of Revelation (12.1–6, 13–17) describes the vision of a "woman clothed with the sun, and the moon under her feet, and upon her head a crown of twelve stars." She is pursued by a dragon (the Devil) who is determined to kill her child, his mortal enemy. Lutherans interpreted the figure of the Virgin as a symbol of the Reformed Church, the forerunner of the New Jerusalem, pregnant with the true faith, while the persecuting dragon was the Roman Church. The Catholic interpretation, conversely, held that she was the Virgin Mary, the new Eve, who bore the Messiah and was the mother of the true Apostolic Church.

The alchemical version of the Apocalyptic Woman is an allegory of the laboratory process of *cibatio* ("feeding") in which the distilled spirits are reunited with the calcinated ashes of their original chemical source. According to medieval commentators, Mary in her role as the Mother of God had been empowered to secure God's grace for sinful humanity. Mary was the fountain of life, like Christ, at which all could quench their thirst. In this context, the Apocalyptic Virgin in Maier's treatise is breast-feeding a crystalline fluid to her infant, the *lac virginis* ("virgin's milk"). This was a volatile spirit believed to be the purest quintessence, the substance of the aetherial stars caught in a flask. The fourteenth-century French alchemist, John of Rupescissa, had created an alchemical elixir from the quintessence

---

[30] The text appears as "Addam et processum sub forma missae, a Nicolao Cibinensi Transilvano, ad Ladislaum Ungariae et Bohemiae regem olim missum," in *Theatrum chemicum*, vol. III (Basel: Lazarus Zetzner, 1602), 853ff.

[31] Jung, *Psychology and Alchemy*, 396–404.

[32] Michael Maier, *Symbola aureae mensae duodecim nationum* (Frankfurt: Lucas Jennis, 1617), 509.

that he called the "coelum" ("heaven," that is, star-liquid). It was intended to drive away the infirmities of old age and extend life. He distilled it from wine which conferred a sacramental connotation on the elixir.[33] In the same period, Arnald of Villanova in his *Rosarium*, as well as the anonymous author of the treatise *Aurora consurgens*, had openly referred to the elixir as being the alchemical form of the blood of Christ. The *Aurora consurgens* was later printed in a popular compendium of alchemy, the *Artis auriferae* (1593), but the editor eliminated its first section (containing the seventh parable) in which the original author had compared the philosopher's stone to the communion bread.[34]

Maier's engraving also recalls the topic of the *Emerald Table*, a brief text attributed to the pagan Hermes Trismegistus, but actually composed in Alexandria in about the second century CE. It describes an entity stated to be the child of the moon, who is carried in the womb of the wind. He rises up to the heavens and sinks down to the earth repeatedly.[35] The medieval Arabic and European alchemists interpreted the *Emerald Table* as an allegory of the distillation process in which volatile spirits were separated by heat from the prime matter and purified. The dregs left behind in the flask were next burnt free of their impurities (calcinated) until the ashes turned white. Eventually the ashes were reunited with the spirits, the process being compared to the Christian resurrection in which the souls of the dead were believed to be rejoined with their bodies on Judgment Day. Paul the apostle had written that during the communion rite Christ was present in his form as the Judge of humanity (1 Cor. 11.27–34). This was signified by an Aramaic expression used in the liturgy, "Maranatha" that meant "Come Lord!" (1 Cor. 16.22). It threatened with damnation those who partook of the body and blood of Christ in a state of sin. The meaning of the communion mass was that it foretold the banquet that would take place after the Universal Judgment in the New Jerusalem. To this feast Christ would invite only those who had been redeemed (Rev. 19.7–9; 21.2).[36] This apocalyptic meaning was also transferred to the alchemical mass.

Maier's illustration depicts a moment within the Catholic ritual of the consecration of the bread and wine. Prior to this particular scene, the chalice with the wine had been blessed with the Words of Institution, those that

---

[33] Michela Pereira, "Un tesoro inestimabile: Elixir e 'prolongatio vitae' nell'alchimia del '300'," in *Micrologus: Nature, Sciences and Medieval Societies*, vol. I: *Discorsi dei Corpi* (Turnhout: Brepols, 1993), 161–187.

[34] *Artis auriferae* (Basel, 1593), 185–246.

[35] Stanton J. Linden (ed.), *An Alchemy Reader* (Cambridge: Cambridge University Press, 2003), 27–28.

[36] Geoffrey Wainwright, *Eucharist and Eschatology* (London: Epworth Press, 1971), 61, 66, 81, 83, 94–95.

Christ had spoken at the Last Supper, "This is my blood." Then the bread had been blessed with the words "This is my body." The Elevation of the Chalice and the Host follows thereafter. Subsequently, the priest proceeds to the section called "Unde et Memores" (Memorial) in which he refers to Christ's requirement in the Gospels that he be remembered by the repetition of the Words of Institution. The sacrifice of the body and blood of Christ in the mass is designated ritually as the "Oblatio." The priest recalls that this ritual sacrifice signifies the promise of eternal life and he speaks the words: "panem sanctum vitae aeternae et calicem salutis perpetuae." The grace of God is sought so that the offering of his Son at the hands of the priest should be acceptable to him ("Supplices").[37] However, Cibinensis' alchemical version of the mass is not the full ritual, but a truncated version of it, as Jung has pointed out.[38] In fact, Cibinensis has failed to locate the chemical transmutation at the central moment of the mass, that is, at the consecration of the bread and wine when they become the body and blood of Christ. Instead he ends his text before that. His alchemical mass jumps, in fact, from the "Secret" at the Offertory stage, straight through to the post-communion texts. Most important of all, Cibinensis never specifically identifies Christ with the philosopher's stone in his text, clearly because he feared reprisals. It was the later Lutheran Paracelsians that were to develop the full allegory of the alchemical mass.

JACOB BOEHME'S CONCEPT OF THE MASS

In the same years Jacob Boehme (1575–1624) produced a similar alchemical and astrological account of the communion rite in *De testamentis Christi, oder Von Christi Testamenten* (1623). Boehme was a theosophist who used alchemical symbolism in his discourse. He stated in Paracelsian terms that the miracle of transubstantiation was produced by the forces of Nature, in which Christ was spiritually present, acting on the elemental construction of the communion materials. Boehme compared the wine to the alchemical tincture.[39]

In fact, the Paracelsian version of alchemical transmutation had more in common with Roman Catholic dogma than with the Lutheran doctrine

---

[37] Joseph A. Jungmann, *The Mass of the Roman Rite: Its Origins and Development*, vol. II (New York and Boston: Benziger Bros., 1955), 186–237.

[38] Jung, *Psychology and Alchemy*, 489.

[39] Jacob Boehme, "De testamentis Christi, oder Von Christ Testamenten (1623)," in Will-Erich Peuckert, *Boehme: Sämtliche Schriften*, vol. VI (Stuttgart: Frommanns Verlag, 1957), 34ff.

of consubstantiation. Luther had taught that the communion bread and wine remained unchanged in material form, though it did indeed somehow become the physical body and blood of Christ. More significantly, the Lutherans altered the meaning of the communion ritual from being the enactment of Christ's original sacrifice on the cross to that of a commemorative meal, using the term *Abendmahl* ("supper"). In the case of the Paracelsian alchemists who were still Lutheran in religious persuasion, their anomalous application of Catholic Eucharistic symbolism to their alchemy may be explained by the inadequacy of the Lutheran *Abendmahl* to express the process of transmutation. The Catholic mass, in contrast, was a perfect equivalent.

THE MASS IN THE ALCHEMICAL LABORATORY

There exists a probable prototype for Maier's engraving, one that had appeared in Khunrath's *Amphiteatrum* (1595) where an alchemist was shown praying in his laboratory before an altar. The liturgical missal of the altar had been replaced by a book of magic displaying two geometrical diagrams (fig. 4). One of the diagrams took the form of a pentacle and the other of a circle in a square. The pentacle, or *annulus* as Khunrath called it, was modeled on Agrippa's mystical geometry in the *Occulta philosophia* (1533).[40] In Khunrath's context the five-pointed star was used to signify Christ-Anthropos as the alchemical fifth essence, or "azoth." The other diagram, that of the circle squared, symbolized Christ's miraculous incarnation through which he had reconciled God (the circle) with matter (the square). The altar in Khunrath's engraving stands within a luxurious Turkish tent that recalls the tabernacle tent, the portable shrine of the Jewish exile for forty years in the desert (Exod. 25–31; 35–40). The innermost part of the shrine had been the Holy of Holies, housing the Ark of the Covenant. In Heb. 9.1–10, 25 the Old Testament account of the tabernacle had been converted into a Christian allegory.

The famous Dutch artist Jan Vredeman de Vries (1527–ca. 1604) had designed the engraving of the alchemical laboratory for Khunrath (testified by an inscription on the 1595 version). De Vries had as a Calvinist escaped from the Netherlands at the time of their occupation by the troops of the Catholic Duke of Alba in 1567. He gained employment as an architect

---

[40] Heinrich Cornelius Agrippa von Nettesheim, *Opera*, 2 vols. (London, 1600; repr. Hildesheim and New York: Georg Olms, 1970), book II, 226–235; book III, 390–396.

for Rudolf II in Prague, but also traveled in Italy, eventually returning to Antwerp.[41] The spatial construction of de Vries' picture consists of a sophisticated, single-point perspective system that is more than a decorative element. The abstract geometry underlying the realistic details of the scene is a symbolical expression of the doctrine of Christ's incarnation in the communion mass. Khunrath's engraving recalls similar depictions carved on the front doors of tabernacles housing the communion wafer in Italian churches. It was a common visual genre that had originated in Desiderio da Settignano's tabernacle doors for the main altar of the Church of S. Lorenzo in Florence (ca. 1461). The scene was that of an empty hallway in the form of a geometrical construction known as a "pavimentum diminutionis" in which the vertical lines run together into a vanishing-point located in an open doorway at the back.[42]

CHRIST AS THE UNIVERSAL JUDGE IN AN ALCHEMICAL CONTEXT

There appears yet another important variant in late Renaissance iconography of the alchemical Christ in his role as Judge of the Last Day. This engraving is found in Stefan Michelspacher's *Cabala: Spiegel der Kunst und Natur* (1616). Michelspacher was a Tyrolean medical practitioner and also, most surprisingly, a visual artist, working in Augsburg ca. 1618–1623. He must have designed his own illustrations. His alchemical imagery is a hybrid of Roman and Protestant teachings since his real sympathies seem to lie with dissident spiritual groups alienated from institutionalized belief systems. According to his own admission, his work was a tribute to the Rosicrucian Brotherhood to whom he dedicated the 1616 edition of his treatise.[43] Little is known about Michelspacher to whose name the texts append his place of origin, "Tyrolensis." The name "Pacher" originates in south Tyrol and is still commonly encountered in the Alto Adige of the present day, although it does not originate historically in any one family, being simply a generic name for a wayfaring pack-bearer. A thriving network of Paracelsian alchemists had existed in the Tyrol during the early seventeenth century despite the repression of the Counter-Reformation. Ferdinand of Habsburg (Holy Roman Emperor, 1619–1637) had expelled all Protestant preachers, teachers, and scribes from Inner Austria in

---

[41] Adolf K. Placzek, "Introduction," in Jan Vredeman de Vries, *Perspectiva, Leiden: Henricus Hondius, 1604* (New York: Columbia University Press; Dover, 1968).

[42] Szulakowska. *Alchemy of Light*, 129–137.

[43] Urszula Szulakowska, "The Apocalyptic Eucharist and Religious Dissidence in Stefan Michelspacher's Cabala," *Aries. Journal for the Study of Western Esotericism* 3 (2003), 200–223.

1598–1601. The Protestant faith was secured only in the mountain valleys of the Tyrol.[44] Among the Tyrolean Paracelsians, Carlos Gilly has identified Adam Haslmayr of Heiligen Kreutz as a central figure. His text *Propheceyung vom Löwen auss Mitternacht* was modeled on Paracelsian prophecy, and for this reason from 1603 he was persecuted by the Jesuits.[45] In 1618, the Jesuits accused Haslmayr of heresy and he was sent to the galleys in 1623. This appalling history of persecution may have caused Michelspacher to remove himself from the oppressive climate of the Tyrol to the more tolerant atmosphere of Augsburg.[46]

Michelspacher's engraving shows the crowned figure of Jesus Christ enthroned symbolically in a baptismal font (fig. 5). It is labeled *Der Brun des Lebens* ("The Source of Life"). He administers a wine-cup to two kneeling figures, male and female, who are crowned with the symbols of the sun and the crescent moon respectively. They represent the alchemical Sulphur and Mercury and also the human soul and body. The sacraments of Baptism and the Eucharist were the only two recognized by Luther. They were an integral part of religious eschatology, since they prepared the individual for judgment and for bodily resurrection. Michelspacher locates his scene of judgment in the center of a vineyard that surrounds Christ on three sides. At the top right of the picture there is a small image of Christ carrying the cross. He is shown standing in a wine-press that is operated by a hovering angel. His blood streams down the picture to fill the baptismal font. It should be noted that the motif of Christ in the wine-press is a Roman Catholic image. It had become especially popular during the Reformation as a polemical defense of the Catholic doctrine of transubstantiation. Hence, it is extraordinary to find the emblem in a Protestant context. The lower level of the picture describes, in contrast, the Lutheran communion rite since wine is being given by Christ the Priest-King to the laity, an action that was prohibited by Catholic authorities at that time.

At the top left of the picture is inscribed the Hebrew form of the name of God, the Tetragrammaton, in a halo of light. Out of this radiance there emerges a dove, the symbol of the Holy Spirit. In its trajectory it flies first to the wine-press and then down to Christ. Meanwhile, in an

[44] Evans, *Rudolf II*, 84–115; R. J. W. Evans, *The Making of the Habsburg Monarchy, 1550–1700: An Interpretation* (Oxford: Clarendon Press, 1979), 346–449.

[45] Carlos Gilly, *Adam Haslmayr: Der erste Verkünder der Manifeste der Rosenkreuzer* (Amsterdam: In de Pelikaan, 1994), 93–105.

[46] Jurgen Bücking, *Kultur und Gesellschaft in Tirol um 1600* (Historische Studien, 401; Lübeck: Matthiesen, 1968).

underground cave there stand six figures, male and female, symbolizing the six base metals. The cave represents the space of Purgatory in which imperfect souls are purified before ascending to heaven. One of the figures lifts a pair of bellows towards Christ as if pleading with him to stoke up the alchemical fire so that the six metals may be purified.

Read within an apocalyptic context, the engraving becomes an alarming prediction concerning the damnation by God of the Paracelsians' political and religious persecutors. The image of the vineyard has a very dark aspect as described in Rev. 14.17–20, which is an account of the gathering and pressing of the grapes (humanity) on the Last Day. The wine-press signifies the punishment that will be inflicted on the unjust and unfaithful.[47] Michelspacher's image also recalls a passage from Isa. 5.1–7 where the lord of the vineyard casts the vines that have born wild grapes into the eternal fire.

THE KABBALISTIC ALCHEMY OF ROBERT FLUDD

One last very important example of the discourse of the alchemical Christ needs to be mentioned, although it takes only textual form, or manifests in abstract geometrical diagrams, rather than in any realistic depictions of Christ himself. The kabbalistic-alchemical Christ is encountered in the Paracelsian medicine of the English physician Robert Fludd (1574–1637), who has attained a lasting historical reputation for the originality of his visionary work. Fludd in his own time achieved notoriety due to his early support of the Rosicrucian Manifestos in his *Apologia* (1616), expanded into the *Tractatus apologeticus* (1617).[48] He gained an international name due to his authorship of a colossal encyclopedia, the *Utriusque cosmi . . . historia* (1617–1626).[49] Fludd had a successful public life as physician to the court of James I. At one stage, nonetheless, he had to pen an *Apologia* defending his Paracelsian medicine against the suspicions of the king who was unnerved by the magical arts.[50]

Fludd regarded his medical practice as the purest expression of sound Christian faith, and he aimed to employ the same miraculous healing power

---

[47] Richard Bauckham, *The Climax of Prophecy: Studies on the Book of Revelation* (Edinburgh: T&T Clark, 1993), 96–98.

[48] Robert Fludd, *Apologia compendiaria fraternitatem de Rosae Cruce . . .* (Leiden: Gottfried Basson, 1616); Robert Fludd, *Tractatus apologeticus integritatem societatis de Rosae Crucis . . .* (Leiden: Gottfried Basson, 1617).

[49] Robert Fludd, *Utriusque cosmi maioris scilicet minoris metaphysica . . .* (Oppenheim: J. T. de Bry, 1617–26).

[50] C. H. Josten, "Truth's Golden Harrow," *Ambix* 3 (1949), 91–150; William H. Huffman, *Robert Fludd and the End of the Renaissance* (London: Routledge, 1988).

that had been given to Christ's disciples in the Gospels. In addition, he appropriated the theology of the sacrament of Communion for his own healing purposes. In his early *Tractatus theologo-philosophicus* (1617) Fludd drew ideas, as was customary, from the Protestant apocalyptic writings.[51] Like Khunrath he also devised an extensive kabbalistic system whose direct source was Agrippa and Reuchlin. He also seems to have been familiar with the original Hebrew corpus of texts, specifically the *Sefer Yetzirah*, the well-spring of kabbalistic theology. He knew the text perhaps from a reading of Guillaume Postel's translation published in Paris in 1552.[52] Fludd identified the divine Spirit of Christ with the kabbalistic Angel Metatron, the heavenly form of the Jewish Messiah. His resting place was the tabernacle of the sun, guarded by the archangel Michael, who was another form of the messianic figure. The sacred Spirit of Christ-Metatron was emitted in the sun's rays to the earth where it animated nature. It was also absorbed into the human lungs and blood.[53]

At the heart of Fludd's medical alchemy there was a recipe for a red elixir, the alchemical quintessence, that he regarded as a "catholic" (i.e. universal) medicine. It was said to be the alchemical equivalent of human blood, a spiritual tincture extracted from the red oil of wheat. This liquid attracted to itself the heavenly Spirit of Christ, in the same manner as the Eucharistic liturgy.[54] The sun played the central role in this process, transmitting the virtue of the heavens to the substance. Fludd, like other Paracelsian alchemists, most notably Boehme, believed that the Communion miracle was enacted by means of astral influences, not solely by the grace of Christ.[55] In the *Medicina catholica* (1629–1631) Fludd elaborated on therapeutic procedures that relied on the healing power of the sacrament of Communion. In this context, he also pondered the mystery of common bread which was chosen to be the material for the miracle of transubstantiation. He traced all mentions of bread in the Old and New Testaments, emphasizing its physical and spiritual potency and its sacramental nature. Such alchemistic appropriation of the Christian sacraments of Baptism and Communion was not welcomed by the governing churches. None of them

---

[51] Robert Fludd, *Tractatus theologo-philosophicus* (Oppenheim: J. T. de Bry, 1617), 89–126.

[52] Ithamar Gruenwald, "A Preliminary Critical Edition of Sefer Yezira," *Israel Oriental Studies* 1 (1971), 132–177; Guillaume Postel (ed. and comm.), *Sefer Jezirah* (Paris, 1552).

[53] Allen G. Debus, *Robert Fludd and the Philosophicall Key* (New York: Science History Publications, 1979), fols. 106v–108v.

[54] C. H. Josten (ed.), "Robert Fludd's 'Philosophicall Key' and his Alchemical Experiment on Wheat," *Ambix* 11 (1963), 1–23.

[55] Andrew Weeks, *Boehme: An Intellectual Biography of the Seventeenth-Century Philosopher and Mystic* (New York: State University of New York Press, 1991), 46–48, 55, 88–89.

could accept a chemistry that claimed to produce substances equivalent to the body and blood of Christ, administering the same grace of spiritual and physical healing. Fludd, when attacked, claimed to be an adherent of Anglican doctrine in his *Clavis philosophiae* (1633). Communion, he claimed to accept, was a commemoration, rather than an enactment of the original sacrifice of Christ.[56] In spite of these disclaimers, Fludd's position in regard to Anglican belief is highly irregular, as his contemporaries were well aware. The French cleric and mathematician Marin Mersenne and the theologian Pierre Gassendi subjected Fludd's theosophy of the alchemical blood to stringent criticism. In his *Clavis philosophiae* (1633) Fludd tried to defend his position by claiming that he intended his original statements to be treated as a metaphor, rather than taken literally.[57] Nonetheless, the fervor with which he described the distilling of the red oil and the precipitation of the stone belies these excuses.

From the early sixteenth century Lutheran alchemists associated with the school of Paracelsus had referred in their books and illustrations to the miracle of transubstantiation in the mass. As the philosopher's stone redeemed the metals, so Christ in the alchemical process redeemed the soul of the alchemist. On the model of Christian eschatology, the alchemists further believed that their materials were reborn in the course of their work in a glorified form. The imagery of resurrection in medieval Christian iconography had become associated with the popular belief in purgatory, a waiting-place in which souls were purged before their entry into heaven.[58] Alchemical iconography appropriated the whole scenario of purgatory, resurrection, and judgment. The alchemists followed the teachings of Paul concerning the resurrection of the body. He had devised an analogy with the dying seed for the process of the death and resurrection of the body, rising not as carnal flesh, but as a "spiritual body" (1 Cor. 15.21–54). This teaching is echoed in the *Liber de arte chymica*, written by an anonymous German alchemist of the sixteenth century. The body of the perfected stone, he states, when perfectly harmonized is like that of Christ. Since he was sinless and divine in essence, his corporeal elements were so perfectly harmonized that he would have remained immortal, had he not sought death of his own free will. In like manner, the philosopher's stone is glorious. Yet, for the sake of its imperfect, diseased brothers and sisters, it dies and

[56] Robert Fludd, *Clavis philosophiae* (Frankfurt: William Fitzer, 1633), 37.

[57] Fludd, *Clavis philosophiae*, 25, 28, 37–39, 46–47, 74.

[58] Jacques le Goff, *The Birth of Purgatory* (London: Scolar Press; Chicago: University of Chicago Press, 1984), 289–292, 356–359.

1. Woodcut of Christ as the philosopher's stone rising from a tomb in the "Rosarium Philosophorum," in Eberhard Zetzner (ed.), *Theatrum chemicum*, vol. V (Strassburg: Heredium Eberhard Zetzner, 1622), 191.

rises again, glorious and redeemed. It tinctures its siblings so that they gain eternal life, making them perfect like pure gold. God the Son is the *homo glorificatus* (glorified man) like the "lapis philosophorum," the Son of Man in the microcosm of the laboratory.[59]

[59] Jean Jacques Mangetus, *Bibliotheca chemica curiosa*, vol. II (Geneva: Chouet *et al.*, 1702), 686.

2. A circular image depicting Christ in an aureole of light from Heinrich Khunrath,
Amphitheatrum sapientiae aeternae (Hamburg, 1595; Hanau, 1609).

3. Alchemical Mass from Michael Maier, *Symbola aureae duodecim nationum*
(Frankfurt: Lucas Jennis, 1617), 509.

4. An alchemist in his laboratory from Heinrich Khunrath, *Amphitheatrum sapientiae aeternae* (Hamburg, 1595; Hanau, 1609).

5. Fourth image of Christ distributing the Eucharist from Stefan Michelspacher, *Cabala: Spiegel der Kunst und Natur* (Augsburg: David Francke, 1616).

BIBLIOGRAPHY

SOURCES

Agrippa von Nettesheim, Heinrich Cornelius, *Opera*, 2 vols. (London, 1600; repr. Hildesheim and New York: Georg Olms, 1970).

Arndt, Johannes, "Judicium über die vier Figuren des grossen Amphiteatrum Henrici Khunraths," in Heinrich Khunrath, *De igne magorum philosophorumque*... (Strassburg: Zetzner, 1608), 107–123.

[Cibinensis, Nicolaus], "Addam et processum sub forma missae, a Nicolao Cibinensi Transilvano...," in *Theatrum chemicum*, vol. III (Basel: Lazarus Zetzner, 1602), 853ff.

Claren, Lutz and Joachim Huber (eds.), *Rosarium philosophorum*, 2 vols. (Weinheim: VCH, 1992).

Fludd, Robert, *Apologia compendiaria fraternitatem de Rosae Cruce*... (Leiden: Gottfried Basson, 1616).

    Tractatus apologeticus integritatem societatis de Rosae Crucis... (Leiden: Gottfried Basson, 1617).

    Tractatus theologo-philosophicus (Oppenheim: J. T de Bry, 1617).

    Utriusque cosmi maioris scilicet minoris metaphysica... (Oppenheim: J. T. de Bry, 1617–26).

    Clavis philosophiae (Frankfurt: William Fitzer, 1633).

Khunrath, Heinrich, *Amphiteatrum sapientiae aeternae* (Hanau, 1609).

Maier, Michael, *Symbola aureae mensae duodecim nationum* (Frankfurt: Lucas Jennis, 1617).

Mangetus, Jean Jacques, *Bibliotheca chemica curiosa*, vol. II (Geneva: Chouet et al., 1702).

Mertens, Michèle (ed.), *Zosime de Panapolis, "Mémoires authentiques,"* vol. IV: *Les alchemistes grecs* (Paris: Les Belles Lettres, 1995).

Peuckert, W.-E., *Boehme: Sämtliche Schriften*, vol. VI (Stuttgart: Frommanns Verlag, 1957).

Postel, Guillaume (ed. and comm.), *Sefer Jezirah* (Paris, 1552).

Reuchlin, Johannes, *De arte kabbalistica (1517)* (Stuttgart: Friedrich Frommanns Verlag, 1964).

"Rosarium philosophorum," in *De alchimia opuscula* (Frankfurt, 1550); reprinted in *Artis auriferae* (Basel, 1593).

Zetzner, Eberhard (ed.), *Theatrum chemicum*, vol. V (Strassburg: Heredium Eberhard Zetzner, 1622).

LITERATURE

Barnes, Robin Bruce, *Prophecy and Gnosis* (Stanford: Stanford University Press, 1988).

Bauckham, Richard, *The Climax of Prophecy: Studies on the Book of Revelation* (Edinburgh: T&T Clark, 1993).

Bücking, Jurgen, *Kultur und Gesellschaft in Tirol um 1600* (Historische Studien, 401; Lübeck: Matthiesen, 1968).

Copenhaver, Brian P., *Hermetica* (Cambridge: Cambridge University Press, 1992).

Debus, Allen G., *The Chemical Philosophy: Paracelsian Science and Medicine in the Sixteenth and Seventeenth Centuries*, vol. I (London: Heinemann, 1977).

Robert Fludd and the Philosophicall Key (New York: Science History Publications, 1979).

Dickson, Donald R., *The Tessera of Antilia* (Leiden: Brill, 1998).

Edighoffer, Roland, "Rosicrucianism," in Wouter J. Hanegraaff *et al.* (eds.), *Dictionary of Gnosis and Western Esotericism*, vol. II (Leiden: Brill, 2005), 1009–1014.

Evans, R. J. W., *Rudolf II and his World: A Study in Intellectual History* (Oxford: Oxford University Press, 1973).

The Making of the Habsburg Monarchy, 1550–1700: An Interpretation (Oxford: Clarendon Press, 1979).

Geyer, Hermann, *Johann Arndts "Vier Bücher vom wahren Christentum"...* (Berlin: Walter de Gruyter, 2001).

Gilly, Carlos, *Adam Haslmayr: Der erste Verkünder der Manifeste der Rosenkreuzer* (Amsterdam: In de Pelikaan, 1994).

Gruenwald, Ithamar, "A Preliminary Critical Edition of Sefer Yezira," *Israel Oriental Studies* 1 (1971), 132–177.

Hartlaub, Gustav Friedrich, "Signa Hermetis," *Zeitschrift des deutschen Vereins für Kunstwissenschaft* 4 (1937), 93–162.

Huffman, William H., *Robert Fludd and the End of the Renaissance* (London: Routledge, 1988).

Josten, C. H., "Truth's Golden Harrow," *Ambix* 3 (1949), 91–150.

Josten, C. H. (ed.), "Robert Fludd's 'Philosophicall Key' and his Alchemical Experiment on Wheat," *Ambix* 11 (1963), 1–23.

Jung, C. G., *Psychology and Alchemy* (London: Routledge and Kegan Paul, 1993).

Jungmann, Joseph A., *The Mass of the Roman Rite: Its Origins and Development*, vol. II (New York and Boston: Benziger Bros., 1955).

Klein, Thomas, *Der Kampf um die zweite Reformation in Kursachsen, 1586–91* (Cologne and Graz: Böhlau, 1962).

Kraeling, Carl H., *Anthropos and Son of Man* (New York: Columbia University Press, 1927).

Le Goff, Jacques, *The Birth of Purgatory* (London: Scolar Press; Chicago: University of Chicago Press, 1984).

Linden, Stanton J., "Alchemy and Eschatology in Seventeenth-Century Poetry," *Ambix* 31 (1984), 102–124.

Linden, Stanton J. (ed.), *An Alchemy Reader* (Cambridge: Cambridge University Press, 2003).

Moran, Bruce T., *The Alchemical World of the German Court: Esoteric Philosophy and Chemical Medicine in the Circle of Moritz of Hesse* (Stuttgart: Franz Steiner Verlag, 1991).

Obrist, Barbara, *Les débuts de l'imagerie alchimique (XIVe–XVe siècles)* (Paris: Le Sycomore, 1982).

Pereira, Michela, "Un tesoro inestimabile: Elixir e 'prolongatio vitae' nell'alchimia del '300'," *Micrologus: Nature, Sciences and Medieval Societies* 1, *Discorsi dei Corpi* (1993), 161–187.

Placzek, Adolf K., "Introduction," in Jan Vredeman de Vries, *Perspectiva, Leiden: Henricus Hondius, 1604* (New York: Columbia University Press; Dover, 1968).

Poynter, F. N. L. (ed.), *Chemistry in the Service of Medicine* (London: Pitman, 1963).

Scholem, Gershom, *Major Trends in Jewish Mysticism* (New York: Schocken Books, 1973).

Szulakowska, Urszula, *The Alchemy of Light* (Leiden: Brill, 2000).

"The Apocalyptic Eucharist and Religious Dissidence in Stefan Michelspacher's Cabala," *Aries. Journal for the Study of Western Esotericism* 3 (2003), 200–223.

The Sacrificial Body and the Day of Doom (Leiden: Brill, 2006).

Tilton, Hereward, *The Quest for the Phoenix: Spiritual Alchemy and Rosicrucianism in the Work of Count Michael Maier (1569–1622)* (Berlin: Walter de Gruyter, 2003).

Wainwright, Geoffrey, *Eucharist and Eschatology* (London: Epworth Press, 1971).

Weeks, Andrew, *Boehme: An Intellectual Biography of the Seventeenth-Century Philosopher and Mystic* (New York: State University of New York Press, 1991).

Yates, Frances A., *The Rosicrucian Enlightenment* (London: Routledge and Kegan Paul, 1972; rep. 1986).

CHAPTER 7

Son of the Son of God: the feminine Messiah and her progeny, according to Guillaume Postel (1510–1581)

Jean-Pierre Brach

A COURSE AFTER MIRACLES

Guillaume Postel[1] was born in a small village in Normandy, to parents of humble means, after whose early death he soon moved to Paris. Originally self-taught in the Liberal Arts and in oriental languages, he also attended lessons at the Collèges of Sainte Barbe and Cardinal Lemoine, and later met some of the most important French Humanists (such as Jean Dorat, Guillaume Budé, and Lazare de Baïf), as well as certain representatives (for instance, Jean de Ganay) of the *milieu* of the French theologian and humanist Jacques Lefèvre d'Étaples, some of whom actually taught there or at the Collège de Navarre. After a while, the young, unknown, and penniless Postel came in contact with some well-connected individuals who, favorably impressed by his learning, endeavored to promote him at the French Court.

Royal attention first manifested itself by sending him, in a minor diplomatic capacity, to Tunis and Istanbul, on a quest for oriental manuscripts destined to enrich the library of King Francis I (1535–1537). He came back through Venice, where he stayed for about two months and became acquainted with several well-known erudites and printers, Jewish or Christian, like Teseo Ambrogio and Daniel Bomberg.

In 1538, his first books (*Alphabetum XII linguarum, De originibus linguæ hebraicæ*) were published in Paris, while the year 1539 saw his appointment as royal lecturer in oriental languages and mathematics at the recently founded Collège Trilingue, later to become the Collège de France. As soon as 1540, however, he felt the first tremors of a profound and lasting

---

[1] William J. Bouwsma, *Concordia Mundi: The Career and Thought of Guillaume Postel (1510–1581)* (Cambridge, Mass.: Harvard University Press, 1957); Georges Weill and François Secret, *Vie et caractère de Guillaume Postel* (Milan and Paris: Archè-Les Belles-Lettres, 1987).

spiritual crisis[2] which, along with the sudden and unexpected disgrace of his principal protector, Chancellor Guillaume Poyet (1541), gradually made him turn aside from the quest for an official position, or for an ecclesiastical benefice, and the financial rewards entailed thereby. At approximately the same time, he acquired the conviction of having heard divine voices, ordering him henceforth to dedicate his life to the purpose of establishing a universal religious concord. Having unsuccessfully attempted to persuade King Francis I of the necessity of reforming his kingdom and his private life in the face of impending divine anger, and having written his important *De orbis terræ concordia* during the winter of 1542–1543, Postel left Paris on foot for Rome, where he arrived in March 1544, to try and join the newly formed Company of Jesus, which he believed to be a uniquely appropriate setting for developing his own reformist goals. He remained in that city until the spring of 1546, and was ordained as a priest in the meantime by the then Vicar General of the city, Filippo Archinto (1495–1558). Yet, unable to make him abandon his already firmly grounded conviction of being the "angelic pope" announced by Joachim of Flora, as well as several other opinions (e.g. about the authority of the Council prevailing over that of the Pope, or the universal monarchy ultimately belonging to the king of France) which were proving equally unsavory to Ignatius of Loyola and his first companions, the Jesuits finally rejected his application. Free, therefore, to move about as he pleased, Postel traveled in Italy and eventually arrived in Venice (late 1546),[3] first taking up residence at the Ospedaletto san Zanipolo (hospital St. John and Paul) as chaplain,[4] and meeting there a fifty-year old woman he was soon to call his "Madre Zuana" (Mother Joanna), and the "Venetian Virgin,"[5] on account of the consecrated existence she was seemingly leading. While ministering for years to the poor and the orphans in the care of this establishment, this woman was apparently living an intense mystical life (including the reception of the stigmata), and was endowed with visions and prophetic revelations. Although very little is known about

[2] Jean-François Maillard, "Postel le cosmopolite: quelques documents nouveaux," in Sylvain Matton (ed.), *Documents oubliés sur l'alchimie, la kabbale et Guillaume Postel... offerts à F. Secret...* (Geneva: Droz, 2001), 208–209.

[3] Guillaume Postel, *Le thresor des prophéties de l'univers* (ed. François Secret; The Hague: M. Nijhoff, 1969), 8–13.

[4] Giuseppe Ellero, "G. Postel e l'ospedale dei Derelitti (1547–49)," in Marion-L. Kuntz (ed.), *Postello, Venezia e il suo mondo* (Florence: L. S. Olschki, 1988), 137–161, who states that it was a well-known meeting-place of the Jesuits in Venice.

[5] Marion-L. Kuntz, *G. Postel, Prophet of the Restitution of All Things* (The Hague: M. Nijhoff, 1981), 69–142; other bibliographical references about her can be found in Guillaume Postel, *Des admirables secrets des nombres platoniciens* (ed. and trans. Jean-Pierre Brach; Paris: Vrin, 2001), 85 n. 131 and Yvonne Petry, *Gender, Kabbalah and the Reformation: The Mystical Theology of Guillaume Postel* (Leiden: Brill, 2004), 95–116.

her biographic details (and certain, relatively striking, parallel elements between her life and that of Saint Catherine of Genova's [Caterina Fieschi] might partly be attributed to later imitation or reconstruction), it has been suggested that she may in all likelihood have been a member of the Venetian branch of the Confraternita del Divino Amore (Fraternity of Divine Love).[6]

If this were true, it would therefore be quite unsurprising to find her sharing with Postel – even before their meeting – certain views concerning the universal religious concord and the upcoming *restitutio* of humankind.

Indeed, ideas of this kind were then prevalent in such circles, Italian as well as French.[7] Having rapidly elected him as her confessor, it seems she went on to encourage his personal claims to the role of *pastor angelicus* (angelic or latter-day pope), a rather infectious contemporary conviction, which he had encountered and begun to nurture for himself while traveling in Italy. Given the situation, it was almost inevitable that Postel should, in turn, look upon her as possessing a profound spiritual wisdom, notwithstanding her illiteracy. However, since Postel moved in February 1548 from the *Ospedale dei Derelitti* to the house of one of his local friends, the printer Jan della Speranza,[8] it would appear that the two were in close contact no longer than at most eighteen months. Postel, nevertheless, was to remain a lifelong enthusiast of his "Venetian Virgin," whose private revelations (including, of course, those concerning his own mission) he found confirmed on every page of the *Zohar* and numerous other kabbalistic texts he was actively meditating on, translating, or actually composing (*Or ha-Menorah / Candelabrum Typicum*, 1548) during this Venetian sojourn.

From the summer of 1549 until after Easter 1551, Postel – sponsored by his long-time friend Daniel Bomberg – traveled to the Middle East and visited Jerusalem and again Istanbul. On his return to Venice, "Mother Joanna" was dead.[9]

After several more trips across Europe, which led him to Besançon, Basle, and Vienna (where he actively collaborated with Johann-Albrecht von Widmanstetter in the eventual first printing, in 1555, of the Syriac New

---

[6] Giuseppe Ellero, "Postel e Venezia," in *Guillaume Postel (1581–1981): Proceedings of the Avranches International Conference, 5–9 Sept. 1981* (Paris: G. Tredaniel, 1986), 28, n. 19. On Caterina Fieschi (1447–1510) and her link to this important milieu of pre-Tridentine Catholic reformers, see Daniela Solfaroli Camillocci, *I devoti della carità: Le confraternite del divino amore nell'Italia del primo cinquecento* (Naples: Città del Sole, 2002).

[7] Jean-Pierre Brach and PierLuigi Zoccatelli, "Courants renaissants de réforme spirituelle et leurs incidences," *Politica Hermetica* 11 (1997), 31–43.

[8] Maillard, "Postel le cosmopolite," 198.

[9] Either in 1549 (at an unspecified date) or on 29 August 1550, according to Postel's own contradictory statements; cf. Jean-Pierre Brach, "Dieu fait femme: Guillaume Postel et l'illumination vénitienne," in Michel Cazenave (ed.), *La face féminine de Dieu* (Paris: Noêsis, 1998), 45 n. 14.

Testament),[10] Postel went back again to Venice, where he presented himself in March 1555 before an inquisitorial court, deploring the inscription of his name to the *Index prohibitorum librorum* and requesting that his works and doctrines be examined anew, for eventual emendations.[11] He probably counted at first on the court's leniency, since it was headed by his old acquaintance, Filippo Archinto. As it turned out, he barely escaped with his life by being officially declared insane and spent the following three and a half years in the Roman prison of Ripetta. Eventually released by a popular upheaval following the demise of Pope Paul IV (1555–1559), he resumed his peregrinations throughout Europe (Basle again, Augsburg, Italy, Lyon) before settling definitively in Paris (1562). The first of his two last great opportunities of spiritual exaltation occurred in 1566, the year of the famous "miracle of Laon" (a public exorcism of a woman, named Nicole Obry, performed with the help of the Eucharist), to which Postel dedicated several tracts, upholding the event as demonstrative of Roman Catholic views on the nature of the sacrament, and contradicting the Protestant tenets he knew quite well, having opposed them all his life.

The second occurred in 1573, when he briefly came under the spell of yet another woman, a young widow named Marie Villeneuse, who claimed to have been made pregnant by the Holy Spirit. A few years later, in 1581, he died peacefully under the regime of mild confinement he had been sustaining for several years at the monastery of St Martin des Champs, having persevered with his – albeit private – teaching, writing, and publishing, almost until the end.

A FEMALE JESUS CHRIST?

If the examples of Nicole Obry and Marie Villeneuse, briefly mentioned above, establish anything, it is of course Postel's lifelong tendency to construe the feminine gender as a privileged vehicle for the physical manifestation of the divine. Such a tendency is even more blatantly present in his relationship with the "Venetian Virgin," whom we shall examine more closely.

Well-known contemporary studies have attracted attention to some unexpected feminine aspects of Jesus Christ, cultivated by certain

---

[10] Robert J. Wilkinson, *Orientalism, Aramaic and Kabbalah in the Catholic Reformation* (Leiden: Brill, 2007), 95–135; Robert J. Wilkinson, *The Kabbalistic Scholars of the Antwerp Polyglot Bible* (Leiden: Brill, 2007), 49–59. I am grateful to Valerie Rees (School of Economic Science, London) for first calling my attention to this (then unpublished) research during an engrossing May 2006 conversation held in Esalen, California.

[11] Weill and Secret, *Vie et caractère*, 110 and 281–282 n. 170.

important historical trends of western mysticism.[12] In Postel's and "Mother Joanna"'s cases, however, the crux of the matter lies not in the devotion to Jesus' feminine characteristics, but revolves around the certainty of his second incarnation within a feminine body (that of the "Madre Zuana," obviously), soon to be mysteriously transferred upon Postel himself. It appears, moreover, that even before their first meeting, at the end of 1546, the Venetian Virgin was already entertaining a firm belief in an imminent "Restitution" of humankind. Common though it was at the time, the conviction was more precisely understood by her – and soon enough, by Postel himself – as an erasing of the supposed bodily stain occasioned by original sin. This perspective obviously implied a complete change or renewal of the corporeal substance of the *electi*, who would be the first to be submitted to such a transformation, before its extension to humankind in general.[13]

As one who felt she was among these chosen few, and had also been designated to provide a crucial impulse to the whole process, which she viewed as having begun around the year 1540,[14] "Mother Joanna" succeeded in transmitting to Postel her conviction of the physical dimension of sin,[15] and of the necessity of a corporeal remedy to it, namely the Eucharist. This last she incited him to perform, in the year 1547, as a universal, once-and-for-all consecration of every kind of food and drink (for which stood bread and wine), designed to graft back humanity as a whole onto the Body of Christ.[16] It is hardly necessary to state that neither of them intended the meaning of this act as merely symbolical but, on the contrary, invested it with its fully realistic and tangible implications, so that, according to them, a complete substantial change would gradually occur in the nature of each man and woman partaking in the *Restitutio*.[17] Such is the real basis of Postel's obsession with the material or even corporeal dimension of sin, spirituality, divinity, and the sacraments, an obsession that he apparently shared with his "Mother."

---

[12] Foremost, here, is Caroline W. Bynum, *Jesus as Mother: Studies in the Spirituality of the High Middle Ages* (Berkeley: University of California Press, 1983).

[13] François Secret, "Guillaume Postel en la place de Realte," *Revue de l'histoire des religions* 192 (1977), 74–81.

[14] Weill and Secret, *Vie et caractère*, 116–117.

[15] And of the actual existence of a "body of sin," Postel, *Des admirables secrets*, 35 and n. 9.

[16] François Secret, "L'herméneutique de Guillaume Postel," in Enrico Castelli (ed.), *Umanesimo e ermeneutica* (Padua: Cedam, 1963), 108 and n. 78; Secret "Guillaume Postel en la place de Realte," 80–86.

[17] Jean-François Marquet, *Philosophies du secret: Etudes sur la gnose et la mystique chrétiennes (XVIᵉ–XIXᵉ siècles)* (Paris: Cerf, 2006), 136–154.

Quite clearly, their outlook is dependent, in this respect, on an exaggeratedly literal understanding of some Pauline texts.[18] Recurrent, also, in the Postellian works of the Venetian period, and throughout the Italian booklet entitled *La vergine venetiana*,[19] is the theme of the final struggle against sin. This was apparently a favorite of "Madre Zuana" as well and, of course, very much in evidence during those years of Catholic reform and high messianic expectations, right at the opening of the Council of Trent (1545–1563).[20]

There exists a natural link between these perspectives and the theme of religious concord. As the era of the "Restitution" must come – according to Postel – as the fourth historical period, after those corresponding to the Laws of Nature, Scripture (Torah), and Grace (Gospel), so the rational unification of all men in the fold of *ecclesia generalis* must itself coincide with this fourth and penultimate age in the history of salvation, which will witness the definitive disappearance of sin and the redemption of sinners. We cannot therefore be surprised to read, in Postel's exactly contemporary *Commentarius in Apocalypsim* (Venice, 1548)[21] that these eschatological issues constitute the "mystery revealed . . . to the new Eve [Joanna] in whom Christ operates the mysteries of his second Coming."[22] For this was the central revelation which the "Venetian Virgin" had hitherto kept to herself, but ultimately confided to her French confessor: that she was in fact Jesus' bride, and that Postel was to become "their substantial son." This was certainly a step up from merely being the "angelic pope" but – unexpected though it may sound to the modern reader – nevertheless quite in line with Postel's theology and mystical anthropology.

Without having here the space to delve into Postel's complex doctrine of the Eucharist, we have seen above that both he and Joanna understood the effects of this sacrament quite literally. In particular, the usual Christian statement about "the members of Christ's body" is taken by them to mean a real participation of the brethren in the actual substance of Jesus Christ, with no mitigating reservation other than the exclusion of Christ's properly

---

[18] Claude-Gérard Dubois, "Rationalisme et ésotérisme dans l'œuvre de Guillaume Postel (1510–81)," in James Dauphiné (ed.), *Créations littéraires et traditions ésotériques (XV°–XX° siècles)* (Biarritz: Infocompo, 1991), 57–68.

[19] Guillaume Postel, *Le prime nove dell'altro mondo, cioe . . . La Vergine Venetiana* (Padua, 1555).

[20] Marion-L. Kuntz, *Venice, Myth and Utopian Thought in the Sixteenth Century: Bodin, Postel and the Venetian Virgin* (Aldershot: Ashgate/Variorum, 1999); Ottavia Niccoli, *La vita religiosa nell'Italia moderna. Secoli XV–XVIII* (Rome: Carocci, 1998).

[21] Today Ms. B. L. Sloane 1409, ff. 229v°–419v° (unpubl.; f. 393v°); cf. François Secret, *Bibliographie des manuscrits de Guillaume Postel* (Geneva: Droz, 1970), 109–110.

[22] Bouwsma, *Concordia Mundi*, 64; 273–292; Secret, "Guillaume Postel en la place de Realte," 64–66 and 65 n. 1 (Latin text).

divine essence from the process. Seen from this perspective, it is no longer very surprising that Postel should have come to consider his "Mother" – who claimed, rather classically, to be Jesus' bride – as the true consort of Jesus Christ, in other words as the Second or New Eve, which was to the new or second Adam as the biblical Eve to the first Adam, that is taken out of him and, thus, "flesh of his flesh."[23] And just as, for the biblical Adam, it was "not good that the man should be alone," the second Adam – or Jesus – must possess "une aide spirituelle et maternelle extraite de sa glorieuse substance" (a spiritual and maternal helpmate, extracted from his glorious substance).[24]

Subintended here, but explicit in many other instances, the classic Latin pun on *mater* and *materia* ("maternal" and "material") is designed to help Postel's readers convince themselves that what is being said about Joanna encompasses in fact both a physical and a "personal" dimension.

The Second Eve is thus assimilated to the "inferior part of the substance of Jesus Christ," and therefore corresponds to the lower part of human nature (mainly, the body) which, according to Postel, has not been redeemed by the Incarnation of Jesus Christ himself. As a matter of fact, being *sub specie aeternitatis* the second person of the Trinity, Christ is construed by Postel as not having been in a position, with his first coming, to assume the human *person*, but only human *nature* in general. Now, *persons* being essentially responsible for committing sin, the entire human *person* (the individual, that is, thus including the body itself) is therefore in dire need of redemption as well. It follows, for Postel necessarily so, that the Messiah must come again as a woman, to redeem in turn that lower part of man which had hitherto been left out of the process of salvation. It is only in this sense, of course, that sin may definitely be erased in its present, most *substantial* sense. In order to achieve this, the second, feminine advent of Christ cannot, for Postel, be other than that of his "lower half," or the New Eve herself, whose direct relation to the physical side of human individuality is rendered even more evident from the correspondences our author establishes between the feminine and *materia* (body), on the one hand, and the masculine (Adam) and *forma* (soul), on the other hand. Didn't Jesus Christ himself, for his Incarnation, receive his physical body from a woman as well?[25] The important link between *mater* and *materia* is confirmed here,

---

[23] Gen. 2.18–25.

[24] *La nouvelle Eve mère du monde* (written in January 1552), in François Secret (ed.), *Apologies et rétractions* (Nieuwkoop: B. de Graaf, 1972), 23.

[25] Indeed, initially after their meeting, Postel was prone to present Joanna as the "second Mary" (Secret, "Guillaume Postel en la place de Realte," 65 and n. 1), and even to call her "Mariohanna" (Weill

since the material, bodily aspect of sin is in fact redeemed by the "maternité générale du monde" (general motherhood of the world) represented by the "Mother of the world" Joanna, whose name – interpreted by Postel as *Jochanna* or *Jehochanna* – means for him (in Hebrew) "grace of God" and testifies to the divine presence within her.[26] Predictably enough, given what I have already said, the ontological relationship between Jesus and Joanna is conceived of in terms of Aristotelian "form" and "matter," the first carrying more intrinsic dignity, since it confers being to all things, but depending on the second for assuming its outward, corporeal dimension or, as Postel puts it: "[les formes priment en elles-mêmes la matière en dignité, puisqu'elles donnent l'être à toutes choses], néantmoins si faut-il que leur estre actuel et manifeste soit de la puissance de matière déduict, ainsi comme en toute la nature se veoit"[27] ([compared to matter, forms retain a superior dignity, since they confer being to all things]; their actual, exterior being, however, must of necessity be drawn from the power of matter, as shown in the whole of nature).

As the "inferior part of Jesus' substance," Joanna manifests in material existence the correlative higher part (to which we shall return), which is to her as form is to matter. We have seen that, for Postel, in her resides the principle of the *personal* differentiation and, as such, she had been (that is, before actually coming into historical existence as Joanna) "cachée (à cause de la divine Personne) comme son inférieure, latérale ou seconde partie sous le voile de la Nature et générale substance humaine qu'Il pour tout le monde a pris" (hidden [on account of the divine Person] as his inferior, lateral[28] or second part behind the veil of Nature and of the general human substance which He has assumed for the whole world).[29] In other words, we are being told that the "Venetian Virgin" existed in fact from all eternity in Jesus, as his indissoluble "lower part," the historical manifestation of which (rendered impossible during the Incarnation by the presence of the divine Person) conditioned the extension of salvation to the entire human *person* and entailed a second, physically feminine advent of the Christian Messiah.

---

and Secret, *Vie et caractère*, 77), before recanting this opinion (Secret [ed.], *Apologies et Rétractions*, 13; Secret, *Bibliographie des manuscrits*, III n. 1).

[26] She is referred to as "Jehohannaiesuo" (*sic*) in Ms. B. L. Sloane 1410, f. 265r° (Postel's Latin translation of the *Bereshit* section of the *Zohar*, carried out in Venice), and also as "Jesusiohanna" (*ibid.*, f. 498), cf. François Secret, *Postel revisité: Nouvelles recherches sur Guillaume Postel et son milieu* (Première série; Paris and Milan: Séha-Archè, 1998), 191.

[27] *La nouvelle Eve*, 32.   [28] Here, the allusion is to Adam's rib (Gen. 2:21–22).

[29] *La nouvelle Eve*, 29.

In this manner, we may understand more easily how, for Postel, and beyond any play on words, the "material" aspect of the New Eve links up with the "maternal," since her "universal motherhood" is in fact inseparable from her eternal existence in Jesus, and the final, corporeal redemption of humankind (one aspect, of course, of her "maternity") is brought about by her individual presence "in the flesh."

But there is yet a final side of her motherhood to be taken into account. As already noted, it is also as Christ's "lower half" that Joanna claimed to be Jesus' bride and, just as the first Adam and Eve begat Cain, so the second must also engender a son and, considering that sin came into this world through the agency of the biblical Adam, Eve, and Cain, "il fault qu'en leurs lieux soient Christ Adam nouveau, Jehochannah Eve nouvelle et Jehochanan René Caïn nouveau restitués"[30] (in their stead must Christ the New Adam, Jehochannah the New Eve and Jehochanan the new Rene [= reborn] Cain, be restituted). It is hardly necessary to state that "Jehochanan René Caïn" is of course none other than Postel himself, so that in the end he does become the "substantial son of the New Eve and of her spouse Jesus"!

One may ask, with reason, why Postel did not content himself with pledging to have witnessed Jesus' Second Advent in the person of the New Eve, and chose to give the story a sequel by setting himself up as Cain *restitutus*. Yet, that would be reckoning without three essential factors: his obvious desire to assume for himself the role of a major eschatological figure; the fact that the "Mother" died without revealing herself or her messianic function to the world, a disclosure she had entrusted him with; and, lastly, that she had promised him that he would in due time receive "sa substance et celle de Jésus mon père" (her substance and that of Jesus my father), and that he was in fact tangibly expecting the fulfillment of her promise.

The second and third aspects are too obviously connected to require any extended explanation: receiving the "substance" of his mystical parents would of course fully enable Postel to proceed to the final, public proclamation of his and Joanna's joint mission.

It remains now to examine what exactly Postel meant by this mysterious "substance" and how, accordingly, he imagined that it could be communicated to him; in other words, *how* he was to become the son of the second Adam and Eve?[31]

---

[30] *Ibid.*
[31] Indeed, Postel had first deemed himself Adam *restitutus*, consort – rather than son – of the second Eve, Secret, *Postel revisité*, 193–198; Postel, *Des admirables secrets*, 143 and n. 321.

THE SECRETS OF THE SOUL(S)

To explain what Postel intended by "substance," and the means of its transmission, one must take into account his curious mystical anthropology and theology, greatly influenced by certain kabbalistic tenets.

Already in his book *De nativitate mediatoris ultima*,[32] Postel was developing a doctrine of the four successive advents of Christ. Drawing on a theory of the three modes of divine presence classically defined before him by Saint Bernard of Clairvaux (1090–1153),[33] Postel added a fourth one, that of the *sapientia creata*, which serves as an intermediary between the Word – considered *in divinis* – and creation as such. At the same time, this "created wisdom" is construed by him as inseparable ontologically from its uncreated counterpart – "as one side of a coin to the other," Postel tells us – so that it is essentially through it that God acts and communicates with individual beings: "ledict Esprit Saint faict communicable par la (*sic*) Esprit créé et mobile à luy unie"[34] (the said Holy Spirit made communicable through the created and mobile Spirit united to it).

Soon enough, during his Venetian stay, he began to identify Joanna with the manifestation of this "sapience seconde," equated in turn with the "lower, interior part" concealed within Jesus from all eternity.

Postel is faithful to a classic doctrine of a fourfold soul (or of a quaternarian distribution of the different powers of the soul), ultimately derived from Lucretius and of which he could also find examples in his beloved Augustine. This doctrine mentions a superior intellect or *mens*, accompanied (in descending order) by a *spiritus*, an *animus* (or rational soul) and an *anima* (living soul). Postel is thus convinced that, before as well as after his Incarnation, Christ is in fact present to the world, and active in it as well, through his *mens* united to his *spiritus*. If we follow our author, it is through their joint agency that Enoch and Elijah were carried off to the heavens, or that spiritual influences are permanently attached to relics or

---

[32] Basel: Johann Oporinus, 1547; Carlos Gilly, "Guillaume Postel et Bâle," in *Guillaume Postel (1581–1981)*, 41–77; Carlos Gilly, *Die Manuskripte in der Bibliothek des Johannes Oporinus... Hommage à F. Secret* (Basel: Schwabe, 2001).

[33] I.e. the eternal mode, that is *in divinis*, the sacramental – by and through the sacraments, principally the Eucharist – and the historical one, in other words the Incarnation; Brach, "Dieu fait femme," 50 n. 27.

[34] *La nouvelle Eve*, 24. Although grammatically impossible in French, the feminine "la" translates the fact that such an "Esprit créé" is for him the feminine counterpart of the (masculine) divine Spirit; Jean-Pierre Brach, "'Deux en une seule chair': Guillaume Postel et le Messie feminin," in *Féminité et spiritualité* (Cahiers du G.E.S.C., n° 3°, Paris and Milan: Archè, 1994), 39 n. 18. About the relation of "created wisdom" to the divine one, see Postel, *Des admirables secrets*, 126–127 and n. 263.

tombs of saints.[35] Even more importantly, they have supposedly adumbrated the "Venetian Virgin" while she was in this life. Considering these elements, the deduction is therefore relatively unsurprising that Joanna, as the "inferior part of Jesus Christ," represents in fact his *animus* conjoined to his *anima*, in other words the lower, feminine half of his substance, ultimately (re)manifested in a woman's body.

This is of course why a feminine Messiah, according to Postel, was needed to accomplish the redemption of the lower soul and body of humankind in such a manner that "Adam nouveau avec Eve nouvelle ensemble par la substance de la Mente (*mens*) et de la Esprit (*spiritus*) unis à la divinité de Jésus communiqué pour faire la substance d'Eve nouvelle, tout le monde soit en âme (*animus/a*) et en corps restitué" (so that the New Adam and the New Eve [being] together, by the substance of the *Mens* and Spirit united to the divinity of Jesus, [and] communicated to make the substance of the New Eve, the whole world should be restituted in soul and body).

The most important point here is that Postel fully confirms (and attempts to justify) his controversial certainty that the "Venetian Virgin" was really a full-fledged Messiah, in the sense that she shared her "substance" with Jesus Christ and, through being united to his upper soul(s), also partook of the divine nature. In other words, he really construed her as Jesus Christ come again as a woman, and even felt perfectly convinced that in her "se manifestait la plénitude corporelle de la Divinité"[36] (the corporeal plenitude of divine nature was manifested).

We shall see what became of this aspect of things in the later course of events, when Postel himself imagined he underwent in his own turn some such transfer of "substance." For the time being, we may simply note that, following the same train of thought, he did not refrain from generously endowing Joanna with many traditional attributes of the Messiah, even calling her *Mens Messiae*, an entity he assimilates to the "created wisdom" mentioned above, and considered *sub specie aeternitatis*. Whereas, as we have seen, the "Mother" only represents, strictly speaking, the "inferior part" of Jesus-Christ, she is as such indissolubly united to the "higher part," which explains that, according to perspective, she may also be identified with the eternal reality of the Messiah, considered either *in divinis* or before the actual creation of the physical world.

---

[35] *La nouvelle Eve*, 27.

[36] Letter to Andreas Masius (19 May 1549) quoted in Weill and Secret, *Vie et caractère*, 78. The sentence replicates Col. 2.9.

A fundamental tenet of Postel's thought,[37] the *Mens Messiae* is for him the same thing as the Law, or the divine plan about creation as contained in the *mens divina*, which is of course one of the reasons for its identification with the Wisdom of God.[38] As shown by one of the quotations above, and even though Postel puts less insistence on it, Jesus also possesses, to all intents and purposes, a *spiritus* closely united to his *mens*, and an *animus* coupled to an *anima* as well.

In certain texts belonging to the Venetian period, like his *Des admirables secrets* [1549], the *anima Christi* is identical to the *anima Messiae*, a theme which is quite important to Postel, in the sense that it is for him the root and the driving force behind the *Gilgul*, or *revolutio animarum*, another key feature of Postel's thought, based on Hebrew tenets of metempsychosis.[39]

As to the modalities of this "circulation" of the souls, they were sometimes declared by him knowable to God alone,[40] and sometimes interpreted as a process mandatory in order to reunite the matching upper and lower souls of each human being, dissociated at the time of the Flood by the activity of Satan. One must remark, by the way, that here is just another aspect of the "material" consequences of sin, which proves again (if need be!) that, for Postel, all things – "spiritual" and otherwise – are interconnected in this world, and strictly dependent on one another. In this light, it comes as no surprise to learn that the era of "Restitution" is precisely meant to coincide with this general reunion of predestined human souls, an accomplishment which, until then, only Jesus Christ and the "Venetian Virgin" have been privileged with.[41] In much later works, where "Madre Zuana" herself is not however forgotten, the theme of the *anima Christi* is still present, and its source, as well as that of the fourfold human soul(s),[42] referred to the *dator formarum*, or Active Intellect, which earlier treatises, such as the *Des admirables secrets*, identified in turn with the *Mens Messiae*.[43] Again, the reunion of the Active with the Passive Intellect, like that of the upper and lower soul(s), and whether we consider it in Jesus Christ, Joanna, or any

---

[37] Secret, "L'herméneutique de Guillaume Postel," 107.   [38] Cf. Wis. 7.22–28; Bar. 4.1.

[39] Postel, *Des admirables secrets*, 196–209 (in particular p. 203 and n. 511). Jean-Pierre Brach, "Das Theorem der 'messianischen Seele' in der christlichen Kabbala bis zur *Kabbala Denudata*," in Andreas B. Kilcher (ed.) *Die* Kabbala Denudata: *Text und Kontext. Morgen-Glantz. Zeitschrift der Christian Knorr von Rosenroth-Gesellschaft* 16, Sulzbach–Rosenberg, 2006, 243–258; I must confess to have inadvertently neglected Francesco Zorzi's passing mention of the theme in question (in his *Problemata* of 1536), yet already pointed out by Secret, "L'herméneutique," 106.

[40] Postel, *Le thresor des prophéties*, 36–37 (introduction).

[41] Postel, *Des admirables secrets*, 203–204 and nn. 516–517.

[42] Ms. BnF lat. 3401 [*Apologie à G. Lindan*, 1578], ff. 5v°–7r; Secret, "L'herméneutique," 108, n. 81; Secret, *Bibliographie des manuscrits*, 85–87.

[43] *Des admirables secrets*, 268–271 and n. 850.

ordinary human being, elicits for Postel strong eschatological innuendos: when every higher soul is again matched with its predestined lower part, the *Gilgul* will cease and, with it, all other cosmological cycles, including the celestial ones; in other words, the world as we know it will then meet its end.[44]

The quaternarian human soul is thus divided into two halves, of which the upper one (*mens* + *spiritus*) is considered masculine, and the lower one (*animus* + *anima*) feminine:

Le Mente, la Esprit unis tout en un comme la lumière en l'air, sont pour la partie supérieure et qui vient en nous du dehors et du ciel. Ceste nature est tellement prédestinée que jamais ne cessera qu'elle n'aye amené à salut ung anime et une âme ensemble, qui sont la seconde et inférieure nature de laquelle ay parlé (The *mens* and spirit united in one, as light to air, make up the superior part which comes into us from outside and from heaven. This nature is so strongly predestinated that it will not cease until it has brought to salvation an *animus* and a soul together, which constitute the second and inferior nature I have been speaking of).[45]

Within this structure, Postel introduces a double hierarchical split, so to speak, in the sense that within both parts the first term is held as male and the second as female, whereas the relations between the two parts operate as follows: the *mens* corresponds to the *animus* and directly influences it, while the *spiritus* plays the same role as regards the *anima*. Such notions are not without their relevance, for it is against such a "psychosophical" background – and the *regime* of *Gilgul* and predestination – that Postel's becoming the son of Joanna "and of her spouse Jesus" is interpreted and understood by the French illuminate himself.

SOUL MATES

Back in Venice from the Middle East around Easter 1551, and confronted with the news of the "Venetian Virgin"'s death, as we have seen, Postel came back to France, where he spent the following months, pondering what to do next and, in all likelihood, somewhat anxiously waiting for a confirmation of his mission, and for an intimation of the fulfillment of Joanna's spiritual promises. In October 1551, he accompanied Gabriel Bouvery, bishop of Angers, to Paris and remained there with him until the days of the Epiphany 1552.[46]

---

[44] Jean-Pierre Brach, "L'Orient messianique chez Guillaume Postel," in Mohammed Ali Amir Moezzi and John Scheid (eds.), *L'Orient dans l'histoire religieuse de l'Europe: L'invention des origines* (Turnhout: Brepols, 2000), 127; Maillard, *Postel le cosmopolite*, 208.

[45] *La nouvelle Eve*, 22.   [46] Weill and Secret, *Vie et caractère*, 89–90.

Struck by illness on the eve of the feast of the Epiphany, Postel thought he felt the approach of death. One or two nights later, convinced that he was actually dying, and having accordingly drafted his will and received the Eucharist, Postel felt like he had "passed away" (!) and his soul was undergoing judgment, in "great tremor and agony." Granted a merciful delay for penance, his *animus*, he fancied, was separated on the following night from his *anima* and body, so that Postel felt carried up into the celestial realm where he had a vision of Jesus Christ and, next to him, of his bride "Mother Joanna," in her *spiritus*, which he calls her "corps spirituel (ou éthéré)" (spiritual [or ethereal] body).

Furthermore, having circulated "par toutes les parties du ciel" (through all sections of the heavens), his *animus*, he imagined, was integrally sub-stituted by Joanna's *spiritus* and, thereby, changed and "immuted" into her own "substance"; after which, on that same third night, he says, his transformed *animus* was reintroduced in him and conjoined again to his *anima* and body, an operation accompanied by great physical pain: "l'Esprit investit l'anime et l'âme, mais aussi le corps, pour obvier aux effets du péché originel et de l'action de Satan"[47] (the spirit invests the *animus* and the soul, and the body as well, in order to obviate the consequences of the original sin and of Satan's activity), a sentence which fully confirms the pervasiveness of sin – and of its material dimension – underlined above, in Postel's and Joanna's spiritual outlook.

Having therefore properly incorporated, as he thought, Joanna's "ethe-real body," Postel could hardly fail to persuade himself he had become her "substantial" son and that of Jesus Christ since, moreover, Postel saw his "Mother"'s *spiritus* as indissolubly linked to the "substance" of Jesus Christ: "je fus immué et faict fils substantiel de Jésus mon Père, excepté sa divinité . . . je receus la substance totale de mon Père Jésus, sauf la divinité, laquelle substance ma Mère m'avait promise à Venise quand j'écrivis le *De nativitate Mediatoris ultima*"[48] (I underwent "immutation" and was made the substantial son of Jesus my Father, but for his divinity . . . I received the total substance of my Father Jesus, with the exception of his divinity, substance which I had been promised in Venice by my Mother, when I was writing the *De nativitate*).

According to Postel, the three main consequences of his famous 1552 "immutation" were, thus, his "death and judgment," his "change of sub-stance," and, finally, his inauguration of the mystical era of the Restitution as "Caïn René." One must note, however, that even then, he neither

---

[47] *La nouvelle Eve*, 25.   [48] *La nouvelle Eve*, 43.

claimed for himself – as he did for Joanna – to be "consubstantial" to the divine part of Jesus' nature as well, nor to be invested with a specifically messianic function.

Furthermore, Postel was henceforth convinced of his own corporeal immortality, which had been promised to him by his "Mother" during his "immutation," and felt moved by an irrepressible desire to exhibit proof of it to all and sundry, the more so as he believed it to bear undeniable testimony to his spiritual *adumbratio* and mission. Eventually, he did proceed to announce these to the world and, first of all, to the Parisian political and theological authorities, whose reaction was stern.[49]

The hour of a more widespread public revelation of his "immutation," through the agency of printing this time, did not come, though, until the following years: 1553 and 1555 saw a string of booklets in French and Italian, mentioning the "Venetian Virgin" for the first time and alluding to her mystical role and Postel's related "restitution." Needless to say, they almost immediately aroused a full-fledged religious and political scandal, which again sent Postel on the roads of Europe.[50]

"JE" EST UN AUTRE?

Considering what precedes, it is obviously tempting to dismiss Postel's mystical experiences as mere illusion, and/or wish-fulfillment, the more so since we have seen that, in the period prior to Epiphany of 1552, he was particularly eager for a confirmation of his mission and of the means to prove it to the world.

Even though direct access to the actual contents of such an experience eludes us, and we must obviously content ourselves with its written traces, no one could fail to recognize in his "immutation" the theme, both classic and central in many religions, of *theosis*, that is, deification. That Postel should have construed it as an assimilation of – or identification with – the "substance" of Jesus, can come as no surprise in this context. As we have seen, the "spiritual body" of his "Mother" is for him contained, so to speak, in the "substance" of her mystical spouse, which enables him to see her continuing to play, even within his own experience of transmutation, her role of universal mediation, that of the "Maternité générale du monde." Moreover, the theme of deification and that of Christ's mystical inhabitation within us mean the same thing to Postel.

---

[49] Weill and Secret, *Vie et caractère*, 89–99.
[50] Jean Dupèbe, "Poursuites contre Postel en 1553," in *Guillaume Postel (1581–1981)*, 29–39.

Again, confronted with the story of his "immutation," no one will miss
the unmistakable eucharistic flavor of such an assimilation, or substitution
of substances, as Postel claims to have experienced.[51] Early on, his extensive
reading of Scripture, and particularly of Paul, had led him to interpret
all form of spiritual transformation from the perspective of a material
alteration of substance in individual persons and, correlatively, of a concrete
participation in the divine nature. Of this, the Eucharist is of course the
central Christian paradigm, central also, for various reasons, in Postel's
thought and writings, where this particular sacrament is held to be the
privileged means of actually nourishing and regenerating the "ethereal
substance" of the body of immortality destroyed by Satan.

Convinced, as he was, to have been dead and revived during his "immutation" and thus to have been made participant in Christ's agony, death and
resurrection (a participation which was the key to his assuming Joanna's
spiritus), it is equally clear that Postel was in fact reproducing, albeit in
rather peculiar fashion, the general and well-known theme of Imitatio
Christi. This was an ideal that he turned into a lifelong pursuit.

There is of course little doubt that a certain amount of wishful thinking,
induced by a perhaps unconscious desire to play, as mystical reformer, a
part which his menial birth denied him on the social or political plane
(a tendency already denounced early on by the Jesuits), was involved in
the layout of his "immutation." Yet, judging by his entire life and its later
developments, it seems rather unlikely to imagine that Postel simply staged
his 1552 experience in cold blood, in order to impress his entourage.

But whatever may (or may not) have befallen him on that night, it
is nevertheless certain that Postel was partly reading his own whim into
reality, that is reinterpreting possible facts according to a set doctrinal
framework, in narrow relationship with his own spiritual claims. That even
concerning these he was sometimes not immune to fits of disquiet and self-
doubt may also have played a part in triggering his "immutation," as has –
undoubtedly – his lasting confidence in Joanna's promises. Postel being our
only source about her, it is of course quite impossible to fathom her own
outlook, or reconstruct her exact part in their mutual exchanges with any
degree of precision; but they most probably developed a forceful spiritual
emulation, by reciprocally confirming each other's mystical aspirations.

As for certain spiritual attitudes which the relationship of Postel and
Joanna exhibit,[52] they are all salient features of early modern, particularly

---

[51] Petry, Gender, Kabbalah and the Reformation, 127–130.
[52] Such as the (otherwise relatively frequent) claim to being "Jesus' bride", the focus on the Eucharist
and its frequent reception, the link with charitable institutions, and the – partial, at least – reversal
of spiritual authority between confessor and dirigée.

Italian, urban spirituality.[53] For this reason, what is most remarkable here is in fact the seemingly perfect and spontaneous agreement on the literal and utterly *physical* understanding of some of these attitudes reached by two individuals who were as unlike, in principle, as the illiterate Venetian mystic and the erudite French Christian kabbalist.

BIBLIOGRAPHY

SOURCES

Postel, Guillaume, *De nativitate Mediatoris ultima* (Basel, 1547).
  Le prime nove dell'altro mondo, cioe . . . La Vergine Venetiana (Padua, 1555).
  Le thresor des prophéties de l'univers (ed. François Secret; The Hague: M. Nijhoff, 1969).
  Apologies et rétractions (ed. François Secret; Nieuwkoop: B. de Graaf, 1972).
  Des admirables secrets des nombres platoniciens (ed. and trans. Jean-Pierre Brach; Paris, Vrin, 2001).

LITERATURE

Bouwsma, William J., *Concordia Mundi: The Career and Thought of Guillaume Postel (1510–1581)* (Cambridge, Mass.: Harvard University Press, 1957).
Brach, Jean-Pierre, "'Deux en une seule chair': Guillaume Postel et le Messie féminin," in *Féminité et spiritualité* (Cahiers du G.E.S.C., 3; Paris and Milan: Archè, 1994), 35–42.
  "Dieu fait femme: Guillaume Postel et l'illumination vénitienne," in M. Cazenave (ed.), *La face féminine de Dieu* (Paris: Noêsis, 1998), 41–61.
  "L'Orient messianique chez Guillaume Postel," in Mohammed Ali Amir Moezzi and John Scheid (eds.), *L'Orient dans l'histoire religieuse de l'Europe: L'invention des origines* (Turnhout: Brepols, 2000), 121–130.
  "Das Theorem der 'messianischen Seele' in der christlichen Kabbala bis zur *Kabbala Denudata*," in Andreas B. Kilcher (ed.), *Die* Kabbala Denudata*: Text und Kontext. Morgen-Glantz: Zeitschrift der Christian Knorr von Rosenroth-Gesellschaft 16* (Sulzbach–Rosenberg, 2006), 243–258.
Brach, Jean-Pierre and PierLuigi Zoccatelli, "Courants renaissants de réforme spirituelle et leurs incidences," *Politica Hermetica* 11 (1997), 31–43.
Bynum, Caroline W., *Jesus as Mother: Studies in the Spirituality of the High Middle Ages* (Berkeley: University of California Press, 1983).
Dubois, Claude-Gérard, "Rationalisme et ésotérisme dans l'œuvre de Guillaume Postel (1510–81)," in James Dauphiné (ed.), *Créations littéraires et traditions ésotériques (XV°–XX° siècles)* (Biarritz: Infocompo, 1991), 57–68.
Dupèbe, Jean, "Poursuites contre Postel en 1553," in *Guillaume Postel (1581–1981): Proceedings of the Avranches International Conference, 5–9 Sept. 1981* (Paris: G. Tredaniel, 1986), 29–39.

---

[53] Solfaroli Camillocci, *I devoti della carità*, 37–48.

Ellero, Giuseppe, "G. Postel e l'ospedale dei Derelitti (1547–49)," in Marion-L. Kuntz (ed.), *Postello, Venezia e il suo mondo* (Florence: L. S. Olschki, 1988), 137–161.

"Postel e Venezia," in *Guillaume Postel (1581–1981)*, 23–28.

Gilly, Carlos, "Guillaume Postel et Bâle," in *Guillaume Postel (1581–1981)*, 41–77.

Die Manuskripte in der Bibliothek des Johannes Oporinus . . . Hommage à F. Secret (Basel: Schwabe, 2002).

Kuntz, Marion-L., *G. Postel, Prophet of the Restitution of All Things* (The Hague: M. Nijhoff, 1981).

Venice, Myth and Utopian Thought in the Sixteenth Century: Bodin, Postel and the Venetian Virgin (Aldershot: Ashgate/Variorum, 1999).

Maillard, Jean-François, "Postel le cosmopolite: quelques documents nouveaux," in Sylvain Matton (ed.), *Documents oubliés sur l'alchimie, la kabbale et Guillaume Postel . . . offerts à F. Secret . . .* (Geneva: Droz, 2001), 197–222.

Marquet, Jean-François, *Philosophies du secret: Etudes sur la gnose et la mystique chrétiennes (XVIᵉ–XIXᵉ siècles)* (Paris: Cerf, 2007).

Niccoli, Ottavia, *La vita religiosa nell'Italia moderna. Secoli XV–XVIII* (Rome: Carocci, 1998).

Petry, Yvonne, *Gender, Kabbalah and the Reformation: The Mystical Theology of Guillaume Postel* (Leiden: Brill, 2004).

Secret, François, "L'herméneutique de Guillaume Postel," in Enrico Castelli (ed.), *Umanesimo e ermeneutica* (Padua: Cedam, 1963), 91–117.

Bibliographie des manuscrits de Guillaume Postel (Geneva: Droz, 1970).

"Guillaume Postel en la place de Realte," *Revue de l'Histoire des religions* 192 (1977), 57–92.

Postel revisité: Nouvelles recherches sur Guillaume Postel et son milieu (Première série; Paris and Milan: Séha-Archè, 1998).

Solfaroli Camillocci, Daniela, *I devoti della carità: Le confraternite del divino amore nell'Italia del primo cinquecento* (Naples: Città del Sole, 2002).

Weill, Georges and François Secret, *Vie et caractère de Guillaume Postel* (Milan and Paris: Archè-Les Belles-Lettres, 1987).

Wilkinson, Robert J., *Orientalism, Aramaic and Kabbalah in the Catholic Reformation* (Leiden: Brill, 2007).

The Kabbalistic Scholars of the Antwerp Polyglot Bible (Leiden: Brill, 2007).

CHAPTER 8

The seminal essence of divinity:
Swedenborg's understanding of Jesus Christ

Wouter J. Hanegraaff

A PIETIST CONVERSION . . .

In the spring of 1744, a Swedish scientist and mining expert made a business trip to the Netherlands to consult libraries and supervise the printing of a large monograph on human anatomy.[1] The name of this fifty-six year old gentleman was Emanuel Swedenborg, a member of the nobility with excellent connections to the royal court, who earned his living as an assessor at the Swedish Board of Mines and was known as the learned author of many voluminous studies on subjects ranging from mineralogy to brain physiology, and much else beside.

For his trip to the Netherlands he had decided to keep a travel diary. From these notes – the hasty and often almost illegible jottings of "a man in his nightshirt"[2] – we learn that in the night before March 25, when Lutherans celebrate the Annunciation of the Lord, Swedenborg had a series of no less than six dreams. In one of them he was standing by a machine and got himself entangled in the spokes of a turning wheel. He commented that this must refer both to the anatomy of the "lungs in the womb" on which he was currently writing and to "difficulties" from which he could not escape.[3] In another dream he saw a fine bed in an herb garden, and desired to own it; but the garden turned out to be infested by bugs or "invisible creeping things," and Swedenborg finally caught one of them and threw it on a white linen cloth, next to a woman.[4] He commented that this referred to the "impurity" that had to be rooted out of him. In

[1] Emanuel Swedenborg, *Regnum animale anatomice, physice et philosophice perlustratum*, vols. I–II (The Hague: Adr. Blijvenburg, 1744).

[2] Anna Fredrika Ehrenborg, *Reflexioner i oktober 1859 öfver de nyligen uppdagade Swedenborgs drömmar 1744 hvilka derjemte oförändrade bifogas* (Stockholm: Riis, 1860); here quoted according to Lars Bergquist, *Swedenborg's Dream Diary* (West Chester: Swedenborg Foundation Publishers, 2001), 8.

[3] Entry # 18, in Bergquist, *Swedenborg's Dream Diary*, 94.

[4] Entry # 19, in *ibid.*, 95–96. The woman most probably stands for carnal temptation: there are many references in the Dream Diary to Swedenborg's sexual desires.

yet another dream he descended a huge stairway which transformed into a ladder, under which was a dark hole in which he threatened to fall. He reached out his hand to others, to help them cross over. He commented that this represented "the danger in which I am: of falling into the abyss unless I receive help."[5]

These dreams proved to be the beginning of a long series, turning Swedenborg's notes into what is now considered history's first example of a dream diary. With hindsight it seems significant that the dream cycle began on the day of the Annunciation, for the series would culminate around Easter in an ecstatic vision of Christ himself.[6] The first dreams are also highly significant in other respects. To begin with the image of the machine: intellectually Swedenborg was an adherent of the post-Cartesian school, a typical man of the Enlightenment whose earlier attempts to explain even the soul in strictly mechanical terms have caused him to be compared to such radical materialists as La Mettrie, the author of *L'homme machine* (1748).[7] But increasingly, he found himself torn between the Lutheran piety that had dominated his youth[8] and the ultimately atheist implications of his scientific work: his great anatomical studies were explicit in their hopeful reference to the human body as the "kingdom of the soul";[9] but by the time of his trip to the Netherlands, Swedenborg had still not succeeded in his project of discovering traces of the soul or any other divine activity within the "machine" of the human organism.

In other words: far from leading him upward to the divine reality of the soul, the detailed explorations of his *Regnum animale* had been leading him downward into the realm of pure matter, at the bottom of which he now threatened to fall into the abyss of atheism and nihilist despair. In this situation, the voice of Swedenborg's Lutheran upbringing returned with a vengeance, telling him essentially that the pietist faith of his youth had been right all along, but that he had been too blind or too busy to see it.[10] His

---

[5] Entry # 20, in *ibid.*, 96–97.

[6] Of course the Annunciation is supposed to culminate in the birth of Christ; but in Swedenborg's personal narrative, the salvational "birth of Christ" in his own heart and soul was more reminiscent of a resurrection from the "grave" of atheism and materialism.

[7] Inge Jonsson, *Visionary Scientist: The Effects of Science and Philosophy on Swedenborg's Cosmology* (West Chester: Swedenborg Foundation Publishers, 1999), 42–43.

[8] Swedenborg's father, Jesper Swedberg, had been a minister and bishop with strong pietistic leanings. An impressive personality by all accounts, he was also an extremely prolific religious author.

[9] Swedenborg, *Oeconomia regni animalis in transactiones divisa*, 3 vols. (London and Amsterdam: Francois Changuion, 1740–1741); Swedenborg, *Regnum animale*.

[10] Swedenborg's Lutheran upbringing seems more than sufficient to explain what happened to him in 1744; but I do not mean to deny the possible significance, in this regard, of his contacts with the Moravian community, which would require a separate discussion.

scientific attempts at discovering the soul in the realm of matter had been nothing but intellectual hubris, for how could the finite human intellect pretend to penetrate the very mysteries of the divine? And in any case, how could Swedenborg have been so blind as to believe that such spiritual mysteries would be disclosed to a person as filled with impure thoughts and worldly desires as himself?

In short, Swedenborg realized that he did not have the resources to save himself: reason and science, on which he had relied all his life, were drawing him inexorably towards the abyss, and he would certainly fall into it "unless he received help." And so he chose the only option left to him: he turned to Jesus Christ in a blind leap of faith, beseeching him to pardon this sinner and save him from himself. On the night before April 2 (Maundy Thursday) he dreamt of receiving "two splendid loaves of bread," signifying the Lord's supper; and indeed, on a ledger of the old German Lutheran congregation in The Hague we find Swedenborg's name inscribed as one of the communicants on that day.[11]

The next night, before Good Friday, Swedenborg dreamt of two persons visiting him at his home, which was untidy and out of order; one of them came up to him and announced that he would be punished on the next Maundy Thursday, unless he took flight. When Swedenborg responded that he did not know how to get out, the person told him he would show him the way. The conclusion: he had been so bold as to "invite the highest" although he was still in a state of moral impurity; but even though he deserved to be punished for this, he had graciously been offered a way out of his sinful condition. On the night before Holy Saturday, Swedenborg dreamt that he was lost in darkness, but was then shown the direction towards the light and liberation.

I awoke. There came then a thought, spontaneous as it were, about the *prima vita*, and thereafter, about the *altera vita*, and it seemed to me that everything was full of grace. I fell to crying because I had not been loving but rather had offended Him who has led me and shown me the way even unto the kingdom of grace, and that I, unworthy one, have been restored to favour.[12]

With hindsight we know that the experiences around Easter 1744 mark the dividing line between Swedenborg's "first life" as a scientist and his subsequent "second life" as a visionary author. The next night, in anticipation of Easter Sunday (April 5), he dreamt of approaching the table of the Holy Supper, and singing a beloved Easter hymn from his youth: *Jesus is*

---

[11] Bergquist, *Swedenborg's Dream Diary*, 108.
[12] Entry # 36, in Bergquist, *Swedenborg's Dream Diary*, 114.

my Best of Friends.[13] Having thus called upon Jesus and having participated in the Lord's Supper that Sunday, Swedenborg was assailed by "temptations" of "the evil one" the following night. In his dreams, the tempter took the shape of an old acquaintance from Sweden, the court marshal Erland Broman, who had been in charge of entertaining King Fredrik I (1676–1751). Swedenborg, who had been a regular guest at the royal court, remembered the king and his marshal as being quite obsessed by sex, and fond of theatrical spectacles of the most vulgar sort; hence Broman, for Swedenborg, represented sensuality, superficiality, and impiety, and Swedenborg now found himself struggling with Broman's "lapdog," which had taken the shape of a "crawling, dark-gray snake."[14] He finally told it to "shut up," and apparently with success, for during several further dreams the same night, Swedenborg began drifting into a "mystical series" of states of consciousness, where he felt "enveloped by strange and indescribable circumvolutions" and finally reached a state of indescribable bliss which he described as "heaven."[15] According to his account, this ineffable condition of "heavenly ecstasy" continued even while he was awake.

The next day, Swedenborg made a long walk to the town of Delft, during which he was "granted the deepest spiritual thoughts, deeper and more beauteous than ever,"[16] although at other moments he was still "tempted" to let his own thinking interfere with his unconditional submission to the Lord. That night (April 6 to 7), having gone to bed at ten o'clock, he felt that "the tempter" was leaving. A few hours later, somewhere between midnight and two o'clock, there occurred what would prove to be the turning point of his life:

[s]uch a strong shivering seized me, from my head to my feet, as a thunder produced by several clouds colliding, shaking me beyond description and prostrating me. And when I was prostrated in this way, I was clearly awake and saw how I was overthrown. I wondered what this was supposed to mean, and I spoke as if awake but found that the words were put into my mouth. I said, "Oh, thou almighty Jesus Christ, who of thy great mercy designest to come to so great a sinner, make me worthy of this grace!" and I clasped my hands and prayed. Then a hand emerged, which pressed my hands firmly. In a little while, I continued my prayer, saying, "Thou hast promised to receive in grace all sinners; thou canst not otherwise than keep thy words!" In the same moment, I was sitting in his bosom and beheld him face to face, a countenance of a holy mien. All was such that I cannot describe. He was smiling at me, and I was convinced that he looked like this when he was alive.[17]

[13] Entry # 37, in *ibid.*, 115. Bergquist gives the complete hymn in English translation on pp. 116–117.
[14] Entry # 41, in *ibid.*, 119.   [15] Entry # 43–44, in *ibid.*, 120–121.
[16] Entry # 50, in *ibid.*, 124.   [17] Entry # 51–54, in *ibid.*, 126.

Christ then asked him whether he had a "health certificate" (*sundhetspass*): a puzzling detail that is most plausibly explained as a reference to Swedenborg's moral health.[18] To the answer "Lord, thou knowest better than I," the response was "Well then, do!" which Swedenborg understood as meaning "Do love me" or "Do as promised." From that moment on and to the end of his life, Swedenborg would be convinced not only that Christ had personally saved him from spiritual perdition, but that he had also sent him on a mission from God. We saw that the Annunciation of the Lord's coming was accompanied by the vision of an abyss underneath a ladder, and it is therefore fitting that the very night after his encounter with Christ, the abyss had vanished: "All night my dreams were about how I went far down, on ladders and through other rooms, but got back safe and sound, so the depths were of no danger to me."[19] And furthermore, it is significant that even in his very first dream of the ladder and the abyss, he had seen himself reaching out his hands to others so as to help them: having been saved himself, he right away saw it as his task to help the rest of humanity to avoid the abyss.

. . . CORRESPONDING TO A RATIONAL CONVERSION

The new focus of Swedenborg's activity was a logical one, not only in view of his religious conversion as such, but also in terms of his scientific and philosophical speculations before 1744. A few years earlier, around 1741/1742, he had written a short but crucial work called *Clavis hieroglyphica*,[20] in which he developed what would turn out to be the theoretical foundation of his later religious worldview. Quite different from what the occult-sounding title might lead one to expect, the *Clavis* is a dry and highly technical exercise in formal logic, ultimately on a geometrical foundation, in which Swedenborg developed a system of *regulae* governing the relation between

---

[18] It has been suggested that the term was somehow meant to echo the traumatic experience of his first visit to England, as a young man, when he had defied the strict quarantine laws by leaving the ship without a "health certificate" and was almost put to death as a result. To me this explanation, which puts Christ in the role of a customs officer, seems quite unlikely: it simply does not make sense in the given context. Bergquist (*ibid.*, 127) is more convincing in arguing that "in the context of the diary, questions of sickness, torment and health refer to moral states. Thus, the question may be whether he has sufficiently liberated himself from temptation and the bondage of the senses to be able to relate to the Godhead. From Swedenborg's point of view, a certificate of sanity surely meant mastery of temptation and implied a mobilization of his own will to turn toward God completely and submit fully."

[19] Entry # 62, in *ibid.*, 137.

[20] Swedenborg, *Clavis hieroglyphica arcanorum naturalium et spiritualium, per viam repraesentationum et correspondentiarum* (London: Robert Hindmarsh, 1784).

the material world, the world of the human psyche, and metaphysical reality. The conclusion was that these are three autonomous realms that stand in a relation of *correspondence*.

What this means may be illustrated by an example.[21] A symphony consists of sound frequencies that can be registered by scientific equipment and analyzed to the smallest details. However, the meaning, coherence, and emotional significance that the symphony may have for listeners can be neither deduced from, nor reduced to, the patterns of physical frequencies that physicists may pick up. Although the physical and musical levels stand in a relation of strict correspondence, they are nevertheless wholly autonomous. To make the comparison with Swedenborg complete we may, furthermore, take the example of a composer such as Johannes Brahms, who claimed that his music came from a divine source: "straightaway the ideas flow in upon me, directly from God."[22] If one believes this, there is even a third level, consisting of metaphysical realities corresponding to the levels of music and frequencies, but once again autonomous in the sense that one cannot be derived from or reduced to the other.

This theory had far-reaching implications for Swedenborg. For many years he had devoted himself to an ambitious project of trying to discover and explain the activity of the soul in the "kingdom" of the human body, and thereby finding a way to overcome the Cartesian split between *res extensa* and *res cogitans*. If the theory of correspondences was correct, not only did this explain why he had still not succeeded, but it also made any further attempts futile: a scientist had about as much chance to find the soul in the realm of matter as a deaf physicist might succeed in finding musical meaning and significance in a computer print-out of frequency charts. Of course the scientist in Swedenborg resisted such a conclusion, and this helps account for the emotional struggle that culminated in 1744; but the logician in him had to admit that if he wanted to say anything about the soul or divine realities at all, continuing his scientific project was a waste of time.

It would be incorrect, therefore, to interpret Swedenborg's conversion of 1744 as a simple rejection of science and rationality in favor of religious piety; rather, it was the entirely logical outcome of a process of strict intellectual speculation. And what is more, the new focus of Swedenborg's activities followed no less compellingly from these same premises. The

---

[21] The analogy is developed in more detail in Wouter J. Hanegraaff, *Swedenborg, Oetinger, Kant: Three Perspectives on the Secrets of Heaven* (West Chester: Swedenborg Foundation, 2007), 6–9.

[22] Arthur M. Abell, *Talks with Great Composers* (Garmisch-Partenkirchen: G. E. Schroeder, 1964), 21.

"book of nature" that scientists tried to decipher was traditionally sup-posed to correspond to the "book of revelation," the Bible; and therefore it makes perfect sense that, once having decided to abandon natural sci-ence, Swedenborg now devoted himself to the science of Scripture: biblical exegesis. From 1748 to 1756 he worked on his *magnum opus*: a gigantic, eight-volume commentary on Genesis and Exodus interspersed with amaz-ingly detailed accounts of visionary travels to heaven and hell, including long discussions with angels and the spirits of the deceased. The thesis cen-tral to this work as a whole, known as the *Arcana coelestia*, is formulated in its first sentence:

The Word in the Old Testament contains the mysteries of heaven, and every single aspect of it has to do with the Lord, his heaven, the church, faith, and all the tenets of faith; but not a single person sees this in the letter.[23]

In other words, underneath the literal text of the Bible lies a hidden meaning. And just as the soul cannot be found in matter, on the level of biblical exegesis too, it is categorically impossible to discover this spiritual meaning on the basis of the literal text as such: this meaning can *only* be disclosed by immediate divine revelation. Swedenborg now claims to have been chosen as the unique recipient of the latter: since 1744, he writes, God had granted him the privilege of freely moving around in the world of spirits and angels, and the true meaning of Scripture has been revealed to him by Christ himself.

The exegetical parts of *Arcana coelestia* are based upon an extreme form of allegorical interpretation, in which each and every word turns out to correspond with an "inner" or "spiritual" meaning. Sometimes there is a rather obvious analogy, as when it turns out that "cloud" means "the Word according to its literal meaning" or "ears" means "obedience"; but Swedenborg continues by explaining that, for example, "earth" means "the church" (and hence an "earthquake" means an "alteration in the state of the church"), "Egypt" means "factual information," "horse" means "intellect," "road" means "truth," "sea" means "(religious) knowledge," and so on and so forth through each and every verse of Genesis and Exodus.[24] By means of this process of relentless "decoding," Swedenborg manages to tell a coherent story: Genesis is really all about the internal development of Christ and of

---

[23] Swedenborg, *Arcana coelestia, quae in scriptura sacra seu verbo domini sunt detecta: nempe quae in Genesi et Exodo una cum mirabilibus quae visa sunt in mundo spirituum et in caelo angelorum*, 8 vols. (orig. 1749–1756; London: Swedenborg Society, 1949–1973), # 1. Translation according to the New Century Edition, *Secrets of Heaven* (trans. Lisa Hyatt Cooper).

[24] See further examples in Hanegraaff, *Swedenborg, Oetinger, Kant*, 38.

religious consciousness,[25] and Exodus narrates the development of the true church.

So what about Jesus according to the *Arcana coelestia*? His story begins in Genesis 12. The events as described on the literal level Swedenborg considers historically accurate; but the inner meaning is not about Abraham and his descendants at all, but about the inner development of "the Lord" in his years of infancy, childhood, and boyhood. This development, according to Swedenborg, led him from a state of spiritual darkness to one of light, thus providing an ideal model of the development that each human individual should undergo. Readers who expect a coherent "biographical" account, however, will be disappointed: while the descriptions do convey a sense of how Jesus only gradually became aware of his true identity and his mission, Swedenborg hardly presents this in a narrative form but mostly speaks in highly abstract terms about the various aspects of his spiritual maturation.

For example, he points out that the phrase "Go from your land" means that the Lord was to withdraw from bodily and worldly concerns;[26] that "there was famine in the land" refers to the scarcity of knowledge that still affected him when he was young;[27] that "Abraham went down into Egypt to reside as an immigrant" means that the Lord was taught concepts from the Word;[28] that the wars described in Genesis 14 mean the spiritual battles he fought; and so on. These discussions tend to become quite technical and abstract, for example when Swedenborg describes in great detail the precise processes by which Jesus' human quality came to be joined to his divine quality (represented by Lot and Abraham, respectively); by which his rational side came to fruition through "the influence of his inner self on his outer self's desire for information";[29] by which truth was connected with goodness within this rational side;[30] by which "the heavenly part of the spiritual dimension influenced and united with facts on the earthly level";[31] and so on and so forth.[32] Throughout, these discussions bear the imprint of Swedenborg's systematic scientific mind: Jesus' gradual awakening to divine consciousness is described by means of an incredibly dry and precise technical language, as if it concerned a complicated series of chemical procedures observed in a laboratory. Swedenborg seems to have been a likeable person by all accounts, but a sense of humor is certainly not prominent among his virtues...

---

[25] See *ibid.*, 40 for a chart that shows exactly how these two strands are subdivided over the chapters of Genesis.
[26] *Arcana coelestia, Ibid.*, # 1407.   [27] *Ibid.*, # 1459–1460.   [28] *Ibid.*, # 1461.   [29] *Ibid.*, # 1890.
[30] *Ibid.*, # 1898–1902.   [31] *Ibid.*, # 5396b.   [32] *Ibid.*, # 3012–3212.

BORN FROM THE FATHER

By far the most detailed discussions of how Swedenborg saw Jesus Christ can be found in his last great work, *Vera christiana religio*, published a year before his death in 1772. As stated in the subtitle, it is written as "A Comprehensive Theology of the New Heaven and the New Church" which Swedenborg believed was now emerging as the legitimate successor to the existing Christian churches. Not surprisingly, this makes it his most polemical work by far: it contains a systematic attack on the many errors and misperceptions that, in his view, had made the Christian churches into a travesty of the true church. Most pernicious of all were the Protestant doctrine of justification by faith alone, and the concept of the Trinity as three divine persons co-existing from eternity.[33] The first three chapters of *Vera christiana religio* are devoted to what should really be understood by the trinity of "God the Creator," "The Lord the Redeemer," and "The Holy Spirit and Divine Action."

Central to Swedenborg's theology is his radical emphasis on the unity of God the Creator. God's inmost, underlying divine being is beyond human understanding,[34] because it is impossible for the finite human mind to grasp the infinite.[35] But some understanding of this mysterious divine reality can be gained by conceiving of him as follows:

1. The one God is called Jehovah from "being," [*Esse*] that is, from the fact that he alone is and was and will be, and that he is the First and the Last, the Beginning and the End, the Alpha and the Omega.
2. The one God is substance itself and form itself. Angels and people are substances and forms from him. To the extent that they are in him and he is in them, to that extent they are images and likenesses of him.

---

[33] For a useful introduction that discusses the relation of Swedenborg's theology to the Apostles' Creed, the Nicene Creed, the Athanasian Creed, and the Lutheran *Book of Concord*, and his relation to contemporary Protestant theology generally, see R. Guy Erwin, "On True Christianity: An Introduction to Swedenborg's Most Comprehensive and Systematic Theological Writing from the Standpoint of the Religion of his Contemporaries," in Emanuel Swedenborg, *True Christianity, Containing a Comprehensive Theology of the New Church that was Predicted by the Lord in Daniel 7:13–14 and Revelation 21: 1, 2*, vol. I (West Chester: Swedenborg Foundation, 2006), 53–101. In modern studies of the doctrine of the trinity Swedenborg tends to be ignored altogether; it is interesting, however, to see that closer to Swedenborg's own time he was still taken seriously, as shown notably by the example of the famous church historian Ferdinand Christian Baur, *Die christliche Lehre von der Dreieinigkeit und Menschwerdung Gottes in ihrer geschichtlichen Entwicklung*, vol. III (Tübingen: Osiander, 1843), 718–750.

[34] Swedenborg, *Vera christiana religio, continens universam theologiam novae ecclesiae a domino apud Danielem cap. VII:13–14, et in Apocalypsi cap. XXI:1, 2. praedictae* (Amsterdam: n.p., 1771), # 18; and cf. # 6.

[35] *Ibid.*, # 28.

3. The [divine Being] is intrinsic reality [*Esse in se*] and is also an intrinsic capacity to [come into existence] [*Existere in se*].
4. The [divine Being] and intrinsic capacity to [come into existence] cannot produce anything else divine that is intrinsically real and has an intrinsic capacity to [come into existence]. Therefore another God of the same essence is impossible.
5. The plurality of gods in ancient times, and nowadays as well, has no other source than a misunderstanding of [divine Being].[36]

So there we have it: the Trinity as commonly understood in fact implies such a plurality of three gods. Swedenborg considers this incompatible both with sound reason and with biblical faith, and he never ceases to expose it as the error of all errors because it destroys the unity of divine creation at its very core. Due to this false doctrine, "a kind of brain fever [*phrenesis*] spread throughout the whole theology and infected the church that calls itself Christian."[37] It is an "insane" concept that has "deranged human minds" so that they no longer know whether there is one God or three, and it is the ultimate cause of the "materialist philosophy that rules today."[38] It is both a rational and psychological impossibility and the summit of impiety, as reflected in the fact – to which Swedenborg keeps returning in his "eyewitness accounts" of heavenly realities – that angels are utterly incapable of even pronouncing the plural "gods."[39] And the converse is true as well: having entered the spiritual world after death, orthodox theologians expose themselves as the polytheists they really are, as shown by the case of a bishop who angrily walked away from a debate with Swedenborg in heaven:

After this exchange the bishop and his ministers left. While he was walking away, he turned back and wanted to shout, "There is one God," but he could not do it, since his thought stopped his tongue. Instead he opened his mouth and thundered, "There are three gods!" When the people who had been standing nearby saw this bizarre occurrence they burst out laughing and went elsewhere.[40]

So what is Swedenborg's alternative? His concept can be summarized as follows. There is indeed a Trinity of Father, Son, and Holy Spirit; but instead of separate persons, these are "three essential components of one

---

[36] *Ibid.*, # 18. All translations before # 463 are mostly according to the recent "New Century Edition": Swedenborg, *True Christianity*. Occasionally I depart from the NCE translation, and indicate this by putting the relevant words in brackets; in some cases I have also inserted words or short passages from the Latin original, again in brackets. The paragraphs starting with # 463 are in vol. II of the NCE, which was not yet available at the time of writing.
[37] *Ibid.*, # 4.   [38] *Ibid.*, # 4; cf. # 6, 23, 90.   [39] *Ibid.*, # 6, 8, 25.   [40] *Ibid.*, # 16; cf. III.

God."[41] The model according to which this must be understood is the triune nature of the human person, who consists of his *soul*, his *body*, and his *actions*. Now, on the level of the divine, this combination occurred only in the "Lord Jesus Christ." What happened is that God, or the Lord Jehovah, himself came down and took on a human manifestation, in which he lived as the soul lives in the body, and which made it possible for him to be active in the world (his actions being meant by the Holy Spirit). The Trinity is therefore not eternal, and there is no such thing as a Son procreated or born "from eternity." Instead, the Trinity came into existence only when God became flesh, and Jesus Christ was much more than the Son of God sent down to earth by his divine Father who remained in heaven: he *was* "the Lord" himself walking this earth.

To understand this innovative concept of Christ and the Trinity, it is crucial to see that Swedenborg considered it superior to any other interpretation *not* just because the angels had told him so, but because it allowed him to give a rational account grounded in a scientific theory of sexual reproduction. Because post-Cartesian scientists rejected any concept of "vital" forces or occult qualities and sought to understand the world with reference only to inert matter and motion, they were forced to assume a doctrine of the preexistence of germs. Each germ was believed to contain a fully formed miniature embryo that had been created by God at the very beginning of time, and which merely needed to grow and evolve in order to become a fully developed human being.[42] As formulated by Nicolas Malebranche in 1763,[43] the infinite divisibility of matter implied that there could be infinite trees concealed in each seed, and all the bodies of men and animals could have been created together in the beginning. All these germs were being passed on from generation to generation, and existed in the female ovum; in order for a human being to be born, they merely needed to be activated and start growing. The stimulus to do so came, interestingly (and rather problematically, given the mechanical principle), not from the male sperm as such, but from a non-material germinative or seminal spirit contained in it.[44]

---

[41] *Ibid.*, # 163.

[42] John Farley, *Gametes and Spores: Ideas about Sexual Reproduction 1750–1914* (Baltimore and London: The Johns Hopkins University Press, 1982), 16.

[43] Nicolas Malebranche, *De la recherche de la verité: Où l'on traite de la nature de l'esprit de l'homme et de l'usage qu'il en doit faire pour éviter l'erreur dans les sciences* (Paris: Vrin, 1962–1964 [1673]), Bk. I, ch. 6.

[44] Farley, *Gametes and Spores*, 17, with reference to Hieronymus Fabricius, William Harvey, and Jan Swammerdam.

This "ovist" theory of reproduction came to be challenged by a "spermist" or "animalculist" alternative based upon the independent discovery, by Antoni van Leeuwenhoek in 1677 and Nicolas Hartsoeker one year later, of spermatozoa. These tiny "animals" swimming in the male semen were, again, believed to be preexistent from the beginning, and to contain a fully formed miniature adult: the famous homunculus.[45] This male "animalcule" now took over the central role formerly assigned to the female egg, as formulated by van Leeuwenhoek: "It is exclusively the male semen that forms the foetus and . . . all that the woman may contribute only serves to receive the semen and feed it."[46] This view reduced the womb essentially to an incubator: a supportive environment that allowed the animalcule to grow to maturity.

Swedenborg, who had met van Leeuwenhoek during his first research trip to the Netherlands, was a firm supporter of the spermist or animalculist view; and this allowed him to interpret Jesus Christ as being born directly from the father, with Mary only in a support role, as the human "vessel" that made incarnation possible. To him this also implied that she contributed only to Christ's bodily constitution:

As for "the son of Mary" meaning just the human manifestation, this is obvious from human reproduction. The soul comes from the father, the body from the mother. The soul is in the father's semen (*semini enim patris inest anima*); it is clothed with a body in the mother. To put it another way, everything we have that is spiritual comes from our father; everything (material) comes from our mother.

In the Lord's case, the divine nature he had came from Jehovah his Father; the human nature he had came from his mother. These two natures united together are "the Son of God."[47]

Swedenborg finds it very important to emphasize that in calling Christ "the Son of Mary," as usual among Catholics, Christians have fallen prey to a "hallucination":[48] admittedly he was born as Mary's son at the time of the incarnation, but as he carried out his acts of redemption during his life (to this we will return), "he put off his human nature from his mother and put on a human nature from his Father."[49] Swedenborg claims that he met Mary herself during one of his trips to heaven, and she confirmed to him

---

[45] *Ibid.*, 20, with an image from Hartsoeker.

[46] Antoni van Leeuwenhoek, *Alle de brieven van Antoni van Leeuwenhoek* (Amsterdam: Swetz and Zeitlinger, 1941), vol. II, 335, as quoted in Farley, *Gametes and Spores*, 20.

[47] Swedenborg, *Vera christiana religio*, # 92; cf. # 82.

[48] *Ibid.*, # 102: "sed in hoc Orbis Christianus hallucinatur" (the New Century Edition has "This is a blunder, though, on the part of the Christian world").

[49] *Ibid.*, # 102.

that "she adores him as her God and does not want anyone to see him as her son, because everything in him is divine."[50] Again, this view of the son being "born from the father" is defended on the basis of a spermist theory of reproduction:

The soul we get from our father is our true self [*homo in se*]. The body we get from our mother is part of us but is not our true self. It is only something that clothes us, woven out of substances belonging to the [natural] world. Our soul is woven out of substances belonging to the spiritual world.[51]

Admittedly, although this theory allowed him to explain how Christ had been "born from God," critics might well have responded that the result was exactly what Swedenborg was so desperately trying to avoid: two divine persons, the one born from the other, just like a human son is born from a human father. Swedenborg seems to have been aware of this embarrassing implication, but refers to it only in passing, during one of his conversations in heaven:

A mother cannot conceive a soul. That idea completely contradicts the design that governs the birth of every human being. Neither could God the Father have given a soul from himself and then withdrawn, the way every father in the world does. God is his own divine essence, an essence that is single and undivided; and since it is undivided it is God himself. This is why the Lord says that the Father and he are one, and that the Father is in him and he is in the Father, as well as other things like that.[52]

So that is where the spermist theory breaks down: the divine seed, in contrast to the human one, can never be separated from its originator, and therefore the Father and the Son are one in essence.

We have seen that, already in *Arcana coelestia*, Swedenborg described how Jesus only gradually became aware of his true nature. Originally he was "an infant like any infant, a child like any child"; but whereas other human beings develop slowly and get stuck somewhere in their development towards perfect understanding, Jesus completed the entire ideal process within one single lifetime. In this process, Swedenborg distinguishes between two states. The first one is described as *exinanitio* ("being

---

[50] *Ibid.*

[51] *Ibid.*, # 103. Cf. in same paragraph: "In the sperm that conceives each of us, there is a whole graft or offshoot of our father's soul that is wrapped in substances from nature. Our body is formed by means of this in our mother's womb. The formation of our body may lean toward a likeness of our father or a likeness of our mother, but the image of our father remains inside and constantly tries to assert itself. If it cannot manifest itself in the first child, it successfully manifests itself in the younger children."

[52] *Ibid.*, # 110.

emptied out"), meaning that he was being "humbled before the Father,"[53] and had to undergo trials and suffering that were preparing him for his divinization, including the moment he thought his Father had abandoned him. At other moments, however, for example when he was performing miracles and during the Transfiguration, he was in the second state, that of glorification, or union with the Father.[54] As will be seen, the final and complete glorification occurred only at the crucifixion.

During his life – that is to say, *not* during the crucifixion or because of it[55] – the Lord carried out the process of redemption. Redemption is defined by Swedenborg very precisely, as a threefold process: "gaining control of the hells [*subjugatio Infernorum*], restructuring the heavens [*ordinatio Caelorum*], and thus preparing for a new spiritual church [*praeparatio ad novam Ecclesiam spiritualem*]."[56] Or in a bit more detail:

> The acts of redemption through which the Lord made himself justice were these: carrying out the Last Judgment, which he did in the spiritual world; separating the evil from the good and the goats from the sheep; driving out of heaven those who had joined the beasts that served the dragon; assembling a new heaven of the deserving and a new hell of the undeserving; bringing both heaven and hell back into the divine design; and establishing a new church.[57]

This process of redemption had to be carried out in an orderly fashion: the hells had to be controlled before a new angelic heaven could be formed, and that heaven had to be there in order for a new church to be instituted. Typical of his concept of the Bible[58] as an inseparable unity, the whole of which speaks about the Lord, Swedenborg appears to see no problem in the fact that scriptural proof of how the Lord "fought battles against the hells" can hardly be found in the New Testament but occurs almost exclusively in the Old Testament Prophets.[59] The process as a whole is compared to that of driving out an army of rebels from a country, chasing away flocks of wild animals who have invaded a city, or weeding out swarms of locusts or caterpillars that have infected the crops.[60] Once the Lord had brought everything back under his control, he proceeded to restore order to his domain, by restructuring heaven and hell so as to realign them to the divine design; and having accomplished this, he finally created a new church to be its visible correspondence here on earth.

---

[53] *Ibid.*, # 104.   [54] On the two states: *ibid.*, # 104–106.   [55] *Ibid.*, # 95.
[56] *Ibid.*, # 114–115.   [57] *Ibid.*, # 95.
[58] On Swedenborg's understanding of the biblical canon, see Hanegraaff, *Swedenborg, Oetinger, Kant,* 28.
[59] See, e.g., *Vera christiana religio*, # 116.   [60] *Ibid.*, # 117.

All this was done on the spiritual level while the Lord was living in the world as a human being, and Swedenborg emphasizes that the redemption could not have been carried out otherwise. Jehovah God in his infinite essence "could not come near hell, let alone enter it": if he were only to breathe on those who are in hell, "he would instantly kill them all."[61] Furthermore, the gap between God's pure spiritual being and the material world would have prevented him from carrying out the redemption: just like "an invisible person cannot shake hands with a visible one,"[62] and "one cannot do work without arms,"[63] Jehovah had to become visible and take on a human body in order to interact with the human world and even with heavenly reality.

Having carried out his task of redemption, the Lord finally achieved the complete (re)union with his Father. This happened during the crucifixion, which should really be defined as the moment of his ultimate and final "glorification." The "seminal essence of divinity" reestablished its full identity with its source, while taking leave completely of its human component, that is to say, his body. This is why Jesus now addressed Mary as "woman" instead of "mother," and gave her to John to be his mother:[64] he was the "Son of God" no longer.

THE SECOND COMING BY PRESS RELEASE

This, in a nutshell, is how the "Great Work" of redemption was accomplished at the beginning of the Christian era. However, the new church quickly began to degenerate again, first with the crypto-paganism of Roman Catholicism and its false doctrine of the Trinity, and then with the Reformation and its equally pernicious doctrine of justification by faith alone. The results had been disastrous:

At the time of the Lord's First Coming the hells had risen so high that they filled the entire world of spirits that is midway between heaven and hell . . . the whole planet had completely alienated itself from God by practicing [idolatry and magic]; and the church that had existed among the children of Israel and later among the Jews had been utterly destroyed by their falsifying and [adulterating] the Word[65] . . . during his First Coming the hells were swollen with [idolaters, magicians], and falsifiers of the Word. During this Second Coming the hells are

---

[61] *Ibid.*, # 124.   [62] *Ibid.*, # 125.   [63] *Ibid.*, # 84.   [64] *Ibid.*, # 102.

[65] On the antisemitic side of Swedenborg's thought, see Wouter J. Hanegraaff, "Swedenborg, the Jews, and Jewish Traditions," in Peter Schäfer & Irina Wandrey (eds.), *Reuchlin und seine Erben: Forscher, Denker, Ideologen und Spinner* (Pforzheimer Reuchlinschriften, 11; Ostfildern: Jan Thorbecke, 2005), 135–154.

swollen with so-called Christians – some who are steeped in materialist philosophy, and others who have falsified the Word by using it to sanction their made-up faith [*fabulosae fidei*] about three divine persons from eternity and about the Lord's suffering as the true redemption.[66]

Therefore a new redemption was badly needed, and Swedenborg claims that this process is now well underway. In a small work called *De ultimo judicio, et de Babylonia destructa* (published in 1758),[67] he had described how the Last Judgment has actually taken place already, but only in the spiritual world. It took place in 1757, to be exact, and Swedenborg was allowed to watch it first-hand. Since heaven and hell had therefore been brought to order again, the foundations were established for the emergence of a New Church. On June 19, 1770, very briefly before the publication of *Vera christiana religio*, the Lord "called together his twelve disciples, who are now angels, and sent them out to the entire spiritual world," to preach the gospel anew, like they had done in the physical world eighteen centuries before.[68]

The Second Coming is happening as well, but it does not mean a renewed appearance of the Lord as a person. This time, he will appear as "the Word," which is "divine truth." According to the opening of the Gospel of John, the Word (or Logos) is with God and is God himself, and therefore the coming of the Word is equivalent to the Coming of the Lord.[69] Swedenborg's explanation of what that means has been particularly shocking to contemporary theologians:[70] the Second Coming means nothing more or less than the publication of his own *Vera christiana religio*!

This second coming of the Lord is effected by means of a man to whom He has manifested himself in person, and whom he has filled with his spirit, that he may teach the doctrines of the New Church from the Lord by means of the Word . . . he will [come and establish a new church] by means of a man who is able not only to receive these doctrines by his intellect but also to publish them by the press. That the Lord manifested himself before me, his servant, and sent me to this office, that he afterward opened the eyes of my spirit and thus introduced me into the spiritual world and granted me to see the heavens and the hells, and also to talk with angels and spirits, and this now continuously for several years, I affirm in truth; as also that from the first day of that call I have not received anything

---

[66] *Vera christiana religio*, # 121.

[67] Swedenborg, *De ultimo judicio, et de Babylonia destructa: Ita quod omnia, quae in Apocalypsi praedicta sunt, hodie impleta sint. Ex auditis & visis* (London: John Lewis Hyde, 1758).

[68] *Vera christiana religio*, # 4, 108, 791.   [69] *Ibid.*, # 776–777.

[70] See in particular the case of Friedrich Christian Oetinger, as analyzed in Hanegraaff, *Swedenborg, Oetinger, Kant*, 79–83.

whatever pertaining to the doctrines of that church from any angel, but from the Lord alone while I have read the Word.[71]

And with this, the circle is closed: after having manifested himself to Swedenborg at Easter 1744, the Lord Jesus Christ had been directly inspiring all his biblical interpretations ever since, so that now it was finally possible for him to return to the world: in the form of Swedenborg's last book, printed in Amsterdam in 1771.

Swedenborg himself died one year later, convinced that the redemption had been accomplished and the world was entering a new era in which a new church would be born. He did not attempt to establish any such organization himself, but his followers did: nowadays there are various denominations claiming the title of New Church,[72] and June 19 is widely celebrated among believers as the beginning of the new dispensation. However, important though these churches have been in preserving and continuing Swedenborg's legacy, his influence is by no means limited to them. Starting already during his own lifetime, his writings were studied widely and quite eclectically by readers who had little interest in his biblical interpretations or his project of reforming the church, but were fascinated by his visionary accounts of "things heard and seen" in heaven and hell. A wide range of theologians, philosophers, esotericists, artists, writers, poets, and composers have taken inspiration from these materials, and a variety of new religious movements, esoteric or otherwise, adopted aspects of Swedenborg's work in creating their own worldviews.[73]

Outside the New Churches, few readers shared Swedenborg's preoccupation with the Trinitarian doctrine, his strict Biblicism, or his belief in the centrality of churches to human salvation. As a result, the many voluminous works written in dry and scholastic Latin by an Enlightenment scientist and self-made theologian made an impressive career that Swedenborg himself could not have foreseen and would certainly not have appreciated: separated from their original biblical and theological context, they were turned into a basic source for the development of esoteric religiosity during the nineteenth and twentieth century. Most attractive to his

---

[71] *Vera christiana religio*, # 779.
[72] For a short overview with references to further studies, see Jean-François Mayer, "Swedenborgian Traditions," in Wouter J. Hanegraaff *et al.* (eds.), *Dictionary of Gnosis and Western Esotericism* (Leiden and Boston: Brill, 2005), 1105–1110.
[73] For a beautifully illustrated overview, see Robin Larsen (ed.), *Emanuel Swedenborg: A Continuing Vision* (New York: Swedenborg Foundation, 1988). See also Erland J. Brock *et al.* (eds.), *Swedenborg and his Influence* (Bryn Athyn: The Academy of the New Church, 1988) and particularly the excellent recent volume by Jonathan S. Rose, Stuart Shotwell, and Mary Lou Bertucci (eds.), *Scribe of Heaven: Swedenborg's Life, Work, and Impact* (West Chester: Swedenborg Foundation, 2005).

new readership were Swedenborg's theoretical concept of correspondences as such, and his colorful descriptions of heavenly realities. Of Swedenborg's Christology, not much more seems to have been retained than the general concept of Jesus as the "perfect human being": an ideal model for personal self-development leading to divinization, congenial even to the contemporary New Age.

BIBLIOGRAPHY

SOURCES

Swedenborg, Emmanuel, *Arcana coelestia, quae in scriptura sacra seu verbo domini sunt detecta: nempe quae in Genesi et Exodo una cum mirabilibus quae visa sunt in mundo spirituum et in caelo angelorum*, 8 vols. (London: Swedenborg Society, 1949–1973).

Oeconomia regni animalis in transactiones divisa, 3 vols. (London and Amsterdam: Francois Changuion, 1740–1741).

Regnum animale anatomice, physice et philosophice perlustratum, vols. I–II (The Hague: Adr. Blijvenburg, 1744).

De ultimo judicio, et de Babylonia destructa: Ita quod omnia, quae in Apocalypsi praedicta sunt, hodie impleta sint. Ex auditis & visis (London: John Lewis Hyde, 1758).

Vera christiana religio, continens universam theologiam novae ecclesiae a domino apud Danielem cap. VII:13–14, et in Apocalypsi cap. XXI:1, 2. praedictae (Amsterdam: n.p., 1771).

Clavis hieroglyphica arcanorum naturalium et spiritualium, per viam repraesentationum et correspondentiaum (London: Robert Hindmarsh, 1784).

The True Christian Religion Containing the Complete Theology of the New Church as Foretold by the Lord in Daniel 7: 13, 14 and in Revelation 21: 2, 3, 2 vols. (trans. John Chadwick; London: Swedenborg Society, 1988).

True Christian Religion, Containing the Universal Theology of the New Church Foretold by the Lord in Daniel 7:13–14 and Revelation 21:1–2, 2 vols. (trans. John C. Ager; West Chester: Swedenborg Foundation, 1996).

True Christianity, Containing a Comprehensive Theology of the New Church that was Predicted by the Lord in Daniel 7:13–14 and Revelation 21: 1, 2, vol. I (New Century Edition; trans. Jonathan S. Rose; West Chester: Swedenborg Foundation, 2006).

A Disclosure of Secrets of Heaven Contained in Sacred Scripture or the Word of the Lord. Here First Those in Genesis. Together with Amazing Things Seen in the World of Spirits & in the Heaven of Angels, vol. I (New Century Edition; trans. Lisa Hyatt Cooper; West Chester: Swedenborg Foundation, 2008).

LITERATURE

Abell, Arthur M., *Talks with Great Composers* (Garmisch-Partenkirchen: G. E. Schroeder, 1964).

Baur, Ferdinand Christian, *Die christliche Lehre von der Dreieinigkeit und Men-schwerdung Gottes in ihrer geschichtlichen Entwicklung*, vol. III (Tübingen: Osiander, 1843).

Bergquist, Lars, *Swedenborg's Dream Diary* (West Chester: Swedenborg Foundation Publishers, 2001).

Brock, Erland J. *et al.* (eds.), *Swedenborg and his Influence* (Bryn Athyn: The Academy of the New Church, 1988).

Ehrenborg, Anna Fredrika, *Reflexioner i oktober 1859 öfver de nyligen uppdagade Swedenborgs drömmar 1744 hvilka derjemte oförändrade bifogas* (Stockholm: Riis, 1860).

Erwin, R. Guy, "On True Christianity: An Introduction to Swedenborg's Most Comprehensive and Systematic Theological Writing from the Standpoint of the Religion of his Contemporaries," in Emanuel Swedenborg, *True Christianity, Containing a Comprehensive Theology of the New Church that was Predicted by the Lord in Daniel 7:13–14 and Revelation 21:1, 2*, vol. I (West Chester: Swedenborg Foundation, 2006), 53–101.

Farley, John, *Gametes and Spores: Ideas about Sexual Reproduction 1750–1914* (Baltimore and London: The Johns Hopkins University Press, 1982).

Hanegraaff, Wouter J., "Swedenborg, the Jews, and Jewish Traditions," in Peter Schäfer and Irina Wandrey (eds.), *Reuchlin und seine Erben: Forscher, Denker, Ideologen und Spinner* (Pforzheimer Reuchlinschriften, 11; Ostfildern: Jan Thorbecke, 2005), 135–154.

Swedenborg, Oetinger, Kant: Three Perspectives on the Secrets of Heaven (West Chester: Swedenborg Foundation, 2007).

Jonsson, Inge, *Visionary Scientist: The Effects of Science and Philosophy on Swedenborg's Cosmology* (West Chester: Swedenborg Foundation, 1999).

Larsen, Robin (ed.), *Emanuel Swedenborg: A Continuing Vision* (New York: Swedenborg Foundation, 1988).

Leeuwenhoek, Antoni van, *Alle de brieven van Antoni van Leeuwenhoek*, vol. II (Amsterdam: Swetz and Zeitlinger, 1941).

Malebranche, Nicolas, *De la recherche de la verité: Où l'on traite de la nature de l'esprit de l'homme et de l'usage qu'il en doit faire pour éviter l'erreur dans les sciences* (Paris: Vrin, 1962–1964 [1673]).

Mayer, Jean-François, "Swedenborgian Traditions," in Wouter J. Hanegraaff *et al.* (eds.), *Dictionary of Gnosis and Western Esotericism* (Leiden and Boston: Brill, 2005), 1105–1110.

Rose, Jonathan S., Stuart Shotwell, and Mary Lou Bertucci (eds.), *Scribe of Heaven: Swedenborg's Life, Work, and Impact* (West Chester: Swedenborg Foundation, 2005).

CHAPTER 9

Christ in Hinduism: traditional views and recent developments

Bradley Malkovsky

INTRODUCTION

Much has been written by Hindu and Christian authors, especially since the latter half of the twentieth century, about the modern Hindu discovery, appreciation, and appropriation of Christ. The focus of the literature has, for the most part, been on some of the most renowned figures of nineteenth- and twentieth-century India, with the nineteenth-century Hindu Renaissance of Bengal taking a prominent position in the discussion.[1] In what follows I begin by offering some preliminary remarks about Hinduism, focusing on those features of the religion that are especially important for understanding the context out of which Hindu Christologies have emerged. Thereafter I present summaries of the way some of the most well-known Hindus of the past two hundred years have understood the meaning and significance of Christ. These include Ram Mohan Roy, Keshub Chunder Sen, Sri Ramakrishna Paramahamsa, Swami Vivekananda, Mahatma Gandhi, and Sarvepalli Radhakrishnan.[2]

The subsequent section of this chapter will examine more recent developments in the Hindu understanding of Christ, which, although integrating previous interpretations, move beyond them to engage new issues. These newer Hindu Christologies at times reveal greater familiarity with mainstream Christian doctrine and method, although they tend, as before, to sharply distinguish themselves overall from Christian theology, often rejecting it as rigidly dogmatic and spiritually deficient.

[1] Cf. especially Ronald Neufeldt, "Hindu Views of Christ," in Harold Coward (ed.), *Hindu–Christian Dialogue: Perspectives and Encounters* (Maryknoll: Orbis, 1989), 162–175; Jacques Dupuis, *Jesus Christ at the Encounter of World Religions* (Maryknoll: Orbis, 1991), 15–45.

[2] Lack of space prevents me from discussing the approaches to Christ taken by Sri Aurobindo Ghose (1872–1950) and Swami Akhilananda (d. 1962), both of whom held Christ in great esteem, as well as the position of Swami Dayananda Saraswati (1824–1883), who regarded Jesus as immoral and unspiritual.

For the non-Hindu reader what perhaps first stands out is the sheer variety of Hindu interpretations of Christ, an array equal to if not greater than that found in any other religion. This is true even when we restrict ourselves to an examination of Hindu writings in English. It will be seen that Jesus has been variously regarded as a teacher of spiritual wisdom, a social reformer with supreme moral authority, a great guru, a miracle worker, a mystic of non-duality, and an incarnation (*avatara*) of the divine.[3] We shall further see that what Hindus reject in regard to traditional Christian claims about Christ is as revealing about their Christology as what they affirm about him. Such Hindu Christologies, especially contemporary ones, have evoked responses from a number of Christian theologians, who have found Hindu interpretations of Christ challenging to their own understandings.

Despite these many different Hindu Christologies it must be said that most Hindus have probably never heard of Jesus, since two-thirds of the Indian population still resides in rural villages and because Christians comprise less than two and a half per cent of the total Indian population. Hindu Christologies, for the most part, have been formulated by highly educated urban dwellers.

SOME CENTRAL FEATURES OF HINDUISM AS THE PRESUPPOSITION FOR HINDU CHRISTOLOGY

Hinduism is usually designated as the world's third-largest religion[4] and sometimes regarded, even by non-Hindu scholars, as the world's oldest tradition of faith, dating back to 3000 BCE and earlier. It is nowadays commonplace among both Western and Indian scholars to point out that "Hinduism" is not a unified or monolithic religious entity. The word "Hinduism" acts rather as an umbrella term, grouping together adherents of quite varied ways of social and religious life who often enough share very little in terms of doctrine or praxis.

Though "Hinduism" is notoriously difficult to define or essentialize, a number of widely held tenets do stand out across its manifold permutations. The following eight points focus on those elements that are collectively the presupposition for the emergence of specifically Hindu Christologies:[5]

---

[3] Dupuis, *Jesus Christ*, 19, distinguishes "moral, devotional, philosophical, theological, ascetic, and mystical" Hindu approaches to Christ.

[4] After Christianity and Islam. Hindus number somewhere between eight hundred and nine hundred million.

[5] The following points are therefore not meant to be exhaustive. An obvious omission in this list is the caste system.

1. It has often been stated that one of Hinduism's defining characteristics has been its *lack of a centralized teaching authority* or "magisterium" to adjudicate what ought to constitute orthodox Hindu doctrine. This lack of a supreme teaching office makes possible the emergence of a dynamic plurality of competing and mutually completing understandings of the divine, its relation to the world, and its saving activities. But it also allows for doctrinal tensions and contradictions within Hinduism as a whole.

2. There is, then, *no unified Hindu understanding of the divine and no unified ontology*. One finds among Hindus strict monotheisms, many brands of polytheism, and very often the affirmation of a supreme Reality co-existing with lesser deities. We find affirmations of divine personhood, but also teachings advocating a non-relational impersonal absolute. As to the ontological status of the world, it may be understood in various ways, for example as the body of the divine and, therefore, ontologically very real, but it may also be regarded as an illusion. One should therefore not be surprised to discover also a great many Hindu interpretations of Christ, since they emerge out of very different theological, ontological, and historical contexts.

3. One may distinguish between *enlightenment and devotional spiritualities and soteriologies* (teachings of salvation or liberation). Of these two very different Hindu spiritualities, the numerically smaller one is oriented almost purely to meditation and enlightenment,[6] eschewing any notion of a personal and interactive God in favor of an impersonal absolute, while the great majority of Hindus over time do in fact pray to a supreme, grace-giving personal Lord and world-creator, expressed through an enormous variety of theologies extolling usually Vishnu, Shiva, or the Goddess (Shakti, Kali, Durga, *et al.*) as the highest reality.

4. Among the devotionalists there are further doctrinal distinctions to be made, perhaps the most important of which is whether or not the divine, out of a desire to rescue humanity and restore divine order, chooses to periodically descend to earth to *take on an embodied form (avatara)*. This doctrine is especially associated with worshippers of Vishnu, the so-called Vaishnavites or Vishnuites. In traditional Vaishnavite theology there are ten such avatars, both human and animal, with Krishna usually regarded as the most popular. In addition to this classical avatar teaching whereby God descends from above in a limited number of perfect earthly forms, a new teaching has emerged in modern times. In this new understanding

---

[6] For example, adherents of Advaita Vedanta and practitioners of classical yoga.

every human person is potentially an avatar or, perhaps better, is already an avatar but needs to awaken to that fact.

5. Reincarnation and karma are near-universal Hindu beliefs and pre-suppose an anthropology, regardless of variation, in which *the spiritual is valued over the material and bodily.*

6. With few exceptions, the ultimate goal of life for Hindus, whether understood as a blissful awakening to a non-dualistic and non-relational Absolute or as a permanent loving union with a supreme and merciful Person, is conceived of as a *final state devoid of materiality,* once the final earthly body has been shed. Even given widely varying Hindu anthropologies it can be generally stated that in Hindu thought the human person in its finitude and bodiliness is not finally so much transformed as transcended altogether in the state of liberation.

7. There continues an ancient Hindu conviction that *the paths to spiritual liberation and release from suffering are many;* in modern times this recognition has expanded beyond purely Hindu paths to include the ways and practices of other faiths.

8. *The ultimate liberating Truth is changeless and immediately available to all in the depths of one's consciousness;* it is not therefore grounded in or dependent upon historical circumstances or special saving events. No one historical event can be regarded as determinative for the liberation of all people.

All eight of these features have impacted the way Christ has been assessed, appropriated, and sometimes rejected by Hindus during the past two hundred years.

CHRIST IN PRE-MODERN INDIA

What Hindus in ancient India thought about Jesus is impossible to know, simply because there are no references to him in early Common Era Hindu literature. How extensively Hindus of antiquity were even aware of Jesus' existence is unknown. In this regard it is irrelevant as to when the Christian faith actually reached India's shores, whether through the Apostle Thomas in the first century CE, as south Indian Christians have long claimed, or not until the third century in Syrian form. Even Shankara, the famous eighth-century Advaitin, who hailed from an area in what is now present-day Kerala, a region in which Christians had by Shankara's lifetime been present for several centuries, makes no reference whatever to Christianity or to Christ in his voluminous writings. Although he attacks Buddhism and many varieties of Hinduism, he is silent on Christianity. Either he was unaware of the existence of south Indian Christians or he may have felt that Christianity did not present a serious enough theological or missiological challenge to elicit from him a response. In any event there are no documented Hindu responses to Christ or Christianity until after Catholic and Protestant missions begin their work in the sixteenth and eighteenth centuries respectively.

CHRIST IN EARLY MODERN HINDU THOUGHT

The nineteenth century and the first half of the twentieth witness to Hindu interpretations of Christ which emerged for the most part as a reaction against widespread aggressive European Christian mission, which asserted itself against what was perceived by the missionaries to be an inferior Hinduism.[7] Hindus were put on the defensive by attacks on their teachings, practices, caste system, and even avatars. The bitter Indian experience of the alliance of Christian mission with exploitative and repressive British colonialism only served, in the minds of many Hindus, to bring into discredit standard Christian claims about Christianity's moral superiority. Christ himself, however, was immediately attractive to many Hindus, who recognized in his spirituality, message, and way of life similarities with their own values and teachings, especially his non-violence, renunciation, and compassion.[8] Thus Christianity, experienced as powerful, exploitative, and European, was contrasted with its founder, whose teaching and spirit were deemed essentially "Asiatic" and even Hindu.

What follows is a brief summary of some of the most important and influential Hindu interpreters of Christ from this period.

Ram Mohun Roy (1772–1833), the "Father of Modern India," the "first great international Hindu of the modern period,"[9] and socio-religious reformer, helped to legally abolish forced widow immolation (*sati*), polygamy, and child marriage, and promoted the education and legal rights of women. He was also opposed to polytheism, ritual, and what

---

[7] Cf. Chakravarthi Ram-Prasad, "Hindu Views of Jesus," in Gregory A. Barker (ed.), *Jesus in the World's Faiths* (Maryknoll: Orbis, 2005), 82–83.

[8] See Anantanand Rambachan, "A Hindu Looks at Jesus," in *The Hindu Vision* (Delhi: Motilal Banarsidass, 1994), who writes, p. 42: "But perhaps in its concern to stress the uniqueness and originality of Jesus, Christianity has ignored some of the identities in the definition of the spiritual life which Jesus shares with the tradition of Hinduism . . . The Hindu who is steeped in the values of his own tradition feels a natural affinity for the self-evident and radiant spirituality of Jesus, and wishes in the enthusiasm of this recognition to welcome him into his home."

[9] Eric J. Sharpe, "Neo-Hindu Images of Christianity," in Arvind Sharma (ed.), *Neo-Hindu Views of Christianity* (Leiden: Brill, 1988), 6.

he saw as idolatry.[10] Roy was attracted to Jesus above all by his moral commandments. In a letter to a friend in 1815 Roy wrote:

The consequence of my long and uninterrupted researches into religious truth has been that I have found the doctrine of Christ more conducive to moral principles and better adapted for the use of rational beings than any others which have come to my knowledge.[11]

In Christology he was close to the Unitarians and thus faced the animosity of Christian evangelicals, who failed to convert him to traditional high Christology with its emphasis on the divinity of Christ. Roy's summary work, *The Precepts of Jesus: The Guide to Peace and Happiness* (1820), presented the moral teachings of Jesus as gleaned from the four Gospels, but it excluded any talk of miracles, incarnation, Trinity, atoning death, apocalyptic, and resurrection. He was critical of Christians who spent too much time pondering the mystery of Christ's alleged divinity while neglecting Jesus' call to ethical discipleship. Jesus was for Roy the ideal or exemplary human being, who teaches us to submit our will to the moral commandments of God and thereby find salvation.

Keshub Chander Sen (1838–1884), like Roy a social and religious reformer of the Bengal Renaissance, displayed a fervent love and devotion to Christ, though his exact understanding of Christ's relation to God is difficult to define. At times Jesus is regarded as a morally perfect human filled with the divine spirit, made possible by the perfect conformity of his will with the divine will. Here the emphasis is on communion between the human and the divine, not a strict identity of the two or the negation of one in favor of the other. At times Sen goes even further, speaking of Christ as a divine descent into the world for the purpose of manifesting God in an unparalleled fashion. Sen was more mystically inclined than Roy, seeing in Christ's death, for example, not an atonement, but rather the most perfect symbol of the universal need to crucify selfishness and desire to attain mystical union with God. Christ represents the most perfect fulfillment of the human search for happiness and oneness with the divine. He completes all Hindu spiritual striving and at the same time breaks the bonds placed on him by western dogmatic theology. Sen also tended towards syncretism, borrowing from both Christianity and Hinduism in

---

[10] Roy's embrace of monotheism seems to have originated with his two-year study as a boy at a Muslim madrasa in Patna.

[11] Cited in M. M. Thomas, *The Acknowledged Christ of the Indian Renaissance* (Madras: Christian Literature Society, 1970), 9.

his establishment of the Church of the New Dispensation, with himself as self-appointed prophet and head.

Ramakrishna Paramahamsa (1836–1886), though not a social reformer, is one of the two or three greatest spiritual figures and mystics in modern Hinduism. While he held Kali, the Mother Goddess, to be the highest reality, he also immersed himself in the teachings and paths of other religions, including Islam and Christianity, and subsequently validated their truth through his own religious experience. During the time he committed himself to Christian spirituality his devotion to Christ was total and exclusive. Initially Ramakrishna's primary source of knowledge of Christ was the New Testament, which was read aloud to him by a fellow Hindu. Eventually his faith in Christ would give way to direct experience, for him a more immediate source of understanding. One day as Ramakrishna gazed on a picture of the child Jesus on his mother's lap the picture suddenly became alive, emitting rays of light that overwhelmed him and caused in him an even greater devotion to Christ. Soon thereafter he encountered Christ directly in a vision, as a fair-complexioned and beautiful divine figure approaching him. At that moment out of his own depths Ramakrishna heard a voice rising up: "Behold the Christ, who shed his heart's blood for the redemption of the world, who suffered a sea of anguish for love of men . . . It is he, the Master Yogi, who is in eternal union with God. It is Jesus, Love Incarnate."[12] Such an experience confirmed for Ramakrishna that Jesus was a true avatar of God, though not the only incarnation, as Christians claimed. He saw the two special weaknesses of Christianity to be its near-fanatical insistence on dogmatizing its understanding of God and Christ, in particular the claim that Jesus was uniquely divine, as also its excessive preoccupation with sin.

Swami Vivekananda (1863–1902), the most famous disciple of Ramakrishna, still exerts enormous influence on popular Hindu theologies of religion today, and much of contemporary Hindu pride derives from Vivekananda's apologetics. He was the first Hindu missionary to the West, appearing at the World Parliament of Religions in Chicago in 1893. Like his master Ramakrishna he taught that all religions lead to the Divine. But, unlike Ramakrishna, he constructed a theology of religions in the form of a hierarchy, the religions being assessed according to their capacity to mediate realization of one's innate divinity.[13] Enlightenment spirituality, especially Advaita Vedanta, was ranked higher than Hindu and Christian

[12] Quoted by Thomas, *The Acknowledged Christ*, 112.
[13] See Bradley Malkovsky, "Swami Vivekananda and Bede Griffiths on Religious Pluralism: Hindu and Christian Approaches to Truth," *Horizons* 25 (1998), 217–237.

devotional theism, which Vivekananda regarded as a primitive dualism of God and world rather than a higher unity of pure identity. According to the Swami, Jesus taught both higher and lower stages of religion and wisdom, depending on his audience, but he was essentially an Advaitin, or rather an avatar who came to teach Advaita or non-duality. As an Advaitin, Jesus represents a mysticism beyond relation. He calls us to awaken to our innate but hidden divinity. His teaching was therefore in opposition to most of standard Christian orthodoxy. Vivekananda rejected, too, the notion that Christ was the only avatar and also Christ's death and resurrection. "Christ was God incarnate," he wrote, "they could not kill him. That which was crucified was only a semblance, a mirage."[14]

Vivekananda also argued that no religion can lay claim to be the one true religion for humankind if its authority rested merely on unverifiable claims, such as the existence of a savior-person from long ago or on an alleged saving event of history. For if the historical facticity of the person or event could eventually be challenged, as it does in fact happen through modern critical awareness, the credibility of the whole religion is undermined and should therefore be dismissed as unreliable. Thus true religion must be founded on unchanging eternal principles that are experientially accessible and verifiable to all, which is, for example, the teaching of Advaita Vedanta. Hence Vivekananda saw it as absurd that the rescue of humankind would be dependent on the work of a single avatar like Christ.[15]

Mohandas K. Gandhi (1869–1948), leader of the Indian independence movement, like Roy and Sen, stressed the ethical character and message of Jesus, especially as articulated in the Sermon on the Mount. The Sermon summarized all that was important in Jesus' teaching, with its emphasis on nonviolence, patience, kindness, and a readiness to suffer out of love. Christ was so inspiring to Gandhi that for a time he considered converting to Christianity, but finally concluded that there was nothing in Christ's teaching that was not already in Hinduism.[16] And yet Christ was exemplary in the way he actually lived out his message of non-violence, service, and love, so much so that Gandhi once wrote, "The example of Jesus' suffering is a factor in the composition of my underlying faith in non-violence, which rules all my actions, worldly and temporal."[17] And elsewhere he stated, "My interpretation, in other words, is that in Jesus' own life is the key of His nearness to God; that He expressed, as no other could, the spirit

[14] Quoted in Thomas, *The Acknowledged Christ*, 126.
[15] See Malkovsky, "Swami Vivekananda," 225–226.
[16] Cf. Robert Ellsberg, *Gandhi on Christianity* (Maryknoll: Orbis, 1991), 12.
[17] Mohandas K. Gandhi, *The Message of Jesus Christ* (Bombay: Bharatiya Vidya Bhavan, 1964), 79.

and will of God."[18] Thus, he concluded, "I shall tell the Hindus: your lives will be incomplete unless you reverently study the teaching of Jesus."[19]

But Gandhi did not see Christ as a universal savior; he was rather one of many embodiments of divine Truth. And even more important than the historical Jesus and the inspiring example he set was the Sermon on the Mount itself.

I must say that I have never been interested in a historical Jesus. I should not care if it was proved by someone that the man called Jesus never lived, and that what was narrated in the Gospels was a figment of the writer's imagination. For the Sermon on the Mount would still be true to me.[20]

It is also worth noting how emphatically Gandhi rejects the possibility of resurrection. "As for Jesus raising the dead to life, well, I doubt if the men he raised were really dead . . . He brought to life not people who were dead but who were believed to be dead."[21]

Sarvepalli Radhakrishnan (1888–1975), Spalding Professor of Eastern Religions and Ethics at Oxford University (1936–1952), President of India (1962–1967), "the foremost apologist in the twentieth century for *advaita* Vedanta in particular and for Hinduism in general,"[22] fashioned a new understanding of avatarhood linked to the idea of evolution. The eternal Divine gradually manifests itself in human history as more and more individuals realize their innate divine potentiality. The focus here is not so much divinity descending into the human realm as people ascending into perfect non-dualistic awareness by following their individual religions. The purpose of all religions is to lead to the "religion of the Spirit" and interiority. Thus Jesus, far from being the uniquely perfect incarnation of Spirit, is one of many, with many more still to come. Radhakrishnan finds much similarity between Jesus' otherworldly teaching and the spiritual orientation of Hinduism and Buddhism. And, like Gandhi, Vivekananda, and other Hindus of the modern period, he contrasts the simple message of Jesus with the exclusivist and dogmatizing interpretations given Jesus by Christianity. Further, he rules out the notion of divine suffering. "A suffering God," he wrote, "a deity with a crown of thorns, cannot satisfy the religious soul."[23]

Thus we find, by way of summary, widely varying Hindu interpretations of Christ with a number of significant commonalities. Without question, all

---

[18] Ellsberg, *Gandhi on Christianity*, 27. Passage written in 1941.
[19] Gandhi, *The Message of Jesus Christ*, 42.   [20] Gandhi, *The Message of Jesus Christ*, 37.
[21] Ellsberg, *Gandhi on Christianity*, 26. Passage from 1937.
[22] Bob Robinson, *Christians Meeting Hindus* (Carlisle and Waynesboro, Ga.: Regnum, 2004), 11.
[23] Sarvepalli Radhakrishnan, *The Philosophy of Rabindranath Tagore* (London: Macmillan, 1918), 15.

six thinkers find in Christ a great source of moral and spiritual inspiration. They seek therefore to emulate him and draw strength from his example, but they do not worship him or pray to him, except Sen. Nor does following Christ require membership in any church, especially since the churches appear to be governed by a different spirit than that of Christ. Additionally, all of these thinkers, with the exception of Roy, see Christ as an embodiment of the divine. The most frequently used term in this regard is *avatar*, though the particular avatar theology varies from thinker to thinker, some emphasizing the divine initiative to descend, while others place greater emphasis on human perfectibility and Self-realization attained through human striving. Moreover, Christ is regarded as only one of many divine embodiments, and therefore cannot be a sole or universal savior. That he is one of many avatars also rules out the need for him to have existed at all. That he suffered is accepted by most, but it is a suffering that does not in any way touch the divine. Most of the Hindu figures covered accept Christ's death as real – though Radhakrishnan acknowledges only an apparent death – but Christ's death is never interpreted as an atonement. In sum, Christ's message and spirituality are interpreted in a new way, largely Hindu, though the manner in which Christ actually lives out his message is regarded as incomparable and unsurpassed.

Many of these features of classical Hindu Christology are incorporated into contemporary models. But there are also some new approaches to understanding the person and work of Christ that are of great significance.

RECENT DEVELOPMENTS IN HINDU CHRISTOLOGY

India's independence from British colonial rule in 1947 made Hindu responses to Christian mission and mainstream Christian Christology less urgent.[24] There was no longer the need to continue a defensive posture which attempted to prove the equality or even the superiority of Hinduism over Christianity. Yet with the arrival of Independence Hindu reflection on Christ did not come to an end nor did Hindu interest in Jesus wane. In fact, the opposite might be the case. Recently a number of Hindu scholars living in the West have noted a widespread popular devotion to Christ among Hindus, both in India and abroad. "Jesus Christ is an ineradicable part of modern Hinduism," writes Seshagiri Rao. "Hindus adore Christ."[25] Chakravarthi Ram-Prasad notes that Jesus

[24] Cf. Ram-Prasad, "Hindu Views," 83.
[25] Chakravarthi Ram-Prasad, "Hindu–Christian Dialogue: A Hindu Perspective," *Hindu-Christian Studies Bulletin* 14 (2001), 10.

is probably more pervasive in popular Hindu devotion than ever in the past. It is frequently noted that pictures of Jesus, especially some dominant Catholic images like the Sacred Heart and the Baby Jesus, are found as part of the collection of sacred posters that are hung in shops, restaurants, and homes, and which function as something between formal shrines and *aide-memoire* to private prayer. To the best of my knowledge, there has been no proper theorization of this popular assimilation of Jesus into Hindu devotionalism, which in form, but also in theological substance, lies some way away from the ideas of Sen, Vivekananda, Radhakrishnan, and the rest.[26]

Ram-Prasad adds that "the aspect of earlier Hindu views of Jesus that retains influence now is the recognition of Jesus as unquestionably divine in some way."[27] This is the most important element of continuity between past and present Hindu Christologies.

In the following I take up the inquiry into what is new in contemporary Hindu understandings of Christ. Instead of striving for completeness, I restrict myself to listing a few of the new perspectives and claims that must be taken into consideration. Any attempt at moving beyond early modern Hindu views of Christ to summarize contemporary Hindu Christology must be necessarily incomplete, not only because the Hindu encounter with Christ is ongoing and dynamic, but also because it is under-researched.[28] The focus here will be more on ideas, theological method, and growing tendencies and less on summarizing the writings and work of individual Hindu thinkers.

Jesus in India

It is sometimes stated that Jesus visited India either during his "missing years," that is, roughly during the ages of twelve to thirty, a period of Jesus' life about which the New Testament is silent, or after his persecution, when he escaped death, or both.[29] Though this claim was never asserted among the standard nineteenth- and twentieth-century Hindu interpreters of Christ I have summarized, it is often stated as fact today. In the words of one Christian theologian and longtime missionary to India, there exists a

---

[26] Ram-Prasad, "Hindu Views," 86.   [27] Ram-Prasad, "Hindu Views," 86.

[28] But a very helpful summary of contemporary views – along with classical ones – has recently appeared in Sandy Bharat, *Christ across the Ganges: Hindu Responses to Jesus* (Winchester and Washington, D.C.: O Books, 2007). The author assesses the positions of Hindus living both in India and the West and presents important new material based in part on first-hand interviews.

[29] Similar claims are found in the Islamic Ahmadiyya movement and in the contemporary West. These are discussed in the chapters by Jan Hjärpe and Olav Hammer in the present volume.

widespread popular belief that Jesus visited India in the so-called "hidden years" before he began his public ministry, and that he sat at the feet of some Hindu saint from whom he derived his teaching... On the cross he did not die but merely swooned, and then set off for the East... Implicit in this story is the claim that Christians have misunderstood Jesus.[30]

This assertion is repeated by such famous Hindu swamis as Paramahansa Yogananda.[31] Bharat similarly refers to a "well-established Hindu belief" that Jesus lived in India during the missing years not reported in the New Testament, that he there learned the basic teachings and practices of Yoga and Vedanta, somehow survived the crucifixion in Palestine through the use of special yogic powers, returned to India, where he then died, and that his shrine is located in Kashmir, where it is visited by Hindus and Sufis today.[32]

It is difficult to trace back to its origins this story of Jesus' travels to India. Eric Sharpe suggests that the 1894 publication of a Russian journalist, Nicholas Notovitch, called *La vie inconnue de Jesus-Christ*[33] was instrumental in spreading this belief. Notovitch claims to have seen two Tibetan scrolls in a Buddhist monastery in Ladakh that witnessed to Jesus' life and visits to both India and Tibet, where he studied the wisdom of Buddhism, Hinduism, and Jainism before returning to Galilee. Notovitch's book was an instant success, having gone through eight printings in France its first year.[34]

Such a publication, of course, offers supporting evidence for those who would deny Jesus' death and subsequent resurrection. But the story of Jesus surviving his crucifixion and heading to India also contradicts those Hindus who do accept the execution of Jesus as fact, even though they interpret its meaning in ways very different from its mainstream Christian rendering.

Many resurrections

While the resurrection of Jesus continues to be of little interest to most Hindus, it is no longer always ignored or dismissed. Indeed, the resurrection

---

[30] Roger Hardham Hooker, *Themes in Hinduism and Christianity* (Frankfurt and New York: Peter Lang, 1989), 358–359.

[31] Paramahansa Yogananda, *Man's Eternal Quest* (Los Angeles: Self-Realization Fellowship, 1945), 285. That Jesus lived in India was also accepted by Swami Sivananda (1887–1963). Cf. Bharat, *Christ across the Ganges*, 41.

[32] Bharat, *Christ across the Ganges*, 6 n. 4. Diana Eck, *Encountering God* (Boston: Beacon Press, 1993), 113–114, in her chapter comparing Christ's incarnation with Hindu avatar teaching, gives an account of her visit to the tomb in Kashmir. There Jesus is known as Yuz Asaf, "son of Joseph."

[33] Translated into English as *The Hidden Life of Jesus Christ*, and also translated into German, Spanish, and Italian.

[34] Sharpe, "Neo-Hindu Images of Christianity," 11.

of Christ is taken by some Hindus as historical fact. But unlike the traditional Christian claim that Jesus alone has been resurrected from the dead,
some Hindus now assert that Jesus' resurrection is not unique. The claim
is made that some of Hinduism's greatest sages and yogis have returned
from the dead and appeared to their disciples or have even raised the dead
themselves.[35] Sri Ramakrishna is supposed to have appeared to his disciples
after his death, and Swami Yogananda, in chapter 3 of his *Autobiography of
a Yoga*, relates to the reader his direct experience with his resurrected guru,
Sri Yukteswar.[36]

It is important to note, in addition, that the Hindu understanding of
the resurrection event and the resurrection body is very different from that
of mainstream Christian faith and theology. For one, there is no talk that
the resurrection of Hindu sages and saints is the work of a personal God or
Absolute; the deceased sage simply reappears after the death of the body,
and there is no reference to a rescue or transformation or a post-mortem
appearance caused by the Supreme. The implication to be drawn is that
the realized sage is himself the master over life and death.

Further, resurrection in this Hindu understanding is not the transformation of the whole human person as it is in Christian thought, but rather
the visible return of the master as spirit or in the form of a "subtle" body. In
summarizing the thought of Swami Satprakashananda (1888–1979) on resurrection as presented in his book, *Jesus Christ and his Teachings in the Light
of Vedanta*,[37] Bharat remarks, "For Swamiji, resurrection and eternal life do
not depend on bodies as spirit is our true nature."[38] More recently, Deepak
Chopra has offered a dualistic understanding of Jesus' resurrection when he
summarizes the Easter event as meaning that "a flesh-and-blood man was
transformed into completely divine substance – the Holy Spirit."[39] He does
not contrast his conception with more holistic Christian understandings.

Finally, it is evident that Hindu resurrections never figure prominently
in Hindu soteriologies. While the faith and hope of most Christians is
founded in large part on the facticity of Jesus' resurrection, in Hindu

---

[35] The followers of Bhagavan Shri Satya Sai Baba (1926–) claim that he has demonstrated his
omnipotence by causing the resurrection of others. Cf. Norris W. Palmer, "Baba's World: A Global
Guru and his Movement," in Thomas A. Forsthoeffel and Cynthia Ann Humes (eds.), *Gurus in
America* (Albany: SUNY Press, 2005), 103.

[36] Cf. Bharat, *Christ across the Ganges*, 61.   [37] Vedanta Society of St. Louis, 1975.

[38] Bharat, *Christ across the Ganges*, 61. Similarly, many years ago I heard Dr. Usharbudh Arya, now
Swami Veda Bharati, at the Meditation Center in Minneapolis publicly refer to the resurrection
appearances of Jesus as the encounter of the disciples with their "disembodied master."

[39] Deepak Chopra, *The Third Jesus: The Christ we Cannot Ignore* (New York: Harmony Books, 2008),
136. Chopra is by birth half-Hindu and half-Sikh. While he does not count himself as a member of
any religion today, his main teachings are recognizably Hindu.

soteriology the role of resurrection – whether that of Jesus or of any other holy figure – is finally quite insignificant. And by virtue of the fact that Hindu resurrection talk has emerged only in very recent times, one gets the impression that this particular teaching is merely a late and rather unimportant appendage grafted on to the main body of Hindu doctrine.

Making use of uncertainties in Christian biblical exegesis

Hindus who assert the essential Hinduness of Christ's teaching are often enough aware of the *problems surrounding modern historical and exegetical research in attempting to determine what can be known with certainty about the historical Jesus and his proclamation.* Since even Christian biblical exegetes cannot arrive at a clear understanding of the essential nature of Christ and his mission, the possibility emerges, they contend, that new Hindu interpretations of Jesus should now be regarded as valid as traditional Christian ones. Sita Ram Goel (1921–2003), one of modern India's most vociferous critics of Christianity, drew the conclusion after having studied the Gospels and modern biblical exegesis that the evidence for Jesus' historical existence and the content of his life was scant indeed, as they are confined to New Testament documents of faith. His position on Christ has been summarized by Sandy Bharat as follows: "The real identity of this enigmatic historical figure is now up for grabs."[40] The uncertainties of Christian biblical exegesis open the door to the legitimacy of Hindu views.

Similarly, in his recent best-seller, *The Third Jesus: The Christ we Cannot Ignore*, Deepak Chopra has gone to some length to inform the reader about the problem of determining who Jesus actually was on the basis of current New Testament studies. He cites such problems as the inability to determine the original wording of biblical verses or the timeline of events in Jesus' life. And, too, the Gospels contain many glaring omissions about the life of Jesus, especially after the age of twelve. The Gospel writers are therefore required at times to insert words into Jesus' mouth, such as during the agony in the garden, when no disciple could have heard him. Chopra continues,

The writers of the gospels set out not to tell the facts of a life but to convert nonbelievers and support their own belief in Jesus as the Messiah. To this end they almost certainly exaggerated events, invented miracles, and put words into Jesus' mouth.[41]

---

[40] Bharat, *Christ across the Ganges*, 107.   [41] Chopra, *The Third Jesus*, 133.

Given these uncertainties surrounding the traditional four Gospels, Chopra suggests that such non-canonical texts as the *Gospel of Thomas* and the gnostic Gospels should therefore be treated as equal in authority with New Testament texts.[42] After presenting many of the quandaries of New Testament exegesis, he then concludes as follows:

The search for the real Jesus will continue for as long as anyone can fore-see... Despite the strictures of the Church, which hold that only priests and saints have authority in this area, today there is a level playing field in religion: Anyone can devise a new interpretation of the New Testament. Unfortunately, this great text is ambiguous and confusing enough to support almost any thesis about its meaning.[43]

The language of "Christ-consciousness" and "God-consciousness"

Chopra's own interpretation, like that of many Hindu gurus and swamis today, is to treat Jesus as a man filled with and wanting to mediate to others direct experiential awareness of the Divine.[44] He contrasts this spiritual-ity with that of Christianity, which traditionally emphasizes "worship over self-transformation, prayer over meditation, and faith over inner growth."[45] Accordingly, Jesus' teaching, in unison with all the great wisdom traditions of the world, is "the project of transcending the physical world to reach the realm of the soul."[46] Jesus' mission, then, is to lead others to "God-consciousness" or enlightenment. The content of Chopra's message is not new; he stands in the neo-Vedantic tradition of Hinduism which, in regard-ing all people as potential Christs or avatars, would overcome mainstream Christianity's proclivity towards exclusivism and the condemnation of non-Christians to hell. In this Christology Christ mediates to others a mystical consciousness that is universal to religion. This higher consciousness is sometimes called by Hindu swamis and gurus "*Christ consciousness*." The

---

[42] Chopra, *The Third Jesus*, 133.

[43] Chopra, *The Third Jesus*, 139. For Chopra the first Jesus is the historical person about whom we can know very little. The second Jesus is the Christ of Church dogmatics and ecclesial oppressors, who know nothing about spirituality. The third Jesus, the real Jesus, is the spiritual teacher of God-consciousness and the highest wisdom.

[44] Cf. Chopra, *The Third Jesus*, 130, and also Swami Satprakashananda, *Hinduism and Christianity: Jesus Christ and His Teachings in the Light of Vedanta* (St. Louis: Vedanta Society of St. Louis, 1975), 88.

[45] Chopra, *The Third Jesus*, 87.

[46] Chopra, *The Third Jesus*, 52. Cf. also p. 139: "The salvation Jesus offered was the same as Buddha's: release from suffering and a path to spiritual freedom, joy, and closeness to God. In that light, the real Jesus is as available today as he ever was, perhaps more so. Instead of relying on faith alone, we can go beyond worship to find a body of teachings consistent with the world's wisdom traditions, a corroboration in Christian terms that higher consciousness is real and open to all."

term is used by Swami Yogananda[47] and the Ramakrishna mission.[48] Here the historical Jesus is subsumed within a "greater cosmic Christness," not limited to any one historical figure and potentially available to all.[49]

Reevaluating Hindu presuppositions

In marked contrast to the above four developments, one finds today a number of Hindu scholars who do not shy away from critiquing fellow Hindus for interpreting Jesus exclusively through pre-given Hindu categories and assumptions. Such an approach makes a growth of knowledge all but impossible. Anantanand Rambachan writes:

> As a Hindu, one has to resist the inclination to see and interpret Jesus in the categories of Hinduism. This approach was very common in the nineteenth and early twentieth centuries and it is not unusual today. The attempt is often made to see his life and teachings in the categories of the Hindu tradition of *advaita* (non-dualism). This, however, is only possible through a very selective use of the records of his sayings, and the dismissal of the way in which he has been traditionally understood by most Christians. It is an approach which claims to place little importance on dogma and doctrine, and, therefore, dismisses the significance of differences in this sphere. In reality, however, such differences must be acknowledged. Dismissing them in sweeping generalizations does not contribute much to the process of mutual understanding.[50]

K. R. Sundararajan expresses very similar views about the traditional Hindu appropriation of Jesus into Hindu categories, an attitude which is not sufficiently respectful of differences.[51]

> In the present mind-set of the Hindus, the tradition has everything one needs and there is nothing to learn from "others." I personally feel that the sound basis for inter-religious dialogue goes beyond mere curiosity, and should be motivated by what I describe as "the existential need" to learn from others and be conceptually broadened and spiritually benefited.[52]

Sundararajan finds legitimacy in both Hindu and Christian teachings about Christ. He says that "In some ways Hindus cannot avoid 'Hinduizing' Jesus if they want to understand/appropriate him." But he also calls for

---

[47] Cf. Yogananda, *Man's Eternal Quest*, 292. Cited in Bharat, *Christ across the Ganges*, 68.

[48] Bharat, *Christ across the Ganges*, 78.

[49] Bharat, *Christ across the Ganges*, 169. Bharat personally takes this position in keeping with her master, Swami Yogananda.

[50] Rambachan, *The Hindu Vision*, 45. Rambachan teaches at St. Olaf College in the USA.

[51] Sundararajan is a professor at St. Bonaventure University in the USA.

[52] In Bharat, *Christ across the Ganges*, 180. Sundarajan's statement was part of a response to a questionnaire sent to him and other Hindus by Bharat.

"the expansion of and a deepening of one's own understanding of 'being religious.'"[53] In particular, Sundararajan suggests the need to move beyond Docetic understandings of Christ and to consider the "possibility of a 'suffering God.'"[54]

The theme is taken up by another Hindu scholar residing in the West, Chakravarthi Ram-Prasad.[55] Rather than simply subsuming Jesus into the avatar pantheon as just one more example of a divine embodiment, he suggests that Jesus, while not superior to other divine manifestations, may be regarded "as being for many the most spiritually apt and emotionally satisfying and ethically fulfilling manifestation of divinity. This is not, of course, the Christian view of Jesus. But neither is it simply a Hindu reduction of Jesus to some subordinate role in a Hindu schema."[56] This approach, he feels, safeguards "what is Christian about belief in Jesus – his uniqueness – while recognizing the possibility of legitimate Hindu views of Jesus."[57]

CONCLUSION AND FURTHER QUESTIONS

As we have seen, both early modern and contemporary Hindu understandings of Christ display a wide range of views.[58] We find first of all significant disagreements, for example, both affirmations and denials by Hindus of Jesus' suffering, his death, his resurrection, and his divinity, from the early nineteenth century until the present day. But we also find a broad, though

---

[53] Cited in Bharat, *Christ across the Ganges*, 117.

[54] Bharat, *Christ across the Ganges*, 181. Cf. also *ibid.*, 179.

[55] Ram-Prasad is Senior Lecturer in Indian Religion, Lancaster University, UK.

[56] Ram-Prasad, "Hindu Views," 91. In similar fashion Rambachan lauds Jesus' "practical spirituality." "The dimension of Jesus' character to which I am referring is his outstanding demonstration of what genuine spirituality means in the process of actually living in the world. I think that he has provided some of the most concrete and finest examples of practical spirituality, or what the spiritual life means when it is translated into human relationships. In his life he has given us some of the fullest instances of the fruits of the spiritual life in action. I find no difficulty, as a Hindu, in deriving guidance and inspiration from these ... I find that Jesus' emphasis on a living spirituality which informs and pervades all our relationships and even our smallest actions to be very meaningful ... At the same time, I think that there is a need for contemporary Hinduism to seek more urgently to gather and emphasize the practical implications in society of its profound philosophical views about the nature of ultimate reality." Rambachan, *The Hindu Vision*, 42–44.

[57] Ram-Prasad, "Hindu Views," 90.

[58] Space does not allow the examination of other perspectives of Hindu relations to Christ, such as ISKCON's (International Society of Krishna Consciousness, also called the Hare Krishna movement) subordination of Christ to Krishna, or the appeal of the suffering Christ to the oppressed Dalit communities of India. Also useful would be the way that the Jewishness of Jesus, with its implications for social justice and human dignity and equality, has been received by Hindu scholars, especially those living in the West.

not unanimous, consensus that Jesus is a great and holy avatar, though finally only one of many, and therefore not to be reckoned as the sole or universal savior. Except for a few individuals,[59] Jesus is regarded by Hindus as a great messenger of morality and spirituality to a humanity suffering under the cloud of ignorance, desire, delusion, and selfishness. His example of selfless sacrifice is often regarded as unparalleled and therefore an inspiration to many. His death as atonement for sin, if this is understood as the propitiation of an angry God, is rejected by all.

In part, the intention and goal of Hindus publicly reflecting on Christ is to force Christians to address challenging theological questions such as these: Should the possibility be ruled out altogether that Christ has appeared to Hindus or that very different experiences of Christ – by those of other faiths – are possible? And how do Christians respond to the challenge, first formulated among Hindus by Swami Vivekananda in the nineteenth century, that modern biblical exegesis is powerless to prove that the Christ of official Christian dogmatics is in fact the authentic one? And what, finally, might Christians learn from Hindus with their very different interpretations of Christ?

I conclude with two quotations, one from a Christian, the other from a Hindu, both warning against the folly of reducing the understanding of Christ to the limitations of a single perspective. The first is from the late Murray Rogers (1917–2006), an Anglican priest who lived many years in India strengthening Hindu–Christian ties and promoting inter-religious dialogue:

I begin to see – seemingly against much of my original upbringing and teaching – that the fundamental message of any of our religions, including my own, lies deeper and beyond the framework in which that message may have been given to the world. The Lord Jesus Christ was not a Christian! True, his message, his work of salvation, was lived out and revealed in a Jewish setting, but it was too strong a message to be confined within that spiritual and cultural packaging. It outgrows every framework in which we out of love and devotion enshrine it.[60]

And, finally, we hear the ringing words of Swami Vivekananda: "I pity the Hindu who does not see the beauty of Jesus Christ's character. I pity the Christian who does not reverence the Hindu Christ."[61]

---

[59] For example, Swami Dayananda Saraswati of the nineteenth century and the late Sita Ram Goel.

[60] Murray Rogers, "Hindu Influence on Christian Spiritual Practice," in Harold Coward (ed.), *Hindu–Christian Dialogue: Perspectives and Encounters* (Maryknoll: Orbis, 1989), 204.

[61] Swami Vivekananda, *Collected Works* (Calcutta: Advaita Ashrama, 1918–1922), vol. III, 219.

BIBLIOGRAPHY

SOURCES

Chopra, Deepak, *The Third Jesus: The Christ we Cannot Ignore* (New York: Harmony Books, 2008).

Ellsberg, Robert (ed.), *Gandhi on Christianity* (Maryknoll: Orbis, 1991).

Gandhi, Mohandas K., *The Message of Jesus Christ* (Bombay: Bharatiya Vidya Bhavan, 1964).

Radhakrishnan, Sarvepalli, *The Philosophy of Rabindranath Tagore* (London: Macmillan, 1918).

Rambachan, Anantanand, *The Hindu Vision* (Delhi: Motilal Banarsidass, 1994).

Rogers, Murray, "Hindu Influence on Christian Spiritual Practice," in Harold Coward (ed.), *Hindu–Christian Dialogue: Perspectives and Encounters* (Maryknoll: Orbis, 1989), 198–206.

Satprakashananda, Swami, *Hinduism and Christianity: Jesus Christ and his Teachings in the Light of Vedanta* (St. Louis: Vedanta Society of St. Louis, 1975).

Vivekananda, Swami, *Collected Works* (Calcutta: Advaita Ashrama, 1918–1922).

Yogananda, Paramahansa, *Man's Eternal Quest* (Los Angeles: Self-Realization Fellowship, 1945).

LITERATURE

Amaladoss, Michael, *The Asian Jesus* (Maryknoll: Orbis, 2006).

Bharat, Sandy, *Christ across the Ganges: Hindu Responses to Jesus* (Winchester and Washington, D.C.: O Books, 2007).

Dhavamony, Mariasusai, *Jesus Christ in the Understanding of World Religions* (Rome: Editrice Pontificia Universita Gregoriana, 2004).

Dupuis, Jacques, *Jesus Christ at the Encounter of World Religions* (Maryknoll: Orbis, 1991).

Eck, Diana, *Encountering God: A Spiritual Journey from Bozeman to Benares* (Boston: Beacon Press, 1992).

Hooker, Roger Hardham, *Themes in Hinduism and Christianity* (Frankfurt and New York: Peter Lang, 1989).

Klostermaier, Klaus K., *Indian Theology in Dialogue* (Madras: The Christian Literature Society, 1986).

Malkovsky, Bradley, "Swami Vivekananda and Bede Griffiths on Religious Pluralism: Hindu and Christian Approaches to Truth," *Horizons* 25 (1998), 217–237.

Neufeldt, Ronald, "Hindu Views of Christ," in Harold Coward (ed.), *Hindu–Christian Dialogue: Perspectives and Encounters* (Maryknoll: Orbis, 1989), 162–175.

Palmer, Norris W., "Baba's World: A Global Guru and his Movement," in Thomas A. Forsthoeffel and Cynthia Ann Humes (eds.), *Gurus in America* (Albany: SUNY Press, 2005), 138–175.

Paradkar, Balwant A. M., "Hindu Interpretations of Christ from Vivekananda to Radhakrishnan," *Indian Journal of Theology* 18 (1969), 65–80.

Ram-Prasad, Chakravarthi, "Hindu–Christian Dialogue: A Hindu Perspective," *Hindu-Christian Studies Bulletin* 14 (2001), 10.

  "Hindu Views of Jesus," in Gregory A. Barker (ed.), *Jesus in the World's Faiths* (Maryknoll: Orbis, 2005), 81–91.

Robinson, Bob, *Christians Meeting Hindus* (Carlisle and Waynesboro, Ga.: Regnum, 2004).

Sharpe, Eric J., "Neo-Hindu Images of Christianity," in Arvind Sharma (ed.), *Neo-Hindu Views of Christianity* (Leiden: Brill, 1988), 1–15.

Sheth, Noel, "Hindu Avatara and Christian Incarnation: A Comparison," *Philosophy East & West* 52.1 (January 2002), 98–125.

Staffner, Hans, *Jesus Christ and the Hindu Community* (Anand: Gujarat Sahitya Prakash, 1988).

Thomas, M. M., *The Acknowledged Christ of the Indian Renaissance* (Madras: Christian Literature Society, 1970).

Tsoukalas, Stephen, "Krishna and Christ: The Body–Divine Relation in the Human Form," in Catherine Cornille (ed.), *Song Divine: Christian Commentaries on the Bhagavad Gita* (Leuven: Peeters, 2006), 145–163.

CHAPTER 10

Christ in Mormonism

Douglas J. Davies

INTRODUCTION

Max Müller amongst the greatest nineteenth-century founders of comparative religion, thought that each should have "the liberty of believing in his own Christ" while doubting whether "the fragments left to us of the real history of the life and teaching of Christ" were sufficient to bear the weight of "interpretation and reconstruction" that many sought: certainly, he objected to his contemporary, Renan's, highly contentious *Life of Jesus* with its "idyllic Christ."[1] Subsequent theological scholarship generated an enormous venture in Jesus studies[2] with several historical-social studies focusing on Jesus in American life exemplified in Fox's valuable *Jesus in America.*[3] Sub-titled, "Personal Savior, Cultural Hero and National Obsession," he showed how this "elastic identity" served many ends, including that of boundary-marking. Similar idealizations underlie Prothero's *The American Jesus,*[4] which could, itself, be partly contextualized in Noll's *America's God,*[5] explored from "Jonathan Edwards to Abraham Lincoln." These works help contextualize a Mormonism often identified as a quintessential, perhaps even *the* quintessential, American religion.[6] If sound, that description would suggest that an analysis of Christ in Mormonism would offer some insight into American religiosity at large with its dynamic

---

[1] Max Müller [1823–1900], *My Autobiography* (London: Longman Green, 1901), 279. Ernest Renan's [1823–1892], *Vie de Jésus* of 1863 was highly controversial.
[2] E. P. Sanders, *The Historical Figure of Jesus* (London: Penguin Books 1993) reflects one, well-known, project in Jesus Studies.
[3] Richard Fox, *Jesus in America: Personal Savior, Cultural Hero, National Obsession* (San Francisco: Harper-Collins, 2004), 12, 26.
[4] Stephen Prothero, *American Jesus, How the Son of God Became a National Icon* (New York: Farrar, Straus, and Giroux, 2003).
[5] Mark A. Noll, *America's God, From Jonathan Edwards to Abraham Lincoln* (Oxford: Oxford University Press, 2002).
[6] Harold Bloom, *The American Religion* (New York: Simon and Schuster, 1992), 77–128, has Mormonism as "an America Original."

authentication of identity and sense of manifest destiny. Such an analysis, however, will take us beyond historical-textual study and into the realm of visions.[7]

To document Christ in Mormonism is, at the outset, to describe the group that set his title within its name. Initially founded in 1830 as The Church of Christ, this organization renamed itself The Church of Jesus Christ of Latter-day Saints in 1838.[8] In 1995 church leaders accentuated the "Jesus Christ" part of the title, giving it larger font size in key printed contexts, and in 2001 expressed a preference for secondary references to speak of "the Church of Jesus Christ."[9] After the death of the founding prophet, Joseph Smith in 1844, his movement split into numerous groups with the largest following Brigham Young westwards into what later became the State of Utah. Others remained behind, established themselves as The Reorganized Church of Jesus Christ of Latter Day Saints under the leadership of one of Joseph's sons, with a major centre at Independence, Missouri, but did not subscribe to many of the features that became characteristic of Utah Mormonism such as polygamy, baptism for the dead, and secret-sacred temple rituals of endowment that prepared believers to become gods in the afterlife.[10] Remaining more identifiably Protestant, they accepted the ordination of women to the priesthood in 1984 and in 2001 renamed themselves The Community of Christ. The Christ-focus in the names of both the LDS and RLDS groups over the turn of this century reflects the strong emphasis on Jesus in American religion at large. Here we consider only the LDS view because it is particularly distinctive, the RLDS-Community of Christ being essentially at one with mainstream Christian doctrines of Christ.

CHRIST AND THE PLAN OF SALVATION

The way a church sets Jesus within its doctrinal scheme affects how he appears in its liturgical expression, ethical perspectives, and social life.[11]

---

[7] Phillip H. Wiebe, *Visions of Jesus: Direct Encounters from the New Testament to Today* (Oxford: Oxford University Press, 1997).

[8] *Doctrine and Covenants* (115.3–4), hereafter abbreviated DC. This was a revelation from God to the prophet leader of the church, then Joseph Smith. Published by Church of Jesus Christ of Latter-day Saints, Salt Lake City, Utah.

[9] Douglas J. Davies, *An Introduction to Mormonism* (Cambridge: Cambridge University Press, 2003), 226.

[10] Conventional reference is to The Church of Jesus Christ of Latter-day Saints (LDS), and The Reorganized Church of Jesus Christ of Latter Day Saints (RLDS).

[11] Brigham Young University Studies Staff, *"We Rejoice in Christ": A Bibliography of LDS Writings on Jesus Christ and the New Testament, Brigham Young University Studies*, 34.3. (Provo, Ut.: Brigham Young University, 1994–1995).

For Mormons that framing key is called The Plan of Salvation,[12] a story of eternity and destiny pivoting around Jesus as the Christ, chosen by his heavenly father to bring about the salvation of humanity. It describes a heavenly council pondering the future state of a humanity that will disobey divine commandments and lie in need of salvation. Lucifer, an angel, offers to save humankind but was rejected by the heavenly father in favor of Jesus, whose approach would effect salvation at great personal cost while Lucifer's would abuse human free-agency in a scheme of compulsion. Angry at his rejection, Lucifer rebels, is cast from heaven, gains identity as Satan whose goal is to frustrate godliness and tempt humanity. Jesus, in "the meridian of time," is born of Mary as a result of direct physical intercourse with the heavenly father, who in LDS belief possesses a physical, though glorified, body. Jesus lives a life of perfect obedience – itself the dominant LDS theological virtue – and brings this to its consummation in his act of atonement for the sins of humankind: his resurrection then guarantees theirs.

GETHSEMANE

While acknowledging the sacrificial death of Jesus on the cross and the expression of divine love manifest there, Mormons traditionally accentuated the role of Jesus in Gethsemane to an even greater degree. In what came to be popularly called his "Gethsemane experience" LDS theology focused on the obedience by which Jesus entered into an experience of the sins of the world. This was a kind of interior, mental encounter with all evil from all times and places. It was a self-willed form of self-sacrifice of such a morally cataclysmic nature that it resulted in Jesus sweating drops of blood. While this blood can, partially at least, be equated with the blood of sacrifice, it also captures something of that human resolve that is fully set upon an ultimate moral goal which, in LDS terms, is understood in terms of obedience. This scene carries a further degree of symbolic and theological sense in Mormonism because it echoes and consummates the scene of the Heavenly Council when Jesus, the obedient son, offered a way of achieving atonement at the cost of personal suffering. Though not a Mormon usage, we can interpret this event as one in which we see a "proactive Christ,"

---

[12] Summary account in Chauncey C. Riddle, "Devils," in Daniel H. Ludlow (ed.), *Encyclopedia of Mormonism* (New York: Macmillan, 1992), 379–382. One popular story-form is Nephi Anderson, *Added Upon* (Independence, Mo.: Zion's Printing and Publishing Co, 1898). Cf. John Taylor, *Mediation and Atonement* (Salt Lake City: Deseret News, 1882; repr. Heber City, Ut.: Archive Publishers, 2000), 91–98.

in contrast to the more passive Christ of tradition who goes "as a lamb to the slaughter."[13] Some contemporary LDS reflection seems to redress this emphasis with a renewed stress upon Christ's crucifixion.[14]

Reflecting the longstanding Gethsemane scene, the LDS Church and its theology developed an activist ethic, favoring proactivism over passivity, and stressing that what the LDS Christ did in that Garden of Gethsemane set the standard for an LDS ethic of activism at large. To reinforce this point we find early Mormon portrayals of Christ as one of dynamic endeavor. Even in the period immediately following his "death" he does not "rest" but, rather, goes into the realm of spirits, to the "spirit-prison"[15] where he preaches his gospel of salvation to those awaiting it there. This is a kind of LDS version of the harrowing of hell but one that depicts Jesus more as a redemptive-missionary figure than in the *Christus Victor* mode of some traditional Christian theology where Jesus triumphs over evil and Satan.[16] This episode has also served popular LDS folk-belief as a way of explaining what may happen to other church leaders or, for example, to missionaries who die young. Their "death" is not pointless but deeply meaningful as they continue in salvation-related "activity," where "activity" is a social virtue in Mormonism.

SALVATION AND RESURRECTION

Salvation itself, however, is both a simple and a complex issue in Mormonism. It begins in the basic belief that, after making atonement in Gethsemane and at Calvary, Jesus experienced a resurrection, gained a glorified body, and guarantees a resurrection for all other people. This traditional Christian belief becomes more complex, however, in that his glorified body serves to reinforce the LDS theological affirmation that his heavenly father also possesses a glorified body. In other words the father and the son can now, in one sense, be more closely aligned with each other in terms of experience gained and status achieved. This factor is related to the canonical form of the First Vision of Joseph Smith in which both personages appear together, share a great likeness, and begin to set Joseph Smith's mind in the direction of new beginnings that will result in new

---

[13] Douglas J. Davies, *The Mormon Culture of Salvation* (Aldershot: Ashgate, 2000), 48–59.

[14] Andrew C. Skinner, *Golgotha* (Salt Lake City: Deseret Books, 2004).

[15] Sometimes viewed as a place of cleansing "before the resurrection." See Clyde J. Williams, "Telestial Kingdom," in Daniel H. Ludlow (ed.), *Encyclopedia of Mormonism* (New York: Macmillan, 1992), 1443.

[16] Gustaf Aulén, *Christus Victor: An Historical Study of Three Main Types of the Idea of the Atonement* (trans. A. G. Herbert; London: SPCK, 1953 [1930]).

resources of salvation in the form of the Church, Book of Mormon, novel revelations, rites, or ordinances.

In the simplest doctrinal terms salvation means freedom from sins and from death itself. Because Jesus was resurrected from the dead which, in Mormon terms, means that his spirit and body were conjoined and transformed so as to be glorified, his act of atonement guarantees the resurrection of every human being. It is, in this sense, that Mormon theology speaks of grace. It is by a pure act of grace that sins are forgiven, death conquered, and a new resurrected identity conferred. All this is devoid of any human effort. By grace all are resurrected. This is a subtle but vitally important theological point as far as understanding Mormonism by other Christian groups is concerned. It is after personal resurrection that the process of salvation becomes both more complex and of particular importance for understanding LDS Christology for, following resurrection, people are judged on the basis of how they lived their lives. They are "brought before the bar of God, to be judged according to our works."[17] Here, great emphasis is placed upon the freedom of each person in the necessity of repentance and the requirement that they devote their free agency to obedience in living according to divine commands, revelations, and the teachings and practices of the LDS Church. For those who died in their sins and who had hardened their hearts against God there remains the negative possibility of a "second death," a death to righteousness, whose traditional idea of a "lake of fire and brimstone" is made all the worse in that those entering it, having already been resurrected, are no longer able to "die": "seeing there is no more corruption."[18]

To each is given a reward commensurate with their effortful achievement, and this is expressed, positively, in terms of being given access to the three afterlife "degrees of glory" in, respectively, the highest Celestial, then the Terrestrial, and finally the Telestial Kingdoms. These kingdoms were conceptualized by Joseph Smith, following Pauline ideas, in terms of degrees of light and glory: the sun being greatest, followed by the moon and then the stars.[19] Entry into the Celestial glory is open only to temple-married and Melchizedek Priesthood-holding couples and, in that domain, they are said to benefit from the presence of the heavenly father. Those in the Terrestrial Kingdom, including many who lived honorably but did not strive as they might have done, are said to experience the presence

---

[17] Alma 12.12. Alma 12 stresses the place of the "plan of redemption."
[18] Alma 12.18.
[19] See Paul in 1 Cor. 15.40–41, though Smith seems to coin the word "telestial."

not of the heavenly father, but of the son, of Jesus Christ himself.[20] This gradation in which Jesus comes after his heavenly father reflects not simply a hierarchical attitude within LDS organization, but the more important principle of progressive development in which achievement and advancement relate to a kind of spiritual-cosmic stature. In this the heavenly father has a greater degree of experience than Jesus as the divine son. Jesus, however, is not only the son of the father, he is also the "elder brother" of all other people. This motif of elder brother stresses the importance of family ideals within LDS theology and practice, and Prothero sees it as expressing an attitude that holds Jesus "at arm's length," with Latter-day Saints "approaching their Savior with at least a modicum of formality."[21] To this idea we will return below, for the moment we simply note the relative difference in status between the divine father and son of a kind that would attract criticism from mainstream orthodox teaching on the equality of persons in the Trinity.

JESUS AND TRINITY

One problem surrounding any discussion of such LDS doctrine concerns the significant differences that exist between the *Book of Mormon*, published in 1830, and post-1830 texts that appear as *The Doctrine and Covenants* and the *Pearl of Great Price*.[22] For the *Book of Mormon* is, essentially, an application of Protestant theological views to an innovative epic that links ancient Israel and America. It traces the rise and fall of migrant communities in the new world through a theological currency of faith, repentance, disbelief, and wickedness, all in relation to prophets and the future coming of Christ. Indeed, Christ is so central to the book that it is perfectly understandable that the Church has, more recently, come to speak of it, and sub-title it, as "Another Testament of Jesus Christ." The other "Standard Works" just mentioned, however, take some quite different theological directions, and seem to be driven by a variety of philosophical and religious ideas of more speculative kinds.[23] The *Book of Mormon* view of Jesus is, itself, often impelled by central biblical perspectives, not least by key themes of John's Gospel as, for example, in a text reckoned to be the

---

[20] DC (76.77–78).

[21] Stephen Prothero's chapter on LDS in his *American Jesus*, 161–199, is entitled "Mormon Elder Brother."

[22] All published by The Church of Jesus Christ of Latter-day Saints.

[23] John L. Brooke, *The Refiner's Fire: The Making of Mormon Cosmology, 1644–1844* (Cambridge: Cambridge University Press, 1994), explores European Hermeticism as a potential influence on Joseph Smith.

words of Jesus during his post-resurrection appearance in America when he says: "whoso believeth in me believeth in the Father also; and unto him will the Father bear record of me, for He will visit him with fire and with the Holy Ghost . . . for the Father, and I, and the Holy Ghost are one."[24] These biblical expressions of Father, Son, and Spirit relationships have been more influential within Mormon understandings of Jesus and the Trinity than have the post-scriptural creeds of Christendom. When Mormons did set out to explain the threefold relation in any detail they tended to focus on the Father and Son as the two embodied "personages" of deity whose unanimity was, itself, the work of the Holy Spirit. This perspective is very clear in *The Lectures on Faith*: these assert that "there are two personages who constitute the great, matchless, governing and supreme power over all things," viz., the "Father and the Son," while the Spirit is described in terms of being of "the same mind with the Father, which mind is the Holy Spirit."[25] It is this feature of the Spirit as the basis of the unanimity between Father and Son, and not as a self-contained "personage," that emerges as a crucial aspect of LDS Trinitarian dynamics that would, probably, be deemed inadequate by traditional Trinitarians for whom a "unanimity" would be quite different from a shared "substance."

Historical Trinitarian orthodoxy emphasizes the equality of Father, Son, and Holy Spirit and opposes any inequality or subordination of one to another. As already mentioned, for reasons of progressive development, Mormonism sees hierarchical difference as perfectly proper, especially given the priority it accords to the family model of relationships and to its particular ideological view of the cosmos itself. In short LDS philosophical theology starts from the basic assumption that everything has always existed in some form or other. All "matter is spirit," albeit in different stages of development or "refinement"; this means that instead of talking of creation Mormons speak of organization. Because the gods organize preexisting material, the traditional Christian idea that God created things "from nothing," or *ex nihilo*, is rendered inappropriate. That *ex nihilo* motif, however, also served the philosophical-theological purpose of differentiating between God and the things God created. And this is what constitutes the core of traditional Christian doctrine on the Holy Trinity and Christ's place in it in respect of all other "things." Traditionally, all three members of the Trinity are reckoned to be constituted of the same divine "stuff" or, in more technical terms, they are all "of one substance." It is that "substance"

[24] 3 Nephi 35–36. Compare with John 14.22; 15.26; 17.21.
[25] Joseph Smith, *Lectures on Faith* (repr.; Salt Lake City: Deseret Books, 1985 [1835]), 53–54.

that distinguishes the "nature" of each of the three persons of the Trinity from all other created entities. Accordingly, the nature of the "origin" of the divine Son is accounted for by the term "begotten" and not "created." Were the Son to be "created" he would not be of the same substance as the father and thus would not be divine. The key theological question over the traditional doctrine of the Incarnation following from this asked how a human being could also be divine or, conversely, how a "person" who was "of one substance with the Father" could also be human? The solution to this problem was to assert that Jesus possessed two natures in one person: "Godhead and Manhood, were joined together in one Person, never to be divided."[26] Just how that might be was much debated within Christian tradition, but that it was so became a mark of orthodoxy.

The LDS outlook is quite different from this. As already intimated, all things have always existed and are, essentially, of the same "stuff," albeit at different stages of development or "refinement." This applies in particular to the notion of "intelligences." This concept describes the eternally existing basis of a process by which the heavenly father ultimately shaped his "spirit children." In a form of "begetting" the divine father is said to have, as it were, looked about him in the eternal world and seen these intelligences that were less developed than himself and was, in some way, able to transform them into more self-aware or purposeful agents. Some would also speak of a role for a divine mother figure in this LDS process of "begetting" which turned such "intelligences" into "spirit-children."

Jesus is distinctive in that he was the first-begotten of these spirit-children of his heavenly father. He was followed by very many others, not least by Lucifer,[27] who disobeyed and fell from his heavenly "first estate," as did a third of the heavenly population. These fallen spirit entities have never, however, had the benefit accorded to spirit-children who remained obedient to the heavenly father in their "first estate" of the preexistence and who were given the opportunity to be born as human babies. In LDS theological anthropology a spirit comes to a human body and then becomes the integrated entity of a living soul.[28] This use of "soul" differs from conventional Greek-informed conceptions. When taking a body in this human or "second estate," people have the opportunity to extend their loyal obedience to God that once they showed during their "first estate." At death, the "soul" is broken into its body and spirit components that will be

---

[26] Article 2 of The Thirty Nine Articles of the Church of England represents this orthodoxy.

[27] Lucifer is also described as a pre-mortal Angel. Here I assume Lucifer was a spirit-child of the heavenly father and not some entity of a different kind from that of Jesus.

[28] Following Gen. 2.7 (AV) where the breath of life makes dust-formed man into "a living soul."

united in a glorified body at the time of its appropriate resurrection.[29] All human beings, therefore, share with Jesus in being of the same substance as the heavenly father, they differ only in degree of development. This means that there is no need for any discussion of Jesus possessing "two natures" in one person and renders the normal language of traditional creeds redundant.

Consonant with this LDS view is the further belief that all people are "gods in embryo," and that the goal of eternity, of humanity's "third estate" after death, is to engage in a progressive development of divine quality of existence. This is expressed in terms of men and women being kings and queens, gods and goddesses as they rule their ever increasing family-kingdoms and rule over future worlds. This expansionist goal underlies the teachings that inform certain temple rituals and establish Mormonism not only as a religion of death-conquest, through the grace-governed resurrection, guaranteed through Christ's act of atonement, but also as a religion of eternal opportunity grounded in each person's obedient and reward-attracting achievements. The scheme of development from eternal intelligences into God's spirit-children, then into human beings, and then into both resurrected and glorified beings is all of a piece in a scheme of ontological progressive development. It is a process of glorification, where "glory" is a major LDS concept embracing many ideas aligned with divine attributes. This process makes more immediate sense of deification than that traditional form of Christian orthodoxy identified as *theosis*, a process of sanctification by which the believer comes so to share in the life of Christ that human nature begins to engage in some way with the divine nature of God.[30] There is a sense in which traditional Christian formulations so divided God from humanity that great effort has to be made in bringing them together. This also has consequences for ideas of the afterlife and, also, raises the issue of worship. At first glance this may sound an odd problem, especially if it were to be posed in the form of the question, "Do Mormons worship God?" The obvious answer is a resounding affirmative as the music, hymns, choirs, prayers, and other activities of Mormon spirituality indicate. But a second thought introduces a qualification, for temple rites ascribe great significance to the activity of believers and to their covenanting with God in the process of pursuing eternal glories of their own. More theologically speaking, Orthodox Christianity grounds worship, as a primary activity, in the very distinction between man and God. It

---

[29] Faithful Saints anticipate the advantage of the "first resurrection" when they may "reign with Christ"; others experience the later, "second resurrection" (Rev. 20.4–5).

[30] As alluded to in Rom. 8.30, Eph. 1.10, and Col. 1.27.

is because humans are not "of one substance" with God, but are redeemed creatures, that worship is evoked. It is also precisely because Jesus possesses the divine nature that he, too, can be worshiped. To worship anything of lesser nature than God is to engage in idolatry. As for the afterlife, that has, regularly, been couched in terms of a heavenly worship. This, however, is not quite the same in Mormonism, where the afterlife is said to be framed by the various presences of Father and Son in Celestial and Terrestrial Kingdoms, and of the Holy Spirit in the Telestial Kingdom.[31] A key feature of the LDS afterlife lies in the ongoing purposeful activity of priesthood holders in developing their own kingdoms and become increasingly filled with glory themselves. It is at this stage of LDS theology that the role of Christ would seem to change and not to be an essential focus of worship as an integral aspect of celestial progression.

CREEDS, TRUTH, AND STATUS

Having considered Christ in Trinitarian terms, it remains to consider the status and role of creeds and their ambiguous status in Mormon life. The prime problem lies in the LDS view that, in response to disobedience, God removed the priesthoods and full understanding of true doctrine from the earth shortly after the first generation of Christians, only restoring them in the 1820s to 1840s. The period of creedal development in the second to fourth centuries thus coincided with a Great Apostasy. Nowhere was the effect of that period of error greater than when later Christian churches spoke, for example, of God as "one living and true God, everlasting, without body, parts, or passions."[32] Many LDS leaders deemed that incredible, denying that God, as the divine father, possessed a body. This antipathy towards creeds as doctrinal instruments was, however, set against the advantage of creeds as a mark of Christian authenticity. Mormons sought and seek a status as authentic Christians, indeed as *the* authentic form of Christianity and this makes it difficult both to reject and own creeds at one and the same time.

 Here we encounter another dimension of authenticity, that which takes authenticity as a driving feature of American life and asks how that may be related to Christ. Certainly, the paths to authenticity are numerous. They include the invoking of tradition and sacramental authority as in

---

[31] DC 76.86.
[32] In the first of The Thirty Nine Articles of the Church of England. Much criticized by LDS thinkers, cf. B. H. Roberts, *The Mormon Doctrine of Deity: The Roberts–Van Der Donckt Discussion* (repr.; Salt Lake City: Signature Books, 1998 [1903]), 11.

Catholicism and of true biblical interpretation associated with spiritual rebirth as in Protestant Evangelicalism. Mormonism incorporated elements of both when pursuing the path of Restoration and arguing that it possessed the true authority of divine priesthoods and important texts that enhanced biblical understanding. In all of this Mormon theology depended upon the prior existence of a Christianity deemed inauthentic. This also meant that the place of Christ in Mormonism was and remains a contested place. How could Jesus in Mormonism be more authentic than the Jesus of other churches?

CHRIST IN AMERICA

It is here that a vision of Christ makes an importance appearance in the religious experience of the boy Joseph Smith who became the Prophet, Seer, and Revelator of the church now so identified with him.[33] Mormons stress the importance of the First Vision to Joseph dated to the spring of 1820. Responding to the prayers of a confused teenager pondering which church was the true church, itself a quandary of authenticity, God the Father and Jesus his Son appeared in a vision of light above young Joseph's head. One indicated that the other was the Son and told Joseph to listen to him. So it was that Jesus made his appearance in America and a youthful prophetic call began. Instead of having a true church pointed out to him, Joseph was told that all erred and that he must await true manifestations. These would include the reported discovery of ancient scriptures telling how peoples migrated from the Holy Land to America and set up civilizations there about 600 BCE. Their "American" life resembled Old Testament-like patterns of obedience and disobedience in respect of prophets and led to their ultimate demise, except for the native Americans whose descendents they were. Central to that epic narrative which constitutes the Book of Mormon is Jesus Christ. It is not divided into anything like an Old and New Testament so that, in the era before his birth, Christ is much discussed as the promised Savior. The Book of Jacob, for example, which LDS reckon to date from the fifth or sixth century before Christ, justifies the production of written records with these words: "that they may know that we knew of Christ . . . many hundreds of years before his coming." It also speaks of "the atonement of Christ, his Only Begotten Son, that ye may obtain a resurrection."[34] The book does, however, tell of a crucial appearance of

---

[33] For visions in the USA, see Ann Taves, *Fits, Trances and Visions* (Princeton, N.J.: Princeton University Press, 1999).
[34] Jacob 4.4, 11.

Jesus in America at the very time of his resurrection in the Holy Land.[35] At this American first advent he appointed twelve disciples, paralleling those made in the biblical Gospels.[36] However, just as there was a great apostasy in the Jewish-Christian Holy Land, so too an apostasy befell this American-Jewish civilization whose last named survivor, Mormon, made final records of its sad demise that would remain hidden until God restored them to Joseph's care, centuries later.

Joseph, in his new experience of Jesus and the Father, set about establishing a church whose initial message was millenarian, Adventist, and Jesus-focused. Its goal was to call all to repent, believe, and gather with Joseph to await Christ's second coming to the world and, especially, to America as the base for his millennial reign. From its inception in 1830 this call became a successful venture, not least because of thousands of Europeans who migrated as converts to swell the numbers of local Americans who aligned themselves with Joseph's visionary call, restored truths, and newly produced Book of Mormon. Much preaching on the evils of the day and the signs of the times kept Jesus' advent to the fore. In all of this the focus on Jesus resembled that of other Protestant Adventist groups. Christ would come again on the clouds of heaven and the faithful would be blessed as they reigned with him and, finally, witness an ultimate conquest of evil and the establishing of the reign of God.

However, differences became increasingly apparent in the years more immediately preceding Joseph Smith's killing in 1844. While initial Mormonism was scriptural, largely Protestant, and Christ-focused, Joseph now introduced a variety of novel ideas as part of the restoration of the fullness of truth as he believed it to be. Some have seen his experience of Freemasonry and its initiatory ritual and lodges as deeply influential on these changes and on the new ritual-style Mormonism that emerged.[37] Prothero speaks of "the gradual transformation of Mormonism from a religion of words into a religion of rites" as not only distancing it "from historical Christianity," but as also leaving "little room in the religion for Jesus."[38] But this is only partially true and is, perhaps, too influenced by one image of Jesus, for while a "religion of rites" does emerge and become dramatically important from the later 1840s, a religion that accompanied the Saints westward and into the settlement of Utah, it was a religion operating within the

---

[35] 3 Nephi 11.7–41.

[36] Some LDS believed that he also made twelve apostles amongst the Lost Tribes of Israel.

[37] David John Buerger, *The Mysteries of Godliness: A History of Mormon Temple Worship* (San Francisco: Smith Research Associates, 1994).

[38] Prothero, *American Jesus*, 183.

church deemed to be Christ's own church. The alliance of Jesus Christ and church qualified the significance of the title "Jesus Christ," preparing for an institutional dimension to the LDS Christ.

JESUS AS JEHOVAH AND FATHER

From the 1840s this Church of Jesus Christ of Latter-day Saints increasingly became a sub-culture firmly located in its new territory, existing in varying degrees of tension with mainstream American politics and Christian creeds. A sense of itself as a kind of "ancient Israel" with Brigham Young as its "American Moses"[39] drove Mormonism forward, not least in respect of polygamy. Here was a chosen people which had suffered persecution and had undergone a form of wilderness wandering before entering a desert that became their promised land. Priesthoods, temples, fathers viewed as patriarchs and wives as "mothers in Israel," and ritual workers deemed to be "Saviors in Zion," all conduced to a view of Jesus that took his identity in new directions, most especially into being "Jehovah." To identify Jesus as the divine figure identified as Jehovah in the Authorized Version of the Bible was an unusual move since broad Christian views tended to associate ancient Israel with God the Father, the time and life of Jesus with the divine Son, and the ongoing period of Christian church history with the Holy Spirit.[40] This idea of "dispensations" or periods of special divine activity helped many ordinary Christians link the abstract notion of the Trinity with more narrative approaches to their faith. The conceptual shift adopted by the LDS created a dissonance that helped form a theological boundary marker for the Restoration movement that was Mormonism. It also gave a new significance to Jesus. Elder Theodore M. Burton expressed this quite clearly in a way that brings together the issue of the heavenly father's begetting of spirit children with that of Christ's divine status.

Jesus was the firstborn of the spirit children of God and that as Jehovah, the Creator, He was the god of this earth before he became manifest in the flesh as Jesus Christ. He is the eternal God of this earth who gave His laws and commandments to the prophets of old before he came to earth as the Son of Man.[41]

---

[39] Leonard J. Arrington entitled his magisterial biography, *Brigham Young: American Moses* (Urbana: University of Illinois Press, 1985).

[40] Though not on Mormonism, but for a distinctive American cultural critique, see Harold Bloom, *Jesus and Yahweh: The Divine Names* (New York: Riverhead Books, 2005): "Jesus and Yahweh are such different personalities" (p. 180). Cf. Thomas J. Jenkins, *The Character of God* (New York: Oxford University Press, 1997), 72, who treats Harriet Beecher Stowe's "remarkable strategy" of declaring that "all appearances of Jehovah in the Old Testament were really 'pre-appearances' of Christ."

[41] *Millennial Star* 131.3 (March 1969), 50 (a Mormon journal published from 1840 to 1970).

The status accorded to Jesus in this reference, and it does not stand alone, is extremely high and, effectively, replaces the "God" figure that much practical Christianity had accepted for millennia and in whose terms the Father was replaced by the Son. In nineteenth-century LDS eyes that would not, of course, be the best way of expressing the issue since it operates on too narrow a view of deity and the cosmos. For Mormons this world was but one of myriads of worlds, and the issue of the number of gods that related to those worlds was open. God, the Father of Jesus, had far more with which to concern himself than simply this earth. Indeed, a feature of LDS religion that contrasts with the early Christian centuries, when doctrines were generated and creeds composed, is precisely that of scope. Ancient Israel and New Testament Christianity tend to be this-worldly in their theologies of salvation, though the latter brings a strong creative role into the attributes of Jesus as the divine Son through whom "God . . . created the world";[42] it also sees cosmic consequences arising from salvation.[43] Mormons, however, thought much more in terms of multiple universes and future realms, in which glorified human beings would, themselves, be gods. This differed from the traditional sense of a future kingdom of God whether in some heavenly domain or on earth; in either case the focus fell singly on God.[44] What Mormonism did was to highlight the role of Jesus as the God of this earth. This integrated role served to unite "Old" and "New" Testament themes in an even stronger way than had been the case in dispensationalist Christian traditions. This process was not without its difficulties, however, not least because the English word "Jehovah" largely came into use through the Authorized Version of 1611 with its very selective use of "Jehovah" to render the Hebrew tetragrammaton YHWH (or JHWH).[45] A sense of piety towards the divine name had long made it customary for Jews to say *Adonai* (meaning Lord) when the text had *YHWH* (perhaps originally spoken as Yahweh, Jahveh or even as Jah). Later, vowel-sound marks for *Adonai* were placed with the consonants for YHWH in a combination that signaled and led to the selective use of the word Jehovah, even though the Authorized Version often used LORD or GOD instead. Historically speaking, at least one analogous case occurs in Richard Carlile's sermon at Cambridge when speaking of how "Jesus Iehoua" (*sic*) preached the Gospel to Adam during Christ's Descension into hell. Just how these issues relate to the use of the word Jehovah in Book of Mormon texts, reckoned by LDS dating to

---

[42] John 1.3; 1 Cor. 8.6; and Heb. 1.2.   [43] Rom. 8.19–23.   [44] Rev. 5.13.

[45] Richard Carlile, *A Discourse Concerning two Divine Positions, That the Souls of the Faithful Fathers Deceased Before Christ Went Immediately to Heaven . . . Touching the Descension of our Saviour Christ into Hell* (London: Roger Ward, 1582), 73.

belong to the sixth century BC,[46] is a hermeneutical issue for others to explore.

The other title used for Jesus that is problematic for non-LDS Christians is that of "Father." One route for this comes from the belief in the similarity between Jesus and his heavenly father following Christ's death and resurrection so that, Jesus "is today a Being like unto the Father in all essential characteristics."[47] Other reasons are connected with the desire to interpret and harmonize LDS scriptures with broader theological interpretations. Texts such as, "Behold I am Jesus Christ, I am the Father and the Son,"[48] led the First Presidency to make a Doctrinal Exposition on this topic in 1916. This explained how Jesus served as "the executive of the Father (Elohim), in the work of creation." Being "the Creator," Jesus is "consistently called the Father of heaven and earth," and is "very properly called the Eternal Father of heaven and earth."[49] Similarly, Jesus is "Father of the righteous . . . through the Second Birth, the Baptismal Regeneration," as also when he represents "Elohim His Father in power and authority." What is more, this status can apply to his pre-mortal state as, for example, in his "labors as a disembodied spirit in the realms of the dead."[50] These many titles symbolize the fact that authority and function are closely allied within LDS thought and emphasize the need for contextual interpretation. So, too, with Christ's marital status. The emphasis placed on kinship, marriage, and eternal families inevitably invited consideration of his eternal status. "Jesus Christ, as Lord of Lords and King of Kings must have a noble race in the heavens, or upon the earth, or else he can never be as great . . . as the scriptures declare."[51] Indeed, one LDS folk tradition accepts that Jesus did in fact marry, as one sermon expressed it: "we say it was Jesus Christ who was married [at Cana to the Marys (*sic* plural) and Martha] whereby he could see his seed before he was crucified."[52]

REMEMBERING THE SON

More important for everyday LDS faith is the focus on Christ that comes in regular congregational activities, especially the Sunday meeting when, amidst the hymns, prayers, readings, and testimonies of church members,

---

[46] See 2 Nephi 22.2. Within a longer passage verses 1–6, that mirrors Isa. 12.1–6.
[47] James Talmage, *Jesus the Christ* (repr.; Salt Lake City: Deseret Books, 1962 [1915]), 39.
[48] Ether 3.14. See also Mosiah 15.10–13.
[49] D. M. Reay and S. Vonda, *Selected Manifestations* (Oakland, Cal.: n.p., 1985), 188–189.
[50] *Ibid.*, 192.   [51] *Millennial Star* 14.29 (1852), 455.
[52] James H. Snowden, *The Truth about Mormonism* (Philadelphia: Westminster Press, 1926), 129–130, a passage referring to Orson Hyde Sermon 3.

there are two fixed prayers said as blessings in the Sacrament Meeting, before the bread and then the water are distributed for all to eat. Two teenage priests from within the Aaronic Priesthood say these prayers. Kneeling at a table prepared with a cloth and holding the elements of bread and water they address "God, the Eternal Father" in the name of his "Son, Jesus Christ," asking that the elements be blessed "to the souls" of those who partake, that they may eat and drink "in remembrance" of the body and the blood "of Thy Son," and that "they may witness unto thee, O God, the Eternal Father, that they do always remember him, that they may have his Spirit to be with them. Amen."[53]

There is certainly a threefoldness of divine personages involved in this liturgically contextualized prayer. Just how to interpret the dynamic relations expressed in it is not easy. At its simplest it stresses the overall status of the Eternal Father and a very strong memorialist location of Jesus Christ who is to be remembered. That sense of historical location as someone existing in the past is, however, immediately complemented by reference to "his Spirit" as that which is desired to be "with them" in the present. Indeed, a sense of the presence of the Spirit holds a crucial place in the LDS emotions of spirituality. To "feel," to "sense," to be aware of an interior presence or motivation is a mark of religious identity in Mormonism which, popularly, speaks of such things as a "burning in the breast," as an indication of divine interaction. In practical terms this sense of presence frames the doctrinal place of Christ in LDS life and is both fostered and expressed by the hymns sung at the Sacrament Meeting.

CHRISTOLOGICAL INTIMACY AND DISTANCE

One remaining topic over the place of Jesus Christ in Mormonism concerns a certain intimacy and distance that may, perhaps, be best approached in terms of a regular Testimony Meeting aligned with the Sacrament Meeting at which it is common to hear members speak, often with that emotion just mentioned, of aspects of personal or family life and of what their church membership has meant in terms of support, care and love. Incidents are specified and feelings expressed before concluding the testimony with an assertion of *knowing* this to be the true church, its leadership to be authentic, that Joseph Smith is a prophet of God, all affirmed by saying "this in the name of Jesus Christ. Amen." The congregation responds with its "Amen." The significance of such a testimony in relation to the paradox

---

[53] DC 20.76–79. See 3 Nephi 18.11.

of intimacy and distance is that the emotional sense of intimacy with the divine and the community seems to be allied with the Holy Spirit as that Spirit operates within the true church which is the Church of Jesus Christ. The "distant" factor is the church organization, including the fact of a living prophet and twelve apostles who are, in some sense, regarded as nearer the mind and will of Christ. In practice the intimate element of the emotional life of faith combines with the more distant organization of the church, yet there is some dynamic tension present here that is reflected in Prothero's assessment that, "Although Mormons have gravitated in recent years towards more intimate relationships with Jesus as a companion and friend, most continue to hold him at arm's length, approaching their Savior with at least a modicum of formality."[54] He interprets this formality in terms of Jesus' status as "Elder Brother" within LDS theology. And while there is some truth in that, a wider issue concerns the very nature of a church organization in relation to its members, for there is a sense in which Jesus Christ is inseparable from the church organization as such, and there is, inevitably, a formality inherent in attitudes of members to the overarching institution to which they belong, and which confers a deep sense of identity upon them. Here a comparison with wider Christianity might be illuminating in that, for example, many a Protestant evangelist seeks to convert people to Jesus Christ, emphasizing that "companion and friend" element of the Savior who died for an individual sinner and who may now be invited into the repentant sinner's "heart." The spiritual rebirth language of conversion enhances notions of intimacy as well as helping to generate that authenticity discussed earlier. While such an evangelist would probably not worry over which denomination the convert joined, as long as it was Evangelical in some way, that would not be possible in Mormonism: salvation and exaltation lie within processes of the Church of Jesus Christ of Latter-day Saints and not in some private alliance with Jesus. The fact that a small number of Mormons have begun to focus on a more privatized intimacy with Jesus within the overall structure of the church is, however, an interesting factor, perhaps related to the profile of that idea in American Evangelicalism at large, and perhaps because the church is now large and powerful enough in the USA that it no longer needs to be overly careful about Jesus-language, especially in "born-again" terms, as a boundary marker between it and others.[55] But also relevant may

---

[54] Prothero, *American Jesus*, 198.

[55] See Richard N. Ostling and Joan K. Ostling, *Mormon America* (San Francisco: HarperSanFrancisco, 1999) for some recent engagements of Mormon and Protestant Evangelical discussions. Also, Donald W. Musser and David L. Paulsen (eds.), *Mormonism in Dialogue with Contemporary Christian Theologies* (Macon, Ga.: Mercer University Press, 2007).

be the pastoral needs of people aware of their imperfections in a church with high demands and for whom more familiar Protestant-like accounts of grace, acceptance, and divine love may find ready application.[56]

Still, many older Mormons attest to the fact that the "born-again" idiom was alien to their tradition. This is understandable in the context of those whose spirituality comes to circle the core of LDS life in the temple ordinances where the role of Christ is much enhanced, where he plays a dramatic role, and where they engage with him in symbolic terms. There they are taken back into the narrative of the Plan of Salvation with its dramatic portrayal of world-organization, fall, and promised restoration and engage in establishing covenant relationships of their own amidst these divine figures of father, son, and other key players including Lucifer. The stage is full, and church members come to be counted amongst this extensive list of *dramatis personae*, mindful of their own destiny as deities. The daily reminder of this is the temple garment worn under ordinary clothes and not, for example, a cross around the neck.

This almost trivial comparison brings us to a final reflection couched in the words of LDS artist, James Christensen, who once spoke of how "we each invent our own image of the Savior," whilst acknowledging that "artists are expected to work within" those images.[57] This chapter has outlined numerous conceptual images of Jesus evident within the Mormon Christological kaleidoscope that is, itself, the narrative Plan of Salvation. Begotten from an eternal intelligence in the pre-mortal world by his heavenly father and born on earth through the physical intercourse of that father with Mary, he is the volunteering Savior-Son. Within the strong kinship-rooted church he is also deemed both a father and an elder brother while, as the prime God of this world he is identified both with the Jehovah of Israel and the Christian Adventist Messiah. Instead of his expected return on heavenly clouds, the Latter-day Saints developed an earthly desert kingdom out of which emerged a church that spread Zion across the world. Within this ecclesial-bureaucratic expansion Christ has come to serve a double function as both a resource for personal piety and as an executive figure mediated by a leadership hierarchy. In all this, the genius of early Mormonism created such a deep pool of potential orientations to Jesus Christ as to provide future generations with many adaptive possibilities of theological exploration.

[56] See Stephen E. Robinson, *Believing Christ* (Salt Lake City: Deseret Book Company, 1992). Robert L. Millett, *Christ Centred Living* (Salt Lake City: Bookcraft, 1994); Robert L. Millett, *A Different Jesus: The Christ of the Latter-Day Saints* (Cambridge: Eerdmans, 2005).

[57] James C. Christensen, "That's not my Jesus: An Artist's Personal Perspective on Images of Christ," *Brigham Young University Studies* 39.3 (2000), 7–17, 11.

BIBLIOGRAPHY

Anderson, Nephi, *Added Upon* (Independence, Mo.: Zion's Printing and Publishing Co., 1898).

Arrington, Leonard J., *Brigham Young: American Moses* (Urbana: University of Illinois Press, 1985).

Aulén, Gustaf, *Christus Victor: An Historical Study of Three Main Types of the Idea of the Atonement* (trans. A. G. Herbert; London: SPCK, 1953 [1930]).

Bloom, Harold, *Jesus and Yahweh: The Divine Names* (New York: Riverhead Books, 2005).

   The American Religion (New York: Simon and Schuster, 1992).

Brigham Young University Studies Staff, *"We Rejoice in Christ": A Bibliography of LDS Writings on Jesus Christ and the New Testament, Brigham Young University Studies* 34.3 (Provo, Ut.: Brigham Young University, 1994–1995).

Brooke, John L., *The Refiner's Fire: The Making of Mormon Cosmology, 1644–1844* (Cambridge: Cambridge University Press, 1994).

Buerger, David John, *The Mysteries of Godliness: A History of Mormon Temple Worship* (San Francisco: Smith Research Associates, 1994).

Carlile, Richard, *A Discourse Concerning Two Divine Positions, That the Souls of the Faithful Fathers Deceased before Christ Went Immediately to Heaven... Touching the Descension of our Saviour Christ into Hell* (London: Roger Ward, 1582).

Christensen, James C., "That's not my Jesus: An Artist's Personal Perspective on Images of Christ," *Brigham Young University Studies* 39.3 (2000), 7–17.

Davies, Douglas J., *An Introduction to Mormonism* (Cambridge: Cambridge University Press, 2003).

   The Mormon Culture of Salvation (Aldershot: Ashgate, 2000).

Fox, Richard, *Jesus in America: Personal Savior, Cultural Hero, National Obsession* (San Francisco: Harper-Collins, 2004).

Jenkins, Thomas J., *The Character of God* (New York: Oxford University Press, 1997).

Müller, Max, *My Autobiography* (London: Longman Green, 1901).

Millett, Robert L., *A Different Jesus: The Christ of the Latter-Day Saints* (Cambridge: Eerdmans, 2005).

   Christ Centred Living (Salt Lake City: Bookcraft, 1994).

Müller, Max, *My Autobiography* (London: Longman Green, 1901).

Musser, Donald W. and David L. Paulsen (eds.), *Mormonism in Dialogue with Contemporary Christian Theologies* (Macon, Ga.: Mercer University Press, 2007).

Noll, Mark A., *America's God, From Jonathan Edwards to Abraham Lincoln* (Oxford: Oxford University Press, 2002).

Ostling, Richard N. and Joan K. Ostling, *Mormon America* (San Francisco: HarperSanFrancisco, 1999).

Prothero, Stephen, *American Jesus, How the Son of God Became a National Icon* (New York: Farrar, Straus, and Giroux, 2003).

Reay, D. M. and S. Vonda, *Selected Manifestations* (Oakland, Cal.: n.p., 1985).

Riddle, Chauncey C., "Devils," in Daniel H. Ludlow (ed.), *Encyclopedia of Mormonism* (New York: Macmillan, 1992), 379–382.

Roberts, B. H., *The Mormon Doctrine of Deity: The Roberts–Van Der Donckt Discussion* (repr.; Salt Lake City: Signature Books, 1998 [1903]).

Robinson, Stephen E., *Believing Christ* (Salt Lake City: Deseret Book Company, 1992).

Sanders, E. P., *The Historical Figure of Jesus* (London: Penguin Books 1993).

Skinner, Andrew C., *Golgotha* (Salt Lake City: Deseret Books, 2004).

Smith, Joseph, *Lectures on Faith* (repr.; Salt Lake City: Deseret Books, 1985 [1835]).

Snowden, James H., *The Truth about Mormonism* (Philadelphia: Westminster Press, 1926).

Talmage, James, *Jesus the Christ* (repr.; Salt Lake City: Deseret Books, 1962 [1915]).

Taves, Ann, *Fits, Trances and Visions* (Princeton, N.J.: Princeton University Press, 1999).

Taylor, John, *Mediation and Atonement* (Salt Lake City: Deseret News, 1882; repr.; Heber City, Ut.: Archive Publishers, 2000).

Wiebe, Phillip H., *Visions of Jesus: Direct Encounters from the New Testament to Today* (Oxford: Oxford University Press, 1997).

Williams, Clyde J., "Telestial Kingdom," in Daniel H. Ludlow (ed.), *Encyclopedia of Mormonism* (New York: Macmillan, 1992), 1443.

CHAPTER II

The conception of Christ in the Theosophical tradition

James A. Santucci

CHRIST AND MESSIAH

One of the most intensely scrutinized terms and concepts in many religious traditions has been the understanding and implication of the Greek designation "Christ(os)" or its Hebraic-Aramaic-Greek form, "Messiah." The accepted orthodox doctrine adopted by the church – that Christ Jesus was true God and true Man – only came about after sustained and intense discussions within the Christian community. Contrary to orthodox teaching, Jesus is viewed in Theosophy as human – not an ordinary human, but rather an exceptional teacher whose gifts and charisma were due to a power that "overshadowed" him at a specific moment in his life. This power, the "Christos," furthermore, does not fuse with Jesus but remains distinct from him, so that toward the end of the life of Jesus, the power departs leaving Jesus at the mercy of his captors.

Theosophical teaching departs even further from the orthodox view when the leading writer of the Theosophical movement, Helena P. Blavatsky (1831–1891), poses the question whether the Jesus of the first century CE is indeed the overshadowed teacher. In her opinion there is ample evidence to suggest that someone identified as Jesus, the teacher-adept who disclosed an ancient wisdom that both antedated and transcended orthodox Christianity, himself appeared much earlier, in the second century BCE to be exact.

The wisdom taught by Jesus is a wisdom located not in the establishment doctrines of the church, but in what might be termed heterodox Christianity. In Theosophical terminology, esoteric Christianity is the designated phrase, in opposition to exoteric or orthodox Christianity. This perception of a binary teaching within Christianity ultimately reflects the teaching of Pythagoras as described by St. Hippolytus of Rome.[1] Therein, it is written

---

[1] St. Hippolytus of Rome, *Refutation of all Heresies* I.2. Online at http://www.newadvent.org/fathers/050101.htm. Internet sites quoted here were last checked and active on 11 August 2008.

that Pythagoras divided his pupils into esoteric and exoteric classes, with the former receiving the advanced doctrines and the latter consigned only a watered-down version of the teaching. A more recent discussion – one that may have been familiar to Theosophists, especially the most prominent of Theosophists, H. P. Blavatsky – appears in Godfrey Higgins' *Anacalypsis*, who repeats this division between exoteric and esoteric religion, and Esoteric Christianity in particular. Therein, he writes of Clement of Alexandria mentioning "that the rudiments of celestial wisdom, taught by Christ, may be found in the philosophy of the Greeks; this is Esoteric Christianity."[2]

Theosophical teaching does not reinterpret the orthodox Christian teachings on Jesus and the Christos, but rather claims to base its teachings on sources that are older and, by implication, more genuine, unsullied by the misinformation that has entered into the Christian mainstream over the millennia.

THEOSOPHY

Theosophy herein refers specifically to that synthesis of teachings developed by H. P. Blavatsky – especially in her seminal works, *Isis Unveiled* (1877)[3] and *The Secret Doctrine* (1888)[4] – and her presumed Masters: the latter communicating their teachings through a series of letters addressed principally to A. P. Sinnett (1840–1921), who in turn summarized their teachings in *Esoteric Buddhism* (1883),[5] and finally in the works of later Theosophical commentators. Theosophy not only comprises a body of theological-philosophical teachings, but also refers to an independent movement consisting of a society founded in 1875 and its numerous offshoots. The provenance of Theosophy's tenets is envisioned by Blavatsky

---

[2] Godfrey Higgins, *Anacalypsis* (New Hyde Park, N.Y.: University Books, 1965 [1833]), vol. II, 130. Elsewhere in the volume (p. 367), he explains esoteric and exoteric Christianity: "There are *two* clear and distinct Christianities – the *exoteric* and the *esoteric*. The exoteric consists of the atonement, imputed righteousness, &c., absurd degrading doctrines, and accounted for by an absurd story about a man eating fruit contrary to the order of God . . . The *esoteric* doctrine was a secret. It might be meant to be described, but it was not meant to be explained. What little is found has escaped from the crypt, and coming into the hands of such men as Irenæus, Papias, Augustine, Athanasius, &c. it has ended in being what might be expected from such persons, incomprehensible nonsense."

[3] Helena Blavatsky, *Isis Unveiled* (New York: J. W. Bouton, 1877, several reprints). Hereafter designated *I.U.*

[4] Helena Blavatsky, *The Secret Doctrine* (New York: Theosophical University Press, 1888, several reprints).

[5] The two Masters who according to Theosophical understanding are responsible for the letters are Morya and Koot Hoomi. For a more complete explanation, see my article "The Notion of Race in Theosophy," *Nova Religio* 11 (2008), note on 56–57, and Blavatsky's *The Key to Theosophy* (London: Theosophical Publishing Company; New York: W. Q. Judge, 1889, several reprints; see below and note 19).

and her followers to be inclusive in nature as opposed to orthodox Christianity's exclusivistic bent. Its teachings are therefore located in any number of religious and philosophical sources, including the sacred compositions of the traditional religions (Hinduism, Buddhism, Zoroastrianism) and the great teachers and philosophers (Buddha, Jesus, Plato, Pythagoras, Patañjali, Kṛṣṇa, and Śaṅkara). Indeed, Blavatsky's vision is so inclusive that it is global in scope: global not only from the geographical perspective, but also from methodological and ecumenical perspectives. Thus a new methodology is added – science – to complement philosophy and religion. An ecumenical approach is added to complement Western esoteric traditions with elements of Hindu and Buddhist teaching, such as Vedānta philosophy and aspects of Mahāyānist and esoteric (Vajrayānist) Buddhist teachings.

THE THEOSOPHICAL MASTERS

For the purpose of this chapter, the teachers of the Theosophical Movement may be divided into three major categories: (1) the great teachers of the past; (2) the Mahatmas or Masters of the nineteenth century, among whom are those who have directly transmitted the teachings to their disciples or agents; (3) and these same disciples or agents, among whom are H. P. Blavatsky, A. P. Sinnett, and others.

The existence of a lineage of great teachers conveying the ancient Wisdom tradition was a favorite theme from Plutarch (46–120) in his *De animae procratione in Timaeo* ("On the birth of the spirit in Timaeus") to Blavatsky and Alexander Wilder (1823–1908)[6] and beyond. In fact, the theme of the lineage was almost as popular and important as the content of the teachings. This is evident in Blavatsky's first major contribution disclosing the ancient teachings, "A Few Questions to 'HIRAF'," [7] and in the earliest lecture on Theosophy by a co-founder of the Theosophical Society, Charles Sotheran (1847–1902), "Ancient Theosophy; or Spiritism in the Past," wherein a lineage is mentioned beginning with Zoroaster and including "Pythagoras, Buddha, Apollonius, Christ and the Sages."[8] The prominence of modern Masters or Mahatmas before the public eye was

---

[6] Wilder wrote *New Platonism and Alchemy: A Sketch of the Doctrines and Principal Teachers of the Eclectic or Alexandrian School* (Albany, N.Y.: Weed, Parsons and Company, Printers, 1869), a work that was to have a deep impact on Blavatsky during her New York years (1873–1878) and beyond.

[7] *H. P. Blavatsky Collected Writings*, vol. I, 101–119. Hereafter references to the *Collected Writings* are designated *C.W.* followed by the volume number.

[8] Charles Sotheran, "Ancient Theosophy; or Spiritism in the Past," *Spiritual Scientist*, 4.7 (April 20, 1876), 76.

established in the popular publication of A. P. Sinnett's *Occult World* in 1881, who wrote that they "constitute a Brotherhood, or Secret Association, which ramifies all over the East, but the principal seat of which for the present I gather to be in Thibet . . ."[9]

Charles W. Leadbeater, who follows in the lineage of A. P. Sinnett's brand of Theosophy, states in *A Textbook on Theosophy*[10] that the Mahatmas or Adepts are called the "Great White Brotherhood," a designation that takes on considerable popularity in Theosophical circles.

In *The Key to Theosophy*, Blavatsky summarizes what is known as the "Masters" or "Theosophical Mahatmas." They are neither "Spirits" nor "some other kind of supernatural beings." Rather, they are "men of great learning, whom we term Initiates, and still greater holiness of life." Though not ascetics, they are nonetheless removed from modern Western society and therefore "do *not* guide the [Theosophical] Society, not even the Founders [Blavatsky and Olcott] . . . they only watch over, and protect it."[11]

JESUS

According to Theosophical teaching, Jesus was considered an initiate, adept, and Master. This view originates from heretical teachings – teachings that deviated from the conventional, orthodox views that were developing over the first four centuries of Christendom – and which were often equated to so-called "Gnostic" teachings, for example in the writings of Irenæus (?115–125 – ?200 CE).[12] One of the most important issues that led to continued disputes over the early centuries of the church revolved around the doctrine of the Incarnation. What was to arise from discussions in the early councils and later codified in the great creeds – the Nicene, Apostles, and Athanasian – was stated in simple terms that there was "one Christ, at once human and divine, flesh and spirit."[13] The outcome of such a proclamation was in keeping with the goal of one teaching, one church, and one understanding. This authoritarian approach increasingly became the norm, with the eventual outcome defined in no uncertain terms in the Nicene Creed, which proclaims Jesus to be "the only Son of God . . . God

[9] A. P. Sinnett, *The Occult World* (8th edn., London: Theosophical Publishing Society, 1908), 20–22.
[10] Charles W. Leadbeater, *A Textbook on Theosophy* (Adyar, Madras: The Theosophical Publishing House, 1912), 12–14.
[11] Blavatsky, *The Key to Theosophy*, 288–299.
[12] Michael A. Williams, *Rethinking "Gnosticism": An Argument for Dismantling a Dubious Category* (Princeton: Princeton University Press 1996), 36.
[13] J. N. D. Kelly, *Early Christian Doctrines* (London: A. & C. Black, 1977 [1958]), 143.

from God . . . true god from true God . . ." Yet, despite the certitude in the
Nicene Creed, many still questioned the doctrine, which is evident from
the itemization of twenty-eight heretical views appearing in Athanasius' *de
Synodis* 2.27. A selected list of these "false teachings" include the following:

(1) But those who say that the Son was from nothing or from other subsistence
    and not from God, and that there was time or age when He was not, the
    Holy and Catholic Church regards as aliens.
(2) Again we say, Whosoever says that the Father and the Son are two Gods, be
    he anathema.
(6) Whosoever shall pretend that the essence of God is dilated or contracted, be
    he anathema.
(9) Whosoever says that the Son from Mary is man only, be he anathema.
(19) Whosoever says that the Father and the Son and the Holy Ghost are one
    Person, be he anathema.

The Theosophical teachings of Blavatsky and her successors focusing on
the nature and person of Jesus would certainly engender similar condemnation. Indeed, a good starting point in establishing the Theosophical
position is the response from "a Theosophist" (probably Blavatsky) to a
letter addressed to the editor of the *Poona Observer* by a correspondent who
identifies himself (?) as "Zero." His criticism of the Theosophical position
is summarized as follows:

(1) They attempt "to identify Jesus Christ and the apostle Paul with the
    ancient adepts in Occultism."
(2) They suggest that Jesus and St. Paul were adepts.
(3) Some Theosophists deny the existence of St. Paul and Jesus in order to
    overcome the difficulties in assigning adeptship to them.
(4) Theosophists wish to "overturn all existing religions, and first of all and
    especially the Christian religion."[14]

Most of the information about Jesus is located in Blavatsky's *Isis Unveiled*,
and what is stated therein is retained and confirmed in her later writings.
There is no doubt that her view is fundamentally different from the orthodox view, since she denies Jesus' divinity. This denial is perhaps based upon
the teachings of the early Christian sect, the Ebionites, who infused their
Christianity with the Jewish notion that there could be but one God, thus
denying any claim that Jesus was divine.[15] This argument was progressively
weakened with the rising influx of Gentiles into the Christian communities. What was, therefore, a relatively influential movement in the formative

---

[14] "A Word with the Theosophists," *C.W.*, vol. IV, 357–358.
[15] For an early view of the Ebionites, see G. R. S. Mead, *Fragments of a Faith Forgotten* (New Hyde
Park, N.Y.: University Books, 1960), 126–130.

years of the Christian movement was weakened as early as the Jewish war (66 CE).[16] Blavatsky agrees with Epiphanius' description of the Ebionite opinion that "Jesus was but a man 'of the seed of a man.'"[17] Elsewhere, she states: "If we do not accept Jesus as God, we revere *him as a man.*"[18] Indeed, in an article posthumously published,[19] Blavatsky is quite clear in her assessment of Jesus:

Was Jesus as "Son of God" and "Saviour" of Mankind, unique in the World's annals? . . . Or was He only the "son of his deeds," a pre-eminently holy man, and a reformer, one of many, who paid with His life for the presumption of endeavouring, in the face of ignorance and despotic power, to enlighten mankind and make its burden lighter by His Ethics and Philosophy? The first necessitates a blind, all-resisting faith; the latter is suggested to every one by reason and logic.[20]

These observations follow that of an early opponent to Christianity, Celsus (second century CE), whose position was summarized in *The Arguments of Celsus against the Christians*[21] and Origen's *Contra Celsus* (1.28), that Jesus pretended to be born of a virgin rather than of a poor woman abandoned by her husband because of an act of adultery committed with a Roman legionary named Panthera,[22] that he worked during the years of his youth in Egypt, where he learned the magical arts. This ability led him to proclaim that he was "a God." These and other stories about Jesus were incorporated in the *Life of Jesus* (*Toledot Yeshu*), most likely a later work that incorporated some of the oral accounts of the Jews of his time. Quoting from the *Sepher-Toldos Jeshu* (her spelling of the *Toledot Yeshu*), Blavatsky[23] recounts the story of Jesus' training under Rabbi Elhanan and Rabbi Johosuah ben Perachiah (Jehoshua ben-Perahiah), the latter, his grand uncle, initiating Jesus into the "*secret* knowledge." Forced to flee Judea due to the King's (Janneus) order to slay all initiates, Jesus and his Rabbi fled to Alexandria where he continued to train in the secret wisdom of the Jewish *Kabala* and the wisdom of Egypt. It is in this context that Jesus is called an initiate,[24] specifically of the Egyptian Mysteries,[25] and one

---

[16] Kelly, *Early Christian Doctrines*, 139.
[17] *I.U.*, vol. II, 182 (note). The full quote appears in Epiphanius' *The Gospel of the Ebionites*.
[18] *I.U.*, vol. II, 530.   [19] "Facts Underlying Adept Biographies," *C.W.*, vol. XIV, 137–162.
[20] "Facts Underlying Adept Biographies," *C.W.*, vol. XIV, 143.
[21] *Arguments of Celsus, Porphyry, and the Emperor Julian against the Christians; Extracts from Diodorus Siculus, Josephus, and Tacitus, Relating to the Jews* (trans. Dr. Lardne; London: Thomas Rodd, 1830), 4–5.
[22] This is repeated in a note in "A Word with 'Zero'," *C.W.*, vol. IV, 361.   [23] *I.U.*, vol. II, 201.
[24] H. P. Blavatsky, "A Word with 'Zero'," *C.W.*, vol. IV, 362; "The Esoteric Character of the Gospels," *C.W.*, vol. VIII, 200; "Miscellaneous Notes," *C.W.*, vol. X, 91.
[25] H. P. Blavatsky, "Traces of the Mysteries," *C.W.*, vol. XIV, 283–284.

who intended to restore the ancient wisdom.[26] Because he revealed the occult wisdom that was never intended to be divulged by its guardians, the Pharisees, Jesus was imprisoned, flogged, "stoned as a blasphemer," and then paid the ultimate price of dying on the cross.[27] Jesus' achievement as adept is summarized in Eliphas Levi's *La science des esprits* (1865): "He had divined the occult theology of Israel, had compared it with the wisdom of Egypt, and found thereby the reason for a universal religious synthesis."[28]

The identification of Jesus with Jehoshua ben-Perahiah (whose father was Panthera) confirmed for Blavatsky that Jesus, or Jehoshua, was actually born in Lydda (Lod) in today's Central District of Israel around 120 BCE[29] and not in the first century CE ("1 to the year 33"), which was a myth invented in the first century by the writers of the Gospels and after by "interested fanatics," such as the fathers of the church. As a myth, she continues, all the actions of Jesus in the New Testament are based upon "the programme of the Cycle of Initiation, a cycle founded on the Precession of the Equinoxes and the Signs of the Zodiac."[30]

The earlier date assigned to Jesus was taken up by later Theosophical writers[31] such as Annie Besant, Charles W. Leadbeater, Gottfried de Purucker, and G. R. S. Mead, the latter examining the Talmudic account in great detail in his *Did Jesus Live 100 BC?* This is probably the main source of later discussions, such as Annie Besant's *Esoteric Christianity*, wherein is mentioned the birth of Jesus in Palestine in 105 BCE "during the consulate of Publius Rutilius Rufus and Gnaeus Mallius Maximus."[32] Charles W. Leadbeater also mentions the early date of Jesus in his *The Christian Creed*[33] and quotes Besant's outline of the early life of Jesus. About thirty years later, G. de Purucker briefly stated that the date of Jesus must be calculated according to the Messianic Cycle lasting 2,160 years. He calculated that Jesus was born "within a few years of 2040 years" from the time of his

---

[26] "Le Phare de l'Inconnu" ("The Beacon of the Unknown"), *C.W.*, vol. XI, 236 (272).

[27] *I.U.*, vol. II, 202.   [28] Quoted from *I.U.*, vol. II, 202.

[29] "Réponse aux fausses conceptions de M. L'abbé Roca relatives à mes observations sur l'ésotérisme chrétien," *C.W.*, vol. IX, 204. Although the date is not mentioned in *I.U.*, the mention of these characters and of Lydda (Lod or Lud) in vol. II, 201–202 suggests that she accepted the date as early as 1877, or at least when she first became acquainted with Eliphas Levi.

[30] "Réponse aux fausses conceptions," 203n.

[31] A good overview of this topic appears in Leslie Price, "Jesus in Theosophical History," *Theosophical History* 1.3 (July, 1985), 38–45.

[32] Annie Besant, *Esoteric Christianity or the Lesser Mysteries* (Wheaton, Ill.: Quest Books; Theosophical Publishing House, 2006 [1903]).

[33] Charles W. Leadbeater, *The Christian Creed* (2nd edn., London and Benares: The Theosophical Publishing House, 1909 [1904]), 12–13.

comment on this issue (1934), that is 106 BCE, all calculated according to the Messianic Cycle of 2,160 solar years.[34]

THE CHRIST

One of the key Theosophical teachings is the fundamental distinction between Jesus and the Christ. It would appear that one of Blavatsky's immediate sources for this opinion was a person she greatly admired from her New York days in the mid 1870s, Alexander Wilder (1823–1908). Following Wilder's opinion that Paul was the true founder of Christianity, she goes on to argue that Paul did not consider Christ "a person, but an embodied idea."[35] Quoting Wilder:

The "Christ of Paul" . . . was something else than the Jesus of the *Gospels* . . . Paul treats of Christ as a personage rather than as a person. The sacred lessons of the secret assemblies often personified the divine good and the divine truth in a human form . . . and this doctrine, emerging from the crypt, was apprehended by churchlings and gross-minded men as that of immaculate conception[36] and divine incarnation.[37]

In other words, Wilder may have understood Christ to be the personification of the divine good or truth, not God nor the Jesus of the *Gospels*. The Theosophical teaching centering on "Christ" focuses on two important associations:
(1) A connection between Christos and Chrestos;
(2) a connection between Jesus and Buddha.
With regard to the Christos–Chrestos connection, Blavatsky states in "The Esoteric Character of the Gospels"[38] that "'the coming of Christ' means the presence of CHRISTOS in a regenerated world, and not at all the actual coming in body of 'Christ' Jesus." This "Christ – the true esoteric

---

[34] Gottfried de Purucker, "The Real Birth-Date of Jesus," in G. de Purucker, *Studies in Occult Philosophy* (Covina: Theosophical University Press, 1945).

[35] *I.U.*, vol. II, 574.

[36] Whether Blavatsky refers to the doctrine of the birth of Mary free from original sin or whether she means an immaculate birth of Christ is unclear. In a later article, "The Future Occultist," she writes: "She [a woman who manifests occult power represented by the Śakti] is moreover gifted with a wonderfully vivid imagination – stronger than man's. And as the phenomenal is the realization or rather the manifestation of the IDEAL, which can be properly and strongly conceived only by a powerful IMAGINATION – a WOMAN-ADEPT can produce high occultists – a race of 'Buddhas and Christs,' born 'without sin.' The more and the sooner the animal sexual affinities are given up, the stronger and the sooner will be the manifestation of the higher occult powers which alone can produce the 'immaculate conception'" (*C.W.*, vol. VI, 262. See also *The Secret Doctrine*, vol. I, 382n).

[37] *I.U.*, vol. II, 575–576.   [38] *C.W.*, vol. VIII, 172–201 (Part One).

SAVIOUR – is no man, but the DIVINE PRINCIPLE in every human being."[39] From the time of the publication of *Isis Unveiled* (1877), Christos is mentioned in conjunction with *chrestos*. In *Isis*,[40] the Essenes are responsible for the association, for Eusebius (265–340) claims that they were the first Christians "long before there had appeared a single Christian in Palestine. Blavatsky adds that the Essenes were *Chrestians* "long before the era of Christianity . . ."[41] The interest in the Essenes was due to Eusebius' observation that "Jesus and his apostles exhibited too close a resemblance to this sect."[42] The term on which Chrestian is based, *chrestos* "good," is of importance to Blavatsky and Theosophical teaching, since she claimed that Justin Martyr referred to "his co-religionists *Chréstians*."[43] Furthermore, Lactantius states that "Christ and Christians, spelt originally *Chrést* and *Chréstians*, were borrowed from the temple vocabulary of the Pagans."[44] Blavatsky takes liberties with the terms reversing the argument made by the church fathers. There is no question that Christ and *Chrestos* appear in the early texts, but *Chrestos* does not appear to be as common or significant as Blavatsky argues. Indeed, in Clement of Alexandria's *Stromateis*, for example, we find in Book II, Chapter 4 this statement: "Those who have shown faith in Christ as God are good (*chrestoi*) in name and fact, just as those of whom a king takes notice are rightly called royal."[45] It is obvious that Blavatsky and others see far more significance with the term than the orthodox Christians. They consider the *chrestoi* (or singular *chrestos*) not merely as descriptive, but as a designation for adepts, high chelas or disciples[46] who have taken on the ascetic life that eventually leads

---

[39] *C.W.*, vol. VIII, 173.   [40] *I.U.*, vol. II, 323.   [41] *I.U.*, vol. II, 323.   [42] *I.U.*, vol. II, 323.

[43] This is mentioned in Blavatsky's *Theosophical Glossary* (Los Angeles: The Theosophy Company, 1973), 84. Justin Martyr states in his *First Apology* (1.4) that "we are accused of being Christian, and to hate what is excellent (Christian) is unjust." Whether this agrees with Blavatsky is open to debate.

[44] Blavatsky, *Theosophical Glossary*, 84. It is rather the other way around: "But the meaning of this name must be set forth, on account of the error of the ignorant, who by the change of a letter are accustomed to call Him Chrestus." This passage is located in Lactantius, *Divine Institutes* 4.7.

[45] *Stromateis* 169. John Ferguson (*Clement of Alexandria: Stromateis Books One to Three* [Washington, D.C.: Catholic University of America Press, 1991] adds in a note that this is wordplay between *Christos* and *chrestos*. Furthermore, he adds that the "Christians were first so called at Antioch where they were nicknamed *chrestoi*, 'goody-goodies,' a name they disowned; however they accepted *Christianoi*, which is further complicated because *Chrestos* is also a name" (169, n. 56). Other wordplays between the two terms are found in Tertullian, *Apology* 3 and Theophilus, *To Autolycus* 1.1.

[46] "The Esoteric Character of the Gospels," *C.W.*, vol. VIII, 187. She states that the term is based on the verb *chráomai*, "consulting an oracle" (184), "to consult a god" (187).

to *Christos*.[47] *Chrestoi* are according to Blavatsky etymologically demon-strated to derive from "oracles" with such terms as *chresterios* "one who belongs to, or is in the service of, an oracle, a god, or 'Master'" and *chreste-rion*, the "vehicle of an oracle, sacrifice and victim."[48] Moreover, the *chrêstês* are the ones who expound or explain oracles. The *chrestoi*, therefore, are those ascetics who belong to oracular temples,[49] all passing through the cycle of initiation, for no "'sacrificial victim' could be united to Christ triumphant before passing through the preliminary stage of the suffering Chrêst who was put to death."[50] This whole discussion points to the con-tention that Chrêstos was earlier than Christianity, that it was connected to Pagan oracular practices, that it was unique to Christianity, that Chrêstos referred to the one on the spiritual path whose ultimate goal was Christos, "the glorified Spirit of 'TRUTH,' the reunion with which makes the soul (the Son) ONE with the (Father) Spirit."[51]

After all is said and done, Jesus was actually a Chrêstos, who, "was like Socrates, like Phocion, like Theodorus, and so many others surnamed Chrêstos, i.e., the 'good, and excellent,' the gentle, and the holy Initiate, who showed the 'way' to the Christos condition, and thus became himself 'the Way' in the hearts of his enthusiastic admirers."[52] In other words, one must be a Chrêstos in order to qualify, as Jesus was,[53] to acquire Christos or "Divine Light."[54]

The second association, the connection between Jesus and Buddha, is partially based upon Essene and Nazarene associations. As early as her first seminal article, "A Few Questions to 'HIRAF***',"[55] Blavatsky men-tions a "well-informed Nazarene – trained as he was in the high school of the Essenes . . ." The Essenes were "converts of Buddhist missionaries who had overrun Egypt, Greece, and even Judea at one time, since the reign of [the Mauryan emperor of the third century] Asoka the zealous propagandist . . ."[56] Jesus, as a pupil of the Essenes, would have come under the influence of the Buddhists, and it was Blavatsky's opinion that he "preached the philosophy of Buddha-Sakyamûni" for the same reason:

---

47 "Notes on Abbé Roca's 'Esotericism of Christian Dogma'," *C.W.*, vol. VIII, 381.
48 "The Esoteric Character of the Gospels," *C.W.*, vol. VIII, 184–185, 387.
49 "Notes on Abbé Roca's 'Esotericism of Christian Dogma'," *C.W.*, vol. VIII, 381.
50 "The Esoteric Character of the Gospels," *C.W.*, vol. VIII, 184–185 and "Notes on Abbé Roca's 'Esotericism of Christian Dogma'," *C.W.*, vol. VIII, 382.
51 "The Esoteric Character of the Gospels," *C.W.*, vol. VIII, 184–185, 189.
52 *C.W.*, vol. VIII, 184–185, 205. The discussion of the Chrêstos also appears in Higgins, *Anacalypsis*, vol. I, 568–574.
53 *C.W.*, vol. VIII, 184–185, 380.   54 *C.W.*, vol. VIII, 184–185, 381.
55 *C.W.*, vol. I, 106.   56 *I.U.*, vol. II, 132.

"to benefit humanity at large by producing a religious reform which should give it a religion of pure ethics."[57] Ten years later, she proclaims that the two "Mahâtmans: Gautama of Kapilavastu and Jesus of Judaea," the two sages and initiates, "proclaimed the same truths."[58] This is no different from her judgment that no matter where the teachings are located – in "Pagan" philosophies, Christianity, Buddhism, or the Hindu Manu[59] – they are in agreement leading her to cite an observation about Mani taken from Neander's *History of the Church*,[60] that "Jesus was a permutation of Gautama; that Buddha, Christ, and Mani were one and the same person, for the teachings of the former two were identical."[61]

The connection between Buddha and Jesus and their convergence of teachings lead to one more rather remarkable pronouncement, if not from the perspective of modern exegesis, that there is also a noticeable similarity between Jesus and Kṛṣṇa – spelled *Christna* – to indicate the union in Christ. Based upon John Lundy's *Monumental Christianity*, there is evidence presented of religions anticipating Christianity, especially through the actions of Christna, Buddha, and Osiris. One figure taken from the book is of a figure of Christna "crucified in space"[62] which is commented upon by Lundy:

It looks like a Christian crucifix in many respects, and in some others it does not. The drawing, the attitude, and the nail-marks in hands and feet, indicate a Christian origin . . . Can it be Plato's second God who impressed himself on the universe in the form of the cross? . . . Plato learned his theology in Egypt and the East, and must have known of the crucifixion of Krishna, Buddha, Mithra, &c. At any rate, the religion of India had its mythical crucified victim long anterior to Christianity, as a type of the real one, and I am inclined to think that we have it in this remarkable plate.

---

[57] *I.U.*, vol. II, 132–133. Compare p. 123.

[58] "Notes on Abbé Roca's 'Esotericism of Christian Dogma'," *C.W.*, vol. VIII, 390. See also "The Esoteric Character of the Gospels," *C.W.*, vol. VIII, 184–185.

[59] The context of this equation is the following quote in *I.U.*, vol. II, 286: "Both Pagan philosophy and Christianity, however, owe their elevated ideas on the soul and spirit of man and the unknown Deity to Buddhism and the Hindu Manu."

[60] Blavatsky quotes this source in a note. An online edition (Google Book) of Augustus Neander's *The History of the Christian Religion and Church during the First Three Centuries* (trans. Henry John Rose, Philadelphia: James M. Campbell, and New York: Saxton & Miles, 1844), 303, contains the following observation: "The pantheistic portion of Manicheeism may be compared, in many respects, with the pantheistic parts of the old Buddhaism. Manes is represented, in fact, to have travelled to the East Indies and China, and many of the later Manichees appeal to the circumstance that Manes, Buddhas, Zoroaster, Christ, and the Sun (the higher spirit which animated the Sun) are the same; that is to say, all these founders of a religion are only different Incarnations of the Sun and therefore, there is, in these different systems, only one religion under different forms."

[61] *I.U.*, vol. II, 286. A similar observation about the Buddha and Jesus is found on p. 290 and 296n.

[62] John P. Lundy, *Monumental Christianity or the Art and Symbolism of the Primitive Church* (New York: J. W. Bouton, 1876), figure 72, 174. Discussed in *I.U.*, vol. II, 557.

Lundy comes to a conclusion that the figure might be of Wittoba (Vittoba), a form or incarnation of Kṛṣṇa, who is "the shepherd-god of Mathura, and kindred to Mithra in being a Saviour – the Lord of the covenant, as well as Lord of heaven and earth – pure and impure, light and dark, good and bad, peaceful and warlike, amiable and wrathful, mild and turbulent, forgiving and vindictive, God and a strange mixture of man, but not the Christ of the Gospels."[63] The coincidence of roles of the two – Jesus and "Christna" or Kṛṣṇa – together with Buddha is then demonstrated very forcibly by comparing the lives and deeds of the three.[64] Furthermore, the spelling of Kṛṣṇa as Christna, borrowed from Louis-François Jacolliot's *Christna et le Christ* and mentioned as early as 1869[65] in his *La Bible dans l'Inde, vie de Iezeus Christna*, is based upon the argument that Christianity had its origins in Brahmanism – referring to the priestly religion of the Brahmins – "in the cult of Krichna."[66] Jacolliot offers a great deal of evidence – more appropriately, speculation – on the connection between the Indian Christna and the Hebrew Christ. Although there was an attractiveness to the Christna–Christ connection, Blavatsky seems to have abandoned it soon after the publication of *Isis Unveiled*.[67]

The observations on the connection of Buddha, Christ, and Christna (Kṛṣṇa) presuppose a common religion antedating the later creedal religions of Buddhism, Christianity, and Hinduism (Brahmanism). This implied a presence of common teachings in all religions, so it is not surprising that a connection was accepted between Christna and Christ based upon dubious evidence. The separation of the Christ from Jesus agrees with this line of reasoning, which is based upon the gnostic notion of Christ as the immortal self – "the divine nature of humanity" – inhabiting humans of both genders.[68] As the Divine Principle or immortal Divine Spirit in

---

[63] Lundy, *Monumental Christianity*, 176. Discussed in *I.U.*, vol. II, 557–558.

[64] *I.U.*, vol. II, 536–541.

[65] Jacolliot was not the originator of this assertion. An earlier reference appears in Higgins, *Anacalypsis*, vol. II, 337.

[66] The quote is taken from *Christna et le Christ*, 332 as translated and quoted in Daniel Caracostea, "Louis-François Jacolliot (1837–1890): A Biographical Essay," *Theosophical History* 9.1 (January, 2003). "Krichna" is a spelling that appears in Eugène Burnouf's *Le Bhâgavata Purâna ou Histoire poétique de Krichna*, 3 vols. (Paris: n.p., 1840–1847).

[67] Her own contribution is a misguided attempt to offer an etymology based upon Sanskrit *Kris* "sacred." One of her assumptions is that Sanskrit is the parent language and Greek the daughter language, so *Christos*, a Greek word, must be explained through the older Sanskrit language. If *Kris* means "sacred," then the name Kṛṣṇa, rendered as "Chris-na" (minus the 't'), must mean "the pure or the sacred," the core meaning of several synonyms assigned to *Christos* (*I.U.*, vol. II, 158).

[68] *C.W.*, vol. IX, 19. Blavatsky states in a note that this has been a "Theosophical doctrine" taught ever since 1875, when the Theosophical Society was founded. A similar statement is "The Esoteric Character of the Gospels," located in *C.W.*, vol. VIII, 173.

man,[69] it is not associated or equated with any person in particular. Therefore, a Horus, Kṛṣṇa, Buddha, or Jesus is imbued with the Christ principle
but is not the Christ. The embodied or carnalized Christ is therefore not
necessarily associated with Jesus.[70]

From the perspective of Christ Consciousness, a term popularized in
neo-Theosophical literature, *Christos* is divine Wisdom, later known as
Buddhi-Manas, a combination of two of seven principles that make up the
human being. The Buddhi represents the discriminating principle and the
Manas the mind principle. In her mature teaching (Instruction No. III),[71]
Blavatsky states that *Christos* or Buddhi-Manas is "of the same essence with
the Universal Spirit, and at the same time the 'Son,' for Manas is the second
remove from the 'Father'," a reference to the Ātman or Divine Spark being
the unstated third element in the monad. Buddhi, discrimination, or the
Spiritual soul is the vehicle (*upādhi*) or base for the Ātman just as Manas,
the mind, or soul is the vehicle for Buddhi. The Ātman, not included in
the equation with *Christos* in the Instruction,[72] must be included since
Buddhi could not exist without it. Ātman is not individualized, but is
rather analogous to the sunlight shining on all things of the earth.[73] Neither
Ātman nor Buddhi are of much importance to the body "*unless the divine
Duad is assimilated by, and reflected in, some consciousness.*"[74] This is the
Manas, which is "inseparably united to the first two"; it is the "glorified
individuality," the Higher Manas or Manas-Taijas (*taijasi*);[75] the Buddhi
and Higher Manas[76] conjoined represent human and divine intellect and
self-consciousness, both in contradistinction to the perishable personality
or the lower Manas[77] of Jesus.[78]

The process wherein the *Christos* joins or inhabits the body comes close to
what we might term "walk-in" or "possession," which today is commonly
interpreted as an altered state of consciousness wherein one personality
replaces another. Blavatsky mentions as the source for this teaching the early

---

[69] *C.W.*, vol. IX, 19; vol. VIII, 173–174 and 183; and vol. XIV, 122.

[70] Note in *C.W.*, vol. VIII, 345.   [71] *C.W.*, vol. XII, 635.

[72] *C.W.*, vol. XII, 635. Nor is it included in "The Dual Aspect of Wisdom," *C.W.*, vol. XII, 313.

[73] Blavatsky, *The Key to Theosophy*, 135.   [74] Blavatsky, *The Key to Theosophy*, 135.

[75] "Pistis-Sophia," in *C.W.*, vol. XIII, 55. This is the Higher Manas because it reflects the light of
Buddhi reflected on it (*The Key to Theosophy*, 159).

[76] The non-material "Ego" as part of the Universal Mind (*C.W.*, vol. XII, 358, 366–367).

[77] The "lower Manas," an emanation of the Higher Manas, is defined as the animal soul (the *nephesh*
in Hebrew) which manifests as instincts and dreams in animals or the mind in humans. Coupled
with the Desire principle (*kāma*) it causes an instinctual action in humans. See "Dreams," in *C.W.*,
vol. X, 246.

[78] "Pistis-Sophia," in *C.W.*, vol. XIII, 55.

gnostic Cerinthus (100 CE)[79] and quotes the *Philosophumena*,[80] which in turn is based upon Irenaeus' *Adversus Haereses*.[81] His teaching had centered on a human Jesus, who had been born not of a virgin, but of normal parents (Mary and Joseph), who had become the temporary vehicle of Christ, who had descended upon him as a dove at the time of Jesus' baptism, who had infused Jesus with the power to work miracles and to proclaim the unknown Father, and who had departed from Jesus after which Jesus suffered from the tortures imposed on him, was crucified, and died only to rise again. Like Cerinthus, Carpocrates (middle of the second century CE) also taught that the natural father of Jesus was Joseph. Carpocrates[82] also taught that a "power descended upon him [Jesus] from the Father."[83] Although this "power" is not identified with the Christ or Christos, it is explicitly identified by Theodotus the Byzantian (late second century CE), who also repeats the teachings of Cerinthus concerning the descent of the Christ into Jesus in the form of a dove at the time of his baptism.[84] Finally, the Christ is identified by Blavatsky as an *aeon*, a sphere of being or power that emanates from the Supreme or eternal Being.[85]

THE CHRIST AS WORLD TEACHER

The teachings of the Christ led to the most significant event in Theosophical history: the coming of the World Teacher. In this later phase of the teaching, a young, impoverished Indian boy, Jiddu Krishnamurti (1895–1986), was selected as the candidate who would be "overshadowed" by the Christ-Maitreya-Kṛṣṇa.[86] Discovered by Charles W. Leadbeater at the Adyar headquarters in 1909, Krishnamurti underwent continuous training and grooming for the next twenty years until he publicly repudiated his

---

[79] "Pistis-Sophia," 55. More information on the teachings of Cerinthus is given in Mead, *Fragments of a Faith Forgotten*, 237–238.

[80] Hippolytus, *Philosophumena or the Refutation of All Heresies* 2.92–93 (7.33) and 166 (10.21).

[81] Irenaeus, *Adversus Haereses* 1.26.   [82] Mead, *Fragments of a Faith Forgotten*, 229–233.

[83] Irenaeus, *Adversus Haereses* 1.25.

[84] Hippolytus, *Philosophumena or the Refutation of All Heresies* 2.93–94 (7.90). So too the Ebionaei: "Wherefore He was named by God Christ and Jesus, since none of them has fulfilled the Law. For if any other had practiced the commandments which are in the Law, he would be the Christ. And they say it is possible for them if they do likewise to become Christs; and that He was a man like unto all [men]."

[85] "The Doctrine of Avataras," in *C.W.*, vol. XIV, 372. The totality of Aeons constitute the "Pleroma or invisible spiritual world, as distinct from the Kenoma, or visible material world" (J. B. Peterson, "Æons," in *The Catholic Encyclopedia* [New York: Robert Appleton Company, 1907]).

[86] A review of the opinions on and reactions to this teaching and project undertaken by the leaders of the Theosophical Society (Adyar) may be found in Govert Schüller, *Krishnamurti and the World Teacher Project: Some Theosophical Perceptions* (Fullerton, Cal.: Theosophical History, 1997).

imminent assumption as World Teacher. From 1929 to his death in 1986, he struck out on his own to establish his own views on the human condition. What would have been, according to Theosophists and his followers, the seminal event in modern times – the coming of the World Teacher – was summarily rejected by Krishnamurti during his talk on August 3, 1929. As a consequence, he dissolved the Order of the Star, the organization promoting his ascendency to World Teacher: "For eighteen years you have been preparing for this event, for the Coming of the World-Teacher . . . I do not care if you believe that I am the World-Teacher or not. That is of very little importance . . ."[87] The reactions to these words led to various interpretations of its significance. Was he the World Teacher despite all that transpired after 1929? Was the doctrine correct regarding the World Teacher but the proposed Vehicle of the Teacher the wrong person? Was the Teaching itself flawed, thereby leading to the failure of the Vehicle? Or was it a success despite the flawed teachings? These questions reflect the views of Theosophists and later writers inspired by Theosophy alike, including Rudolf Steiner, E. L. Gardner, Rom Landau, Alice Bailey, Cyril Scott, Guy Ballard, and Elizabeth Clare Prophet.[88]

   The coming of the World Teacher is illustrative of the continuity and development of Theosophical teachings from the early twentieth century. These later teachings, introduced by C. W. Leadbeater and Annie Besant, were given the pejorative designation "neo-Theosophy" by F. T. Brooks in his book, *Neo-Theosophy Exposed.*[89] Recently, the phrase "Second-Generation Theosophy" has gained increased popularity, replacing the former term.[90] The important issue for many Theosophists has been whether this version of Theosophy, however one wishes to call it, is to be considered in conformity with the earlier version of Theosophy. For many, because the later interpretation is deemed not in agreement with the teachings of Blavatsky and her Masters, it is not genuine.[91]

[87] Quoted in the Foreword by James Santucci in Schüller, *Krishnamurti and the World Teacher Project*, iii.

[88] All are discussed in Schüller, *Krishnamurti and the World Teacher Project*.

[89] F. T. Brooks, *Neo-Theosophy Exposed* (repr., Edmonton: Edmonton Theosophical Society, 1991 [1914]). Brooks is discussed in Michael Gomes, "Nehru's Theosophical Tutor," *Theosophical History* 7.3 (July, 1998), 99–108. Gomes (p. 108, n. 31) mentions that Annie Besant used the term in 1912 in her lecture, *The Growth of the Theosophical Society* (Adyar, Madras: The Theosophist Office, 1912), echoing what others identified as the investigation of past lives by her and her colleague, C. W. Leadbeater, followed by another mention in a letter written in 1913 by Bhagavan Das.

[90] It occurs at least as early as 1996 in Geoffrey Farthing, "The Theosophical Society and its Future Manifesto 1996." Online at www.anandgholap.net/Christian_Creed-CWL.htm.

[91] This is clear from a compilation made by Margaret Thomas, a member of the Theosophical Society of Scotland, Wales and England from 1912 to 1924, entitled *Theosophy and Neo-Theosophy?* (Grand Rapids, Ohio: Isis Books, 1995 [1925]).

Despite this disparity, there is some agreement with Blavatsky's view of Jesus and Leadbeater's view in his *The Christian Creed*, the second edition appearing around the time of his discovery of Krishnamurti. In *The Christian Creed*, Leadbeater states that the phrase that concludes the prayer, "through Jesus Christ our Lord" actually confuses three separate "ideas: (a) the disciple Jesus; (b) the great Master whom men call the Christ . . . and (c) the Second Aspect or Person of the Logos." Discounting the third idea, the first illustrates agreement with Blavatsky. He, quoting Besant's *Esoteric Christianity*, gives the birth of Jesus in Palestine in 105 BCE,[92] which does not differ with the discussion on Jesus given above.

Not so, however, the second observation, namely that the Christ is a Master. Blavatsky never identified Christ as a person; at most, the Christ is a "personage" or, better, an "impersonal Principle."[93] From Blavatsky's perspective, Jesus is imbued with the Christ principle but is not the Christ. Leadbeater states, however, that both "the disciple Jesus and the great Master Christ are men of our own humanity, however far in advance of us they are along the path of evolution."[94]

The distinction between Blavatsky's and Besant–Leadbeater's opinions may be overstated in some cases. When Blavatsky discussed the Christ and Jesus, she explained their relationship within a decidedly gnostic and Talmudic context. If one compares Leadbeater's teachings of the World Teacher with the infusion of Jesus with the Christ, there is certainly disagreement. But with the teaching of the Bodhisattva of Buddhism, there appears something new, a special form of incarnation based upon Tibetan teaching. Reincarnation generally implies the reembodiment of an unenlightened rebirth consciousness that eventually develops into a similar entity based upon past actions. In Tibetan Buddhism reembodiment of the monks and lamas, most notably the Dalai Lama and Panchen Lama, represents something else: the reembodiment of the same being into a new body. The connection is that both previous and current Dalai Lamas are

[92] Leadbeater, *The Christian Creed*, 12.

[93] H. P. Blavatsky, "The Kabalah and the Kabalists at the Close of the Nineteenth Century," *C.W.*, vol. VII, 259. Thomas (*Theosophy and Neo-Theosophy?*, 14–17) also cites the disparities between Blavatsky and the Masters on the one hand and Besant and Leadbeater on the other.

[94] *The Christian Creed*, 15. Christ as a person also appears in Besant's *Esoteric Christianity*, but Besant is more careful and in my opinion closer to Blavatsky's description of the Christ: "[Baptism of Jesus], when the Spirit was seen 'descending from heaven like a dove, and it abode upon Him' (John 1: 32) . . . To that manifested Presence the name of 'the Christ' may rightly be given, and it was He who lived and moved in the form of the man Jesus over the hills and plains of Palestine . . ." Yet, if this is accepted, a reconciliation of dating is in order. Is it the Jesus of 105 BCE or the Jesus of the first century CE?

incarnations of the Bodhisattva of Compassion, Avalokiteśvara. The notion of rule by incarnation was established by the head of the Karmapa sect of Tibetan Buddhism, with the Gyalwa Karmapa, as an incarnation of Avalokiteśvara, continuously reincarnating up to the present incarnation. The Bodhisattva Avalokiteśvara thereby assumes the role of a religious leader participating in human affairs.[95]

This teaching of embodiment gives some credence to the notion of a person in the form of Christ overshadowing or descending upon the person who is to become the Vehicle. One cannot determine whether Leadbeater was familiar with this teaching from some contemporary source other than Blavatsky, from Blavatsky herself, or was arrived at independently by Leadbeater. It is of great interest that she describes a similar process – though within the much broader context of the Ancient Wisdom tradition, that Gautama too was reborn as Śaṃkara, the vedantic commentator.

Was Samkarâchârya Gautama the Buddha, then, under a new personal form? It may perhaps only puzzle the reader the more if he be told that there was the "astral" Gautama inside the outward Samkara, whose higher principle, or Âtman, was, nevertheless, his own divine prototype – the "Son of Light," indeed – the heavenly, mind-born son of Aditi. This fact is again based on that mysterious transference of the divine ex-personality merged in the impersonal Individuality – now in its full trinitarian form of the Monad as Atma-Buddhi-Manas – to a new body, whether visible or subjective.[96]

Or, as is stated in *Esoteric Buddhism:* "Sankaracharya simply *was* Buddha in all respects, in a new body."[97] Leadbeater, belonging to the London Lodge under Sinnett's Presidency in the 1880s, may have been in greater agreement with Sinnett. He certainly was more acquainted with his version of Theosophy, as noted in the section on Theosophical Masters. In Leadbeater's *Masters and the Path*, we find a similar approach to the succession: Lord Maitreya taking up the "office" of Lord Gautama and then arranging the Teachers to appear in different parts of the planet, including "the Buddha Himself, Sri Shankaracharya and Mahavira in India, but also Mithra in Persia, Laotse and Confucius in China, and Pythagoras in ancient Greece."[98] Then, to set up the coming World Teacher, he states

---

[95] Franz H. Michael, *Rule by Incarnation: Tibetan Buddhism and its Role in Society and State* (Boulder, Col.: Westview Press, 1982), 2, 21, 37.

[96] H. P. Blavatsky, "The Mystery of Buddha," *C.W.*, vol. XIV, 391.

[97] A. P. Sinnett, *Esoteric Buddhism* (5th edn., San Diego, Cal.: Wizards Bookshelf, 1981 [1883]), 175. The same statement also appears in Blavatsky, "The Mystery of Buddha," 390.

[98] C. W. Leadbeater, *The Masters and the Path* (Adyar, Madras: The Theosophical Publishing House, 1925), #1041.

that Maitreya himself appeared as an embodiment in Kṛṣṇa in India and as Christ in Palestine.[99]

It is obvious that the primary teachings about Jesus and the Christ are founded on gnostic teachings. In this regard, Blavatsky has remained faithful to her sources. When Leadbeater and to a lesser extent Besant proposed their version of the teaching of the World Teacher, the doctrine was somewhat modified. For one, the appearance of a Master of Wisdom was not due to appear until 1975 according to Blavatsky;[100] Leadbeater, however, already selected Krishnamurti in 1909 as the intended Vehicle for the World Teacher. The descent of the impersonal Christ on Jesus is mirrored in the overshadowing of Lord Maitreya of Krishnamurti. This shift from a principle to a person is not necessarily an invention of Leadbeater, but a partial reflection of Tibetan Buddhist teaching as cited by Blavatsky and mentioned by Sinnett in his *Esoteric Buddhism*. The Tibetan teaching on Incarnations of "Living Buddhas" more closely reflects the expectation of the coming World Teacher. The major difference, however, is that the descent, overshadowing, or possession of Krishnamurti remains a gnostic teaching. Reincarnation or reembodiment was not adopted in the description of the coming World Teacher. What remains is an amalgam of gnostic and Tibetan Buddhist teaching in Leaderbeater's description of the World Teacher. Whether Blavatsky intended to combine or equate Tibetan Buddhist with the gnostic teaching is not certain. What is certain, however, is that the teaching was devised before there was any attempt to introduce Tibetan Buddhist teachings.

BIBLIOGRAPHY

THEOSOPHICAL SOURCES

Besant, Annie, *Esoteric Christianity or the Lesser Mysteries* (Wheaton, Ill.: Quest Books; Theosophical Publishing House, 2006 [1903]).
  The Growth of the Theosophical Society (Adyar, Madras: The Theosophist Office, 1912).
Blavatsky, Helena Petrovna, *H. P. Blavatsky Collected Writings*, vol. I: *1874–1878* (3rd edn., Wheaton, Ill.: The Theosophical Publishing House [TPH], 1988); vol. IV: *1882–1883* (Wheaton, Ill.: TPH, 1988); vol. VI: *1883–1885* (Los Angeles: Blavatsky Writings Publication Fund, 1954); vol. VII: *1886–1887* (Adyar, Madras: TPH, 1958); vol. VIII: *1887* (Adyar, Madras: TPH, 1960); vol. IX: *1888* (Adyar, Madras: TPH, 1962); vol. X: *1888–1889* (Adyar, Madras:

---

[99] Leadbeater, *The Masters and the Path*, #1042.
[100] H. P. Blavatsky, *The Original Programme of the Theosophical Society* (repr.; Adyar, Madras: Theosophical Publishing House, 1974).

TPH, 1964); vol. XI: *1889* (Wheaton, Ill.: TPH, 1973); vol. XII: *1889–1890*
(Wheaton, Ill.: TPH, 1980); vol. XIII: *1890–1891* (Wheaton, Ill.: TPH, 1982);
vol. XIV (Wheaton, Ill.: TPH, 1985).

"The Esoteric Character of the Gospels," in *Collected Writings*, vol. VIII,
172–317. Originally published in *Lucifer* 1.3 (November, 1887), 173–180, 1.4
(December, 1887), 299–310, and 1.6 (February, 1888), 490–496.

"Facts Underlying Adept Biographies," in *Collected Writings*, vol. XIV, 137–162.

"A Few Questions to 'HIRAF***'," in *Collected Writings*, vol. I, 101–119. Originally published in *Spiritual Scientist* (Boston) (July 15 and 22, 1875), 217–218,
224, 236–237.

"The Future Occultist," in *Collected Writings*, vol. VI, 257–263. Originally
published in *The Theosophist* 5.11 (59) (August, 1884), 263–264.

"Instruction No. III," in *Collected Writings*, vol. XII, 581–652.

"The Kabalah and the Kabalists at the Close of the Nineteenth Century," in
Collected Writings, vol. VII, 250–272. Originally published in *Lucifer* 10.57
(May, 1892), 185–196.

"Miscellaneous Notes," in *Collected Writings*, vol. X, 90–92. Originally published in *Lucifer* 2.12 (August, 1888), 472, 497.

"Le phare de l'inconnu," in *Collected Writings*, vol. XI, 212–247 (Translation:
"The Beacon of the Unknown"), 248–283. Originally published in *La Revue
Théosophique* (Paris), 1.3 (21 May, 1889), 1–9; 1.4 (21 June, 1889), 1–7; 1.5
(21 July, 1889), 1–6; 1.6 (21 August, 1889), 1–9.

"Pistis-Sophia," in *Collected Writings*, vol. XIII, 1–81.

"Psychic and Noetic Action," in *Collected Writings*, vol. XII, 350–374. Originally
published in *Lucifer* 7.38 (October, 1890), 89–98.

"Réponse aux fausses conceptions de M. L'abbé Roca relatives à mes observations sur l'ésotérisme chrétien," in *Collected Writings*, vol. IX, 194–215
(Translation: "Reply to the Mistaken Conceptions of the Abbé Roca Concerning my Observations on Christian Esotericism," 216–237). Originally
published in *Le Lotus* (Paris) 2.13 (April, 1888), 3–19 (original French article).

"Traces of the Mysteries," in *Collected Writings*, vol. XIV, 281–293.

"A Word with the Theosophists," in *Collected Writings*, vol. IV, 357–358. Originally published in *The Theosophist* 4.6 (March 1883), 143–145.

"A Word with 'Zero'," in *Collected Writings*, vol. IV, 358–365. Perhaps published
in the Poona Observer, but there is no publication information given.

Isis Unveiled, 2 vols. (Los Angeles: The Theosophy Company, 1982; originally
published in New York: J. W. Bouton, 1877).

The Key to Theosophy (Los Angeles: The Theosophy Company, 1973; originally
published London: Theosophical Publishing Company; New York: W. Q.
Judge, 1889).

The Original Programme of the Theosophical Society (repr.; Adyar, Madras: Theosophical Publishing House, 1974).

The Secret Doctrine, 2 vols. in 1 (Los Angeles: The Theosophy Company, 1974;
facsimile of the original edition; New York: Theosophical University Press,
1888).

Theosophical Glossary (Los Angeles: The Theosophy Company, 1973 [1892]).

Brooks, F. T. *Neo-Theosophy Exposed* (repr.; Edmonton: Edmonton Theosophical Society, 1991 [1914]).

Farthing, Geoffrey, "The Theosophical Society and its Future Manifesto 1996." Online at www.teosofia.com/1996_GAF_Manifesto.html.

Leadbeater, Charles Webster, *The Christian Creed* (2nd edn., London and Benares: The Theosophical Publishing House, 1909 [1904]). Online at www.anandgholap.net/Christian_Creed-CWL.htm.

   The Masters and the Path (Adyar, Madras: The Theosophical Publishing House, 1925). Online at www.anandgholap.net/Masters_And_Path-CWL.htm.

   A Textbook on Theosophy (Adyar, Madras: The Theosophical Publishing House, 1912).

Mead, G. R. S., *Did Jesus Live 100 BC?* (London: Theosophical Publishing Society, 1903). Online at www.gnosis.org/library/grs-mead/jesus_live_100/index.htm.

   Fragments of a Faith Forgotten (New Hyde Park, N.Y.: University Books, 1960). Online at www.sacred-texts.com/gno/fff/fff35.htm.

Purucker, Gottfried de, "The Real Birth-Date of Jesus," in G. de Purucker, *Studies in Occult Philosophy* (Covina: Theosophical University Press, 1945). Online at www.theosociety.org/pasadena/soph/sopqa01.htm#realbirth.

Sinnett, A. P., *The Occult World* (8th edn., London: Theosophical Publishing Society, 1908). First edition online as Google Book at blavatskyarchives.com/sinnettowgateway.htm.

   Esoteric Buddhism (5th edn., San Diego, Cal.: Wizards Bookshelf, 1981 [1883]).

Sotheran, Charles, "Ancient Theosophy; or Spiritism in the Past," *Spiritual Scientist* 4.7 (April 20, 1876), 76.

Thomas, Margaret, *Theosophy and Neo-Theosophy?* (Grand Rapids, Ohio: Isis Books, 1995 [1925]).

CHRISTIAN AND ESOTERIC SOURCES

Arguments of Celsus, Porphyry, and the Emperor Julian against the Christians; Extracts from Diodorus Siculus, Josephus, and Tacitus, Relating to the Jews (trans. Dr. Lardner; London: Thomas Rodd, 1830).

Athanasius, *On the Incarnation of the Word.* Online at www.newadvent.org/fathers/2802.htm.

   De Synodis. Online at www.newadvent.org/fathers/2817.htm.

Augustine of Hippo, *On Christian Doctrine.* Online at www.newadvent.org/fathers/1202.htm and ccat.sas.upenn.edu/jod/augustine/ddc.html.

Catechism of the Catholic Church. Online at www.vatican.va/archive/ENG0015/_INDEX.HTM.

Clement of Alexandria, *Stromateis* (trans. John Ferguson; Washington, D.C.: Catholic University of America Press, 1991). Online at www.newadvent.org/fathers/07014.htm.

Epiphanius, *The Gospel of the Ebionites.* Online at www.earlychristianwritings.com/text/gospelebionites.html.

Gregory Thaumaturgus, *On the Trinity*. Online at www.newadvent.org/fathers/0606.htm.

Higgins, Godfrey, *Anacalypsis*, 2 vols. (New Hyde Park, N.Y: University Books, 1965 [1833]).

Hippolytus, *Philosophumena or the Refutation of All Heresies. Formerly attributed to Origen, but now to Hippolytus, Bishop and Martyr, who flourished about 220 A.D.*, vol. II (trans. F. Legge; London: Society for Promoting Christian Knowledge, 1921). Online at www.newadvent.org/fathers/050101.htm.

Irenaeus, *Adversus Haereses*. Online at www.newadvent.org/fathers/0103126.htm.

Jacolliot, Louis-François, *Christna et le Christ* (Paris: Lacroix, 1874).

   La Bible dans l'Inde, vie de Iezeus Christna (Paris: Librairie Internationale, 1869). Translated into English as *The Bible in India: Hindoo Origin of Hebrew and Christian Revelation* (London: J. C. Hotten; New York: Carleton, 1870). Online at www.archive.org/details/bibleinindiahindoojacorich.

Justin Martyr, *First Apology*. Online at www.newadvent.org/fathers/0126.htm.

Lactantius, *Divine Institutes*. Online at www.newadvent.org/fathers/07014.htm.

The New American Bible. Online at www.vatican.va/archive/ENG0839/_INDEX.HTM.

Tertullian, *Apology*. Online at www.newadvent.org/fathers/0301.htm.

   On the Flesh of Christ. Online at www.newadvent.org/fathers/0315.htm and www.tertullian.org/works/de_carne_christi.htm.

Theophilus, *To Autolycus*. Online at www.newadvent.org/fathers/02041.htm.

LITERATURE

Burnouf, Eugine, *Le Bhâgavata Purâna, ou Histoire poétique de Krichna*, 3 vols. (Paris: n.p., 1840–1847).

Caracostea, Daniel, "Louis-François Jacolliot (1837–1890): A Biographical Essay," *Theosophical History* 9.1 (January, 2003), 12–39.

Gomes, Michael, "Nehru's Theosophical Tutor," *Theosophical History* 7.3 (July, 1998), 99–108.

Haught, John, "Kenosis," in Wentzel Vrede van Huyssteen (ed.), *Encyclopedia of Science and Religion* (New York: Macmillan Reference USA, 2003), vol. II, 500–502.

Kannengiesser, Charles, "Arianism," in Lindsay Jones (ed.), *Encyclopedia of Religion* (2nd edn., Detroit: Macmillan Reference USA, 2005), vol. I, 478–479.

Kelly, J. N. D., *Early Christian Doctrines* (5th edn., London: A. & C. Black, 1977 [1958]).

Lundy, John P., *Monumental Christianity or the Art and Symbolism of the Primitive Church* (New York: J. W. Bouton, 1876).

McKenna, S. J., "Adoptionism," in *New Catholic Encyclopedia*, vol. I (2nd edn., Detroit: Gale, 2003), 119–120.

Michael, Franz H., *Rule by Incarnation: Tibetan Buddhism and its Role in Society and State* (Boulder, Col.: Westview Press, 1982).

Neander, Augustus, *The History of the Christian Religion and Church During the First Three Centuries* (trans. Henry John Rose, Philadelphia: James M. Campbell, and New York: Saxton & Miles, 1844). Google Book online at books.google.com/books?id=xw0QAAAAYAAJ&pg=PA103&lpg=PA103& dq=neander+history+of+the+church+vol+1&source=web&ots= QWsoVAiLR0&sig=rFrebQIZq03ObGH13PQF4C23d2s&hl= en#PPR1,M1.

"The Nicene Creed." Online at www.creeds.net/ancient/nicene.htm.

O'Collins, Gerald, S. J., *Christology: A Biblical, Historical, and Systematic Study of Jesus* (Oxford: Oxford University Press, 1995).

Peterson, J. B. "Æons," in *The Catholic Encyclopedia* (New York: Robert Appleton Company, 1907). Online at www.newadvent.org/cathen/01173c.htm.

Price, Leslie, "Jesus in Theosophical History," *Theosophical History* 1.3 (July 1985), 38–45.

Santucci, James, "Foreword," in Govert Schüller, *Krishnamurti and the World Teacher Project: Some Theosophical Perceptions* (Fullerton, Cal.: Theosophical History, 1997), i–xiii.

  "The Notion of Race in Theosophy," *Nova Religio* 11 (2008), 37–64.

Schüller, Govert, *Krishnamurti and the World Teacher Project: Some Theosophical Perceptions* (Fullerton: Cal.: Theosophical History, 1997).

Wilder, Alexander, *New Platonism and Alchemy: A Sketch of the Doctrines and Principal Teachers of the Eclectic or Alexandrian School* (Albany, N.Y.: Weed, Parsons and Company, Printers, 1869; repr.; Minneapolis: Wizards Bookshelf, 1975). Online at www.theosophy-nw.org/theosnw/books/wil-plat/npa-hp.htm.

Wilken, Robert L., "Nestorianism," in Lindsay Jones (ed.) *Encyclopedia of Religion* (2nd edn.; Detroit: Macmillan Reference USA, 2005), vol. X, 6482–6483.

Williams, Michael Allen, *Rethinking "Gnosticism": An Argument for Dismantling a Dubious Category* (Princeton: Princeton University Press, 1996).

CHAPTER 12

The Aryan Christ: the electrochristology of Ariosophy

Nicholas Goodrick-Clarke

INTRODUCTION

From the 1830s onwards scientists undertook a massive program of empirical experiment in the fields of physics, chemistry, biology, zoology, medicine, geography, anthropology, and ethnography. Radical new hypotheses concerning the properties of matter and the origins of life often posed fundamental questions concerning philosophical and religious views of humanity, creation, and the natural order. As modern science was almost exclusively a Western enterprise, so its discoveries interacted often directly with the scriptural authority of Christianity. Moreover, scientific discoveries were paralleled by comparable advances and discoveries relating to the ancient history and archaeology of early civilizations, the varieties of religion, Bible scholarship, and Christian theology. This study documents the further reaches of this encounter between natural science and Christian theology, involving a dualist theodicy of race and millennial notions of salvation expressed in terms of a pure-blooded Christ. Its context is the notion of an Aryan master race, widespread in European science and scholarship from the 1850s, destined to rule the world as the acme of human perfection, and the concept of selective breeding or eugenics. Its combination led to the reformulation of Christianity along racialist lines among certain German theological and political circles before and during the Third Reich.

This study focuses on the heterodox Christian doctrines of Jörg Lanz von Liebenfels (1874–1954), a former Cistercian monk, scholar, and founder of the Ordo Novi Templi (ONT), his own religious order, but reference will also be made to similar expressions of Aryan and German Christianity within the *völkisch* (nationalist-racialist) precursors of the Third Reich in the period 1900 to 1935.[1] Lanz called his doctrine Ario-Christianity

---

[1] There now exist several full-length studies of Lanz von Liebenfels' life, thought, and works. Scholarly works include Wilfried Daim, *Der Mann, der Hitler die Ideen gab: Von den religiösen Verirrungen eines Sektierers zum Rassenwahn des Diktators* (Munich: Isar Verlag, 1958; 2nd edn, Vienna: Hermann

or Ariosophy, a term combining the notion of the Aryan race with the current vogue of Theosophy, the scientistic-esoteric movement that flourished in Europe, India, and America between 1880 and the 1930s. Ariosophy expounded a gnostic form of Christianity underpinned by Lanz's racial theology of a dualistic antagonism between the divine light-skinned Aryans and the demonic dark-skinned races and buttressed by esoteric biblical exegesis. Lanz also assimilated current scientific discoveries, seeing electricity as a form of divine revelation and inspiration. In his fundamental text *Theozoologie* (1905), he attributed to the divine ancestors of the Aryan race extraordinary electrical powers of telepathy and omniscience. Lanz alleged that Jehovah, the God of Israel, was just such a prehistoric electrical being, while the heathen deities of Israel were all throwbacks to evil cults of interbreeding with the lower (non-divine) beasts, the ancestors of the dark races. Lanz identified Christ as an electrical being who came to redeem a fallen humankind from bestial miscegenation through a revival of the racial gnosis. According to Lanz, Christ was one of the last god-men, but not God. Christ's miracles and magical powers and the Transfiguration confirmed his electrical nature. The electrochristology of Ariosophy represents the redemptive strand of a theology in support of the maintenance and survival of the white race in a global context.[2]

THE INFLUENCE OF SOCIAL DARWINISM AND RACIAL ANTHROPOLOGY

Lanz von Liebenfels' theology was predicated upon modern scientific ideas of evolution, zoological theories of humankind's descent, and racial differences. Earlier theories questioning the fixity of species (a tenet of the biblical account of creation) and suggestive of evolution had been advanced by

---

Böhlau, 1985); Nicholas Goodrick-Clarke, *The Occult Roots of Nazism: The Ariosophists of Austria and Germany 1890–1935* (Wellingborough: Aquarian Press, 1985; 2nd edn, New York: New York University Press, 1992; 3rd edn, London: I. B. Tauris, 2004); Ekkehard Hieronimus, *Lanz von Liebenfels: Eine Bibliographie* (Toppenstedt: Uwe Berg, 1991); Jan Willem de Groot, "Arische Gnosis" (MA dissertation, University of Amsterdam, 2001). Rudolf J. Mund, *Jörg Lanz v. Liebenfels: Die Esoterik des Christentums* (Stuttgart: Rudolf Arnold Spieth Verlag, 1976) is a hagiographical study by a senior member of the Ordo Novi Templi, while Horst Lorenz (ed.), *'Rosen aus Germaniens Bergen': Eine Denkschrift zum 50. Todestag des Begründers des Neutemplerordens Jörg Lanz von Liebenfels (19 VII 1874–22 IV 1954)* (Ilvesheim: Edition Weltwende, 2004) supplies a wealth of detailed material from an insider perspective.

[2] Lanz's electrotheology is discussed at some length in Nicholas Goodrick-Clarke, "The Esoteric Uses of Electricity: Theologies of Electricity from Swabian Pietism to Ariosophy," *Aries* 4.1 (2004), 69–90.

Georges-Louis Leclerc Buffon (1707–1788), Erasmus Darwin (1731–1802), and Jean-Baptiste Lamarck (1744–1829). Charles Darwin (1809–1882) crystallized these theories in his path-breaking *On the Origins of Species by Means of Natural Selection, or the Preservation of Races in the Struggle for Life* (1859) by proposing that species' development was accountable in terms of mechanical short-term adaptation to natural environment. It is notable that Darwin's hypothesis was neither initially nor primarily conceived as a theory of evolution towards some end or goal in the manner of optimistic eighteenth-century teleology, but simply a pragmatic attempt to explain change and development. Darwin's ideas were also politically ambivalent, used alike by protagonists of altruism, socialist egalitarianism, liberal theories of progress as well as by advocates of historical fatalism, the rule of the strong, and racial inequality. However, his sober scientific title anticipated two key themes that would dominate its religious and political interpretation over the next four decades: evolution and the nature of selection.[3]

While biology challenged divine and providential assumptions about the natural order, new discoveries in the human sciences suggested polygenic origins instead of the biblical monogenist account of creation and descent from Adam and Noachite genealogy (through his sons Shem, Ham, and Japhet). Thus had comparative linguistics and anthropology proceeded from the discovery of the Indo-European languages in 1787 by Sir William Jones (1746–1794) to the identification of the Indo-European or Aryan races by the 1820s. The word was derived from Herodotus' *Arioi* (an early name for the Medes and the Persians) and carried linguistic connotations of honor and aristocracy. Through the first half of the century philosophers, philologists, and geographers contributed to a general acceptance of the expansion and civilizing mission of the Aryan races which had given rise to the principal nations of Europe. Racial interpretations of history had begun to appear in the 1840s.[4] Late nineteenth-century studies on the Aryan race proliferated, especially in Germany and Austria, where the putative Aryans were increasingly related to questions of German national identity and destiny. Although increasingly detailed archaeological evidence threw doubt among specialists concerning the existence of a unitary Aryan race speaking a proto-Indo-European language, the notion persisted among a

---

[3] Hans-Günter Zmarzlik, "Der Sozialdarwinismus in Deutschland als geschichtliches Problem," *Vierteljahreshefte für Zeitgeschichte* 11 (1963), 247.

[4] Léon Poliakov, *The Aryan Myth: A History of Racist and Nationalist Ideas in Europe* (London: Chatto Heinemann, 1974), 188–214, 224–233.

number of serious prehistorians and anthropologists and gained ground in popular science and literature.[5]

If the supremacy of putative prehistoric forbears seemingly justified the hegemony of the European powers in the nineteenth century, racial anthropology could also serve cultural pessimism as a narrative involving the eclipse and extinction of the superior races. In his *Essai sur l'inégalité des races humaines* (1853) Count Arthur de Gobineau (1816–1882) described how, although instinctually opposed to cross-breeding with lower races, the white race's increased contact through civilization and conquest would produce alloys or infusions of inferior blood leading to degradation and decline. Gobineau's ideas were massively influential in Germany during the later decades of the nineteenth century finding articulate and effective exponents in such figures as Richard Wagner, Ludwig Schemann, and Houston Stewart Chamberlain.[6]

In Germany the Darwinian theory of natural selection found its major exponent and interpreter in Ernst Haeckel (1834–1919), professor of zoology at Jena and author of numerous specialist and popular books on evolution. His fundamental works on evolution included *Natürliche Schöpfungsgeschichte* (1868, Eng. 1876) and *Anthropogenie oder Entwick-lungsgeschichte des Menschen* (1874, Eng. 1903). During the 1880s and 1890s he sought to apply the laws he had discovered in biological and physical nature to society, thereby anticipating what would become a widespread movement of Social Darwinism in both Germany and the English-speaking world. From 1877 until 1886, Haeckel together with his colleague Ernst Krause edited *Kosmos*, the chief journal of the German Darwinian movement. Krause had written popular biographies of Erasmus and Charles Darwin as well as two influential books on Aryanism and Germanic religion. Specifically, Haeckel espoused a naturalist materialism and a campaign against Christianity, which he regarded as an otherworldly, ascetic belief-system, in whose place he offered a new religion of nature called Monism, as presented in such works as *Der Monismus als Band zwischen Religion und Wissenschaft* (1892, Eng. 1894) and *Die Welträtsel* (1899, *The Riddles of the Universe*, 1900).[7] Far from being a mechanistic materialist, Haeckel actually offered an empirically updated Romantic philosophy of

[5] Rolf Peter Sieferle, "Rassismus, Rassenhygiene, Menschenzuchtideale," in Uwe Puschner, Walter Schmitz and Justus H. Ulbricht (eds.), *Handbuch zur 'Völkischen Bewegung' 1871–1918* (Munich: K. G. Saur, 1996), 441.

[6] Michael D. Biddiss, *Father of Racist Ideology: The Social and Political Ideas of Count Gobineau* (London: Weidenfeld & Nicolson, 1970), 122ff., 256–258; Poliakov, *The Aryan Myth*, 234–238.

[7] Daniel Gasman, *The Scientific Origins of National Socialism: Social Darwinism in Ernst Haeckel and the German Monist League* (London: Macdonald; New York: American Elsevier, 1971), 13, 151.

nature (*Naturphilosophie*), redolent of the idealist scientific explanations involving Platonic "archetypes" or Aristotelian "ends" in natural history, botany, embryology, and palaeontology in the early nineteenth century. Like the Romantic philosophers of nature, Haeckel insisted on the absolute unity, harmony and consistency of nature as an all-embracing whole (*All-Natur*), the animation of the entire cosmos in a pan-psychic notion of the world-soul, and the biogenetic law that ontogeny recapitulates phylogeny.[8] Monism thus reformulated the restricted, pragmatic expression of Darwinism as an ideology of social and racial ideology within an idealistic vision of cosmic purpose and regeneration.

Haeckel found many supporters among the branches of the German Free-Thought Movement, founded by the materialist Ludwig Büchner in 1881, which united its members under the banner of secularism and opposition to Christianity. Haeckel's prominence, his tireless public lecturing, and the best-seller status of *Die Welträtsel* led to the foundation of the Monist League in 1906, which counted many thousands of members. Founding members of the League included writers Wilhelm Bölsche, Bruno Wille, and Wilhelm Schallmayer, one of the founders of the German eugenics movement, while the chemist and 1909 Nobel laureate Wilhelm Ostwald (1853–1932) became the League's director in 1911. Alongside the League journals flourished a number of other allied Monist periodicals, including *Das freie Wort, Neue Weltanschauung*, and *Dokumente des Fortschritts*.[9] Monism formed an early station in Lanz von Liebenfels' intellectual progress. After leaving the Cistercian order in 1899, he joined the Monist League and published several articles in *Das freie Wort*, in which he castigated the supranational Jesuits for undermining the regional and genealogical identity of Catholicism in Europe, supposedly continuous from the conversion of the Germanic tribes in the early Middle Ages. Another article was devoted to the budding topic of political anthropology.[10]

During the 1890s these currents of zoology, physical anthropology and Social Darwinism in Germany and the English-speaking world gave rise to movements of racial hygiene (eugenics) and social hygiene, another ideological milieu within which Lanz von Liebenfels formulated his own alternative theology. The development of Social Darwinism in the Anglo-American world owed its origin largely to the influence of Herbert Spencer's

---

[8] *Ibid.*, 64.   [9] *Ibid.*, 21–22.

[10] Jörg Lanz-Liebenfels, "Die Armee des schwarzen Papstes," *Das freie Wort* 2 (1903), 394–402, 451–459, 721–729; "Der große Kampf des Jesuitismus gegen den Katholizismus," *Das freie Wort* 3 (1904), 49–56; "Leo XIII., der 'Friedenspapst'," *Das freie Wort* 3 (1904), 338–346; "Politische Anthropologie," *Das freie Wort* 3 (1904), 778–795.

philosophy in the context of "laissez-faire" liberalism.[11] Spencer's emphasis on environmental factors also appealed to German Marxists, but German Social Darwinism of an anti-Christian hue was most evident in the influential work of Friedrich von Hellbach (1842–1892) and Alexander Tille (1866–1912), the latter linking Darwinism with Nietzschean philosophy. Imperialistic varieties of Social Darwinism were more familiar in Anglo-Saxon countries where colonial expansion was already more well advanced than in Germany, whereas Social Darwinism appealed to the mood of anxiety and potential decline in Austria following defeat in the Austro-German War of 1866, exclusion from the German Reich under Prussian leadership, and increasing friction within a multinational empire composed of Germans, Magyars, Slavs, and Latins. Hellbach had served as a senior officer in the Austrian army, while the early Austrian sociologists Ludwig Gumplowicz (1838–1909) and Gustav Ratzenhofer (1842–1904) notably employed Social Darwinist concepts of struggle in their studies of state and society.[12]

This older current of Social Darwinism scholarship was succeeded by newer currents by the turn of the century in Germany. A younger generation of racial anthropologists gathered around the journal *Politisch-Anthropologische Revue* (est. 1902) edited by Ludwig Woltmann (1871–1907), and the anthropologist Otto Ammon (1842–1915) who conducted statistical studies of the Baden population.[13] Woltmann had initially trained and practiced as a physician after taking two doctorates in medicine (1895) and the genetic basis of ethics (1896). After travels in Greece and Palestine he became a lecturer in evolution at Haubinda in Germany. Woltmann had joined the German Social Democratic Party by 1898, and his first book related Darwinian theory to socialism. After launching the journal, he published his major work *Politische Anthropologie* (1903), applying the theory of descent to the political development of different races. His next books examined the influence and contribution of the Germanic races in France and in the Italian Renaissance and were key works in promoting a historical, cultural, and aesthetic view of racial anthropology. After leaving the Cistercian order, Lanz von Liebenfels was introduced to Ludwig Woltmann's acquaintance in 1903 and published his first major piece in the pages of his journal.

---

[11] Robert C. Bannister, *Social Darwinism: Science and Myth in Anglo-American Social Thought* (Philadelphia: Temple University Press, 1979), chapters 2 and 3.

[12] Zmarzlik, "Der Sozialdarwinismus in Deutschland," 260–263.

[13] For Woltmann, see George L. Mosse, *The Crisis of German Ideology: Intellectual Origins of the Third Reich* (London: Weidenfeld & Nicolson, 1966), 99–103.

The German racial hygiene movement took further inspiration from a much-publicized prize offered in 1900 by the famous industrialist Alfred Krupp for a study of how selective human breeding could counter the degenerative effects of mass society and urbanization. The prize was won by Wilhelm Schallmayer (1857–1919), a doctor with social democratic and pacifist leanings who had previously addressed this problem in *Über die drohende körperliche Entartung der Kuturmenschheit* (1891).[14] His collaborator in the prize essay, later published as *Vererbung und Auslese im Lebenslauf der Völker* (1903), was the doctor Alfred Ploetz (1860–1940), who had published his *Grundlinien der Rassenhygiene* (1895), started the long-lived journal *Archiv für Rassen- und Gesellschaftsbiologie* (1904–1944) and founded the Gesellschaft für Rassenhygiene (German Eugenics Society) in Berlin in 1905. Ploetz sought a broad base among scientists and scholars with close links to the Monist League of Ernst Haeckel, the anthropologist Richard Thurnwald, and the geographer Friedrich Ratzel, as well as with the *völkisch* ideologues and organizers, Theodor Fritsch and Willibald Hentschel, whose Mittgart-Bund, a racialist utopian community, was later realized in a modified form as the Artamanen agrarian organization after the Great War. In late Wilhelmine society, these movements aiming at the improvement of the population in terms of genetic inheritance, health, and intelligence by means of birth control and family policy, appeared the natural allies of meliorism, emancipation, and scientific advance in the service of society, especially attractive to social planners and the medical profession. As such they were meritocratic rather than racialist and appeared as progressive strands of the broader reform movements dedicated to ecology, natural medicine, nudism, garden cities, land reform, and alternative education.[15] Popularized and politicized, these scientific and social movements of Social Darwinism, racial anthropology, and eugenics had a profound effect on intellectual life and religious belief in the late nineteenth century.[16] These currents were determinant influences on Lanz von Liebenfels' heterodox Christianity after 1900.

---

[14] Sheila Faith Weiss, *Race Hygiene and National Efficiency: The Eugenics of Wilhelm Schallmayer* (Berkeley: University of California Press, 1987).

[15] Jürgen Reulecke, "Rassenhygiene, Sozialhygiene, Eugenik," in Diethart Kerbs and Jürgen Reulecke (eds.) *Handbuch der deutschen Reformbewegungen 1880–1933* (Wuppertal: Peter Hammer, 1998), 197–201.

[16] Ingo Wiwjorra, "Die deutsche Vorgeschichtsforschung und ihr Verhältnis zu Nationalismus und Rassismus," in Uwe Puschaner, Walter Schmitz, and Justus H. Ulbricht (eds.), *Handbuch der 'Völkischen Bewegung' 1871–1918* (Munich: K. G. Saur, 1996), 194–197.

THE OLD TESTAMENT AND ASSYRIOLOGY: BIBLE AND BABEL

So much for Lanz's debt to contemporary science, but what were the theological bases of his Christianity? Adolf Josef Lanz (he later added the aristocratic von Liebenfels) was born into a middle-class Viennese family in 1874. A pious and highly intelligent youth, he completed his schooling at the old Gymnasium in the Rosasgasse and decided "with innermost vocation" to become a monk. In July 1893, at the age of nineteen, he entered the novitiate of the Cistercian order at Heiligenkreuz Abbey in the Wienerwald, the second oldest such foundation in Europe dating from 1133. The monastery effectively provided Lanz with a sound higher education in theology, biblical exegesis and church history. There he was instructed by Dr. Nivard Schlögl (1864–1939), who had himself entered the novitiate in 1884, becoming novice-master in 1890 and taking his doctorate at Vienna University in 1896. From 1896 to 1908 he taught as the professor of Old Testament at the Institutum Theologicum in Heiligenkreuz. From Schlögl Lanz undoubtedly received a thorough training in the Hebrew Bible, with emphasis on the Pentateuch, the prophets and Old Testament apocrypha. Schlögl's influence must partly account for Lanz's enduring interest and focus in this area of exegesis and that so much of his early theological writing was devoted to Hebraic, Jewish, and Old Testament subjects.[17] Although committed to Cistercian ideals and despite his fast progress through the stages of solemn vows, subdeacon, deacon, ordination as priest and promotion to *magister alumnorum*, Lanz abruptly left the monastery in April 1899 for reasons that remain unclear.[18]

At the beginning of 1900, while reading in the Vienna University Library, Lanz found *Niniveh and its Remains* (1849), the famous account of archaeological excavations by Sir Austen Henry Layard (1817–1894) in Assyria over the years 1845 to 1846. Lanz retrospectively described this work as a revelation: "the last veil fell from the mystery, I saw my way clearly ahead."[19] This crucial moment of illumination, the point at which Lanz suddenly

---

[17] Schlögl subsequently developed a form of conjectural criticism based on his conviction that the Bible had been originally written in rhythmic unities, and on this basis he published his Bible translations, which the Vatican regarded as erroneous and placed on the Index of Forbidden Books in January 1922. Schlögl dedicated his translations "to the German people" and by 1920 he proposed the exclusion of any member with Jewish grandparents from Catholic student organisations. It is not clear whether he already held these nationalist and antisemitic views before the First World War. See Alkuin Volker Schachenmayr, *Prägende Professoren in der Entwicklung des theologischen Lehrbetriebes im Cistercienserstift Heiligenkreuz* (Langwaden: Bernardus, 2004).

[18] Cf. full discussion of available sources in Hieronimus, *Lanz von Liebenfels*, 12–13.

[19] Jörg Lanz von Liebenfels, "Chronikon Archprioratus Ord.Nov.Templ. ad Werfenstein Tom.1," undated MS, 19.

grasped a new world-view, involved the integration of new archaeological discoveries and a politicized form of anthropology with his schooling in theology and biblical exegesis, especially that of the Old Testament.

Layard was a British traveler, archaeologist, historian, draughtsman, and diplomat, whose cosmopolitan education and travels had led him from Constantinople to make explorations of the ruins of Assyria, where his curiosity had been first aroused by the ruins of Nimrud on the River Tigris and the great mound of Kuyunjik near Mosul. Layard began digging at Nimrud, biblical Calah, built in 879 BCE as his new capital by King Ashur-nasirpal II (reigned 883–859 BCE). He quickly struck treasure: enormous stone reliefs depicting horses and riders, sieges, captives, archers on chariots, lion hunts, and an anthropomorphic image of a hawk-headed deity seven feet high. Some of the panels carried cuneiform inscriptions, the cryptic wedge-shaped script first discovered by the Italian traveler Pietro della Valle in the early seventeenth century but not deciphered until 1846 by Sir Henry Creswicke Rawlinson (1810–1895). A year later at Nimrud Layard found statues of colossal winged lion- and bull-men, and these enormous artifacts, together with the Black Obelisk of Shalmaneser III, king of Assyria (reigned 858–824 BCE) were shipped to the British Museum.[20]

The ancient Assyrians were reputed for violence and immorality in the Bible and classical authors, but the sheer size and fine execution of the objects in the exhibition drew enormous interest. Layard's book sold 8,000 copies in its first year and an "Assyrian revival" was plainly evident in art and design at the Great Exhibition at London in 1851. Layard received an Oxford DCL in 1849 and then mounted a second expedition to excavate the ruins of Babylon and the mounds of southern Mesopotamia.[21] Assyriology was carried further by George Smith (1840–1876), a young assistant to Henry Rawlinson at the British Museum. Working on the eighty tablets from the library of King Ashurbanipal (reigned 668–627 BCE) at Nineveh, Smith found the familiar story of the Flood. Proceeding to Nineveh in 1873, Smith found further fragments containing the story of man's original innocence,

[20] Austen Henry Layard, *Nineveh and its Remains: with an Account of a Visit to the Chaldaean Christians of Kurdistan, and the Yezidis, or Devil-Worshippers; and an Enquiry into the Manners and Arts of the Ancient Assyrians*, 2 vols. (London: John Murray, 1849); Layard, *The Monuments of Nineveh: From Drawings Made on the Spot* (London: John Murray, 1849); cf. Henry Creswicke Rawlinson, *The Persian Cuneiform Inscription at Behistun: Deciphered and Translated with Memoir on Persian Cuneiform Inscriptions in General* (London: Parker for the Royal Asiatic Society, 1846); Rawlinson, *A Commentary on the Cuneiform Inscriptions of Babylonia and Assyria; Including Readings of the Inscription on the Nimrud Obelisk, and a Brief Notice of the Ancient Kings of Nineveh and Babylon* (London: J. W. Parker, 1850).

[21] Austen Henry Layard, *Nineveh and Babylon: A Narrative of a Second Expedition to Assyria during the Years 1849, 1850 and 1851* (London: John Murray, 1867).

the temptation and the fall.[22] These Assyrian epics of Gilgamesh and creation drew manifest parallels with the biblical account of man's creation, the flood, the Tower of Babel, and the patriarchs in Genesis.

German scholarship next took a hand, when the orientalist Eberhard Schrader (1836–1908) published his study of the cuneiform inscriptions from the excavations as *Die assyrisch-babylonischen Keilinschriften* (1872). Schrader had first achieved distinction for his work on Ethiopian languages and began his academic career as professor of theology at Zurich, subsequently holding chairs at Giessen (1870) and Jena (1873). His initial focus on biblical research enabled him to examine the Assyrian-Babylonian sources of Jewish religion and mythology, as published in his popular work *Die Keilinschriften und das Alte Testament* (1872). Appointed professor of oriental languages at the Friedrich-Wilhelm-Universität Berlin in 1878, Schrader's chief achievements were in the field of Assyriology, where he acquired an international reputation. In 1885 his widely read book was translated as *The Cuneiform Inscriptions and the Old Testament*, while the original German went through three editions. In 1903 it was rewritten by Heinrich Zimmern and Hugo Winckler, who both published key works on biblical and Babylonian prehistory and myth. Schrader's monumental five-volume collection of Assyrian and Babylonian cuneiform texts was published as *Keilinschriftliche Bibliothek* (1889–1896).[23]

Assyriology, cuneiform inscriptions, and a Mesopotamian origin for the oldest records of the Bible had therefore captured the European imagination of the general public and scholars alike during the latter half of the nineteenth century. The implications of an Assyrian and Babylonian source for the Jewish Bible obviously impacted directly on questions of biblical authority, revelation, and the Christian faith. This was dramatically illustrated by the storm of controversy unleashed by the German Assyriologist Friedrich Delitzsch (1850–1922), following his two lectures on "Babel and Bible" delivered on January 13 and February 1, 1902 to members of the Deutsche Orient-Gesellschaft in the presence of Kaiser Wilhelm II

---

[22] George Smith, *History of Assurbanipal, Translated from the Cuneiform Inscriptions* (London: Williams & Norgate, 1871); Smith, *The Chaldean Account of Genesis, Containing the Description of Creation, the Fall of Man, the Deluge, the Tower of Babel, the Times of the Patriarchs, and Nimrod; Babylonian Fables, and Legends of the Gods; from the Cuneiform Inscriptions* (London, 1876).

[23] Eberhard Schrader, *Die assyrisch-babylonische Keilinschriften: Kritische Untersuchung der Grundlagen ihrer Entzifferung* (Leipzig, 1872); Schrader, *Keilinschriften und das Alte Testament* (Giessen, 1872); Schrader, *Keilinschriftliche Bibliothek: Sammlung von Assyrischen und Babylonischen Texten in Umschrift und Übersetzung*, 5 vols. (Berlin: Reuther's Verlagsbuchhandlung, 1889–1896; 3rd edn, ed. Dr. H. Zimmern and Dr. H. Winckler; Berlin, 1903); Heinrich Zimmern, *Biblische und babylonische Urgeschichte* (Berlin: Vorderasiatische Gesellschaft, 1901); Hugo Winckler, *Die babylonische Weltschöpfung* (Berlin: Vorderasiatische Gesellschaft, 1906).

at Berlin. The son of a Lutheran scholar of the Old Testament and Hebrew, Delitzsch initially studied ancient languages, Coptic, and Sanskrit, writing his doctorate on the relationship between Indo-Germanic and Semitic root-words in 1873.[24] A providential meeting at Jena with Eberhard Schrader led him away from Sanskrit studies to the expanding new field of Assyrian, so that he habilitated in Semitic languages and Assyriology in 1874 at Leipzig, becoming professor there in 1877, then at Breslau in 1893, before succeeding Schrader as professor of Assyriology at Berlin in 1899. As co-founder of the Deutsche Orient-Gesellschaft and director of the West Asian department of the Berlin Royal Museums, he was a prominent member of the German academic community, making major contributions to the study of Assyrian and Akkadian and the promotion of Old Testament criticism.[25] His two lectures on Babel and Bible began by recalling that until late into the nineteenth century, the Old Testament formed

a world by itself . . . it spoke of times . . . and peoples of whom there is no mention or only a passing mention among Greek and Roman writers. From about 550 BC onwards, the Bible was the only source for the history of the Near East . . . now at a stroke [with the excavations] the walls that have shut off the remoter portion of the Old Testament scene of action fall and . . . a flood of light . . . illuminates the whole of the time-honored Book . . . because Hebrew antiquity from beginning to end is closely linked with this same Babylonia and Assyria.[26]

Delitzsch recounted Rawlinson's location of the city of Ur of the Chaldees, Abraham's home (Gen. 11.31; 15.7), Smith's discovery of Carchemish, site of Nebuchadnezzar's victory over Pharaoh Necho (Jer. 46.2) in 605 BCE, and the many images of Babylonian life on the excavated reliefs that matched Hebrew experience and customs described in the Bible.

More importantly, as Smith had speculated, Assyrian and Babylonian literature anticipated many themes and events in the Bible. According to Delitzsch, the El-Amarna excavations in Egypt of 1887 had shown how Canaan, home of the twelve tribes of Israel after the Exodus, was "a domain completely pervaded by Babylonian culture" in trade, law, custom, science, language, and literature. Babylonian religious literature and myth described a Sabbath, the temptation of woman by a serpent, pre- and post-deluge

---

[24] Friedrich Delitzsch, *Studien über indogermanisch-semitische Wurzelwortverwandtschaft* (Leipzig: J. C. Hinrichs'sche Buchhandlung, 1873).

[25] Delitzsch's best known scholarly works included *Prolegomena eines neuen hebräisch-aramäischen Wörterbuches zum Alten Testament* (1886), *Geschichte Babyloniens und Assyriens* (1891), *Assyrisches Handwörterbuch* (1894–96), *Das babylonische Weltschöpfungs-Epos* (1897).

[26] Friedrich Delitzsch, *Babel and Bible: Two Lectures Delivered before the Members of the Deutsche Orient-Gesellschaft in the Presence of the German Emperor* (ed. and introd. C. H. W. Johns; London: Williams & Norgate, 1903), 6–7.

calendars, a cosmogony describing a heroic battle between the deity and a fearsome sea-monster and its progeny (Marduk and Tiamât), notions of hell and heaven, intermediary animal-headed demons and winged beings, which all had their echo in the Old Testament's account of the Creation, the Fall, the Flood, Sheol and Paradise, and the Jewish idea of cherubim angels. The book of Job, a special subject of Delitzsch, betrayed a close acquaintance with Babylonian ideas, witness Jehovah's battle with the monsters Behemoth and Leviathan. Even the fifth, sixth, and seventh commandments and the notion of suffering, illness, and death as a punishment for sin also found prototypes in Babel. In Delitzsch's view the Old Testament could no longer be regarded as unique and therefore as a revelation. The fundamental authority of the Old Testament was thereby questioned and the two lectures, the second seeking to mollify outraged theologians, caused a furore that led to some 200 scholarly works in response and went through at least ten editions between 1903 and 1905, as well as being widely translated.[27]

Studies in Assyriology and the history of religion were much documented by Lanz in his published work. The British archaeologists and decoders of cuneiform were foremost: Austen Henry Layard's pioneering accounts of Nineveh and his *Inscriptions in the Cuneiform Character* (1882), George Rawlinson's *Cuneiform Inscriptions* (1861–1896), and the German translation of George Smith's *Die Keilinschrifttexte Assurbanibals* (1887–1889), and his *Miscellaneous Assyrian Texts of the British Museum* (1887). Lanz had frequent recourse to the monumental five-volume *Keilinschriftliche Bibliothek* (1889–1896), edited by Eberhard Schrader. Other Assyriological works consulted included *Die Geschichte Babyloniens und Assyriens* (1885) and *Die altisraelitische Überlieferung* (1897) by Fritz Hommel (1854–1936), professor of Semitic languages at Munich, Thomas Friedrich, *Kabiren und Keilinschriften* (1894), Peter Jensen's *Die Kosmologie der Babylonier* (1890) and *Assyrisch-babylonische Mythen und Epen* (1900) in the *Keilinschriftliche Bibliothek*, Eduard Stucken's *Astralmythen der Hebraer, Babylonier und Aegypter* (1896), and Friedrich Delitzsch's *Das babylonische Weltschöpfungsepos* (1897). Linguistic studies relating to cuneiform and links between Indo-European and Semitic languages included Delitzsch's doctoral thesis *Studien über indogermanisch-semitische Wurzelverwandtschaft* (1873), his *Assyrisches Handwörterbuch* (1896) and *Die Entstehung des ältesten Schriftsystems* (1897), Simon Leo Reinisch, *Der einheitliche Ursprung der Sprachen der alten Welt* (1873), *Aryo-Semitic Speech* (1881) by James

---

[27] Delitzsch, *Babel and Bible*.

Frederick McCurdy (1847–1935), a Hebraist and Sanskritist at Princeton, who then studied for three years with the Lutheran Hebraist Franz Delitzsch at Göttingen and Leipzig until 1885, when appointed to the chair of Assyriology at Toronto, Carl Abel's *Einleitung in ein aegyptisch-semitisch-indoeuropäisches Wurzelwörterbuch* (1896), and Rudolf Meringer's *Indogermanische Sprachwissenschaft* (1897).

THEOZOOLOGY

As an Old Testament scholar at Heiligenkreuz under Schlögl's tuition, Lanz was well prepared to engage in this debate about the Assyrian and Babylonian influences upon the ancient Israelites and the Jewish Bible. Lanz began to publish freelance journalism after the Frankfurt-based journal *Die Umschau* asked him for an essay on Delitzsch's *Babel und Bibel*, a commission Lanz considered very significant in steering him towards his new world-view. If Assyriology had so recently illuminated the Old Testament as a prehistorical record of the Israelites, so racial anthropology provided Lanz with further speculation on the nature of man's origins, evolution and racial differences. Lanz's next article addressed the discoveries of the 25,000 year-old Cro-Magnon man and other skeletal remains of the Upper Palaeolithic era, excavated from 1895 onwards in the Baousse-Rousse caves, the proto-Indo-European homeland, and the racial eugenic theories of Hans Driesmans (1863–1927).[28]

Layard's fine drawings of the Assyrian winged lion-men, bull-men and other anthropomorphic hybrids evidently triggered Lanz's revolutionary interpretation of the Old Testament. The year 1903 brought new academic and editorial contacts. Through the *Umschau*, Lanz got his work accepted by the semi-Monist journal *Das freie Wort* and the newly founded *Politische-Anthropologische Revue*, edited by Ludwig Woltmann, with whom Lanz began to correspond.[29] His first major publication, devoted to the prehistory of the arts, was published in Woltmann's journal in May 1903.[30] His long article "Anthropozoon biblicum" in a periodical for biblical research indicated where Lanz's reading of Layard had led him. From

---

[28] J. Lanz-Liebenfels, "Friedrich Delitzsch: Über Babel und Bibel," *Die Umschau* 6 (1902), 386–389, 407–410; "Der Mensch der 'Grotte des Enfants' (Baoussé-Roussé)," *Die Umschau* 6 (1902), 566–567; "2. Urgeschichtliche Beziehungen der Indogermanen zu den anderen Rassen," *Die Umschau* 7 (1903), 338–339; "3. Die Urheimat der 'Indogermanen'," *Die Umschau* 7 (1903), 649–651; "Rasse und Milieu," *Die Umschau* 7 (1903), 121–123.

[29] Lanz von Liebenfels, "Chronikon," 22.

[30] J. Lanz-Liebenfels, "Die Urgeschichte der Künste," *Politisch-Anthropologische Revue* 2.2 (1903), 134–156.

his analysis of obscure mystery cults described by Herodotus, Euhemerus, Plutarch, Strabo, and Pliny, Lanz concluded that the ancient civilizations had practiced an orgiastic cult involving sexual intercourse with various kinds of beasts: "Hinter den Kabirenmysterien und hinter den anderen Geheimkulten steckt die Sünde mit dem Thier, die Sodomie oder schärfer die systematische, in Cultformen gekleidete Bestialität." Lanz claimed that Layard's excavations at Nimrud, notably the relief of Ashurnasirpal II (883–859 BCE) and the Black Obelisk of Shalmaneser III (858–824 BCE), had enabled him to identify the actual animals used in these cults. These artifacts showed such beasts (*pagutu, bazaati, udumi*) adorned with jewellery being sent as tribute from neighboring kingdoms to the Assyrians. Lanz claimed that these varieties of amphibious scaly anthropoid bipeds were the "*Nicker*" and dwarves of tales and legend. The pygmies of recent anthropological discovery were descendants of the smaller *pagatu* and *bazaati*, while the *udumi* were enormous gorilla-like anthropoids, the giants of prehistory.[31]

This was the core of Lanz's world-view, later apostrophized as the hypotheses of "ariosophical esotericism."[32] For his scientific authorities, Lanz relied on sources ranging from Claudius Aelianus (c. 175–235), the French Protestant theologian Samuel Bochart's *Hierozoicon* (1663), a zoological treatise on the animals of the Bible, which possibly inspired Lanz's basic manifesto title "theozoology," to contemporary zoologists and physical anthropologists, such as Wilhelm Bölsche (1861–1939), author of *Das Liebesleben in der Natur* (1900–1903) and a member of the Monist League, Hermann Klaatsch (1863–1916), professor of anatomy at Heidelberg and Breslau and an authority on evolutionary theory, and Alfred Brehm (1829–1884), the popular zoological writer. The eminent Viennese prehistorian Matthäus Much (1832–1909) and the ethnologists Karl Penka (1847–1912), Heinrich Driesmans (1863–1927), Theodor Poesche (1826–1899), and Ludwig Wilser (1850–1923) supplied Lanz with the contemporary thesis of an "Aryan" race, its origins, migration and superiority. According to Lanz, the pure-blooded Aryans (*Homo Ariacus*) could be traced back to America or the fabled submerged continent of Atlantis, before they settled in northern Germany and the Netherlands. Thereafter all was downhill and the Aryans had progressively mixed with the beast-men to create the black and yellow

[31] J. Lanz-Liebenfels, "Anthropozoon biblicum," *Vierteljahrsschrift für Bibelkunde* 1 (1903–1904), 307–355, 429–469; 2 (1904–1905), 26–60, 314–337, 395–412 (1: 321–328, 341).
[32] J. Lanz von Liebenfels, *Bibliomystikon oder die Geheimbibel der Eingeweihten. I. Anthropozoikon* (Pforzheim: Privatdruckverlag Bibliomystikon, 1930), 87.

colored races.[33] Lanz agreed with Ludwig Woltmann's thesis that the races had not only migrated widely and mixed, but that they formed a conquering upper caste or aristocracy distinguished by lighter skin color wherever they settled in Asia, Africa, America, and Polynesia.[34] Lanz thus considered race more a matter of breeding, rank, and class than of nationality. This formulation accorded well with his own origins in the Austrian multi-national state where Germans formed the nobility and dominant commercial and cultural class. Christian universalism also resonated more with global pan-Aryanism rather than a territorial form of German nationalism. As a result his racial ideology served both as a defense of the late feudal social order of nineteenth-century Austria-Hungary and as a German nationalist reaction to the increasing parliamentary representation of Slavs, Latins, and other "mediterranoid" races in the empire, whom Lanz saw as the "apelings" of racial degeneration. Lanz's speculations concerning pygmies' origin and distribution came from anthropologists Julius Kollmann (1834–1918) and Giuseppe Sergi (1841–1936), the notable Italian anthropologist, who advanced the notion of a "Mediterranean" race and traced the pygmies in Sardinia, Sicily, and southern Italy to tropical Central Africa.[35]

Lanz rhetorically asked what the Bible had to do with all this science, replying that the Bible offered a detailed scientific description of the bestial *Anthropozoa*: an "incomparable monument of the holy genocidal war that Jahve and his chosen people, the ancient Israelites, had waged against this man-beast."[36] Accordingly, the Old Testament or "covenant" was the sacred contract between the Aryans (i.e. the ancient Israelites) and God to exterminate the beast-men, abjure any further acts of miscegenation, and to create "the sons of God" on earth. "It was a practical eugenic policy for the breeding of a superior human race on a purely anthropological basis."[37] By contrast, the New Testament was simply the

---

[33] Lanz-Liebenfels, "Anthropozoon biblicum," 1: 343–355. Lanz's references to the Aryan race and homeland included Theodor Poesche, *Die Arier: Ein Beitrag zur historischen Anthropologie* (Jena, 1878); Karl Penka, *Origines Ariacae* (Teschen-Wien, 1883); Penka, *Die Herkunft der Arier* (Teschen-Wien, 1886); Vacher Lapouge, *L'Aryen* (Paris, 1900); Matthäus Much, *Die Heimat der Indogermanen* (Berlin, 1902), and Ludwig Wilser, *Die Herkunft der Deutschen* (1885). His source for Atlantis was Ignatius Donnelly, *Atlantis: The Antediluvian World* (New York: Harper & Brothers, 1882).

[34] Lanz-Liebenfels, "Anthropozoon biblicum," 1: 346–347.

[35] Guiseppe Sergi, "Ueber europäische Pygmäen," *Mittheilungen der anthropologischen Gesellschaft Wien* 24 (1894) and Julius Kollmann, "Pygmäen in Europa und Amerika," *Globus* (1902), 325; Kollmann, "Die Pygmäen und ihre systematische Stellung innerhalb des Menschengeschlechtes," *Verhandlung der naturforschende Gesellschaft in Basel* 16 (1902). For a historical review of this literature, see Martin Gusinde, "Pygmies and Pygmoids: Twides of Tropical Africa," *Anthropological Quarterly* 28.1 (January 1955), 3–61.

[36] Lanz-Liebenfels, "Anthropozoon biblicum," 1: 351f.   [37] *Ibid.*, 354.

renewal of this forgotten covenant among humankind that had continued to miscegenate through mixed-race unions or still practiced bestiality. However, the purity of the Aryan racial stock was so polluted by the time of Christ that the gospel proclaimed the struggle against the beast within each person, who combined the two natures of the "sons of God" and the "sons of Hades." According to Lanz, many Hebrew words in Scripture had an esoteric meaning: wood and stone referred to the Aryan, while bread, water, wine, and root were cryptic references to the beast-men. Thus, the Eucharist meant the sacrifice of the beasts, the castration of the inferior, so that the sons of God could arise from the "dead," that is the *Anthropozoa*.[38]

In 1905 Lanz published his fundamental statement of doctrine as *Theozoologie oder die Kunde von den Sodoms-Äfflingen und dem Götter-Elektron*, which again combined traditional Judaeo-Christian sources with the new life-sciences: hence theo-zoology. The first section of the book presented the evil realm by examining the origin and nature of the pygmies. The first pygmy, called Adam, spawned a race of beast-men (*Anthropozoa*), which gave rise to the various races of "apelings" in the world.[39] Quite distinct in origin were the earlier and superior god-men (*Theozoa*). Following Euhemerus and Saxo Grammaticus, Lanz believed that these superior forms of life, previously described as *Homo Ariacus*, were in fact gods who had once walked the earth. Impressed by current scientific discoveries in electronics and radiology, Lanz saw electricity as a form of divine revelation and inspiration and attributed to the *Theozoa* extraordinary sensory organs for the reception and transmission of electrical signals. These organs bestowed powers of telepathy and omniscience upon the *Theozoa*.[40] True religion in Lanz's view consisted in endogamous cults of racial purity in order to maintain these divine powers and to counter the temptations of lecherous acts with the bestial apelings, amphibious monsters, pygmies and their crossbreeds.

In place of the originally distinct species of *Theozoa* and apes, there had developed several mixed races, of which the Aryans were the least corrupt. The marvelous electrical organs of the *Theozoa* had atrophied into the supposedly superfluous pituitary and pineal glands in modern humans owing to miscegenation. Throughout all recorded history, the apelings,

[38] *Ibid.*, 355.

[39] J. Lanz-Liebenfels, *Theozoologie oder die Kunde von den Sodoms-Äfflingen und dem Götter-Elektron: Eine Einführung in die älteste und die neueste Weltanschauung und eine Rechtfertigung des Fürstentums und des Adels* (Vienna: Moderner Verlag [1905]), 26ff.

[40] *Ibid.*, 75–79, 83–85.

amphibians, and pygmies had sought to destroy the Aryans by dragging them down the evolutionary ladder by means of their promiscuity. The history of religion recorded a constant struggle between the bestial and endogamous cults. Besides Lanz's citation of gnostic sources, his racial religion also betrays gnostic features. "[The gods] once walked physically on earth. Today they live on in man. The gods slumber in the racially degraded bodies of men, but the day will come when they arise once more." The entrapment of the divine electrical spark within racially inferior bodies transposes gnostic ideas into the modern discourse of physical anthropology and eugenics. Lanz claimed that a universal program of segregation, selective breeding, and genocide could restore these divine powers to the Aryans as the closest descendants of the god-men. Lanz's notion of an "electrical gene" in the purer-blooded representatives of humankind matched his own discovery of a sexo-racial *gnosis*, as a form of eugenic saving or salvific knowledge through which redemption from all the ills, suffering, and evil in the world could be achieved.[41]

According to Lanz, the writings of Herodotus and Strabo, the findings of modern archaeology, and substantial sections of the Old Testament corroborated this cultic practice of bestiality. On the basis of contemporary speculations in zoology and anthropology, and the findings of Assyriology, Lanz articulated a complete theology in which the Fall denoted the racial compromise of the divine pure-blooded Aryans due to wicked interbreeding with lower animal species, deriving from an earlier primitive branch of animal evolution. These persistent sins, institutionalized as satanic cults of miscegenation, led to the creation of several mixed races, which threatened the sacred and legitimate authority of the Aryans throughout the world, especially in Germany, where the fair, blue-eyed Aryans were still most numerous.[42]

THE SECRET BIBLE OF INITIATES

However, for all Lanz's reliance on the speculations of anthropology, ethnology, and anatomy, his prime source remained the Bible and his focus the interpretation of Holy Scripture in this radical and heterodox sense. Given Lanz's view that endogamy was the righteous and divinely ordained cult, his expertise and emphasis on Judaic and Old Testament scholarship was at an obvious premium. Moreover, he was well qualified for this task. "Anthropozoon biblicum" was published in the inaugural volume of

---

[41] *Ibid.*, 91, 133–136.   [42] *Ibid.*, 132, 158–160.

the *Vierteljahrsschrift für Bibelkunde*, whose editor Dr. Moritz Altschüler, a Viennese theologian, enlisted the collaboration of many distinguished Jewish and Christian scholars for specialist studies in the Talmud and patristics. Dr. August Wünsche (1839–1913) at Dresden was one of Germany's most prominent Christian Hebraists, whose studies of rabbinical literature included commentaries on the books of Hosea and Joel, and a concordance of parallel passages of the Talmud and the New Testament. He also made a German translation of the entire *Midrash Rabbah* and the *Midrash to the Five Megillot*, translated the haggadic parts of the *Jerusalem Talmud* (1880) and the *Babylonian Talmud* (1886–1889) and the *Midrash to the Psalms* (1891). He also produced a study of the Kabbalah with Dr. Erich Bischoff. Adolf Büchler (1867–1939) was a Budapest-born Jewish rabbi, who taught Jewish history, Bible, and Talmud at the Vienna Jewish Theological Seminary and became principal of the Jews' College, London in 1906. Professors Emil Schürer (1844–1910) of Göttingen and Bernard Stade (1848–1906) of Giessen were eminent German Protestant theologians. Schürer's *Geschichte des jüdischen Volkes im Zeitalter Jesu Christi* (1886–1890) ran to four editions by 1901 and was translated into English by 1885; he was well known in Britain and America. His major work was revised and updated by Oxford theologians Geza Vermes and Fergus Millar in the 1980s. Stade also wrote an acclaimed two-volume critical history of Israel (1887–1888). George Robert Stowe Mead (1863–1933), an English classical scholar and Theosophist, had authored several works on gnostic and Hermetic texts as well as studies of the Talmud Jesus stories and the Toldoth Jesus.

Lanz's focus on Hebraic and Old Testament (OT) sources and authorities was plainly evident in "Anthropozoon biblicum," where his references to scholarly studies of the ancient Israelites and the Old Testament were much in evidence, including *Der Ahnenkultus und die Urreligion Israels* (1900) by Carl Grüneisen (1802–1878), the Lutheran theologian and court preacher at Stuttgart; *Schöpfung und Chaos in Urzeit und Endzeit* (1895) and *Die Sagen von Genesis* (1901) by Hermann Gunkel (1862–1932), professor of Old Testament at Berlin; the Old Testament apocrypha edition (1900) by Emil Friedrich Kautzsch (1841–1910), the German Hebrew scholar and professor of theology at Halle; the Ethiopic edition of Enoch I by August Dillmann (1823–1894), the orientalist and late professor of theology at Berlin; Emil Schürer and Bernard Stade's histories of Israel; Carl Ferdinand Reinhardt Budde's *Die biblische Urgeschichte* (1883) and *Das Alte Testament und die Ausgrabungen* (1903). Lanz also quoted modern Jewish rabbinical and Talmudic scholarship: footnotes referred to the onomatological study of Proverbs by Zwi Perez Chajes (1876–1927), the Vienna rabbi; the Semitic ancestral researches of Eduard Glaser (1855–1908), the Austrian Jewish orientalist and archaeologist of the Sabians in Yemen, who lobbied Theodor Herzl for the foundation of a Jewish state in Southern Arabia; and the Babylonian Talmud edition (1897) by Lazarus Goldschmidt (1871–1950), the Lithuanian Jewish orientalist who studied with Schrader at Berlin.[43]

Nearly two-thirds of this substantial serial article of 160 pages was devoted to his minute biblical exegesis comparing the Aramaic Targum, Hebrew, Greek, and Latin texts of key passages in the five Books of Moses, Job, the Prophets, and the OT Apocrypha including Enoch, using the German from Kautzsch's recently compiled *Textbibel* (1899) of both Testaments and Apocrypha. The Israelites' eugenic cult and constant struggle to eliminate miscegenation and the monstrous fruits of unnatural unions were apparent in the numerous strictures in the Pentateuch, especially Exodus (22.19) and Leviticus (18.23–30; 20.15–16, 25–26), regarding the taboos on incestuous, homosexual, and bestial sexual relations and the death penalties imposed on man and beast alike.[44] Lanz recalled how Esau was described as "a hairy man" and called "Edom" (clearly a reference to the *udumi*) (Gen. 27.11; 25.11), in order to explain God's hatred of him and nomination of Jacob as his rightful heir.[45] Lanz was fascinated by the monsters Behemoth and Leviathan in Job 40 and 41. In his account these figures were neither sea-dragons (viz. Leviathan in Ps. 74.14; Isa. 27.1), possibly derived from Babylonian cosmological mythology, nor simply the hippopotamus or crocodile of standard exegesis, but the scaly *pagutu* amphibians and anthropoid apes (*bazaati*), whose extermination the furious, restless battle-god Jahve demands of his chosen people. "Behemoth" is none other than God's creature Adam made from "the dust of the earth" (Gen. 2.7) quite distinct from his prior creation of the true Adam or "man in his own image" (Gen. 1.26–27). Paradoxically, these lower creatures were sexually irresistible to women and the subject of strong Israelite taboos.[46] Lanz conjures up a pornographic view of the ancient world: the *paguta*, *bazaati*, and *udumi* beasts appear on the lists of tribute sent to Assyria by all Mediterranean princes, massively exported by Thebes, and shipped for vice on a scale comparable to girls in the modern white slave trade.[47] Lanz found these aberrant and obscene cults described as vile abominations involving "creeping things and loathsome beasts" (e.g. Ezek. 8.6–18), but Jahve determined

---

[43] Lanz-Liebenfels, "Anthropozoon biblicum," 1: 308n–312n, 316n.   [44] *Ibid.*, 2: 41–45.
[45] *Ibid.*, 2: 321.   [46] *Ibid.*, 1: 429–450. cf. Friedrich Delitzsch, *Das Buch Hiob* (Leipzig, 1902).
[47] Lanz-Liebenfels, "Anthropozoon biblicum," 1: 456.

to destroy all these beasts (Ezek. 32.2–8, 12–13).[48] In ancient Judaic scripture Jahve often described Israel as his bride and in other feminine metaphors. In the frequent event of Israel's neglect of the Jahve cult and worship of strange gods and idols, Jahve's jealous anger exploded in accusations of harlotry, promiscuity, and nymphomania (Ezek. 16.1–40). Elsewhere these sexual metaphors become even more graphic describing Jerusalem as a woman "flaunting her nakedness" and doting on her paramours in Egypt whose "members were like those of asses and whose issue was like those of horses" (Ezek. 23.20). Appalled, Lanz concluded that womenfolk maddened by the erotic attractions of the beast-men, had bred degenerates and thereby devastated all civilization.

Der Menschenthierphallus hat die Weiber rasend gemacht und alles verwüstet . . . Durch diese verkehrten Gelüste hat das Weib alle alten Culturvölker hinabgezüchtet. Dies zu verhindern, den Menschen, den Gottmenschen wiederaufstehen zu lassen, das ist der wahrer Inhalt der Moseslehre.[49]

When Jahve, the jealous God, promises to visit "the iniquity of the fathers upon the children to the third and fourth generation" (Deut. 5.9), Lanz sees no moral or theological justification for this, but rather the logic of a eugenic commandment.[50] The intersection of *fin-de-siècle* antifeminist polemic with eugenic visions was complete.

ELECTROCHRISTOLOGY

Lanz asserted in 1904 that both the Old and New Testaments were nothing but political anthropology or a practical cult of endogamy.[51] The historical Christ was only *a* Jesus, only *a* "superman and god-man" but not uniquely *the* god-man. According to his anthropological gospel, Lanz saw humankind attaining through a process of selection to the status of godmen up a long ladder of ever purer racial Christs. Man alone led to God, for the divinity lay nowhere else but in the marrow, brains, bones and muscles of the beautiful and good human being. "You are gods" quoted Lanz approvingly (Ps. 81.6; John 10.34; Acts 17.29).[52] As in the case of his "occult" interpretation of countless passages in the Hebrew Bible, Lanz appeared to respect Holy Scripture, but only in terms of its "hidden" meaning referring to the beast-cults and the exhortation to endogamy to restore the Aryans to their pristine status of *Theozoa* or god-men. A list of biblical terms for the expected Jewish messiah such as "Star" (Num. 24.17), "Wonderful

---

[48] *Ibid.*, 2: 31.   [49] *Ibid.*, 1: 467.   [50] *Ibid.*, 2: 319.
[51] *Ibid.*, 2: 323.   [52] *Ibid.*, 2: 46–47.

Counsellor, Mighty God, Everlasting Father, Prince of Peace" (Isa. 9.6), "ensign to the peoples" (Isa. 11.3), "a stone of offence" (Isa. 8.14), which the "builders [of the houses of Sodom] rejected" (Ps. 109.22) is echoed in Lanz's lexicon of New Testament terms for the Christ such as the "living bread which came down from heaven" (John 6.51; cf. Exod. 14.4), or the "Rock" [stone] (1 Cor. 10.4), and the long list of "cover-words" for Christ (mercy, salt, pearl, plough, gnosis, etc.) in the gnostic text the *Acts of John*. While this esoteric exercise in occult etymology serves Lanz to show how the Bible conceals a hidden meaning, his main point is that Christ's most frequent self-appellation is *ben-ha-elohim* (Son of God), which Lanz equates with the good angels and descendants of Seth, the son of the true Adam made in the image of God, not the *udumu*, *Anthropozoa*, or man of clay, a point attested by Luke's genealogy of Jesus back to Adam, son of God (Luke 3.23–38).[53]

Lanz cites Justin Martyr and Homer to the effect that the pagans also spoke of the sons of Zeus, just as the ancient Germans recalled the sons of the *Asen* (Air-Gods), enabling him to conclude that Christ is but one "son of God" rather than the Son of God. This revisionist interpretation of Christ as a "Gottessohn" (Son of God) is further developed in Lanz's naturalistic and biological account of the Assumption of the Virgin Mary at Nazareth. Lanz suggests that the angel Gabriel was none other than a pure-blooded Scythian from the neighboring city of Beit She'an, which bore the name Scythopolis in the Hellenistic period. Herodotus had given an account of the Scythians as a nomadic tribe who migrated from upper Asia to conquer the Iranian-speaking Cimmerians on the steppes of southern Russia in the eighth and seventh centuries BCE. The Cimmerians were supposedly driven in the latter half of the seventh century in two directions towards Thrace and along the Caucasus into Asia Minor, where the Assyrians called them the *Gimirrai*, also identified with the biblical Gomer, son of Japhet (Gen. 10.2–3). This south-eastern migration of Cimmerians was followed by an invasion of Scythians (Ashguzai, Hebr. *Ashkenaz*), whom the Assyrians welcomed as allies against the Cimmerians, the Medes, and Egyptians.[54] Emboldened by their destruction of the Medes, ca. 626 BCE, the Scythians launched an attack westwards, laying Assyria waste

[53] *Ibid.*, 113–114, 116.

[54] Anon., "Beisan," *Encyclopædia Brittanica* (14th edn; New York, 1929), vol. III, 333–334; V. Gordon Childe, "Scythia," *ibid.*, vol. X, 235–238; for a recent discussion, see Askold I. Ivantchik, *Kimmerier und Skythen: Kulturhistorische und chronologische Probleme der Archäologie der osteuropäischen Steppen und Kaukasiens in vor- und frühskythischer Zeit* (Moscow: Paleograph Press; Deutsches Archäologisches Institut; Center for Comparative Study on Ancient Civilizations, Russian Academy of Sciences, 2001).

and pillaging Syria, Phoenicia, and Palestine (Jer. 4.13).[55] Beit She'an's Hellenistic name probably recalled the Scythian mercenaries from the steppes north of the Black Sea who settled there as veterans. Lanz probably knew of these accounts of Scythian hordes in Palestine from Herodotus (1.103–106; 4.5–27) and Pliny's *Natural History* (5.16). Contemporary ethnology identified the Cimmerians as speakers of an Iranian (i.e. Indo-Aryan) language, while the conquering Scythians also used Iranian words, but also Ugric (i.e. Tartar) words for deities. Lanz's chief interest in Scythopolis was the suggestion that the historical Christ was fathered by a man of Iranian stock, the eastern branch of the Aryans. Lanz further cited a verse in the Koran (19.17) confirming the natural conception of Mary.[56] However, Lanz also seeks to show that Christ as the Logos comes from another supernatural sphere, quoting Hippolytus' report of Sethian Gnostic teachings: "the Son, on beholding the perfect Logos of the supernal light, underwent a transformation, and in the shape of a serpent entered into a womb, in order that he might be able to recover that Mind which is the scintillation from the light" (*Refutation of all Heresies* 10.7).

In Lanz's view, this is the meaning of "The Word became flesh" (John 1.14), and Christ is a *mamzer* or *Mischling* (crossbreed, a technical term in later Nazi eugenics). This also supposedly confirmed the Christian dogma of the two natures of Christ. Christ himself tells the people "You are from below, I am from above; you are of this world, I am not of this world" (John 8.23).[57] To account for this "unworldliness" or supernatural status, Lanz identified Christ as a natural creature yet, like the angels, endowed with electrical powers of revelation and inspiration attributed to the original euhemerist *Theozoa*. This electrical nature is evident in miracles such as the woman with the issue of blood, whose touch of faith evokes his exclamation "I feel that a power has gone forth from me" (Luke 8.46). He can read the unspoken thoughts of his disciples and foretell the future (Matt. 26.23; Mark 14.13; Luke 22.10). Other electrical phenomena are the Transfiguration, when Christ appears in an aura of brilliant light on Mount Tabor and an attendant cloud produces the sonic effect of a voice (Mark 9.2–8; Matt. 17.2–5); he manifests with extraordinary sounds and "cloven tongues of fire" at Pentecost (Acts 2) and strikes Saul down on his way to Damascus with a beam of light (Acts 9.3). In the Aramaic *Life of Jesus*, Christ declares that he is a son of God who revives the dead and makes Tiberius' daughter pregnant by whispering to her. Lanz often favors

---

[55] R. Ghirshman, *Iran: From the Earliest Times to the Islamic Conquest* (Harmondsworth: Penguin, 1954), 96–99.
[56] Lanz-Liebenfels, *Theozoologie*, 117–118.   [57] *Ibid.*, 120.

gnostic texts such as the *Pistis Sophia* to demonstrate the electrical nature of Christ through its recurrent references to light.[58]

The idea of sodomitic crucifixions may have occurred to Lanz as a result of graffiti dating from the second or third century discovered in excavations at the Palatine in Rome. In 1856 a half-clothed, animal-headed creature with exposed lower body upon a crucifix was uncovered.[59] However, Lanz was also aware that this image might have some connection with the pagan dismissal of Christianity as an obscene ass-worshiping sect or the portrayal of a crucified (jackal-headed) Typhon by gnostic Sethians. In due course, he would elaborate a farrago of derivations and links between classical, Indian, and Germanic mythology to interpret the Davidic genealogy supplied by Matthew (1.1–17). Here, Christ was descended from Abraham (Lanz, Brahma), the Nordic god Gambris of the Teutonic Cimbri, and the valkyrie Gambara of the Langobards. Like these gods, Christ was a member of a divine (theonic) prehistoric bio-electrical species, known in the Bible as angels, cherubs, and seraphs, to the classical writers as muses, sibyls, horae, graces, and cupids, and as the norns and valkyries of Germanic mythology. Such "electronic" nature enabled Christ to appear variously as levitated, a lamb, a cloud full of flashing lights (cf. the *chasmal* in Ezek. 1) and the winged phoenix.[60]

The sufferings, death, and resurrection of Christ are interpreted by Lanz in terms of his eugenic ministry reaching its climax through a series of places full of sodomitic apelings seeking to compromise his racial purity through sexual attacks. The passion begins in the Garden of Gethsemane (Lanz, the grove of Sodom-oils), thence to the Gabatha (Pavement; Lanz, the place of Sodom-stones), thence to "the place of the Kranios," Golgotha (Lanz, the place of the ape-men). According to Lanz, crucifixion was both a punishment for and a practice of the sodomitic cults of the Old Testament. If Jahve commands the "hanging" (Lanz, "crucifixion") of Israelites who consorted with the apelings (Lanz's tendentious reading of Num. 25.4; 2 Sam. 21.9; Est. 9.13), "crucifixion" also signified a ritualized form of forced

---

[58] *Ibid.*, 121–122.

[59] This find was analyzed in Ferdinand Becker, *Das Spottcrucifix der römischen Kaiserpaläste* (Breslau, 1866), Franz Xaver Kraus, *Das Spottcrucifix vom Palatin* (Freiburg i. Br., 1872), and J. Reil, *Die frühchristliche Darstellung der Kreuzigung Christi* (Leipzig, 1904). The subject is reviewed in Ernst Grube, "Majestas und Crucifix: Zum Motiv des Suppedaneums," *Zeitschrift für Kunstgeschichte* 20.3 (1957), 268–287.

[60] J. Lanz von Liebenfels, *Bibliomystikon oder die Geheimbibel der Eingeweihten*, IX. Band I. Teil: *Christus und der elekrotheonische Mensch des Uranuszeitalters (Kommentar zu Matthaeus I–XVIII, 11)* (Szt. Balázs, [c. 1934]), 10–21, 48.

sexual intercourse with apelings in the dysgenic cults. Wild and unruly "Sodomsunholde" were fastened to stakes in order to facilitate obscene couplings; persons were also tied to such stakes and sodomized by the lustful apelings (after Lanz, Job 40.24; Lam. 5.13). Christ was "delivered to the Gentiles [Lanz, the rabble]" (Matt. 20.19) which led to a ritualized rape of Christ by the apelings and pygmies of the lower races. Christ's wounds are made by the claws of the lascivious apelings; he does not die on the cross, but is taken off the stake and confined in a tomb. Here he suffers further attempts upon his purity and chastity, for the tombs are notorious as the place of the apeling colonies outside the town (Matt. 8.28; Mark 5.2; Luke 8.27). Lanz continues his farrago of abstruse etymological interpretations of Greek, Hebrew, and Syriac words to give wholly contrived interpretations of biblical references. The miracle of the raising of Lazarus is reduced to Christ's command to take away the stone (Lanz, *Sodomsstein*, apeling) (John 11.39). Just as the graves were the places of sodomy, so Christ is "resurrected" in the sense that he rejects the apelings, renounces their lewd advances and sexual attacks. When Christ "rises from the dead," he has "risen from the Sodom-graves" and conquered sodomy.[61] Death and the grave are but synonyms for the apelings and the destruction of the electrical higher nature of racial purity.

Lanz concludes that the great mystery of the Trinity is an anthropological formula expressing the three evolutionary phases of the higher white race. The "Father" is the oldest stage, the "Spirit" is the next, while the "Son" describes the racial state of humankind at the time of Christ when the *udumu* had almost achieved victory in degeneration. The resurrection can only be achieved by eugenic transformation, and Christ's example is the basis of the New Testament, the renewal of the racial covenant to breed the gods once more on earth.[62]

ARYAN CHRISTIANITY AS "JUDAIZING"

Lanz-Liebenfels' racial gospel is clearly identifiable as a set of beliefs specifically espousing the predominance of traditional German-speaking elites in Austria-Hungary and generally the world-rule of the Aryan Germans. His indebtedness to Social Darwinism, political anthropology and eugenics have been related to his contacts, editors and the academic sources of his work. However, what makes his work eccentric, almost unique,

---

[61] Lanz-Liebenfels, *Theozoologie*, 124–130.   [62] *Ibid.*, 131.

is his attempt to re-interpret the Bible as the canon of this racial *gnosis*, thereby suggesting that orthodox Christianity is erroneous and maintains a false world of degeneration and ruin. Most religiously inspired advocates of racialism recognized the universalistic implications of Christianity and rejected it, either in favor of the hierarchical biology of Monism, thereby rephrasing *Naturphilosophie* in evolutionary selective terminology, or in various neopagan (*deutschvölkisch*) groups which sought to revive the beliefs and customs of the pre-Christian Germanic peoples. Such neo-Germanic religious societies included the Deutschbund (est. 1894), the Germanische Glaubensgemeinschaft (est. 1908), Deutscher Orden (est. 1911), the Gesellschaft Wodan (est. 1912), the Deutschgläubige Gemeinschaft (est. 1917), the Volkschaft der Nordungen (est. 1913), and the Nordische Glaubensgemeinschaft (est. 1928).[63]

On account of his lifelong fascination with Cistercian-monastic ideals (viz. the foundation of his own reforming sectarian New Templar Order) and his training in biblical exegesis and church history, Lanz felt compelled to project his political anthropology onto a biblical narrative complete with Old and New Testament. Moreover, precisely by extolling the ancient Israelites as an Aryan people *maintaining* endogamy and tribal eugenics, Lanz's earlier (pre-1918) thought was philosemitic. Only later, after the collapse of Germany and Austria-Hungary at the end of the war did Lanz embrace the common reactionary currency of a world-conspiracy of Jews, Freemasons, and Bolsheviks and henceforth identify the Jews as *failing* to maintain the endogamous cult, disappointing Jahve and worse, attacking his Son for preaching the racial gospel. But this lay in the future, when a generic antisemitism swept through the far right in Germany. However, in his particular emphasis on the Old Testament, the Targums, and Talmud, Lanz actually did identify with the Israelites as a tribal group. In Ario-Christianity, Frauja-Christ is but a racial evangelist whose promise of salvation has no bearing on his person, his sacrifice, his forgiveness of sins, or the atonement of the cross, but a eugenic example of rejecting sodomy and the exhortation to "love one's neighbor" (Lanz, kinsman). In his emphasis on the tribal principle of Jewish (Aryan) identity and effective denial of Christ's atonement, Lanz paradoxically offers an esoteric form of heresy that approximates traditional charges of "Judaizing." Such a form of redemption through the collectivity of German nation and race as a cryptic

---

[63] Erhard Schlund, *Neugermanisches Heidentum im heutigen Deutschland* (Munich: Franz Pfeiffer, 1924), 40–62; Alfons Steiger, *Der neudeutsche Heide im Kampf gegen Christen und Juden* (Berlin: Germania, 1924); Alfred Müller, *Die neugermanischen Religionsbildungen der Gegenwart* (Bonn: Ludwig Röhrscheid, 1934), 1–26.

imitation of an imagined Jewish cult of endogamy would be enshrined in the political religion of National Socialism.

BIBLIOGRAPHY

(NB – the following list comprises sources and secondary literature specifically used as references in the text, and does not include titles that exemplify Lanz's social and historical context)

SOURCES BY JÖRG LANZ VON LIEBENFELS

"Die Armee des schwarzen Papstes," *Das freie Wort* 2 (1903), 394–402, 451–459, 721–729.

"Der große Kampf des Jesuitismus gegen den Katholizismus," *Das freie Wort* 3 (1904), 49–56.

"Leo XIII., der 'Friedenspapst'," *Das freie Wort* 3 (1904), 338–346.

"Politische Anthropologie," *Das freie Wort* 3 (1904), 778–795.

"Chronikon Archprioratus Ord.Nov.Templ. ad Werfenstein Tom.1," undated MS.

"Friedrich Delitzsch: Über Babel und Bibel," *Die Umschau* 6 (1902), 386–389, 407–410.

"Der Mensch der 'Grotte des Enfants' (Baoussé-Roussé)," *Die Umschau* 6 (1902), 566–567.

"2. Urgeschichtliche Beziehungen der Indogermanen zu den anderen Rassen," *Die Umschau* 7 (1903), 338–339.

"3. Die Urheimat der 'Indogermanen'," *Die Umschau* 7 (1903), 649–651.

"Rasse und Milieu," *Die Umschau* 7 (1903), 121–123.

"Die Urgeschichte der Künste," *Politisch-Anthropologische Revue* 2.2 (1903), 134–156.

"Anthropozoon biblicum," *Vierteljahrsschrift für Bibelkunde* 1 (1903–1904), 307–355, 429–469; 2 (1904–1905), 26–60, 314–337, 395–412.

Bibliomystikon oder die Geheimbibel der Eingeweihten. I. Band *Anthropozoikon* (Pforzheim: Privatdruckveerlag Bibliomystikon, 1930).

Theozoologie oder die Kunde von den Sodoms-Äfflingen und dem Götter-Elektron: Eine Einführung in die älteste und die neueste Weltanschauung und eine Rechtfertigung des Fürstentums und des Adels (Vienna: Moderner Verlag [1905])

Bibliomystikon oder die Geheimbibel der Eingeweihten, IX. Band I. Teil: *Christus und der elekrotheonische Mensch des Uranuszeitalters (Kommentar zu Matthaeus I–XVIII, 11)* (Szt. Balázs, [c. 1934]).

LITERATURE

Bannister, Robert C., *Social Darwinism: Science and Myth in Anglo-American Social Thought* (Philadelphia: Temple University Press, 1979).

Biddiss, Michael D., *Father of Racist Ideology: The Social and Political Ideas of Count Gobineau* (London: Weidenfeld & Nicolson, 1970).

Daim, Wilfried, *Der Mann, der Hitler die Ideen gab: Von den religiösen Verirrungen eines Sektierers zum Rassenwahn des Diktators* (Munich: Isar Verlag, 1958; 2nd edn, Vienna: Hermann Böhlau, 1985).

Gasman, Daniel, *The Scientific Origins of National Socialism: Social Darwinism in Ernst Haeckel and the German Monist League* (London: Macdonald; New York: American Elsevier, 1971)

Ghirshman, R., *Iran: From the Earliest Times to the Islamic Conquest* (Harmondsworth: Penguin, 1954).

Goodrick-Clarke, Nicholas, "The Esoteric Uses of Electricity: Theologies of Electricity from Swabian Pietism to Ariosophy," *Aries* 4.1 (2004), 69–90.

The Occult Roots of Nazism: The Ariosophists of Austria and Germany 1890–1935 (Wellingborough: Aquarian Press, 1985; 2nd edn, New York: New York University Press, 1992; 3rd edn, London: I. B. Tauris, 2004).

de Groot, Jan Willem, "Arische Gnosis" (MA dissertation, University of Amsterdam, 2001).

Grube, Ernst, "Majestas und Crucifix: Zum Motiv des Suppedaneums," *Zeitschrift für Kunstgeschichte* 20.3 (1957), 268–287.

Gusinde, Martin, "Pygmies and Pygmoids: Twides of Tropical Africa," *Anthropological Quarterly* 28.1 (January 1955), 3–61.

Hieronimus, Ekkehard, *Lanz von Liebenfels: Eine Bibliographie* (Toppenstedt: Uwe Berg, 1991).

Ivantchik, Askold I., *Kimmerier und Skythen: Kulturhistorische und chronologische Probleme der Archäologie der osteuropäischen Steppen und Kaukasiens in vor- und frühskythischer Zeit* (Moscow: Paleograph Press; Deutsches Archäologisches Institut; Center for Comparative Study on Ancient Civilizations, Russian Academy of Sciences, 2001).

Lorenz, Horst (ed.), *'Rosen aus Germaniens Bergen': Eine Denkschrift zum 50. Todestag des Begründers des Neutemplerordens Jörg Lanz von Liebenfels (19 VII 1874–22 IV 1954)* (Ilvesheim: Edition Weltwende, 2004).

Mosse, George L., *The Crisis of German Ideology: Intellectual Origins of the Third Reich* (London: Weidenfeld & Nicolson, 1966).

Müller, Alfred, *Die neugermanischen Religionsbildungen der Gegenwart* (Bonn: Ludwig Röhrscheid, 1934).

Mund, Rudolf J., *Jörg Lanz v. Liebenfels: Die Esoterik des Christentums* (Stuttgart: Rudolf Arnold Spieth Verlag, 1976).

Poliakov, Léon, *The Aryan Myth: A History of Racist and Nationalist Ideas in Europe* (London: Chatto Heinemann, 1974).

Reulecke, Jürgen, "Rassenhygiene, Sozialhygiene, Eugenik," in Diethart Kerbs and Jürgen Reulecke (eds.), *Handbuch der deutschen Reformbewegungen 1880–1933* (Wuppertal: Peter Hammer, 1998), 197–210.

Schachenmayr, Alkuin Volker, *Prägende Professoren in der Entwicklung des theologischen Lehrbetriebes im Cistercienserstift Heiligenkreuz* (Langwaden: Bernardus, 2004).

Schlund, Erhard, *Neugermanisches Heidentum im heutigen Deutschland* (Munich: Franz Pfeiffer, 1924).

Sieferle, Rolf Peter, "Rassismus, Rassenhygiene, Menschenzuchtideale," in Uwe Puschner, Walter Schmitz, and Justus H. Ulbricht (eds.), *Handbuch zur 'Völkischen Bewegung' 1871–1918* (Munich: K. G. Saur, 1996), 436–448.

Steiger, Alfons, *Der neudeutsche Heide im Kampf gegen Christen und Juden* (Berlin: Germania, 1924).

Weiss, Sheila Faith, *Race Hygiene and National Efficiency: The Eugenics of Wilhelm Schallmayer* (Berkeley: University of California Press, 1987).

Wiwjorra, Ingo, "Die deutsche Vorgeschichtsforschung und ihr Verhältnis zu Nationalismus und Rassismus," in Uwe Puschner, Walter Schmitz, and Justus H. Ulbricht (eds.), *Handbuch der 'Völkischen Bewegung' 1871–1918* (Munich: K. E. Saur, 1996), 186–207.

Zmarzlik, Hans-Günter, "Der Sozialdarwinismus in Deutschland als geschichtliches Problem," *Vierteljahreshefte für Zeitgeschichte* 11 (1963), 246–273.

CHAPTER 13

Did Jesus die for our karma? Christology and atonement in a contemporary metaphysical church

James R. Lewis

> Jesus, through his death and resurrection, changed the karma of the planet. Before Jesus' time, the law of the planet was "an eye for an eye and a tooth for a tooth," also known as the Law of Moses. Through the Christ action, human beings came under grace, and salvation was won for all of us.
>
> John-Roger

INTRODUCTION

The Church of the Movement of Spiritual Inner Awareness (MSIA) was one of the new religions to emerge out of the spiritual ferment of the 1970s. While this church has often been characterized as "new age," and while the group's core spiritual techniques are clearly related to South Asian Sant Mat practices,[1] MSIA does not fit comfortably into either the New Age or the Sant Mat category. The church is also related to Eckankar, another contemporary new religion.

One clue to this movement's uniqueness is the organization's explicit and reiterated assertion that "Jesus Christ is the head of the Church of the Movement of Spiritual Inner Awareness." Like many other churches in the larger metaphysical-occult subculture, MSIA discourse is peppered with references to the "inner Christ," "Christ consciousness," "master Jesus," and so on. Because so many other metaphysical churches rely on similar terminology, this kind of discourse can initially strike one as a superficial gleaning of terms from the dominant religious culture (i.e., deploying Christian language to express a world-view and a spiritual sensitivity significantly at odds with traditional Christianity). Upon closer examination, however, one finds an unusually orthodox understanding of certain

---

[1] Sant Mat is a north Indian guru lineage. In this regard, refer to Mark Juergensmeyer, *Radhasoami Reality* (Princeton: Princeton University Press, 1995).

key theological notions, particularly the related doctrines of grace and atonement.

The present chapter proposes to discuss this group's Christology, as well as that aspect of the church's soteriology which reflects traditional Christian soteriology. Following an overview of the organization's history and world-view, MSIA's views of Christ and the Bible will be examined. In order to clarify the uniqueness of the role of Christian grace in this movement, MSIA's soteriology will be contrasted with Eckankar's. The discussion will conclude with the question of whether or not MSIA members consider themselves part of a Christian organization.

BRIEF OVERVIEW OF MSIA HISTORY AND WORLD-VIEW

MSIA was founded by John-Roger Hinkins, generally referred to as "John-Roger" or "J-R." In 1963, while undergoing surgery for a kidney stone, he fell into a nine-day coma. Upon awakening, he found himself aware of a new spiritual personality – "John " – who had superseded or merged with his old personality. After the operation, Hinkins began to refer to himself as "John-Roger," in recognition of his transformed self. In 1971 he formally incorporated the Church of the Movement of Spiritual Inner Awareness.

The basic MSIA world-view is related to that of the religious traditions that originated on the South Asian subcontinent – Hinduism, Buddhism, and Sikhism (particularly the latter). In common with these religions, MSIA accepts the notion that the individual soul is trapped in the material world, which is viewed as a realm of suffering. Because of the related processes of reincarnation and karma, the death of the physical body does not free a person from suffering. Only through the practice of certain spiritual techniques, such as the practice of yogic meditation, can individuals liberate themselves from the cycle of death and rebirth.

There are many levels of involvement in MSIA. A useful criterion of participation is whether or not one is actively enrolled in a series of monthly lessons referred to as the Soul Awareness Discourses. After a specified period of time "on Discourses," one may apply for the first formal initiation done physically by an MSIA initiator. There are five formal initiations (though the first two are always done together, meaning that there are only four separate initiation ceremonies), each of which indicates progressively deeper involvement in the spiritual path which is at the core of MSIA's various practices.

Independently of the initiation structure, one may become an MSIA minister (although the general criterion is that a person needs to be an initiate in order to be ordained). The basic MSIA gathering is the home seminar. Thus MSIA ministers do not normally minister to congregations. Rather, ministers are involved in some type of service work, which constitutes their "ministry." While seminary training is not required to receive ordination, MSIA has established an educational institution, Peace Theological Seminary and College of Philosophy (PTS/COP). PTS/COP has become an integral part of MSIA's outreach. The majority of MSIA seminars and workshops are held under the auspices of the Seminary. PTS/COP's relatively new Masters and Doctoral programs have been vigorously expanded to reach students across the United States. The Masters program has also been exported to South America and, most recently, to Australia and England.

As a low-intensity group that does not make excessive demands upon either the time or the resources of most members, MSIA largely escaped the attention of the anti-cult movement until the late eighties. In 1988, the *Los Angeles Times* published a highly critical article on MSIA. A similar article appeared in *People* magazine. Both pieces dwelt on charges by ex-staff members that Hinkins had sexually exploited them. Depending significantly upon the testimony of disgruntled ex-members and drawing heavily on the "cult" stereotype, MSIA was portrayed as an organization that was created for no other purpose than to serve the financial, sexual, and ego needs of John-Roger Hinkins. None of these allegations could ever be proven. As a consequence, after a brief moment in the spotlight reporters turned their attentions to other stories and MSIA disappeared from the mass media.

In common with Sant Mat groups, MSIA pictures the cosmos as composed of many different levels or "planes." At the point of creation, these levels sequentially emerged from God along a vibratory "stream" until creation reached its terminus in the physical plane. The Sant Mat tradition teaches that individuals can be linked to God's creative energy, and that this stream of energy will carry their consciousness back to God. This link-up is accomplished during initiation, though the individual still must appropriate and utilize the link through the practice of certain spiritual exercises. Although there are theological differences and some minor technical variances in the different Sant organizations, the basic tenets are shared by all groups.

Central to the teachings of the Sant Mat tradition is the necessity of a living human master who is competent in initiating disciples into the practice and technique of listening to the inner sound and contemplating the inner light (Surat Shabd Yoga, referred to as "spiritual exercises" in MSIA).

While the Sant tradition refers to the living human master with such honorifics as "guru," "Satguru," "Perfect Master," and so forth, in MSIA the teacher is referred to as the Mystical Traveler. The Mystical Traveler Consciousness is, however, a somewhat different notion from that of "guru."

According to MSIA, each individual on the planet is involved in his or her own movement of spiritual inner awareness, of which the Movement of Spiritual Inner Awareness is an outward reflection. MSIA is devoted solely to supporting people in doing Soul Transcendence, but the organization of MSIA is not necessary to the spiritual work of the Mystical Traveler, which is seen as a consciousness existing on the planet from the very beginning of time. Individuals who wish to develop total awareness and free themselves from the necessity of reincarnation can seek the assistance of the Mystical Traveler, who holds the spiritual keys to Soul Transcendence and can assist students in doing this.

The Mystical Traveler, in the sense of a living person, has a complex relationship with the Mystical Traveler Consciousness (MTC), which is a much larger reality, and much harder to explain. The MTC is said to be somewhat similar to the Christian notion of the Holy Spirit. Like the Holy Spirit, the MTC is an impersonal yet conscious "energy" or "spirit" that seeks to spiritually uplift human beings. The Traveler Consciousness is also said to exist within each person on the planet, though some are more aware of this than others. The human being through whom the energy of the MTC flows is said to "anchor" the MTC into the physical realm – the world of our ordinary, everyday experience. Anchoring the energy allows it to become available for everyone to use for his or her spiritual upliftment. Thus, the MTC is described as being like a conveyer system or an "escalator" into the higher realms of spirit. John-Roger formerly served as the anchor for the MTC, but in 1988 passed that function on to his spiritual heir, John Morton.

In their roles as Mystical Travelers, John-Roger and John Morton are simultaneously greater and lesser than gurus – greater in the sense that the Mystical Traveler Consciousness is a larger notion than that of guruship; lesser in the sense that the person who "anchors" the MTC is an ordinary human being who is not identical with the MTC. Because it is the MTC that is the significant reality, MSIA initiates need not have a personal relationship with John-Roger or John Morton in order to follow the MSIA "path."[2]

---

[2] For general information on MSIA, refer to James R. Lewis, *Seeking the Light* (Los Angeles: Mandeville, 1996).

WHO IS THE CHRIST?

At first glance, MSIA appears to be basically a Sant Mat group, "with some esoteric Christianity added on to make it more Western."[3] Upon closer examination, however, one finds that John-Roger has drunk deeply from the well of metaphysical Christianity, and that MSIA is saturated with the language and the ideology of this strand of spirituality.

Metaphysical Christianity – which includes everything from New Thought denominations to churches oriented more towards Theosophy and Spiritualism – rejects traditional theological views regarding, among other things, sin and hell, and embraces a view of the human being as basically good. We are all part of God and we will all eventually be "saved." In most systems of metaphysical Christianity, Christ becomes a Divine principle and Jesus becomes a human being who is honored as the person who best exemplified the Christ principle in his life. Jesus thus does not save us by "atoning" for our sins. Instead, he serves as a model for human striving by demonstrating perfect "at-one-ment" with God.[4]

MSIA is clearly in this general tradition. In addition to embracing metaphysical Christianity's doctrine of universal salvation (in J-R's words, "Not one soul shall be lost"), MSIA distinguishes between Jesus the historical personage and Christ. The Christ is both a spiritual "office" (like the "president" of this planet) and the designation for the deepest and most real part of the human being. This Christ self – which is alternately designated as the soul, the true self, the cosmic self, Christ Consciousness, and so forth – is also where we are in contact with God, conceptualized simultaneously as personal (a being who can respond to us) as well as impersonal (in the abstract sense of the universal Ground of Being).

One of the points on which MSIA departs from metaphysical Christianity is to stipulate a second spiritual "office," the Mystical Traveler, which overlaps the Christ office in complex and sometimes confusing ways. Both Christ and the Mystical Traveler are concerned with promoting human spiritual evolution and with returning individual souls to God. John-Roger has described the Traveler Consciousness and the Christ as "twin" energies that are so blended at this level that they cannot be distinguished.[5] To further complicate this situation, the historical Jesus held both offices during his lifetime. Furthermore, Jesus continues to hold the Christ office,

---

[3] Andrea Grace Diem, "Shabdism in North America: The Influence of Radhasoami on Guru Movements" (PhD Dissertation, University of California, Santa Barbara, September, 1995), 163.

[4] J. Stillson Judah, *The History and Philosophy of the Metaphysical Movements in America* (Philadelphia: Westminster Press, 1967).

[5] John-Roger, MSIA Tape #7462, "God*Traveler*Christ*You".

and MSIA asserts (1) that Jesus Christ is the head of the Church of the Movement of Spiritual Inner Awareness (J-R has often stated that Jesus Christ is his "boss"), and (2) that "the Traveler's work through MSIA (Soul Transcendence) is based on Jesus' work."[6]

This overlap has many ramifications, one of which is that – as the physical anchor for the Mystical Traveler Consciousness during his lifetime – Jesus taught soul travel, and initiated his disciples into the sound current: "At the time Jesus Christ walked the planet they did soul transcendence, but not as a popular movement. Only Jesus was doing soul travel. That's one of the reasons he was ostracized, picked on and put down."[7]

Furthermore, although there had been Mystical Travelers before Jesus, there was something unique about his approach to Soul Transcendence – some new recasting of the energies involved – that altered the nature of the work for succeeding Travelers; in J-R's words, "If he hadn't done his work, I couldn't have done mine, because my work is based upon that work having been done and having been done correctly . . . I follow right exactly in [Jesus'] format."[8]

Precisely what this new twist on the Traveler role involved is never specified, except that it may relate to the new dispensation of Grace (discussed below) introduced by Jesus' death and resurrection.

As evidence that Jesus taught his disciples shabd yoga, John-Roger has cited the words of the Gospel of John, both in ch. 1 where "In the beginning was the word" is exegeted as referring to the sound current, and in ch. 17, where Jesus is quoted as saying, among other things, "For I gave them the words you gave me and they accepted them" (John 17.8).

In this passage, the "words" are viewed as being the tones that are given to students upon initiation.

Because the Mystical Traveler Consciousness (MTC) can only be anchored by a living person, Jesus let go of that office after he left the physical plane. As people before Jesus had held the "keys" to the MTC, so other people became Mystical Travelers after Jesus' passing. In John-Roger's case, he received the keys during his near-death experience in 1963 and passed them on to John Morton in 1988. It is because MSIA regards Jesus as having been a Mystical Traveler that J-R and his organization can assert that they teach what Jesus taught (i.e., soul travel).

In this regard, it would not be unfair to say that MSIA understands what Jesus taught in terms of what John-Roger teaches, as opposed to attempting

[6] Anon., *Soul Transcendence* (Los Angeles: Peace Theological Seminary & College of Philosophy, 1995), 11.
[7] John-Roger, MSIA Tape #1507, "What Is the Secret Center?"   [8] "Secret Center."

to make MSIA's teachings conform to the traces of Jesus' teachings preserved in the Gospels – the latter being the approach commonly adopted
by traditional Christianity. This is not to say that J-R ignores the biblical record, although his approach to scripture is complex, simultaneously
similar and dissimilar to the approach of metaphysical Christianity.

ROLE OF THE BIBLE

Unlike some metaphysical churches, such as Unity, that embrace the Bible
as the touchstone of their teachings, MSIA's approach is more selective.
Readings from scripture play no role in a typical MSIA gathering, and no
set of John-Roger's teachings focuses on the Bible. At the same time, J-R
often cites and otherwise refers to the Bible as an authoritative text.[9] Furthermore, MSIA participants are encouraged to read and become familiar
with scripture.[10] Although the Bible is authoritative, this authority is not
exclusivistic, as reflected in John-Roger's response to the question, Can
I find the Christ in Hindu scriptures? "Yes, but it won't be spelled that
way."[11]

The aspirant is also warned against over-focusing on scripture. In one
of his talks, J-R asserts that the Travelers always advise one to "seek first
the Kingdom," because, "If you seek first that which is written, and try
to maintain that which is written, then you sacrifice the 'moving within
consciousness' of God."[12]

Congruent with the teachings of other metaphysical churches,[13] John-
Roger tends towards a non-literal reading of scripture: "The Bible sometimes does not give us specific answers to our questions, but you must
understand that the Bible is coded . . ."[14]

How, then, does one go about decoding scripture? MSIA does not
provide explicit guidelines for such a task. Instead, the implicit message
seems to be that one can unlock the deeper meaning of the Bible only after
one has achieved a certain level of enlightenment. Furthermore, even if we
had the keys for interpreting scripture, not all of the mysteries would be
found there because not all of the "hidden teachings" were encoded in the
Bible – "They couldn't all fit."[15] John-Roger notes, for instance, that soul
travel is only alluded to in scripture:

---

9 "I read it often." John-Roger, MSIA Tape #1329, "The Meditation of the Christ."
10 E.g., refer to John-Roger, MSIA Tape #7341, "Are you Living under Law or Grace?"
11 John-Roger, MSIA Tape #1330, "Christmas Eve with John-Roger."
12 "Meditation of the Christ."   13 Judah, *Metaphysical Movements in America*, 17–18.
14 John-Roger. *The Christ within and the Disciples of Christ* (Los Angeles: Mandeville, 1994), 24–25.
15 "Christmas Eve."

The work that we do in soul travel – transcending the physical – is alluded to in the Bible, in a few places. Let me give you two of the references. One, it says, "when you're out of the body, you're with the Lord." It's like, Why would they make a statement like that? It's like, To worship God you must worship God in the spirit (i.e., the Soul).[16]

The other example John-Roger mentions in this taped discussion is the familiar Pauline epistle relating the experience of a man who was "taken up" to the third heaven.

Given the Bible's state of incompleteness, one might well ask why one should bother reading it at all. J-R's answer to this hypothetical question would be that, while the Bible is not necessary for "salvation," it points the way, not unlike how a water almanac points the way to water. One can shake and twist a water almanac all day and never get a single drop of water. Similarly, the Bible does not have a magical potency to "save" anyone. Instead, it points the way to quenching our spiritual thirst:

What is the value of the Book? The value of the Book is it points a direction. The water almanac points a way – a direction – to where water can be found. And [the Bible] points to where the Living Waters can be found. And it points it out very beautifully, very succinctly, and, believe me, I thrill anew each time that I hear it because I've validated it inside of me.[17]

Finally, John-Roger has periodically made the observation that our present-day scriptures will eventually be superseded by a new Bible or Bibles. He has made this assertion in the context of discussions that portray the present period as being the "biblical times" of the future:

Realize that you are biblical scripture now being written and that centuries from now, the lives that are being enthroned in the spiritual records at this time will be the "Bible" of people who will say, "If I had lived in that time, if I could have partaken of that Christ Consciousness, then I, too, could have been saintly. I, too, could have expressed eternal love."[18]

From this passage as well as from many of the other statements cited above, one can see that MSIA departs significantly from tradition. There is, however, one part of MSIA's soteriology – namely its doctrine of atonement – on which the group diverges considerably from the metaphysical churches, and ends up surprisingly close to a traditional understanding of the significance of Jesus' death and resurrection. We might best work our way into this aspect of MSIA's teachings indirectly, via a comparison-contrast with Eckankar.

[16] "Secret Center."   [17] "Christmas Eve."   [18] *The Christ within*, 43.

ECKANKAR AND KARMA

Eckankar is a new religious movement founded by Paul Twitchell in California in 1965. It is an eclectic blend of spiritual influences which draws most of its followers from the same metaphysical/occult subculture from which MSIA participants come. Twitchell claimed that in 1956 he experienced "God-realization" when he was initiated by a group of spiritual masters known as the "Order of the Vairagi Masters" who live and work on a spiritual plane linked to the mystic East, and who assigned him the role of "971st Living Eck Master."

Twitchell was succeeded by Darwin Gross and Gross in turn was succeeded by Harold Klemp, the 973rd Living Eck Master. In terms of the role the Master plays in the life of the disciple, the Living Eck Master is much closer to being like a Sant Mat guru than like MSIA's Mystical Traveler. Eckankar is "the ancient science of soul travel" and "the religion of the light and sound of God." Its basic cosmology is clearly related to that of the Sant Mat tradition.[19]

Like MSIA, as well as most religions originating in South Asia (India), Eckankar assumes the basic validity of the law of karma. In its simplest form, this law operates impersonally like a natural law, ensuring that every good or bad deed eventually returns to the individual in the form of reward or punishment commensurate with the original deed. Karma originally referred to ritual action, which in the Hindu tradition produces concrete results if properly performed (the priest controlled the gods if his rituals were correctly carried out). Karma was later extended to refer to the effects of action in general.

The contemporary notion of karma refers both to the personality patterns that result from past actions as well as the forces at large in the cosmos that bring reward or retribution to the human individual. In yogic psychology, the personality patterns – in the sense of the subconscious motivators of action – shaped by karma are termed samskaras. Karmic forces also compel human beings to take rebirth (to reincarnate) in successive lifetimes. In other words, if one dies before reaping the effects of one's actions (as most people do), the karmic process demands that one come back in a future life. Coming back to another lifetime also allows karmic forces to reward or

---

[19] For concise overviews of Eckankar, refer to Robert S. Ellwood and Harry B. Partin, *Religious and Spiritual Groups in Modern America* (Englewood Cliffs, N.J.: Prentice-Hall, 2nd edn, 1988), 220–225; Roger E. Olson, "ECKANKAR: From Ancient Science of Soul Travel to New Age Religion," in Timothy Miller (ed.), *America's Alternative Religions* (Albany: State University of New York Press, 1995).

punish one through the circumstances into which one is born. Hence, for example, an individual who was generous in one lifetime might be reborn as the child of wealthy parents in her or his next incarnation.

The mainstream of South Asian thinking does not view the cycle of death and rebirth as attractive. Hence the ultimate goal of Indian religions is to escape the cycle of death and rebirth. While many contemporary Westerners would view the prospects of reincarnation positively, the traditional South Asian view is that returning to live another life is distinctly undesirable. Because life in the physical body always involves suffering, we should strive to escape the wheel of rebirth. Getting off the Ferris wheel of reincarnation necessarily involves extracting oneself from the compelling influence of karma, a process sometimes portrayed as a "balancing" of one's karma.

Balancing one's karma is not unlike balancing one's bank account. The effects of morally bad actions (producing "bad karma") are comparable to debts, whereas the effects of good actions produce "dues" to be paid out. Before one can close one's account and finally check out of the reincarnation process, one must settle one's debts as well as collect all of one's "receipts payable," leaving a zero balance. In the words of an Eck Satsang Discourse, "Everything which can be karma can be both good and bad. There are two sides to it and in order to enter into the heavenly state one must balance the two."[20]

However, while the balancing of karma is a necessary concomitant of liberation, it is not, in and of itself, sufficient to produce liberation. Instead, in almost all Indian spiritual systems – including all Sant Mat groups as well as Sant Mat-related systems such as Eckankar and MSIA – one must also become adept at certain mental/spiritual exercises designed to project one's consciousness into higher realms of being. In Sant Mat, Eckankar, and MSIA, this is accomplished by meditating on the sound current, following it back to its source and establishing oneself in the spiritual realm.

The relationship between these two components of liberation – balancing (or "burning out") one's karma and establishing a steady link to the higher realms – is not conceptualized as lucidly as one might wish. Certain passages, such as the one cited above, make it seem that only one component is necessary for achieving an enlightened state. Other passages appear to be saying that one is a precondition for the other.

In all Sant Mat groups, the master has at least some power to "adjust" her or his students' karma – and, in some cases, even to "annul" karma, at least

---

[20] *Eck Satsang Discourses*, 3rd series #4, 6.

partially – for their ultimate spiritual benefit. While this is also the case in Eckankar, it is nevertheless clear that students must work through most of their karma mechanically to become eligible for liberation; for example, "Eventually after many incarnations and working off karma collected in these lives, Soul returns to heaven again."[21] "No Eck Master is going to relieve anyone of his karmic debt unless he feels that it can assist in some way."[22]

While Eckankar's conceptualization of karma is actually more nuanced than it is here being portrayed, enough has been said to constitute a baseline for contrasting MSIA's soteriology with Eckankar's.

MSIA SOTERIOLOGY

As should be clear from the above discussion, the "theory of salvation" found in most South Asian religions – a soteriology which has also been largely adopted by contemporary metaphysical religions – departs significantly from that of traditional Christianity. One can, however, trace out certain rough parallels at a structural level. In other words, both families of religion aim to "save" individuals from suffering, either from the cycle of death and rebirth or, in the case of Christianity, from hell. Both point to higher realms as the ultimate abode of the "saved," although both also believe that the individual can be enlightened/saved while still in the physical body. Finally, both religious traditions point to past actions as being productive of a moral "substance" – sin or karma – that stands in the way of individual liberation from suffering.

With respect to how sin/karma is removed, these two religious families part company. Christianity, especially its Protestant varieties, emphasizes that sin is absolved by the Grace of God. The doorway of Grace was opened to humankind as a consequence of the atoning death of Jesus, who "died for our sins." In contrast, and, despite the oft-mentioned notion of the "grace of the guru," most streams of the South Asian tradition, including Sant Mat, conceptualize the removal of karma in terms of a "balancing" of negative karma with positive karma through moral activity, as noted in the above discussion of Eckankar.

Despite these contrasting soteriologies, the structural similarities are such that proponents of a particular tradition can sometimes sense the parallels. For example, the following passage from an Eck satsang discourse implicitly

---

[21] *Eck Satsang Discourses*, 1st series #1, 5.   [22] *Eck Satsang Discourses*, 1st series #9, 5.

recognizes the parallel between Eckankar and Christian soteriology, while simultaneously rejecting the "saving power" of the latter:

Anyone who has been raised from childhood in the worship of Christianity finds it's almost impossible to escape from a loyalty to Jesus to enter into the works of Eck . . . nobody can follow the teachings of the Mahanta, the Living Eck Master, and at the same time be praying to their traditional religious founder for assistance, understanding and fulfillment.[23]

To the extent that the Mystical Traveler is a parallel figure to the Living Eck Master, MSIA would be in 100 per cent disagreement with this statement. Instead, as has already been indicated, Jesus occupies a pivotal position in MSIA soteriology; namely, "Jesus Christ made it possible for all people to enter the Soul realm. Before that time, this was available only to a few people."[24] Jesus accomplished this "by his death and resurrection [which] reversed the karma of the planet and instituted the law of grace in place of the law of Moses."[25]

Unlike some of the ancient gnostic and modern metaphysical groups who want to say that Jesus did not really suffer and die on the cross, John-Roger teaches a literal, physical death followed by an equally literal resurrection:

It happened to him. I mean, God, they nailed him – you know, bam, bam, bam, three nails and he's on the cross. That probably wasn't fun in the sun . . . His dying did nothing. His resurrection did it all. Because everybody can die. And will. The resurrection, the transformation, is what is taking care of all the sin.[26]

John-Roger has sometimes referred to the mechanical working out of karma as the "Lucifer plan," and the overcoming of karma through grace as the "Christ plan." Echoing traditional theological language, the latter plan is sometimes referred to as a new dispensation. As the author of the karmic plan, Lucifer's rebellion takes place, in MSIA's account, when God allows Jesus to institute the grace plan alongside the original Lucifer plan. Lucifer/Satan then becomes the enemy of Jesus, even playing a role in his death: "They killed Jesus Christ on a cross . . . Thank God that happened, because then starts the Salvation for the Spirit part of us, the Soul . . . Satan

---

[23] *Eck Satsang Discourses*, 3rd series #3, 9.
[24] MSIA correspondence reply, "How Jesus Functions through MSIA" (This and other "correspondence replies" are from "boiler plate" responses used to address frequently asked questions from MSIA Discourse subscribers.)
[25] MSIA correspondence reply, "'Salvation' with Regard to Jesus."
[26] "God*Traveler*Christ*You."

didn't even know he was helping to fulfill the plan. He was just being a jerk."[27]

Precisely how and why the death and resurrection establish the grace plan is never really explicated. Perhaps in a Christian culture, familiar with the general idea of Jesus dying for one's sins, such explanation is unnecessary. The closest John-Roger comes to addressing this matter is where he discusses the resurrection as providing a paradigmatic model – a symbol – for awaking the Christ-self within individual human beings: "Someone will...call forward the Christ out of the burial tomb and resurrect it where it sits behind the eyes. And it's still in its tomb because it's in the head, but it must be freed from that so it floods the entire being."[28]

In a few places, he makes it sound as though Jesus' resurrection altered the spiritual "energy" structure of the planet:

[T]he grace of Christ is that Jesus, through his death and resurrection, brought forward into the planetary energy field a new spiritual consciousness. Where as before his time, every out-of-balance action ["negative karma"] needed to be balanced to the last farthing, now there was grace – the dissolving, or erasing, of negative karma through forgiveness. Jesus also made it possible for people to transcend into the Soul realm; from that realm, karma on the lower levels can be dissolved through love, grace, and forgiveness.[29]

John-Roger's most general attitude, however, appears to be: Accept what-ever explanation you want. It's the results that count: "[A] lot of people say it's done through the blood of Christ. Others say it's done through repentance, receive the Holy Spirit. So there's a lot of different brand names out there saying how it's to be done. Listen, if that's how it's to be done with their group, that's fine."[30]

In spite of all this very traditional-sounding language, however, MSIA's notion of grace is that the great majority of people do not immediately appropriate the full measure of grace because one must learn how to live in grace by practicing a Christ-like life. "When are we forgiven by God? When we do things God's way. Now that's a radical act. And when are we forgiven by Christ? When we come to Christ and become Christ-like or do Christ's way."[31]

[27] John-Roger [Unnumbered MSIA Tape] "Christmas Eve Seminar" (December 24, 1997).
[28] "God*Traveler*Christ*You."
[29] MSIA correspondence reply, "What is the Grace of the Christ?"
[30] "God*Traveler*Christ*You."
[31] John-Roger, *Forgiveness: The Key to the Kingdom* (Los Angeles: Mandeville, 1994), 199.

The traditional view of salvation from sin is that one is completely saved as soon as one completely surrenders. But then how does one deal with the un-Christ-like behavior in which one engages not long after even the most sincere "born again" experience? John-Roger describes such experiences as "[A]sking God for forgiveness and just believing and feeling and sensing that that has been given to you. But if we go and do the same thing over again, then was there forgiveness? Because there's been no change in behavior nor any learning."[32]

Hence, instead of grace being a once-and-for-all threshold, it is, rather, an ongoing, dynamic alternation between grace and law – a growth process through which we progressively learn to live more and more in grace: "It is always our choice [in every moment] to live under the Law of Moses or the grace of the Christ. And that grace manifests as unconditioned loving."[33]

This grace is appropriated by bringing love and forgiveness to bear in every potentially karma-generating situation. The same attitude with respect to one's "hang-ups" from the past will dissolve past karma. Much of the thrust of J-R's more down-to-earth teachings have to do with appropriating grace by learning to respond to every situation from one's Christ-self.

IS MSIA CHRISTIAN?

As a way of bringing this discussion to a close, it seemed appropriate to pose the question of whether MSIA members consider themselves Christians.

In the process of researching the present chapter, a short questionnaire was given to students in the group's seminary program. Twenty-two out of approximately fifty questionnaires were returned. Although I have not referred to these surveys prior to this section, they were of immense usefulness in helping me sort out MSIA's Christology. The final question of the instrument asked, "Is MSIA Christian? If so, Why? If not, why not?" The answers to this item ran the gamut, reflecting a far broader range of opinion than had been elicited by any of the other questions.

While no one emphatically rejected the label, several respondents said that they did not refer to themselves as "Christians" and, further, that MSIA was not "Christian" in any traditional sense. At the same time, these individuals noted that they were "followers of the Christ," and that they studied the teachings of Jesus.

---

[32] "God*Traveler*Christ*You."
[33] MSIA correspondence reply, "The Meaning of Jesus' Death and Resurrection."

At the other end of the spectrum, a half dozen participants responded
"Yes," but then went on to qualify their answer in some way or another.
The most interesting of these answers is worth citing as a representative
response (representative in content if not in tone):

This question – Is MSIA Christian? – is, on one level, insulting to me. Of course it is
Christian, if you mean does it reflect what Christ taught and not the "unChristian"
distortions of Christianity that have polluted and distorted the teachings of Jesus
Christ down through these 2,000 years, not to mention the mistranslations of his
words . . .

The majority of respondents gave yes *and* no answers, often saying that
if one defines "Christian" as meaning such-and-such, then Yes; otherwise,
No. A useful example of this category of responses is the following:

Yes and No. "Yes," in terms of we do follow Jesus' teachings . . . but, "No," in terms
of we do not necessarily follow someone else's interpretation of Jesus' teaching. We
follow our own truth as the Christ is revealed to us, and, if that is being Christian,
then so be it.

There were many variations on this basic idea; for example, one respondent
asserted that the mainstream churches followed the teachings of the apostle
Paul, whereas MSIA follows the teachings of Christ.
    Finally, three or four members of this category of respondents stressed
that truth could not be restricted to Christianity. Rather, one could follow
any of the world's great religions and eventually find one's way to salvation.
In the words of an MSIA member, from a letter to John Morton:

I see Jesus as my teacher and model, as a living Son of God, sent as Messiah, as
was Melchizedek – certainly not a common view. But I honor the light of Buddha,
Moses, Mother Mary, and other saints, past and present. I know the true Lord and
the true Light are one – and they are not found in any one religion.

Alongside this expression of universality, however, MSIA would also assert
that – whether or not one chooses to call oneself Christian – everyone on the
planet benefits from the death of Jesus, because, ever since his resurrection,
everyone can appropriate Grace by the simple act of forgiveness.

BIBLIOGRAPHY

PUBLISHED SOURCES

Anon., *Forgiveness: The Key to the Kingdom* (Los Angeles: Mandeville, 1994).
    Soul Transcendence (Los Angeles: Peace Theological Seminary and College of
        Philosophy, 1995).

Church of the Movement of Spiritual Inner Awareness, *Eck Satsang Discourses*, 1st Series, #1 & #9; 3rd Series, #3 & #4.
John-Roger, *The Christ within and the Disciples of Christ* (Los Angeles: Mandeville, 1994).

UNPUBLISHED SOURCES

MSIA Audio Tapes

#1329, "The Meditation of the Christ."
#1330, "Christmas Eve with John-Roger."
#1507, "What Is the Secret Center."
#7341, "Are you Living under Law or Grace?"
#7462, "God*Traveler*Christ*You."
[Unnumbered], "Christmas Eve Seminar," December 24, 1997.

John-Roger Correspondence Replies ("boiler plate" responses used to respond to frequently asked questions from Discourse subscribers)

"How Jesus Functions through MSIA"
"The Meaning of Jesus' Death and Resurrection"
"'Salvation' with Regard to Jesus"
"What is the Grace of the Christ?"

LITERATURE

Diem, Andrea Grace, "Shabdism in North America: The Influence of Radhasoami on Guru Movements" (PhD Dissertation, University of California, Santa Barbara. September, 1995).
Ellwood, Robert S. and Harry B. Partin, *Religious and Spiritual Groups in Modern America* (2nd edn; Englewood Cliffs, N.J.: Prentice-Hall, 1988).
Juergensmeyer, Mark, *Radhasoami Reality* (Princeton: Princeton University Press, 1995).
Judah, J. Stillson, *The History and Philosophy of the Metaphysical Movements in America* (Philadelphia: Westminster Press, 1967).
Lewis, James R., *Seeking the Light* (Los Angeles: Mandeville, 1996).
Olson, Roger E., "ECKANKAR: From Ancient Science of Soul Travel to New Age Religion," in Timothy Miller (ed.), *America's Alternative Religions* (Albany: State University of New York Press, 1995), 363–370.

CHAPTER 14

World savior in undergarment: the palpable Jesus of The Aetherius Society

Mikael Rothstein

INTRODUCTION

When studying the Jesus mythology of a contemporary UFO religion, some of the points made in the Introduction to this volume should be kept in mind. There is no real or true Jesus. From a historical point of view it is likely that a self-proclaimed rabbi, presumably with the common name of Yeshua (later on Latinized into Jesus), was active in Palestine some 2,000 years ago, but we know virtually nothing about him as an individual. The little that is given to conjecture is almost entirely circumstantial.[1] The Jesus of the Christian religions is a product of the religious-minded imagination. The only thing we can be certain about is what people have ascribed to him, and what they have said about him. Jesus, in that sense, is a mythical character. An alternative Jesus, then, is not alternative because he differs from a historical individual with an original teaching, but because he is constructed within alternative mythological and theological frameworks. In the case before us, the creative context is a small religious group within a Theosophical tradition. Competing Christs, therefore, reflect competing religious groups of people who work on the basis of different mythological elaborations. In effect, talking about Jesus means talking about the people who are constructing, upholding, and changing him in the complex social processes known as religion. The historical reality that has given its impetus to the Jesus myth is of no real importance. The multitude of Jesus-based religions will always – one way or another – claim that their beliefs are rooted in historical facts, but it is their own notions of alleged biblical "events," rather than historical realities, they refer to. Studying Jesus in unconventional contexts is simply to study the varieties and proliferations of a cherished mythological entity, and in doing so we are bound to

---

[1] This is not the place to discuss the study of the historical Jesus in any detail. The reader is referred to the discussions in Bruce Chilton and Craig A. Evans (eds.), *Studying the Historical Jesus: Evaluations of the State of Current Research* (Leiden: Brill, 1994).

encounter some of these agents whose personal initiatives have contributed greatly to the further development of the Jesus figure. Such a person is George King (1919–1997), the prophet and founder of The Aetherius Society, one of among several so-called UFO-religions that came into being in the aftermath of World War II.[2] This link between a creative religious mind and its mythological product is important simply because the qualities of the mythological figure, in many ways, will express the motifs, interests, and longings of its creator or creators. The study of Jesus as conceived by The Aetherius Society, consequently, is indirectly a study of George King, one of the more influential so-called contactees of the 1950s, who, each in their own particular (but usually Theosophical) way, claimed a unique relationship with beings from outer space. This is why Jesus in The Aetherius Society mostly falls within Theosophical categories.[3] Most UFO prophets never became successful beyond a brief period of stardom in the media, but a few, who managed to build organizations and institutionalize their authority, made a lasting impact. King is one of them.[4]

A closer exploration of The Aetherius Society's belief system (including the teachings ascribed to Jesus), however, is not intended here. The main topic of the following discussion is the nature and status of the Cosmic Master Jesus as expounded in George King's texts and narratives.[5]

ENTER JESUS

In a brief statement, commemorating the inauguration of "Operation Starlight," a project that would charge a number of sacred mountains

---

[2] A good introduction to The Aetherius Society is John A. Saliba, "The Earth is a Dangerous Place: The Worldview of The Aetherius Society," in James R. Lewis (ed.), *Encyclopedic Sourcebook of UFO Religions* (New York: Prometheus Books, 2003 [1999]), 123–142. Also see Mikael Rothstein, "The Idea of the Past, the Reality of the Present, and the Construction of the Future: A Case Study of The Aetherius Society," in James R. Lewis (ed.), *Encyclopedic Sourcebook of UFO Religions* (New York: Prometheus Books, 2003), 143–156, and Simon G. Smith, "Opening a Channel to the Stars: The Origins and Development of The Aetherius Society," in Christopher Partridge (ed.), *UFO Religions* (London and New York: Routledge, 2003), 84–102. UFO religions such as The Aetherius Society are commonly understood to have appeared as a response to Cold War fears.

[3] A number of comments regarding King's person shall be made in the following paragraphs, but he himself is not the topic of this chapter. For more details on King, see Mikael Rothstein, "Hagiography and Text in The Aetherius Society: Aspects of the Social Construction of a Religious Leader," in Mikael Rothstein and Reender Kranenborg (eds.), *New Religions in a Postmodern World* (RENNER Studies in New Religions; Aarhus: Aarhus University Press, 2003), 165–193.

[4] See Mikael Rothstein, "The Rise and Decline of the First Generation UFO Contactees: A Cognitive Approach," in James R. Lewis (ed.), *Encyclopedic Handbook of UFO Religions* (New York: Prometheus Books, 2003), 63–76.

[5] The general picture of Jesus in Theosophical interpretations is dealt with elsewhere in this volume; see the chapter by James A. Santucci.

with "cosmic energy" and thus save planet Earth from destruction, George King's close associate, Charles Abrahamson, writes, "Late at night, on July 23rd, 1958, on a barren mountaintop in Devon, England, a Western Master of Yoga held a rendezvous with a Cosmic Master from Planet Venus which forever changed the future of mankind upon Earth."[6]

According to George King's own account, a "Martian Adept" had tele-pathically instructed him to go to a location known as Stoney Cross in the vicinity of the village of Combe Martin at the foot of Holdston Down in Devonshire, England. Once he arrived, he was given further directions and told that he was supposed to physically meet another space being. Later he would recall how he, during his climb towards the summit, realized who that individual would be:

A cold perspiration formed tiny beads upon my forehead. I took one sweeping and dissatisfied look at my past and wondered why such a Holy Being as He Whom I was due to meet should ever trouble any further with us mere mortals. "But then" I thought, "The very essence of His Mission was to be of Sacrifice for Earth" . . .[7]

After having sent up an audible prayer for suffering humankind and peace on Earth, King saw a "bright blue sphere of light skip across the night skies." King continues his narrative (bold and capitals as in the original):

A few minutes passed. Then . . . . HE CAME. **I knew instantly that the God-man who stood silently looking down upon me was Jesus**.

What is more, this was no psychic vision, for He was completely physical. He was dressed from the shoulders to the ground in a robe, which seemed to glow with a bluish-white incandescence. Beneath the outer garment He wore a tightly fitting undergarment, which clung to his tall, lean, rather athletic body as though it was made of a very resilient substance. Around His waist there was a broad, tight band of purple, dotted with jewels, which seemed alive – such was the magnificence of their fire. One large five-pointed jewel in the middle of the front part of the purple belt continually changed colour.

Fascinated by the radiant beauty, I moved my head slowly upwards and gasped when my eyes lighted upon a really magnificent, pointed, star-like jewel upon His chest. The furthermost points of this living crystal must have stretched from His physical heart to the left hand side, to His Spiritual heart on the right. His outer garment covered these two points, yet I could plainly see the radiations coming through the garment, such was the intensity of the living fire which came from this great, scintillating crystal.

---

[6] Charles Abrahamson (ed.), *The Holy Mountains of the World Charged in Operation Starlight* (California: The Aetherius Society, 1994). This account was originally published in the journal *Cosmic Voice* 18 (1958), and subsequently in George King's book *Jesus Comes Again* (London: Aetherius Society, 1984).

[7] Abrahamson, *The Holy Mountains*, 18–19.

His face was, to a simple man like me, so wonderful as to be beyond my limited descriptive abilities. His living eyes clear, bright, shone with the blue flame of the great Cosmic Adept, which He is. Such was the light radiated by Jesus that I could plainly see the colour of those eyes. He was, contrary to popular theological belief, clean-shaven, with a firm chin, soft, kind lips and a well-shaped nose. His skin was tanned a deep golden colour. I did not see a solitary line upon His broad forehead. His long, light-brown hair fell to His broad, straight shoulders.[8]

George King also relates that Jesus was carrying a short wand (apparently, King hypothesizes, a symbol of "The Rod of Power from Venus") that was terminated by a "large crystal in the shape of a five-pointed star." Jesus pointed the wand towards King, and, using King as a device in the spiritual charging of the mountain "a great surge of vivid blue flame coursed through [his] body, along the arms and out of the fingertips." The encounter ended when the tall, silent, radiant Jesus, still holding his wand, fixed King "with a penetrating but kindly gaze for a moment." Then, King recalls, "a wide beam of green light sprang out of a faintly luminous shape hovering a few feet above the ground, about 30 yards away. Jesus moved a few steps to one side, into this beam, and was gone!"[9]

All elements of The Aetherius Society's notions regarding Jesus have their origin in this narrative, which, therefore, shall serve as our backdrop for the rest of this chapter. There was, however, an incident two years earlier that seemed to indicate that George King had met with the remarkable Venusian already in 1956. I shall return to that towards the end of this chapter.

MYTHOLOGICAL INNOVATIONS

George King's account of his initial encounter with Jesus appears in the shape of a simple recollection of an event, which, even if extraordinary, simply happened one late summer's night in 1958. In effect, however, the story carries all the qualities of a religious myth and indeed should be classified within the same category as stories such as those about Moses on Mount Sinai, Muhammad in Hira, and the myth of the transfiguration (Matt. 17.1–2) which may be the one immediate source of inspiration for King's narrative. The fact that Jesus, in King's case, is a space captain should not confuse us. The family resemblance to earlier religious myths, and more specifically to Christian lore regarding Jesus, which also places the events of divine intervention in a mundane setting, are so striking that

[8] *Ibid.*, 20.   [9] *Ibid.*, 20–21.

the historical and thematic connections are obvious. And perhaps even more so than we tend to imagine: the language of Christian doctrine tells of "God's son" who "descended from his Father's heavenly abode into this world," and that he, after his mission, departed and returned to the skies. In traditional Christian beliefs Jesus, clearly, has an extraterrestrial origin, and a permanent dwelling outside of Earth. His presence among people on this planet was temporary. The most important mythical characters of Christianity (God and Jesus) are discursively placed apart from the realm of people, they are literally space beings, which is emphasized by the fact that the third component of the joint Godhead of Christianity, the Holy Spirit, is said to have been sent to Earth to serve as the temporary substitute for Jesus until he shall return from "Heaven" when the planet Earth is on the verge of a great apocalypse.

Through the ages Christians have argued intensely over these concepts, and many different theologies have appeared. George King's Jesus, however, has demystified and rationalized the traditional Christian Jesus by revealing – and making intelligible – what "Heaven" actually means, namely another planet or perhaps a spaceship. Furthermore, like the Christian Heaven, the abode of Jesus and other Cosmic Masters of The Aetherius Society, is perfect: "They live in a paradisal state and place, where old age, disease, natural disasters, and wars do not exist."[10] Such considerations were also relevant to George King and still are to his organization: it is generally argued that biblical texts are not very precise, that they carry many misconceptions, and that no real understanding of them has been possible prior to the explanatory revelations received by George King. Among the things he learned (with reference to Jesus) was that the star of Bethlehem was no star at all: "No, this was a classic example of a UFO, leading three advanced men to a great Interplanetary Master who had been born on this Planet to perform a specific mission."[11] Christian mythology is taken into account – it even serves as a legitimating device – but it is reinterpreted and reevaluated on the basis of King's superior knowledge. In traditional Christendom Jesus carries the authority of God, but in The Aetherius Society he has other associates and co-workers. King explains how a group of space beings known as "The Ancient Ones" work with Jesus and serve as advisors to humanity and control all human life in the solar system, "as well as that on some Planets in other parts of the Milky Way."

[10] Saliba, "The Earth is a Dangerous Place," 129.
[11] George King (with Richard Lawrence), *Contacts With the Gods from Space: Pathway to the New Millennium* (Hollywood: The Aetherius Society, 1996), 39.

But it is Jesus himself who occupies the role of the savior, a notion structurally quite similar to traditional Jesus mythology. This became clear to King during his physical meeting with Jesus, but even more explicit after a series of subsequent revelations received by King. On July 10, 1958, prior to King's meeting with Jesus in Devon, the Master Aetherius (who holds the title of "Cosmic Adept and Representative of the Planet Venus in the Interplanetary Parliamentary System"), using King as a channel, prepared King's associates for an upcoming event: the release of "Twelve Blessings" that would be transmitted to people on Earth with King as the medium, from the Master Jesus residing on Venus. The Twelve Blessings were received one by one from July 27 to October 12, 1958, and were published immediately thereafter (in November) in a book with the same title which includes the following explanation: "The Twelve Blessings were given for the benefit of all humanity through the Everlasting Love of the Cosmic Master – Jesus."

Some of the blessings mirror the teachings ascribed to Jesus in conventional Christianity ("Blessed are They Who Love" [3], "Blessed are They Who Heal" [6]), but others show that the Master Jesus is a Theosophically oriented Venusian with interplanetary responsibility, more than he is a Jewish-Hellenistic carpenter's son from Nazareth. Blessed are: "Those Who Work For Peace" (1), "The Wise Ones" (2), "The Planetary Ones" (4), "The Thanksgivers" (5), "The Mother Earth" (7), "The Mighty Sun" (8), "The Supreme Lords of Karma" (9), "The Galaxy" (10), "The Supreme Lords of Creation" (11), and "The Absolute" (12). Addressing his audience (people gathered to witness King's reception of the new messages) as "my adorable children," Master Jesus seems to magnify or expand the points he is supposed to have made during his earthly presence, involving a new body of superhuman agents in his project, and making his ambitions intergalactic rather than merely a question of the salvation of human beings on Earth. Where the New Testament's Sermon on the Mount (which clearly is the source of inspiration here) stops, The Twelve Blessings continue. Where the Jesus of the traditional churches comes to a halt, Master Jesus of The Aetherius Society makes another move.

The importance of Master Jesus' teachings is emphasized in a final blessing by King, which has been included in later imprints of the book. On April 4, 1959 in London, George King, in a prayer, addressed "the Mighty Brahma" (who apparently is the same being as God) and talked about Jesus as a "Wonderful Angel," asking the Godhead to make himself and his approximately fifty associates (who had witnessed the transmissions) channels for the "Energy" that Jesus would need to "further His Great

Mission upon this Planet."[12] A final text in the book, the "Conclusion," is a speech delivered by yet another space being, "the great Orator and New Age Prophet, known to Earth simply as Mars Sector 6," through King on October 18, 1958. In an introductory remark, The Twelve Blessings is called "the New Age Bible," and the role of Master Jesus is stressed:

Jesus has come again in this twentieth century to extend His Ancient Mission to save this Earth. It is now up to you, the New Disciples who read, to learn and accept these Teachings, to take your rightful place as sowers of the seed of Cosmic Truth throughout your World.[13]

Mars Sector 6 is quite blunt in his way of putting things:

These Teachings were given by the Venusian you murdered. In these Teachings known as The Twelve Blessings, this person you called Jesus, gave an enhanced concept of Reality, so that the men of Terra, in these days, could take these Teachings in the light of scientific knowledge – in the light of proposed Space travel – and broaden their minds accordingly.

Speaking in an adapted King James Bible style he adds: "Think ye well upon these things! Go ye forth – in multitudinous ways – to spread this Word."[14]

As it appears, George King and his followers are positioned in relation to Master Jesus much in the same ways as the disciples of the New Testament in relation to Jesus. The religious notions have changed, but the matrix of authority and relationship between people and divine beings is in several ways borrowed from old-fashioned Christianity. Rather than inventing something new, King claims to have gained insight into the reality of Jesus' mission, while traditional Christians only understand very limited bits and pieces. In doing so he also claims to know the true or real Jesus, thereby inscribing himself into the history of competing theologians in Christian traditions.

King, however, does not take his thoughts to the traditional theological battlefield. Master Jesus' teachings and philosophical maneuverability seem to be constrained by the same kind of esoteric trend that permeates Theosophy. Master Jesus, consequently, is only active in relative secrecy, that is, in the context of The Aetherius Society, where his terrestrial mental channel was operating on behalf of the "Cosmic Intelligences" until his death. It is no wonder, then, that official Aetherius Society documents

---

[12] Anon., The Twelve Blessings: The Cosmic Concept for the New Aquarian Age as given by the Master Jesus in his Overshadowing of George King (California: The Aetherius Society, rev. edn., 1974 [1958]), 60–61.
[13] The Twelve Blessings, 62.   [14] Ibid., 63.

talk very favorably of Christian mysticism (and other kinds of mysticism), while the dogmatic beliefs of the ordinary churches and denominations are considered vulgar, superficial, or wrong.[15] "Mysticism" is quite open to various interpretations, including ufological perspectives, while traditional dogmatism is far more difficult to bend in such a direction.

It is relevant to observe that the emphasis is not only on the teachings of Master Jesus, but also on his personality or perhaps individuality. This, of course, is central to traditional Christian lore as well, where contemplations regarding the god-man's nature are extremely important: salvation is obtained through him as a person, or more precisely, through his tormented, killed, and revivified body. These notions transferred to the ideology of The Aetherius Society mean that it is primarily his function, as a highly skilled and knowledgeable space captain, in charge of the "Energy work" needed to save and spiritually mature people on Earth, that counts. The materiality or physical reality of Master Jesus is therefore also of great importance to George King.

MYTHS OF MATERIALITY

While many Christian traditions have transformed the bodily resurrected god-man into some kind of metaphysical, "spiritual" being, King's Jesus lives his concrete life either on his home planet Venus, on Saturn (his body is especially adapted to the varying conditions), or aboard a Mother Craft, a large vessel floating in space serving as a base for the numerous minor space crafts he is in command of.

But why is the post-ascended Jesus of the Christian churches a strangely transparent and non-concrete figure, when Master Jesus of The Aetherius Society is much more tangible? The answer is probably twofold: Firstly, George King offers a very definite belief system, and it is predictable that concrete notions will trigger concrete expectations. Secondly it is likely that the UFO context, operating with physical vessels flying in space, has allowed The Aetherius Society to employ a much more concrete theology than the metaphysics of traditional Christianity. In general, so it seems, new and non-institutionalized religions will express more concrete religious expectations than old and well-established religions. Time will unavoidably lead to religious fatigue and disappointments in religious groups carried by expectations of imminent cosmic transformations. In order not to nourish such frustrations, religious expectations should not be too demanding and

---

[15] King, *Contacts with the Gods from Space*, 86.

too concrete. Hence the weak articulation of the post-ascended Jesus in the major churches. He is "in Heaven" somehow, but if his return and the apocalypse are not awaited shortly, there is no need to be concrete. New religions with strong beliefs in imminent transformations, on the contrary, will tend to employ rather specific visions of what will transpire.[16] According to The Aetherius Society, we live in a time of great changes, and by means of non-symbolic narratives that are believed to reflect the plain truth, the conditions and implications of these transformations are explained. The palpable Master Jesus of The Aetherius Society is a product of these expectations.

Sometimes the specific environment is also of great importance. On rare occasions, for instance, King's texts describe the interior of the spacecrafts. Most notable, perhaps, is the incident where George King's mother (whose name happens to be Mary), on January 19, 1959, inside the Mother Craft, found herself in close proximity to Master Jesus "hundreds of miles from Earth in the purple magnificence of Star-studded Space."[17] It was "a happening which will eventually have its effect upon the religious beliefs of this World." Once again "an earth person stood face to face with Jesus."[18] Mary King's description, fascinating as it is, shows how the Jesus of The Aetherius Society seems to amalgamate the figure of a traditional religious preacher and a competent space captain.

Following telepathically received instructions, Mary King was picked up by a space craft commanded by one of Master Jesus' associates, Mars Sector 8 (not to be confused with his near namesake Mars Sector 6), who had directed her to carry a copy of The Twelve Blessings published in a single volume by The Aetherius Society: "Bring the Book. This must not be touched by any at Aetherius House [the centre of the movement], save our Mental Channel [i.e. George King]."[19] What transpired after the spaceship had entered Master Jesus' Mother Craft was this: "The Great Master Jesus, Himself, entered, approached the Commander [i.e. Mars Sector 8] and said: 'Give Me the Book.' The Master Jesus then took It in both hands and this is what He said . . ." A prayer to the Supreme Master of All Creation was offered by Jesus, and King is mentioned as "The one Whom Thou didst choose to be a Leader Among men on earth, in this their New Age."[20] Then Jesus placed the book in a special box where it fitted exactly. A wonderful music filled the room, and Mary became so affected and moved that she wept aloud. The "Cosmic Music" ceased, Jesus turned

[16] I have elaborated on this in Mikael Rothstein, Gud er (stadig) blå (Copenhagen: Aschehoug, 2001).
[17] Also see George King, The Nine Freedoms: An Authoritative Metaphysical Treatise on the Progress through Ascension to Cosmic Existence (California: The Aetherius Society, 1974 [1963]), 122f.
[18] The Twelve Blessings, 11.   [19] Ibid., 11.   [20] Ibid., 11.

towards her, still holding the box with the book in his hands, and said, "Blessed is he, who reading this Book doth understand. But exalted is he, even among the Angels, who reading this Book, doth take it to his heart and follow its precepts. Tell my Son, that this Book is now and forever – Holy."[21]

The Twelve Blessings were initially a channeled message delivered through George King, the "terrestrial mental channel," and received by his followers as yet another divine message. The words came out of King's mouth, but they were in fact (which was apparent to every believer witnessing the event) those of Master Jesus. Soon thereafter the message was published as a book, and thereby made available as a written text. In a third stage this text was furnished with a myth of origin that added further religious significance to it. Now, King's followers were told, it was also single-handedly blessed by Master Jesus and made "forever Holy."

The Twelve Blessings, also known as "the Cosmic Concept," therefore support the notion of Master Jesus as being concrete and close to his followers. Not only did he address people in direct speech (through his channel), he also initiated and blessed the printed version of his words, a book in the possession of every member of The Aetherius Society. Furthermore, this astonishing event happened in close proximity to a human witness.

This myth about Mary King aboard Master Jesus' spaceship is perhaps more significant than the story of how King initially was confronted with Jesus, because it serves to legitimize the most cherished theological document of The Aetherius Society, and because the person holding a copy of The Twelve Blessings in his or her hand, according to the Society's doctrines, will establish a direct link to Master Jesus who himself exalted the book. Residing on "the shining Planet, Venus," Jesus is in one way very far from humans on Earth, but through his earthly channel, and through the physical manifestations of his blessings (the book), people may nevertheless experience his presence and closeness. In a way Jesus is always readily available in the same way as in Catholicism and Orthodox Christianity, but by means of another kind of agency. He is not present through the ritual of communion, but through the published version of The Twelve Blessings. The book has, in certain ways, the function of a relic because it represents a direct link to Master Jesus, but also because it is the manifestation of a line of events, where George King's followers were able to *witness* Master Jesus speaking directly to humanity. In a copy of the first imprint of The Twelve Blessings (which is in this author's possession), there is a dedication from one woman to another where the giver, after writing her name, states, "who

---

21 *Ibid.*, 11–12.

was present during the reception of these things, 25.12.1958." One should not be confused by the date, which in traditional Christendom marks the mythological birth of Jesus. In The Aetherius Society "the actual birthday of Master Jesus" is on March 15.[22] Celebrating the birthday of Jesus on this alternative date also indicates a unique access to knowledge about the divinity, and, therefore, to an incomparable religious authority. In many ways this is what the concrete narratives about Master Jesus are all about: providing authority.

CHRISTOLOGY AND AUTHORITY

Any Christology, by its nature, is also a hagiography that takes the biblical character of Jesus into specific, and sometimes entirely new, realms. But in the case of George King and The Aetherius Society the innovative Christology serves a double function. It does not only represent a revised hagiography regarding Jesus, it also contributes massively to the social construction of George King as a religious leader, and to the authority of his organization. As stated by George King in a foreword to the abovementioned *The Twelve Blessings*:

Now the Society is still further privileged by being chosen as the Organisation through which Jesus, Himself, gave the Sacred Truths known as The Twelve Blessings.
  I too feel honoured as the human instrument who was Overshadowed by the Master Jesus so that He could radiate Energies to all men on Earth and also give to them a wide Cosmic Concept in these mystic texts.[23]

The elevation of King, through Jesus, also happens in other ways. One of The Aetherius Society's executives, the reverend Chrissie Blaze of the American Division of the Society's Ecclesiastical Synod, referring to the revelations King received from Master Jesus, writes:

Suddenly, Dr. King was in the spotlight and these messages, far from making him popular, made his life extremely difficult. In 1958, when he received a series of twelve Transmissions from no less a Cosmic Personage than the Master Jesus, he received death threats . . . Dr. King, a man of great strength and courage continued despite these threats; he had a lifelong mission to perform and he would let nothing stand in his way.[24]

---

[22] George King and Kevin Quinn Avery, *The Age of Aetherius* (California: The Aetherius Society, 1982), 47.
[23] *The Twelve Blessings*, 9.
[24] Quotation from Blaze's personal home page: http://www.chrissieblaze.com/drgeorgeking.shtml (accessed April 15, 2008).

In essence what is implied here is that George King is the ultimate authority as far as Jesus is concerned. The theologies of the conventional churches are flawed to say the least, whereas King had direct access to the source itself. In conventional Christian traditions, knowledge of Jesus is based on readings of the biblical texts. In The Aetherius Society this is hardly the case. It is – as we have already seen – George King's first-hand contacts with Jesus, and the texts that subsequently came about as the result of these meetings, that really count. And there is no reason why King's followers should distrust him. In April 1959, the Master Jesus, on behalf of the Cosmic Masters collectively, proclaimed to King: "My Son, you are now one of Us, and We now declare this to all men."[25] Today King, according to his epitaph, resides with his fellow Masters on another planet.

The philosophy of George King, then, is based on a specific authority structure: Master Jesus of Venus taps into the solid authority of rabbi Jesus of Nazareth, or more precisely, King's narratives tap into biblical myths, and in a way the authority of the churches or of the Bible is transferred into the hands of George King, and thereby to The Aetherius Society.

This mechanism, of course, works well inside the organization, but it creates tension towards the surroundings. Indeed the Christian sentiments sometimes raised against the Jesus of The Aetherius Society are predictable. Making radical changes in well-established, heavily institutionalized mythologies will always create a stir.

One rather impressive example is *An Encyclopaedia of False Christs* composed by Shaun Aisbitt and posted on the Internet in 2002. Under the headline: "Is there Another Jesus?" he writes:

In these dark days there are many who say or believe they follow Jesus Christ, but who are following a false Jesus Christ. I come across so many false teachings and cults that confuse people with the argument "But we are Christians, we follow Jesus Christ, just like all Christians do." They may follow what they call Jesus, but it isn't the same Jesus of the Bible. . . . When we say we follow Jesus, we need to make sure the Jesus we are following is the right one. Just saying we follow Jesus and not follow the Jesus of the Bible, leads to following men and demons. This of course leads to a lost eternity . . . As a guidepost, I decided to make an encyclopaedic list of all the false Jesus' out there, and hopefully open the eyes of those following an angel of light into the darkness.[26]

This initiative is, of course, based on the New Testament which itself – probably due to concrete experiences among the early followers

---

[25] Smith, "Opening a Channel to the Stars," 97.
[26] http://www.geocities.com/da_preach/anotherchrist.htm (accessed April 7, 2008).

of Jesus – systematically seeks to protect the authors' idea of Jesus against potential copycats. Aisbitt's Internet site quotes the Gospel of Matthew:

Then if any man shall say unto you, Lo, here is Christ, or there; believe it not. For there shall arise false Christs, and false prophets, and shall show great signs and wonders; insomuch that, if it were possible, they shall deceive the very elect. Behold, I have told you before. Wherefore if they shall say unto you, Behold, he is in the desert; go not forth: behold, he is in the secret chambers; believe it not.[27]

The encyclopedia (which is basically an annotated list) offers no less than 259 entries (with some overlap), one of which is The Aetherius Society, thereby demonstrating the variety of Jesus mythologies at work. Clearly many Christians feel an urge to defend their own Jesus mythology against that of others, including that of The Aetherius Society.

But who, so to say, from a historical point of view, *is* Master Jesus of The Aetherius Society? There is no simple answer, but apparently he is composed of, or inspired by, three different figures: (1) One or more of the masters of Theosophy, (2) the New Testament Jesus, and (3) the Jesus of American-Christian popular religion. The Theosophical nature of George King's Jesus is apparent in several ways, partly through the description of his looks, partly through the teachings ascribed to him. Indeed The Aetherius Society is yet another Theosophical off-shoot, and as the Masters or Adepts are crucial to Theosophical mythology, and given that Jesus has a prominent position in the pantheon of most Theosophical traditions, it is quite predictable that also George King's UFO-inclined version would include notions about him.[28] The legacy of the New Testament, of course, permeates Theosophy as far as Jesus is concerned. The inspiration from the New Testament is therefore filtered through Theosophy, but sometimes a more direct link is also apparent.

The connection with American-Christian popular religion is perhaps less visible, but even so of great importance, especially with regard to Jesus' physical appearance. It may be difficult to determine the more precise connections, but there is a striking resemblance between the image of Jesus that appears in King's description, and the most cherished notion of his looks in American popular culture derived from artist Warner Sallman's paintings (see below), and – perhaps more indirectly – late (or even relatively modern) apocrypha such as the rather influential text known as "Letter of Lentulus." The latter was conceived in the Middle Ages, most likely to

---

[27] Matt. 24.23–26.
[28] A chapter in this volume by James A. Santucci deals with Jesus in Theosophy.

legitimize the way Jesus was portrayed in church art. The text claims to be an eyewitness account of the Senate in Rome, written by one Publius Lentulus, who had met Jesus. The text is still very widely disseminated, and will be found in numerous popular Christian connections. In an English translation from Latin (but not the classical Latin of ancient Rome!) one passage reads thus:

He is a tall man, and well shaped, of an amiable and reverend aspect; his hair of a colour that can hardly be matched, the colour of chestnut full ripe, falling in waves about his shoulders. His forehead high, large and imposing; his cheeks without spot or wrinkle, beautiful with a lovely red; his nose and mouth formed with exquisite symmetry; his beard thick and of a colour suitable to his hair reaching below his chin. His eyes bright blue, clear and serene, look innocent, dignified, manly, and mature. In proportion of body, most perfect and captivating, his hands and arms most delectable to behold.[29]

In a discussion of the text Edgar J. Godspeed concludes:

The "Letter of Lentulus" is evidently a fiction, designed to give currency to the description contained in the printers' manuals about the personal appearance of Jesus. The varying accounts of its provenance are simply devices to explain its survival from antiquity until today. It is probably as old as the thirteenth century; but it was unknown to Christian antiquity, and has no claims to serious attention as throwing any light upon the personal appearance of Jesus.[30]

However, such texts may certainly have helped shape the public notion of what Jesus looked like, and it would only be natural for George King to tap into such ideas. There is no proof that he did so consciously, but given the frequent use of the text in popular religious milieus, it is quite possible that he came across the Lentulus document at some point, directly or indirectly. Similarly, it is most likely that various iconographic representations may have made an impact, for instance, a painting by Warner Sallman (1892–1968), supposedly the best-known Jesus portrait ever in popular culture: following a nightly vision, Sallman drew a sketch of what he had seen, and years later he turned the sketch into an oil painting in 1941. This particular portrait soon became the most reproduced and most widely distributed popular depiction of Jesus in the USA (where George King settled in 1959)

---

[29] The text has been published on several occasions and is easily found on the Internet. On the following webpage the Lentulus text, and a few others of the same kind, is available: http://mariavaltortawebring.com/Pages/015_Jesus_Physical_Appearance.htm (accessed April 15, 2008).

[30] Edgar J. Goodspeed, *Modern Apocrypha: Famous "Biblical" Hoaxes* (Boston: The Beacon Press, 1956), 91.

and beyond, and arguably a fundamental reference in most Americans' and many Europeans' way of imagining the god-man.[31] Relating to the picture, a woman expresses her feelings thus:

> From the image of the head of Christ I see righteousness, strength, power, reverence, respect, fairness, faithfulness, love, compassion. From the way the hair in the image is highlighted in the back and highlights around the front of the head and face there seems to be a Holy radiance emitted from the image, depicting the qualities mentioned above.[32]

It is, of course, circumstantial, but it is certainly possible that George King, as so many other religiously interested people in the West, was inspired in the same way, and that he somehow transferred Sallman's image of Jesus, as in the case of the apocryphal Publius Lentulus-text, into his own image of Master Jesus. The only picture of Jesus, however, to be found in the publicly available material from The Aetherius Society (the web page) is, to my knowledge, a photo of sculptor Bertel Thorvaldsen's famous Jesus statue, probably best known from its very frequent usage in Mormon temples (the original is in the main church of Copenhagen, Denmark). This statue features Jesus in the most typical way, but it is not the Jesus of King's description. Thorvaldsen's Jesus is clad in the robe apparently imagined by Christian artists to be the only possible dress of ancient times. Master Jesus, however, posed in a rather more sophisticated outfit when he stood before George King. But this discrepancy is no problem at all: George King has physically met the Master Jesus in his capacity of a space captain, while the same individual is known to people on Earth in quite another capacity: as Jesus of Nazareth. Hence, Thorvaldsen's statue depicts Master Jesus during his presence on Earth when he would dress like everybody else. By allowing for this difference, members of The Aetherius Society are able to appreciate ordinary Christian art, and identify most conventional iconographic representations of Jesus with their own understanding. What remains impossible for them is to identify with the Christian understanding of who Jesus really was or is. One may assume that this also explains why no iconographic tradition of any significance has emerged in The Aetherius Society. It is simply not necessary.

---

[31] The painting is available at: http://www.warnersallman.com (accessed April 15, 2008). On Sallman's art, see David Morgan and Sally M. Promey, *Exhibiting the Visual Culture of American Religions* (Valparaiso: Brauer Museum of Art, 2000).

[32] http://www.anderson.edu/sallman/headofchrist.html (a sub-page of the abovementioned Internet site) (accessed April 15, 2008).

The Aetherius Society's religious vision requires the believers to actively take part in world transformation processes. King was instructed by the Cosmic Masters to initiate and oversee a number of projects designed to further the spiritual evolution of humankind, and one of his main achievements was to institutionalize these heavily ritualized projects that essentially were designed to channel "spiritual energy" into the planet or otherwise assist the Cosmic Masters in their work. On several occasions Master Jesus encourages his audience to attend these rituals, and quite often the participants will perform according to his specific instructions. One such example is the "Prayer for Spiritual Workers" delivered by Master Jesus through George King on December 22, 1962. The prayer is supposed to strengthen the believer in his or her religious endeavors, and Jesus furnished it with a piece of advice to the users:

Say this Prayer with your heart and with your Soul, when the world is cold to you – and you will be warmed. Say it when you are down – and you will be lifted. Say it when you are alone – and you will be comforted by a Presence. Say it when you fail – and you will succeed. Say it when you die – and you will live. Say it so that you may gain sufficient Power and strength to do greater things.[33]

In reciting the "Prayer for Spiritual Workers" the individual not only supports the work of the Cosmic Masters. He or she will also follow in the footsteps of Master Jesus, who himself originally conceived of and uttered the words. The structure is well known from traditional Christianity, where the most important rituals are related to mytho-historical events involving Jesus, not least the Eucharist. In the prayer Master Jesus asks "mighty God" for strength to face a world of non-believers, and to work above his "Karmic weakness" for the benefit of God's will. In doing so Master Jesus occupies a double position: he is the bringer of knowledge through which humans are able to understand and confront the problems of the world, but he is also the associate of humans, who is struggling to realize the ideals he himself has described. Master Jesus is structurally mediating between heaven and earth, between the divine and the human, but in his prayer for "spiritual workers" he tends to include himself as one among them, rather than being an object for their devotion. This is probably where Master Jesus differs most profoundly from the Jesus of conventional Christianity.

---

[33] King, *The Nine Freedoms*, 199.

Jesus' absolute divinity in the traditional churches, where he is one of the three intertwined gods that constitute the one Godhead, is unquestionable, but in The Aetherius Society the divinity of Master Jesus is relative. The "Mighty God" in George King's belief system is a kind of gnostic construct, which relegates the divine agents of the local solar system to lower strata of the cosmic system. Master Jesus rises high above mortal humans, but he is not at the top of the cosmic hierarchy. This is ritually emphasized in his prayer, which, therefore, serves to create a kind of nearness between the otherwise distant Venusian and his followers on Earth.

There is, however, a ritual perspective that even more directly links Master Jesus with people of Earth. According to George King he witnessed a figure with features and functions exactly as those of Master Jesus perform a very special initiation aboard a spaceship on March 23, 1956, approximately two years before the incident on Holdstone Down in Devon described above. It is never said explicitly, but there is little doubt that this "Tall Master from Venus" was indeed Master Jesus. Amazed by this Master's beauty King asked the Martian instructor who had taken him to the space ship who the amazing individual was. Reluctantly, and with a secrecy reminding the reader of the New Testament's *Messiasgeheimnisse*, the Martian answered with a twinkle in his eyes: "He has been known by many names on Earth."

The initiation carried out by this Venusian Master is described in great detail. A young girl from India was bestowed immortality and glorified by an ascension to a higher realm of existence. She had, however, chosen to continue her life among the mortals of Earth, and King uses this experience to contemplate on the further need for spiritual evolution among human beings. During the course of his description of this initiation, King also describes the Venusian Master entering through the roof in a brilliant white cloud:

The Master from Venus had arrived. He looked ageless, appearing neither old nor young. He was very tall, straight and slim, with long golden hair which hung down to his straight, broad shoulders. Like the locks of some fastidious woman, His hair shone like burnished gold. Gently tinted by the reflection of the blue radiance from the roof, it seemed majestically alive... He was attired in a simple robe of white, drawn in around His slim waist by a broad band which sparkled with the light from a complicated pattern of multi-hued jewels... Even from where I stood, I could see His blue eyes – blue like a cloudless summer sky, they held the depth of Space itself.[34]

[34] *Ibid.*, 133–134.

It is almost unavoidable to identify the Venusian as the Master Jesus that King would later encounter in Devon.[35] More importantly, however, is his function as the provider of soteriologically significant rituals that even makes his brothers in the Cosmic Hierarchy bow in amazement. King's Jesus is no superior god, but he holds the spiritual authority on which humanity depends, and he is in charge of the rituals that will enable us to overcome our current blindness and folly. Structurally he has kept some of the Christian Jesus' key features, but the twist into a Theosophical Master and subsequently a space captain has made him something in his own right. The Master Jesus of Venus is one of the more recent divinities in the history of religions, but also among those with the deepest roots in European religious history.

BIBLIOGRAPHY

SOURCES

Abrahamson, Charles (ed.), *The Holy Mountains of the World Charged in Operation Starlight* (California: The Aetherius Society, 1994).
Anon., *The Twelve Blessings: The Cosmic Concept for the New Aquarian Age as given by the Master Jesus in his Overshadowing of George King* (California: The Aetherius Society, rev. edn., 1974 [1958]).
King, George, *Jesus Comes Again* (London: Aetherius Society, 1984).
  The Nine Freedoms: An Authoritative Metaphysical Treatise on the Progress through Ascension to Cosmic Existence (California: The Aetherius Society, 1974 [1963]).
King, George (with Richard Lawrence), *Contacts with the Gods from Space: Pathway to the New Millennium* (Hollywood: The Aetherius Society, 1996).
King, George and Kevin Quinn Avery, *The Age of Aetherius* (California: The Aetherius Society, 1982).

LITERATURE

Chilton, Bruce and Craig A. Evans (eds.), *Studying the Historical Jesus: Evaluations of the State of Current Research* (Leiden: Brill, 1994).
Goodspeed, Edgar J., *Modern Apocrypha: Famous "Biblical" Hoaxes* (Boston: The Beacon Press, 1956).
Morgan, David and Sally M. Promey, *Exhibiting the Visual Culture of American Religions* (Valparaiso: Brauer Museum of Art, 2000).
Rothstein, Mikael, *Gud er (stadig) blå* (Copenhagen: Ashehoug, 2001).
  "The Idea of the Past, the Reality of the Present, and the Construction of the Future: A Case Study of The Aetherius Society," in James R. Lewis (ed.),

---

[35] It should be noted that King's second meeting with Master Jesus was mentioned in writing prior to the first. I have no explanation why, but presumably it should be explained with reference to missionary strategies.

Encyclopedic Sourcebook of UFO Religions (New York: Prometheus Books, 2003), 143–156.

"Hagiography and Text in The Aetherius Society: Aspects of the Social Construction of a Religious Leader," in Mikael Rothstein and Reender Kranenborg (eds.), *New Religions in a Postmodern World* (RENNER Studies in New Religions; Aarhus: Aarhus University Press, 2003), 165–193.

"The Rise and Decline of the First Generation UFO Contactees: A Cognitive Approach," in James R. Lewis (ed.), *Encyclopedic Sourcebook of UFO Religions* (New York: Prometheus Books, 2003), 63–76.

Saliba, John A., "The Earth is a Dangerous Place. The Worldview of The Aetherius Society," in James R. Lewis (ed.), *Encyclopedic Sourcebook of UFO Religions* (New York: Prometheus Books, 2003), 123–142.

Smith, Simon G., "Opening a Channel to the Stars. The Origins and Development of The Aetherius Society," in Christopher Partridge (ed.), *UFO Religions* (London and New York: Routledge, 2003), 84–102.

CHAPTER 15

Modern Jesus legends

Olav Hammer

THE BUILDING BLOCKS OF LEGEND

The Introduction to the present volume outlines a view of religions as heterogeneous cultural repertoires. The sheer age of the Christian tradition implies that this repertoire by a process of accretion has acquired vast proportions. Jesus narratives from the past 2,000 years are today available to religious innovators. In theory, nothing would prevent a modern Christology from drawing on, for example, alchemical images or on Guillaume Postel's theory of the feminine Messiah. Long-forgotten or neglected religious elements do very occasionally enter popular imagination, and are used as building blocks for new Jesus narratives. In practice, however, a much more limited range of culturally prevalent themes tends to be chosen.

Most fundamental among these themes are the accounts in the canonical Gospels, which are to my knowledge the base line referred to by all modern legends, even if only to be rejected. The figure of Jesus would of course be unrecognizable to contemporary readers if it were not anchored in familiar Gospel stories. The birth narratives, the visit to the temple described in Luke, the three-year ministry and the Passion are frequent elements even in otherwise very heterodox accounts.

Extracanonical material from early Christianity constitutes a second source of themes. The *Gospel of Thomas* is one striking example of how ancient non-canonical texts can be appropriated for new purposes. The sayings in *Thomas* are by modern authors construed as evidence that Jesus was the teacher of a holistic, psychologically based wisdom, the purveyor of a zen-like form of mysticism, or even the promoter of a macrobiotic diet.[1] More unusually, authors can construct accounts resembling the infancy Gospels. In his book *Die Jugend Jesu*, the German prophet Jakob Lorber

---

[1] Dylan Burns, "Seeking Ancient Wisdom in the New Age," in Olav Hammer and Kocku von Stuckrad (eds.), *Polemical Encounters: Esoteric Discourse and its Others* (Leiden: Brill, 2007), 253–289.

(1800–1864) lets Jesus speak and perform numerous miracles as an infant. Lorber's account includes versions of various incidents from the *Infancy Gospel of Thomas*: the young boy Jesus fashions birds from clay and gives them life, causes the death of a child in a fit of rage, is impatient with his teacher's reading lessons, carries water in his cloak, and raises several people from the dead.[2]

Yet another group of themes are topics associated with religious currents outside the Christian mainstream, in particular various forms of Western esotericism and a variety of new religious movements. Unorthodox narratives of this kind include the suggestion that Jesus was an initiate into mystery cults that transmitted a perennial wisdom religion, that he travelled to India, that he was the human receptacle of a spiritual entity emanating from the Sun, that he was married and had children, that he was the son of a Roman soldier, born in the late second century BCE, that he was black, the reincarnation of a person who had once lived on Atlantis, or an extraterrestrial being.

Such themes can be used in a variety of combinations. The theme of *philosophia perennis* affirms that religions (or at least some religions) share certain core elements. Particular leading figures of various religious traditions can in this perspective be understood as the spokespersons of this tradition-transcending wisdom. One version of the theme suggests that Egypt is the homeland of (or the main conduit of) profound religious and philosophical truths. Another version suggests that India, rather than Egypt, is the fountainhead of wisdom. The theme of initiation proposes that religious insight can only be transmitted via an initiatory path. These themes can appear independently of one another, but two, three, or more can easily be combined. A classic work of late nineteenth-century esotericism, Edouard Schuré's *Les grands initiés* (1889), presents a grand synthesis. In his version of religious history, there exists a primeval wisdom tradition into which the founders of the great religions were initiated. Sages from India (Rama, Krishna) and Egypt (Hermes) were particularly important transmitters of this tradition. From India and Egypt, the perennial wisdom tradition was transmitted to representatives in Israel (Moses) and Greece (Orpheus, Pythagoras, and Plato), until it was given its final form by Jesus.

New Jesus narratives can thus be created from the repertoire of already available religious building blocks. The building block metaphor conversely

[2] Jakob Lorber, *Die Jugend Jesu: Das Jakobus-Evangelium* (Bietigheim: Lorber-Verlag, 1936), chs. 279–296.

also implies that every individual element of religious discourse or practice has its own history, and can percolate across the borders of conventionally defined cultural and social domains. They can migrate across textual genres and social milieus, from the controversial to the purportedly scientific and back, between various new religions, move between popular fiction and religious apologetics, be taken up by various subcultural milieus, and so forth. In order to illustrate the ways in which one particular piece of Jesus discourse can be used in so many different ways, a somewhat more elaborate example is called for.

A widespread legend suggests that Jesus came into contact with various Asian religions, and that he may have traveled to India. A fully fledged "Jesus in India" story was presented by Nicolas Notovitch in his *La vie inconnue de Jésus-Christ* (1894). On a journey through Kashmir and Ladakh in northernmost India, the book informs us, Notovitch was told that the best-educated Tibetan lamas were well aware of Jesus, whom they knew as Issa. Some ancient texts concerning Issa had been preserved in Lhasa, and copies or translations into Tibetan could be found in various monasteries in the Tibetan Buddhist area. Notovitch relates that he was lucky enough to find such a set of texts at the Ladakhi monastery of Hemis, had them translated, and summarized the contents in a heavily edited French version, which he produced in order to organize the material chronologically and avoid the many digressions of the original.

This edited version is included as the second half of Notovitch's travelogue. The reader is here first presented with the generally familiar outline of Jesus' childhood. At the age of thirteen, a period in his life not documented in any canonical text, events take a startling new course. The family of Jesus is keen to see him married, a fate that the spiritually minded Jesus is not willing to accept. He therefore leaves his native country and travels eastward. He reaches India and crosses the country from west to east. On his way, he meets Jains in the Western province of Sindh, Hindus in Orissa in the East, and finally Buddhists further north. He learns the sacred languages of the Indians, gets thoroughly acquainted with their religions, and makes himself highly unpopular with the ruling strata of the areas he visits by preaching against their religions. Two elements of Indian culture in particular offend him: the caste system and the polytheism of the local religions. Contrary to many later versions of the legend, the "Jesus in India" motif starts out not as a way to reformulate Christianity in a way that can accommodate the spiritual insights of Buddhists or Hindus, but as a defense of the virtues of Christianity vis-à-vis supposedly corrupt Oriental mores and superstitions.

The "Jesus in India" legend has, however, become far more widely used and known precisely for its ability to bolster the conception that Jesus' message was not very much like the teachings of the churches, and that the true teachings of Jesus were inspired by Asian religions. This shift is partly carried out in *The Aquarian Gospel of Jesus the Christ* (also known as *The Aquarian Age Gospel of Jesus, the Christ of the Piscean Age*) written by Levi Dowling (1844–1911) and published in 1908. The story of Jesus in India can be found in chapters 21 to 37, and constitutes a more detailed account than Notovitch's story. The text was said to have been received from the Akashic records, a theosophical concept denoting a source of revelatory knowledge.

In Dowling's book, the story of Jesus in India also begins after Jesus' twelfth year. An Indian prince visits Israel, gets to know Jesus, and invites him back to India. In this story, Jesus "longs to learn" (ch. 21 v. 16), rather than preach to the inhabitants of India; this, however, does not correspond entirely to the contents of the following chapters. Via Sindh, they reach Orissa (presumably a tacit reference to similar geographical details in Notovitch's book). Jesus spends several years in India, where he astounds the Brahmins with his learning, discusses the evils of the caste system, and answers metaphysical questions. He exhorts his audiences to give up the worship of idols. On the receiving side, he is instructed in Indian medicine by a learned healer in Benares. Some aspects of Jesus' message are rather unorthodox from a mainstream theological point of view. In a pantheist vein, he suggests that even the lowliest worms are sacred because they are "deities, made flesh" (ch. 28 v. 9). Jesus is also an ecumenical preacher, who assures his listeners that Parabrahm (i.e. Brahma), Thoth, Zeus, and Jehovah are different names for the same deity. Nowhere is it suggested that these are doctrines that Jesus has picked up in India. Rather, the Hindu crowds listening to Jesus' discourses are astounded by his words of wisdom.

The anticlerical message of Jesus enrages the Brahmins to such an extent that he continues north to the land of the Buddhists. The chapters that deal with his further journey (chs. 32–35) reveal the theosophical tendency of the book with particular clarity. In a passage on the origin of the human species, Jesus refutes the doctrine of reincarnation held by his Buddhist interlocutor and explains how humans are the thoughts of God clothed in the substance of certain ether planes. Later, Jesus preaches the message of an androgynous Father-Mother-God, and discusses the religion of the coming (astrological) age with the sage Vidyapati. Finally, Jesus passes through Lhasa and Ladakh, before returning home via Persia.

From Dowling's theosophically tinged story, the Jesus in India legend crossed denominational boundaries, and became integrated into the canonical text of an influential African-American religious movement: *The Holy Koran of the Moorish Science Temple of America*, published in 1927.[3] Chapters 6 to 12 of the *Holy Koran* contain the history of Jesus in the years after the age of twelve that the Gospels do not discuss. The account roughly follows Dowling's story and has the same cast of characters: readers encounter by now familiar topics such as the Indian prince in Palestine, Jesus' journey to Orissa, his message of monotheism and equality. Whereas the *Aquarian Gospel* speaks of God, the *Holy Koran* gives the divinity the name Allah. It diverges from the *Aquarian Gospel* mainly by omitting numerous events contained in Dowling's book. While the *Aquarian Gospel* relates Jesus' travels back from India, the *Holy Koran* makes an abrupt transition from chapter 12 (Jesus preaches to a group of Buddhist laypersons gathered at a well) to chapter 13 (Jesus has returned to "Egyptland").

Versions of the same legend have been appropriated by other authors and movements, including Nicholas Roerich, co-founder of a theosophical movement, Swami Abhedananda of the Ramakrishna movement, and Elizabeth Clare Prophet of the Church Universal and Triumphant, who writes at length on this topic in her book *The Lost Years of Jesus* (1987). Although thoroughly debunked by various critics, the Jesus in India legend is at the time of writing (2008) making a new appearance, this time in a film. *The Aquarian Gospel*, which portrays Jesus as a holy man inspired by the religions of India, is scheduled to be released in 2009.[4]

A rather different version on the Jesus in India theme is associated with the heterodox Islamic Ahmadiyya movement, with roots in Pakistan. The founder of the movement, Mirza Ghulam Ahmad (1835–1908) in a book published in Urdu in 1899 (*Masih Hindustan mein*) and translated into English in 1938–1939 as *Jesus in India* suggested that Jesus escaped death on the cross, traveled to India and died a natural death in the city of Srinagar in Kashmir. The original purpose of presenting the idea that Jesus survived the crucifixion and died in India seems to have been embedded both within an Islamic and a more local context. Following Yohanan Friedmann's account, Ghulam Ahmad's religious message was fundamentally at odds

---

[3] Mattias Gardell, "Countdown to Armageddon: Minister Farrakhan and the Nation of Islam in the Latter Days" (PhD dissertation, Stockholm, 1995), 25. The document itself is reproduced at http://www.geocities.com/Heartland/Woods/4623/frontspiece.html. All websites cited in this chapter were checked and active on August 20, 2008.

[4] At the time of writing, the production of this film had been discussed by various media, including the November 19, 2007 issue of *The Guardian*, available online at www.guardian.co.uk/world/2007/nov/19/india.religion.

with the eschatological scenario of mainstream Sunni Islam.[5] According to a widespread conception, Jesus never died on the cross, but was elevated to heaven. At the end of time, he will return to lead a battle against the forces of evil. Christian missionaries in British India could use this idea to point at the similarities between Christianity and Islam, but also to depict Christianity as the superior alternative, since Christ was alive while Muhammad was dead. Ghulam Ahmad's Jesus narrative allowed him not only to reject core Christian claims, but also to appropriate a messianic role for himself. Jesus was dead and could therefore not be the eschatological savior.

The Ahmadiyya legend has been incorporated into Western alternative discourses on Jesus, most notably through the efforts by Ahmadiyya missionaries to publicize this Jesus-in-India theory. Several magazine articles, tracts, and book-length exposés in English and German have provided the transition from Ahmadiyya doctrine to a Western readership. Among Western authors, perhaps the most influential is Holger Kersten, whose German book *Jesus in Indien* (1981) has been translated into English as *Jesus Lived in India* (1986). The main missing link between the South Asian and Western receptions of the Jesus in India legend is the fact that the early German reports were largely based on interviews with Fida Hassnain, former Director of the State Archives, Archaeology Research and Museums in Kashmir. Hassnain is also author of *A Search for the Historical Jesus*, a book which summarizes and endorses much of the Jesus in India narrative.[6]

SOCIAL AND HISTORICAL CONTEXT

The selection of elements from the repertoire and the addition of new elements reflect varying historical and social contexts. A few examples, ranging from the end of the eighteenth century to the present day, show how the interests of each epoch are echoed in emerging alternative Christ themes.

The theme of initiation into secret knowledge has been a recurrent element of alternative Jesus narratives since at least the late eighteenth century, and has been transformed into various versions matching the specific preoccupations of each age. Early versions of the theme of initiation

---

[5] Yohanan Friedmann, *Prophecy Continuous: Aspects of Ahmadī Religious Thought and its Medieval Background* (Berkeley: University of California Press, 1989), 111–118.

[6] For the early German literature on Jesus in India, and on the role of Hassnain, see Günter Grönbold, *Jesus in Indien: Das Ende einer Legende* (Munich: Kösel, 1985), 13–18.

are projections of Enlightenment rationalism and of the masonic milieus of the time. Johann Georg Wachter's (1673–1757) influential *De primordiis Christianiae religionis*, written in 1703 and revised in 1717, presents Jesus as a teacher in the tradition of the Essenes. This group is here described as a link in a long chain of transmission of natural theology, that is, of a moral and philosophical deist tradition that had its origins among the Egyptians and included the kabbalah. From 1730 onwards, masonic authors join into the discussion about the Essenes, who are described in terms that make them appear as precursors of the Freemasons.

The Freemason Karl Bahrdt (1741–1792) is the first writer to have synthesized these themes and to present for the public a detailed version of the legend. In *Briefe ueber die Bibel im Volkston* (1782), Jesus and several other central New Testament characters are presented as members of the Essenes. The Essene faith is portrayed as a form of enlightened humanism, and the life and mission of Jesus are reinterpreted in rationalist terms. In Bahrdt's account, the Essenes spread their humanist faith by staging fake miracles in order to convince the spiritually less-enlightened masses. Jesus survived the crucifixion and was healed by Joseph of Arimathea and Nicodemus, who were also Essenes. Jesus then withdrew from public life and lived into old age. Karl Heinrich Venturini (1768–1849) fleshed out the details of Bahrdt's account further in a four-volume novel, *Natuerliche Geschichte des grossen Propheten von Nazareth* (1800–1802).

Rationalist explanations of the virgin birth also became an important part of this discourse on the non-supernatural Jesus. One hypothesis – based on a passage by Celsus summarized in Origen's *Contra Celsum* – presents him as the son of a Roman soldier by the name of Pantera or Pandera, and suggests that he was actually born in 105 BCE.[7] A version of the theory that Jesus was born long before the beginning of the Common Era has migrated into the annals of (amateur) scholarship, and is a central claim in the book *Jesus – One Hundred Years before Christ: A Study in Creative Mythology* (1999, Swedish original published in 1992) written by the then emeritus professor of English Alvar Ellegård (1919–2008).

As we have seen, Notovitch and his successors described the religions of India in less than flattering terms. The converse idea that true religious wisdom originates in India was a staple of Romantic historiography; much of the material concerning this belief is surveyed in several standard works

[7] Annie Besant, *Esoteric Christianity or The Lesser Mysteries* (London and Benares: Theosophical Publishing House, 1915 [1901]), 129–130. For a fuller discussion, see also James Santucci's chapter in the present volume.

and need not be pursued here.[8] The "Jesus as initiate" and "Jesus in India" elements coalesce in legends that stress Jesus' indebtedness to Oriental traditions. Godfrey Higgins (1772–1833) was one of the first (in his two-volume work *Anacalypsis*, 1833) to suggest that Buddhism was the primeval religion of humanity, and that a process of cultural diffusion had led much of the rest of humankind to adopt parts of this perennial religion. Via the Essenes, Buddhist teachings had passed from India to the eastern Mediterranean area. This brotherhood counted among its ranks Jesus, which effectively meant that Jesus was perceived as the founder of a late offshoot of Buddhism.

The French lawyer Louis Jacolliot (1837–1890) gave Vedic religion a similar role in his book *La Bible dans l'Inde, ou la vie de Iezeus Christna* ("The Bible in India or the Life of Iezeus Christna," published in 1869). Vedic religion, as Jacolliot understood it, included messianic expectations which had given rise to the belief that a savior figure by the name of Christna, supposedly Sanskrit for "sacred," would be born. Iezeus, on the other hand, was a Sanskrit form of the word for "god." By means of massive diffusion, Vedic traditions spread over all of Europe, a process of migration that could be documented by a close study of etymologies. "Jesus Christ" obviously was a rendering of the original Vedic "Iezeus Christna." Despite an etymology that would seem to reduce the name Jesus Christ to a linguistically corrupt version of the title Sacred God, Jacolliot did not rule out that Jesus was a historical figure. He was presumably a Jewish rabbi who had traveled to Egypt and had been initiated into the mystery religions of that land. These were schools that imparted the sacred Vedic teachings. Perhaps, Jacolliot muses in a passage that prefigures Notovitch and other authors of alternative Jesus myths, Jesus had even traveled to India in order to learn of the Vedic mysteries at first hand.

If all major religions contain a core of the perennial philosophy, if the religions of India represent a particularly faithful rendering of this core, and if Jesus was an initiate into this teaching, it stands to reason that Jesus must have defended the doctrine of reincarnation which is so central to most Indian religions. This, at least, is the logic behind yet another prevalent Jesus legend, which has its origins in late nineteenth-century theosophical circles. Briefly, this narrative states that Jesus supported the belief in reincarnation, and that several passages in the Bible hint at this teaching, but that the

[8] See Raymond Schwab, *The Oriental Renaissance: Europe's Rediscovery of India and the East, 1680–1880* (New York: Columbia University Press, 1984), Wilhelm Halbfass, *Indien und Europa: Perspektiven ihrer geistigen Begegnung* (Basel and Stuttgart: Schwabe, 1981), J.J. Clarke, *Oriental Enlightenment: The Encounter between Asian and Western Thought* (London: Routledge, 1997).

church council of Constantinople in the sixth century banned it. Various versions of the legend have circulated in theosophical and post-theosophical writings, and can be found in numerous New Age books even today. Wouter Hanegraaff has followed the legend as far as the writings of Shirley MacLaine in the mid 1970s.[9] More recent books continue to reproduce the legend. Thus, in a book published in 1993, hypnotherapist Brian L. Weiss suggested that his research into the origins of reincarnation beliefs had shown how the doctrine was considered destabilizing by the worldly authorities under the emperor Constantine and was therefore banned.[10]

The theme of Jesus as an initiate, and a teacher of ageless truths, tends to be part of a universalist discourse: most, perhaps all major traditions are said to partake of the perennial philosophy. A quite different version of the theme is found in H. Spencer Lewis' *The Mystical Life of Jesus*, published in 1929. In common with several other alternative Christologies of the pre-war years, this book presents a Jesus legend with a distinctly anti-Semitic slant. Here, Egyptian wisdom is again transmitted to the Essenes, a brotherhood that Lewis specifically describes as not being Jewish, but as an order of pure-blooded descendants of the Aryan race.[11] As transmitters of a universalistic faith, the Essenes had to be a Gentile order, since Judaism was, according to the author, "quite a problem at this time,"[12] and the Jews were only interested in furthering the interests of their own ethnic group. Jesus himself was also "born of *Gentile* parents through whose veins flowed Aryan blood."[13]

The close connection between *Zeitgeist* and alternative Jesus narratives is also apparent in several contemporary or near-contemporary books with quite different claims. A distinct echo of the psychedelic 1960s can be found in a book by John Allegro (1923–1988) entitled *The Sacred Mushroom and the Cross*. Allegro had an established career as a scholar involved in the study and translation of the Dead Sea scrolls, when he in 1970 published a controversial work suggesting that Christianity was founded not on the memory of a human being called Jesus, but on the ritual use of hallucinogenic mushrooms.[14]

[9] Wouter J. Hanegraaff, *New Age Religion and Western Culture: Esotericism in the Mirror of Secular Thought* (Leiden: Brill, 1996), 321–322 briefly surveys the occurrences of this legend in New Age literature.

[10] Brian L. Weiss, *Through Time into Healing: How Past Life Regression Therapy Can Heal Mind, Body and Soul* (London: Piatkus, 2001), 40–41.

[11] Spencer Lewis, *The Mystical Life of Jesus* (San Jose, Cal.: Supreme Grand Lodge of AMORC Printing and Publishing Department, 1964 [1929]), 28.

[12] *Ibid.*, 45.   [13] *Ibid.*, 53; emphasis in the original.

[14] See especially John Allegro, *The Sacred Mushroom and the Cross: A Study of the Nature and Origins of Christianity within the Fertility Cults of the Ancient Near East* (Garden City, N.Y.: Doubleday

More recently, Dan Brown's bestselling *The Da Vinci Code* (2003) incorporates such topical themes (found also in the broader New Age milieu) as anticlericalism and feminine spirituality. Jesus taught a message that was subsequently corrupted by the churches, and which has been relentlessly persecuted up to the present. The core of that message is the supposed fact that Jesus' main disciple was Mary Magdalene, who was the only one of his followers to appreciate that the divine has a feminine aspect.

INDIVIDUAL CREATIVITY

No matter how thoroughly embedded each Jesus narrative may be in its socio-historical context, it is also the product of the labor and creativity of individual authors. As the following examples will demonstrate, the element of personal originality can be considerable.

Rudolf Steiner (1861–1925), the founder of Anthroposophy, stands as the creator of one of the most original Jesus narratives. As documented in detail in an important study by Helmut Zander, Steiner's interpretations of Jesus and Christ (who are clearly distinguished in Steiner's writings) evolved over the period from 1902 to approximately 1912.[15] Steiner's first Christological text, *Der Christentum als mystische Tatsache* (published in 1902) elaborates on the by now familiar theme of Jesus as one of several initiated spiritual masters, who preached a version of the same spiritual wisdom that one finds in Buddhism and among the Essenes. In a number of later speeches and publications, beginning in 1906, Christianity is lifted out of this perennialist context, and is increasingly interpreted as the fulcrum of a unique and superior religious path. There are different initiatory traditions, and all are not equal. Zander tentatively reads this increasingly distinct Christology as a running commentary on developments in theosophical circles, from which Steiner wished to distance himself.

Steiner's growing valuation of Christianity and the Christian scriptures needs, however, to be understood in the light of his claim that the true Christian message only becomes apparent in the light of his own spiritual insights. Steiner's arguably most radical innovation was formulated in a series of lectures on the Gospel of Luke held in September 1909.[16] The two

---

& Doubleday, 1970), 193–195, where Allegro sums up crucial parts of his argument and denies the historicity of Jesus. The biblical narratives cover up the presumed fact that Christianity is one of many Oriental mystery cults based on the use of psychedelic drugs.

[15] Helmut Zander, *Anthroposophie in Deutschland: Theosophische Weltanschauung und gesellschaftliche Praxis 1884–1945* (Göttingen: Vandenhoeck & Ruprecht, 2007), 781–824.

[16] Summarized in Zander, *Anthroposophie in Deutschland*, 808. Steiner's lectures on Luke have been published as volume 114 of the *Gesamtausgabe*.

genealogies of Jesus presented in the Gospels of Matthew and Luke differ from each other in many details. Earlier exegetes have attempted in various ways to harmonize the two lineages. An interpretation found among conservative Bible commentators is, roughly, that Luke records Jesus' ancestry through Mary, while Matthew lists Jesus' legal father Joseph's family background.[17] Steiner proposed a new way of matching these scriptural passages. His account is complex and detailed, and can only be hinted at here.

Two couples, both with the names Joseph and Mary, were the parents of two boys, both of whom were called Jesus. One of these boys, the one mentioned in Matthew, was the reincarnation of Zarathustra. The other, the Jesus in Luke, had not been incarnated before, but became associated with Buddha by an intermingling of his astral body with forces emanating from the Buddha. A complex mystical process then led to the uniting in one single body of the individuality of both children. It was this fused person who would later undergo the baptism in the river Jordan, when Jesus was permeated by the Christ-Being. At the death of the combined Jesus, the Christ-Being poured himself out into the etheric "body" of the Earth, an event referred to as the "Mystery of Golgotha." Ever since then, a gradual spiritualization of humankind has taken place.

DISCIPLINING

Church officials remain intensely wary of innovative Jesus narratives. Some of the Jesus legends we have surveyed differ dramatically from the Gospel accounts, and it is hardly surprising that they should provoke hostile responses. Even when the novel accounts would seem to be much more closely modeled on the Gospel stories, they may be rejected by most clerical institutions. Churches seem to be particularly concerned when such stories are produced by means that appear to short-circuit church monopolies on access to historical and theological "truth." In the Catholic world, one of the most celebrated cases is the revelatory narrative of the Italian Maria Valtorta (1897–1961). Like many other female visionaries, Valtorta was ill and bedridden for many years. In 1943, she had a vision of Jesus. She soon afterward began to write a biography of Jesus that she reported came about through further visionary communications. This biography, which follows the Gospel accounts but is much more detailed, was published as *Il poema*

---

[17] "Roughly," because this attempt at harmonization needs added details in order to tackle further facts that impede easy synthesis of the two accounts, e.g. that the list in Matthew includes far fewer generations than that found in Luke.

del Uomo-Dio, and later translated into English as *Poem of the Man-God*. Although enthusiastically received by many readers, Valtorta's Jesus biography has also generated fierce critique for its purported historical errors and theological deviations.[18]

In more recent years, one of the most publicized and contested cases of religious innovation within a Christian context concerns the prophetic activity of Vassula Rydén (b. 1942). The narrative of Rydén's prophetic activity begins with a conversion story. According to biographical accounts, she was raised in a Greek Orthodox family but was for many years religiously indifferent. In 1985, however, she experienced the sudden presence of a transcendent being that identified itself as the guardian Angel Daniel.[19] After this pivotal experience, Rydén's life has been marked by frequent experiences of communicating with Christ. In the years that have passed, these communications have been put into writing and published under the title *True Life in God* (TLIG).[20] Although the biography of Jesus is not a primary topic of these communications (much less an alternative biography of Jesus), the *True Life in God* books and the prophetic claims made by Vassula Rydén herself have been the topic of a lengthy controversy in Catholic circles, involving aspects of her understanding of Christ. In brief, the discussion can be summed up as a deployment of identity politics, that is, an effort to come to an official stance whether her messages constitute "acceptable" or "unacceptable" religion. Although the details of the case are too complex and lengthy to discuss here, the bare basics are as follows.

In 1996 the Congregation for the Doctrine of the Faith (CDF) issued a Notification that described Rydén's messages as "private meditations," warning its readers that some of the opinions contained in the communications were incompatible with Catholic doctrine. Vassula Rydén was given the opportunity to "clarify" five questions felt to be particularly problematic: the relationship between her communications and Scripture, her attitude as an Orthodox Christian to the Catholic Church, her conception of the Trinity, her view of history and eschatology, and the issue of whether TLIG was a religious movement. In 2004, Cardinal Ratzinger, who at the time was head of the CDF, notified the Presidents of the Episcopal Conferences of five countries that Vassula had indeed provided "useful

[18] An article that sums up a number of such points, and which therefore is quoted by many subsequent critical authors, is Fr. Mitch Pacwa, S. J., "Is the Poem of the Man-God Simply a Bad Novel?," *New Covenant* (February, 1994); Pacwa's text has been posted on several Internet sites, see, e.g., http://www.ewtn.com/library/scriptur/valtorta.txt.
[19] Niels Christian Hvidt, *Christian Prophecy: The Post-Biblical Tradition* (Oxford: Oxford University Press, 2007), 111–119.
[20] See www.tlig.org.

clarifications." Opinions within the Catholic Church remain divided. Most relevant for the present discussion is the third question, and her answer to the suggestion that her discussion of the Trinity was unorthodox. In her response, Rydén goes to considerable lengths to stress her complete orthodoxy, and to defend the position that any interpretation of her communications that implied an unorthodox Christology was due to a literal interpretation of language intended metaphorically.[21]

Vassula Rydén's revelatory accounts are – at least to an outsider – quite close to doctrines routinely promulgated by mainstream churches. Nevertheless, even her narratives have after many years of public attention and polemics with Church institutions still not unambiguously passed the strict criteria of Catholic identity politics, and no definite consensus has been reached by Church officials.

THE LEGITIMATION OF TRUTH CLAIMS

Modern Christ narratives face characteristic problems of legitimacy. The disciplining efforts of spokespersons for the churches and other skeptical voices undermine the credibility of those who suggest, for example, that Jesus traveled to India or taught reincarnation. The fact that many different alternative Christ narratives coexist would also seem to diminish the trustworthiness of any particular legend. In order to provide Jesus narratives with a measure of plausibility, they are rarely if ever presented as flat statements. Legitimacy is conferred by a variety of strategic means, which for analytical purposes can be divided into paratext, frame, and intertextual references.

A host of accompanying materials – paratext, in the terminology of literary critic Gérard Genette – converts a narrative into a publication.[22] The title, author's name, cataloging information, covers and flaps, dedications, mottoes and preface, publisher's flyers and interviews with the author are just a few of these materials. The effect of the paratext is to control the interpretive dimension of the text, to coax the reader into understanding the text in a specific way. A preface that states that "this is a true story" will convey a very different message than a book cover that carries the genre label "a novel." Texts such as Lorber's *Die Jugend Jesu* and Dowling's *Aquarian Gospel*, which are visually structured to resemble Bible translations, will

---

[21] The response can be found at http://www.tlig.org/en/testimonies/churchpos/cdf2005/q3a/

[22] Gérard Genette, *Paratexts: Thresholds of Interpretation* (Cambridge: Cambridge University Press, 1997).

project a rhetorical ethos different from works whose pages look like those of any other book.

A Jesus narrative can be framed by a story that confers authenticity. Some frames stress the empirical, intersubjective validity of the Jesus legend that they present. Notovitch's story of travelling through Kashmir and Ladakh make his story of the discovery of Jesus biography in the monastery of Hemis more plausible. H. Spencer Lewis supports his story by referring to his research in Rosicrucian archives. Whereas Dan Brown in his bestselling *The Da Vinci Code* (2003) presents his account of the family life of Jesus as a fact but embeds it in a clearly fictional mystery novel, several of his immediate predecessors go to great lengths to present arguments for the claim that Jesus was married. Donovan Joyce (*The Jesus Scroll*, 1972), among other rhetorical devices uses scriptural and historical exegesis as well as a dramatic first-person narrative with actually existing characters to support the idea.[23] Some of Joyce's arguments for his views are very similar or even identical to those found in Dan Brown's novel. The suggestion that Jesus married Mary Magdalene is supported by references to a contested passage in the Gospel of Philip where it is stated that Jesus "used to kiss her often." More recently, Laurence Gardner (*Bloodline of the Holy Grail*, 1996) refers to archival sources to make plausible another suggestion that readers of *The Da Vinci Code* will instantly recognize: that the Holy Grail is a scribal error for *sangréal*, the "royal bloodline" of Jesus.[24]

Other frames focus on the spiritual abilities of the authors. The Jesus biographies presented by Jakob Lorber, Levi Dowling, and Rudolf Steiner are presented as legitimate because their authors have accessed higher levels of consciousness. Steiner's very heterodox exegesis of the scriptural account of the birth of Jesus is introduced by a lengthy passage that justifies it as the result of a particular kind of insight accessible to those who have powers of suprasensible perception (i.e., who are *hellsichtig*) and spiritual intuition, different from everyday sensory observation but equally valid.

Legitimacy can be conferred by intertextual references. References to other broadly accepted Jesus narratives or to other sources of legitimacy that already exist in the cultural repertoire will make one's own text more plausible. Although the historicity of the Gospel stories has been repeatedly

---

[23] Important evidence for Jesus' hidden family life is according to Joyce's book a scroll unearthed by an archaeological team led by Yigael Yadin. Yadin (1917–1984) was a prominent Israeli archaeologist also in real life. The scroll, Joyce informs us, has since vanished, presumably stolen because its contents would damage established Christianity; see Donovan Joyce, *The Jesus Scroll* (New York: Dial Press, 1973), 94.

[24] Laurence Gardner, *Bloodline of the Holy Grail: The Hidden Lineage of Jesus Revealed* (Shaftesbury: Element Books, 1997 [1996]).

questioned by historical-critical scholarship, the basic events of the biblical narratives are so familiar that references to them confer plausibility.

Alternative Jesus legends are by no means unique in this respect – mainstream narratives also tend to seek legitimacy by means of an appropriate paratext, a believable frame and supporting intertextual references. It is in the details that specific narratives come across as "alternative." Some authors, like Jakob Lorber, rely on the claim that their narratives are based on a form of gnosis that more traditional writers have lacked. Others such as Notovitch insist that their stories build on research that others have not undertaken. Yet others, such as Barbara Thiering, suggest that their narratives are the result of an empirically valid form of scriptural exegesis that other writers have overlooked.[25] As the writings of Rudolf Steiner show, claims of gnosis, empirical validity, and insightful scriptural exegesis can be combined.

A final, essential element in gaining legitimacy is to undermine that of one's opponents. If Jesus was really married, a teacher of reincarnation, or the person occupying a grave in Kashmir, what should one make of the claims of mainstream theologians and historians? Their stories are routinely denounced as the result of either ignorance or ill will. After Notovitch had discovered the facts about Jesus' final resting place, the Catholic Church did what it could to suppress this truth. Or so Fida Hassnain tells us; if later researchers who have visited Hemis monastery have not been able to find the notorious documents concerning Issa, it is because Church representatives have stolen these scrolls.[26]

The deployment of such strategies of legitimation is, of course, no guarantee of rhetorical success. In the final account, the willing suspension of disbelief may be due to a host of less readily controllable factors. No obvious measure of plausibility would seem to make the proposition "Jesus was dead for several days, and was then brought back to life" more readily acceptable than "Jesus was the name given to two different boys, whose identities merged at age twelve." Nevertheless, the former proposition is seen as historically accurate by many Christians, whereas the latter (which essentially is the core of Steiner's 1909 narrative of the childhood of Jesus) apparently occasioned considerable consternation, not only among Steiner's critics, but also among his anthroposophical followers.[27]

---

[25] See, e.g., Barbara Thiering, *Jesus the Man* (London and New York: Doubleday, 1992).
[26] Fida Hassnain, *A Search for the Historical Jesus from Apocryphal, Buddhist, Islamic and Sanskrit Sources* (The Hollies: Gateway Books, 1994), 32.
[27] Zander, *Anthroposophie in Deutschland*, 809.

As noted in the Introduction, questions of legitimacy loom large even in the scholarly literature on alternative Jesus narratives. This body of writing tends not only to present and interpret these narratives in the light of some theory of religious innovation, but is often crucially concerned with issues of validity. Edgar Goodspeed presents the theological problem succinctly: to distinguish the "genuine" from the "spurious." John Saliba suggests that "the New Age will only neglect historical scholarship to its own detriment."[28] This quest for the putatively authentic is not unproblematic, as Per Beskow notes: "If the early Church was allowed to create poetic fiction about Jesus, and to do so with a clear conscience, why can't we?" A few paragraphs further on, Beskow answers his question in a way that drastically reduces its skeptical implications:

None of the pretended gospels give a deeper view of Jesus. They do not attribute any divine or human qualities to him that could give us a richer picture of him. On the contrary, we consistently get a shallow, sentimental or superficially modernized image of Jesus which maybe is attractive to some people for a while, but which soon reveals its lack of substance.[29]

In the light of historical-critical research, even the oldest and most canonical Jesus narratives are thoroughly legendary. The Gospel stories are nevertheless held up as the absolute standards – aesthetic, literary, historical, and theological – against which all other Jesus narratives are measured.

BIBLIOGRAPHY

SOURCES

Ahmed, Ghulam, *Jesus in India: Being an Account of Jesus' Escape from Death on the Cross and of his Journey to India* (London: London Mosque, 1978).

Allegro, John, *The Sacred Mushroom and the Cross: A Study of the Nature and Origins of Christianity within the Fertility Cults of the Ancient Near East* (Garden City, N.Y.: Doubleday & Doubleday, 1970).

Anon., *Holy Koran of the Moorish Science Temple of America* (n.p., 1927).

Bahrdt, Karl, *Briefe ueber die Bibel im Volkston* (Halle, 1782).

Besant, Annie, *Esoteric Christianity or The Lesser Mysteries* (London and Benares: Theosophical Publishing House, 1915 [1901]).

Brown, Dan, *The Da Vinci Code* (New York: Doubleday, 2003).

Dowling, Levi, *The Aquarian Gospel of Jesus the Christ* (Los Angeles: Leo W. Dowling, 1908).

Ellegård, Alvar, *Jesus – One Hundred Years before Christ: A Study in Creative Mythology* (London: Century, 1999).

[28] John Saliba, *Christian Responses to the New Age Movement* (London: Geoffrey Chapman, 1999), 204.
[29] Per Beskow, *Fynd och fusk i Bibelns värld* (Stockholm: Proprius, 1979), 152; my translation.

Gardner, Laurence, *Bloodline of the Holy Grail: The Hidden Lineage of Jesus Revealed* (Shaftesbury: Element Books, 1997 [1996]).

Hassnain, Fida, *A Search for the Historical Jesus from Apocryphal, Buddhist, Islamic and Sanskrit Sources* (The Hollies: Gateway Books, 1994).

Higgins, Godfrey, *Anacalypsis: An Attempt to Draw aside the Veil of the Saitic Isis, or, an Inquiry into the Origin of Languages, Nations, and Religions* (London: Longman, 1833).

Jacolliot, Louis, *La Bible dans l'Inde, ou la vie de Iezeus Christna* (Paris: Librairie Internationale, 1869).

Joyce, Donovan, *The Jesus Scroll* (New York: Dial Press, 1973 [1972]).

Lewis, H. Spencer, *The Mystical Life of Jesus* (San Jose, Cal.: Supreme Grand Lodge of AMORC Printing and Publishing Department, 1964 [1929]).

Lorber, Jakob, *Die Jugend Jesu: Das Jakobus-Evangelium* (Bietigheim: Lorber-Verlag, 1936).

Notovitch, Nicolas, *La vie inconnue de Jésus-Christ* (Paris: Paul Ollendorff, 1894).

Schuré, Édouard, *Les grands initiés: Esquisse de l'histoire secrète des religions* (Paris: Perrin, 1921).

Steiner, Rudolf, *Der Christentum als mystische Tatsache* (Berlin: Schwetschke, 1902).

Thiering, Barbara, *Jesus the Man* (London and New York: Doubleday, 1992).

Valtorta, Maria, *The Poem of the Man-God* (Isola del Liri: Centro Editoriale Valtortiano, 1986–1990).

Venturini, Karl Heinrich, *Natuerliche Geschichte des grossen Propheten von Nazareth* (Bethlehem [= Copenhagen]: Schubothe, 1800–1802).

Wachter, Johann Georg, "De primordiis Christianae religionis," in Winfried Schröder (ed.), *Freidenker der europäischen Aufklärung*, vol. I.2 (Stuttgart-Bad Cannstatt: Frommann-Holzboog, 1995).

Weiss, Brian L., *Through Time into Healing: How Past Life Regression Therapy Can Heal Mind, Body and Soul* (London: Piatkus, 2001).

LITERATURE

Beskow, Per, *Fynd och fusk i Bibelns värld* (Stockholm: Proprius 1979) [an English language version has been published under the title *Strange Tales about Jesus: A Survey of Unfamiliar Gospels* (Philadelphia: Fortress Press, 1983)].

Burns, Dylan, "Seeking Ancient Wisdom in the New Age," in Olav Hammer and Kocku von Stuckrad (eds.), *Polemical Encounters: Esoteric Discourse and its Others* (Leiden: Brill, 2007), 253–289.

Clarke, J. J., *Oriental Enlightenment: The Encounter between Asian and Western Thought* (London: Routledge, 1997).

Friedmann, Yohanan, *Prophecy Continuous: Aspects of Ahmadī Religious Thought and its Medieval Background* (Berkeley: University of California Press, 1989).

Gardell, Mattias, "Countdown to Armageddon: Minister Farrakhan and the Nation of Islam in the Latter Days" (PhD dissertation, Stockholm, 1995).

Genette, Gérard, *Paratexts: Thresholds of Interpretation* (Cambridge: Cambridge University Press, 1997).

Goodspeed, Edgar, *Strange New Gospels* (Chicago: University of Chicago Press, 1931).

Grönbold, Günter, *Jesus in Indien: Das Ende einer Legende* (Munich: Kösel, 1985).

Halbfass, Wilhelm, *Indien und Europa: Perspektiven ihrer geistigen Begegnung* (Basel and Stuttgart: Schwabe, 1981).

Hanegraaff, Wouter J., *New Age Religion and Western Culture: Esotericism in the Mirror of Secular Thought* (Leiden: Brill, 1996).

Hvidt, Niels Christian, *Christian Prophecy: The Post-Biblical Tradition* (Oxford: Oxford University Press, 2007).

Pacwa, Fr. Mitch, S. J., "Is the Poem of the Man-God Simply a Bad Novel?," *New Covenant* (February, 1994). Online at www.catholicculture.org/library/view.cfm?RecNum=3365.

Saliba, John, *Christian Responses to the New Age Movement* (London: Geoffrey Chapman, 1999).

Schwab, Raymond, *The Oriental Renaissance: Europe's Rediscovery of India and the East, 1680–1880* (New York: Columbia University Press, 1984).

Zander, Helmut, *Anthroposophie in Deutschland: Theosophische Weltanschauung und gesellschaftliche Praxis 1884–1945* (Göttingen: Vandenhoeck & Ruprecht, 2007).

Index